Looking to earn CPE credit?
Download free content from CCH®.

D1196681

Work on CPE at your convenience by downloading *free* CPE content.

Free CCH content includes:*

- Top Federal Tax Issues
- Top Accounting Issues
- Top Auditing Issues
- Multistate Corporate Tax Course

Don't delay — downloading
CCH content is quick and easy.

Access free content at CCHGroup.com/PrintCPE

*A normal grading and administration fee of approximately $12 per credit applies.

CCH is
AdvancingBusiness
with Best in Process™ Solutions
Delivering Faster Answers
and Better Results.

.CCH
a Wolters Kluwer business

2012-0183

2014
Guidebook to
NEW JERSEY
TAXES

Susan A. Feeney

Michael A. Guariglia

Editors

Wolters Kluwer
CCH

CCH Editorial Staff

Reviewing Editors . . . . Irene Goodman, Patricia McDermott,
Brian Nudelman

Production Coordinators . . . . Aaron Rozario, Linda Barnich

ISBN 978-0-8080-3586-2

4025 W. Peterson Ave.
Chicago, IL 60646-6085
800 248 3248
CCHGroup.com

Printed in the United States of America

PREFACE

This *Guidebook* gives a general picture of the taxes imposed by the state of New Jersey and the general property tax levied by the local governments. All 2013 legislative amendments received as of press time are reflected, and references to New Jersey and federal laws are to the laws as of the date of publication of this book.

The emphasis is on the law applicable to the filing of income tax returns in 2014 for the 2013 tax year. However, if legislation has made changes effective after 2013, we have tried to note this also, with an indication of the effective date to avoid confusion.

The taxes of major interest—income and sales and use—are discussed in detail. Other New Jersey taxes, including inheritance taxes, are summarized, with particular emphasis on application, exemptions, returns, and payment.

Throughout the *Guidebook*, tax tips are highlighted to help practitioners avoid pitfalls and use the tax laws to their best advantage.

The *Guidebook* is designed as a quick reference work, describing the general provisions of the various tax laws, regulations, and administrative practices. It is useful to tax practitioners, businesspersons, and others who prepare or file New Jersey returns or who are required to deal with New Jersey taxes.

The *Guidebook* is not designed to eliminate the necessity of referring to the law and regulations for answers to complicated problems, nor is it intended to take the place of detailed reference works such as the CCH NEW JERSEY TAX REPORTS. With this in mind, specific references to the publisher's New Jersey and federal tax products are inserted in most paragraphs. By assuming some knowledge of federal taxes, the *Guidebook* is able to provide a concise, readable treatment of New Jersey taxes that will supply a complete answer to most questions and will serve as a time-saving aid where it does not provide the complete answer.

SCOPE OF THE BOOK

This *Guidebook* is designed to do three things:

1. Give a general picture of the impact and pattern of all taxes levied by the state of New Jersey and the general property tax levied by local governmental units.

2. Provide a readable, quick-reference work for the personal income tax and the tax on corporate income. As such, it explains briefly what the New Jersey law provides and indicates whether the New Jersey provision is the same as federal law.

3. Analyze and explain the differences, in most cases, between New Jersey and federal law.

HIGHLIGHTS OF 2013 NEW JERSEY TAX CHANGES

The most important 2013 New Jersey tax changes received by press time are noted in the "Highlights of 2013 New Jersey Tax Changes" section of the *Guidebook*, beginning on page 11. This useful reference gives the practitioner up-to-the-minute information on changes in tax legislation.

LOCAL TAXES

The *Guidebook* also features a chapter on local taxes that includes discussions of the tax on business tangible personal property of telephone, telegraph, and messenger system companies and the hotel use or occupancy tax. The Atlantic City sales tax, the Trenton business license tax, the Newark, Jersey City, and Elizabeth parking taxes, and the Cape May County tourism tax are also discussed.

FINDERS

The practitioner may find the information wanted by consulting the general Table of Contents at the beginning of the *Guidebook*, the Table of Contents at the beginning of each chapter, the Topical Index, or the Law and Regulation Locator.

The Topical Index is a useful tool. Specific taxes and information on rates, allocation, credits, exemptions, returns, payments, collection, penalties, and remedies are thoroughly indexed and cross-referenced to paragraph numbers in the *Guidebook*.

The Law and Regulation Locator is an equally useful finders tool. Beginning on page 301, this finding list shows where sections of New Jersey statutory law and administrative regulations referred to in the *Guidebook* are discussed.

November 2013

ABOUT THE EDITORS

Susan A. Feeney

Susan A. Feeney is a partner with the law firm of McCarter & English, LLP with offices in Newark, New Jersey; Boston; New York City; Philadelphia; Wilmington, Delaware; and Hartford, Connecticut. She concentrates in the areas of state taxation and local property taxation.

She is admitted to the Bars of the States of New Jersey and New York and is a member of the Essex County, New Jersey, and American Bar Associations and a Fellow of the American Bar Foundation. Ms. Feeney is Past President of the New Jersey State Bar Association (2011-2012), a former trustee of the New Jersey State Bar Association (2001-2006), a New Jersey State Bar Association ABA Delegate and Past Chair (1993-1994) of the New Jersey State Bar Association Taxation Section. She is a member of the New Jersey Supreme Court Committee on the Tax Court. Ms. Feeney is a member of the Sales and Use Tax Review Commission of the State of New Jersey. She lectures frequently on the subject of state taxes and local property taxes to civic and professional groups and has served as an adjunct professor at Fairleigh Dickinson University in the Master of Taxation Program. She is the attorney for the N.J. Association of County Tax Board Commissioners and Administrators. Ms. Feeney is Treasurer and Board Member of Legal Services Foundation of Essex County and President of the Board of Volunteer Lawyers for Justice.

Ms. Feeney is a graduate of Fordham Law School (1981) and she holds an undergraduate degree from Seton Hall University (summa cum laude 1978). She completed a clerkship in the New Jersey Tax Court upon graduation from law school.

Michael A. Guariglia

Michael A. Guariglia is a partner in the law firm of McCarter & English, LLP with offices in Newark, New Jersey; New York City; Boston; Philadelphia; Wilmington, Delaware; and Hartford, Connecticut.

He is admitted to the Bars of the States of New Jersey and New York, the United States Tax Court, the United States Claims Court and the United States Court of Federal Trade. He has served as Chair of the New Jersey Supreme Court Committee on the Tax Court, is a past Chair of the New Jersey State Bar Association Taxation Section and is a member of the State and Local Tax Committee of the ABA Tax Section. Mr. Guariglia also has served as an adjunct professor at Rutgers University School of Management and Business and Rutgers Law School, where he taught State and Local Taxation and participates in the Rutgers Tax Clinic. Mr. Guariglia is a frequent author and speaker on state and local tax topics.

Mr. Guariglia is an honors graduate of Rutgers Law School. He also holds an LL.M degree in Taxation from New York University, as well as an undergraduate degree from Rutgers College.

9

CONTENTS

Chapter | Page

Highlights of 2013 New Jersey Tax Changes 11
Tax Calendar 15

PART I—TABLES

Tax Rates 21
Business Incentives and Credits 23

PART II—PERSONAL INCOME TAX

1. Imposition of Tax, Rates, Exemptions, Credits 33
2. Computation of Taxable Income 47
3. Allocation and Apportionment 65
4. Returns, Estimates, Payment of Tax, Withholding ... 71
5. Estates and Trusts, Partnerships, S Corporations ... 81
6. Administration, Deficiencies, Penalties, Refunds, Appeals 85

PART III—CORPORATION BUSINESS TAX

7. Imposition of Tax, Rates, Exemptions, Credits 89
8. Basis of Tax—Entire Net Income 131
9. Allocation of Income 141
10. Returns, Estimates, Payment of Tax 149
11. Administration, Deficiencies, Penalties, Refunds, Appeals 155

PART IV—SALES AND USE TAXES

12. Imposition of Tax, Basis, Rate 159
13. Exemptions 183
14. Returns, Payment, Administration 205

PART V—INHERITANCE TAXES

15. Inheritance and Estate Taxes 213

PART VI—PROPERTY TAXES

16. Real Property Taxes 223

PART VII—MISCELLANEOUS TAXES

17. Unemployment Compensation Tax (Including Disability Benefits) 235
18. Other State Taxes 247
   Insurance Taxes 247
   Motor Vehicle Registration 250
   Alcoholic Beverage Taxes 250
   Cigarette and Tobacco Products Tax 251
   Realty Transfer Tax 252
   Utilities Taxes 254

Chapter		Page
	Motor Fuels Tax	256
	Motor Fuels Use Tax	258
	Motor Passenger Carrier Taxes	259
	Spill Compensation and Control Tax	259
	Casino Taxes and Fees	260
	Annual Tax Imposed on Internet Gaming Gross Revenues	261
	Major Hazardous Waste Facilities Tax	261
	Sanitary Landfill Facility Taxes	262
	Litter Control Fee	263
	Petroleum Products Gross Receipts Tax	263
	Waterfront Commission Payroll Tax (Joint New York-New Jersey Compact)	265
	Domestic Security Fee	265
	Tax on Certain Cosmetic Medical Procedures	266
	Fees on Outdoor Advertising Space	266
	Interim Assessment on HMOs	266
	Assessment on Licensed Ambulatory Care Facilities	267
	Tire Fee	267
	Mobile Telecommunications Fee	267
	Air Toxics Surcharge	267
	Fur Clothing Retail Gross Receipts Tax and Use Tax	268
	Luxury Vehicle/Gas Guzzler Tax	268
	Non-Residential Development Fee	268

PART VIII—LOCAL TAXES

| 19. | Local Taxes | 269 |

PART IX—ADMINISTRATION AND PROCEDURE

| 20. | State Tax Uniform Procedure Law | 277 |
| 21. | New Jersey Resources | 287 |

PART X—DOING BUSINESS IN NEW JERSEY

| 22. | Fees and Taxes | 289 |

PART XI—UNCLAIMED PROPERTY

23.	Unclaimed Property	293
	Law and Regulation Locator	301
	Topical Index	307

HIGHLIGHTS OF 2013 NEW JERSEY TAX CHANGES

The most important 2013 tax changes received by press time are noted below:

• *Determining Gross Income Tax Residency*

Effective June 27, 2013, charitable contributions shall not be a factor in determining a person's place of domicile for gross income tax purposes. P.L. 2013, c. 73.

• *Qualified Disaster Relief Payments Excluded from Tax*

Qualified disaster relief payments excluded under IRC Sec. 139 are not treated as taxable income for personal income tax purposes. Qualified disaster relief payments excluded under IRC Sec. 139 include amounts paid to cover reasonable and necessary personal, family, living or funeral expenses that were not covered by insurance, and reasonable and necessary expenses to repair or rehabilitate a personal residence or repair or replace its contents to the extent that they were not covered by insurance. Disaster-related payments for lost wage or business income, however, are subject to tax and must be reported for personal income tax purposes. (Notice, Division of Taxation, February 21, 2013.)

• *Regular Place of Business Outside New Jersey Not Required in order to Allocate under Gross Income Tax*

For gross income tax purposes, an unincorporated business that carries on business activities both inside and outside the State of New Jersey may allocate its business income and is not required to maintain a regular place of business outside the State in order to allocate its income. (Notice, Division of Taxation, March 13, 2013.)

• *Neighborhood Revitalization Tax Credit expanded to Gross Income Tax*

Effective June 6, 2013, for tax years beginning on or after January 1, 2012, the Neighborhood Revitalization Tax Credit may be claimed against the gross income tax. The taxpayer must apply to, and be approved by, the Commissioner of the Department of Community Affairs to be eligible for the credit. The available credit shall be a percentage of the taxpayer's gross income tax liability equal to the percentage of the taxpayer's gross income (before exclusions or deductions) attributable to the business through which the qualified project funding was provided. The credit may not exceed the taxpayer's total liability for that year. The amount of credits may not exceed a cumulative total of $10,000,000 in any fiscal year. P.L. 2013, c. 61.

• *Angel Investor Tax Credit Adopted*

For tax years beginning on or after January 1, 2012, the Angel Investor Tax Credit allows a credit against the gross income tax or corporation business tax for individuals or entities making qualified investments in New Jersey emerging technology businesses. The taxpayer must apply to, and be approved by, the Economic Development Authority to be eligible for the credit. The credit is equal to 10% of the qualified investment made by the taxpayer in a New Jersey emerging technology business up to a maximum allowed credit of $500,000 for the taxable year for each qualified investment. The amount of credits may not exceed a cumulative total of $25,000,000 in any calendar year. P.L. 2013, c.14.

• *Corporation Business Tax Nexus for Certain Transportation Companies*

Effective August 7, 2013, for tax years beginning on or after January 1, 2013, a foreign corporation shall not be considered to be doing business in the State of New Jersey and shall not be subject to corporation business tax if its only contact with the

State is the carriage of passengers from a location outside the State to a location inside the State or the carriage of passengers from a location inside the State to a location outside the State by way of a motor vehicle or motorbus operated over the public highways. P.L. 2013, c. 98.

- *Reorganization of Incentive Programs – New Jersey Economic Opportunity Act of 2013*

Effective September 18, 2013, the New Jersey Economic Opportunity Act of 2013 consolidates and expands five tax incentive programs into two programs and extends the two programs to July 1, 2019. The Act expands the Grow New Jersey Assistance Program ("GrowNJ") as the primary job growth incentive program and the Economic Redevelopment and Growth Program ("ERG") as the sole economic development incentive program. Those two programs, administered by the Economic Development Authority ("EDA"), will incorporate aspects of the Urban Transit Hub Tax Credit Program, the Business Retention and Relocation Assistance Grant Program and the Business Employment Incentive Program, which will be phased out by December 31, 2013. The Act is designed to extend eligibility to more businesses within greater geographical boundaries and to lower eligibility thresholds. P.L. 2013, c. 161.

- *Special Olympics Check-off authorized*

Effective for tax years beginning in calendar years 2012 and 2013, taxpayers may make voluntary contributions to the "2014 NJ Special Olympics Home Team Fund" through a "check-off" mechanism on the New Jersey Gross Income Tax return. P.L. 2013, c. 13.

- *Tax Credit Programs and Interns*

June 6, 2013, the Commissioner of Labor and Workforce Development shall undertake a review of gross income tax and corporation business tax credit programs for payments to interns and shall report any findings and recommendations directly to the Governor no later than twelve months from the date of the enactment of the act. Specifically, the commissioner shall examine the impact of, and make recommendations on, tax credit programs for interns as it pertains to increasing long-term employment for future college graduates. P.L. 2013, c. 60.

- *Permitted Amount of Surcharge on Admission Charges at Major Places of Amusement Revised*

The amount of a surcharge that a New Jersey municipality may impose on admission charges at certain major places of amusement located within the municipality has been revised. The law applies to places of amusement, as defined under the sales and use tax law, that seat at least 10,000 patrons, but excluding motion picture theaters, amusement parks and places of amusement owned by, or located on property owned by, the state or an independent state authority. Specifically, the legislation allows a municipality to set the surcharge at an amount up to 5% of the admission charge to a major place of amusement. Previously, the law authorized a municipality to impose a 5% surcharge upon each admission charge to a major place of amusement. P.L. 2013, c.84.

- *Assessment Demonstration Program Authorized*

Enacted January 25, 2013, a new property tax provision creates a real property assessment demonstration program to demonstrate a more cost-effective and accurate process of real property assessment administration. The program specifically addresses the systemic costs that result from the losses due to successful tax assessment appeals. The legislation details how many counties may participate in the program, sets out criteria that the counties must meet and specifies the information that counties must provide to the Director of the Division of Local Government services and the Director of the Division of Taxation in order to implement the demonstration program as a demonstration county. Implementation of the demonstration project takes place October 1, 2013. P.L. 2013, c.15.

• *Legislation Permits Cancellation of Certain Municipal Charges and Fees*

Effective May 9, 2013, the governing body of a municipality may adopt a resolution authorizing a municipal employee chosen by the governing body to process, without further action on the part of the governing body, the cancellation of any New Jersey property tax refund, delinquency or the charges and fees imposed by the municipality of less than $10. P.L. 2013, c.54.

• *Annual Tax Imposed on Internet Gaming Gross Revenues*

New legislation imposes an annual tax on Internet gaming gross revenues in the amount of 15% of such gross revenues, which must be paid into the Casino Revenue Fund. The 8% tax on casino gross revenues will not apply to Internet gaming gross revenues. However, the investment alternative tax will apply to Internet gaming gross revenues, except that the investment alternative tax on these revenues will be 5% and the investment alternative will be 2.5%, with the proceeds thereof used as provided by law. The legislation is effective February 26, 2013, but remains inoperative until the date selected by the Division of Gaming Enforcement pursuant to pending legislation. P.L. 2012, c.27.

• *Use of Fraud Prevention Contractors*

For purposes of all taxes administered by the New Jersey Division of Taxation, legislation was enacted effective January 25, 2013, that authorizes the use of contractors by the Division to supply fraud prevention services for the purpose of assisting the Division. The Director may enter into agreements with one or more private persons, companies, associations or corporations providing fraud prevention services. P.L. 2013, c.20.

TAX CALENDAR

The following table lists significant dates of interest to New Jersey taxpayers and tax practitioners for the tax year 2014.

January 1
Real Property Tax
    Appeals from added assessments must be heard by county tax board by this date
    Property which has materially depreciated in value subsequent to October 1 and prior to January 1 assessed as of this date
    Taxes on realty become a lien as of this date for the year for which assessed

January 10
Real Property Tax
    Assessments of real property to be completed by this date

January 15
Corporation Business Tax
CBT-100 - Annual return for accounting periods ending September 30
CBT-150 - Installment payment of estimated tax for 4th, 6th, 9th, or 12th month of current tax year
CBA-1 - Notice of Business Activities report by foreign corporations with periods ending September 30
Gross Income Tax (Individual)
NJ-1040-ES - Installment payment of estimated tax for fourth quarter of previous tax year

January 21
9-1-1 System and Emergency Response Fee ERF-100 - Quarterly return
Cosmetic Medical Procedures Gross Receipts Tax
CMPT-100 - Quarterly return
Hotel/Motel Occupancy Fee
HM-100 - State occupancy fee and municipal occupancy tax monthly return
Motor Vehicle Tire Fee TIR-100 - Quarterly return
Nursing Home Provider Assessment
NHA-100 - Quarterly return
Recycling Tax
RC-100 - Quarterly return
Sales and Use Tax
ST-50 - Quarterly return
ST-250 - Combined Atlantic City luxury tax and State sales tax monthly return
ST-350 - Cape May County tourism sales tax and tourism assessment monthly return
ST-450 - Salem County sales and use tax quarterly return
UZ-50 - Combined State sales and use tax/Urban Enterprise Zone/Urban Enterprise Zone Impacted Business District sales tax monthly return
Spill Compensation and Control Tax
SCC-5 - Monthly return
SCC-6 - Public storage terminal information return
Sports and Entertainment Facility Tax - Millville
SM-100 - Quarterly return

January 22
Motor Fuel Tax
DMF-10 - Distributor's monthly return
RMF-10 - Combined motor fuel tax return (ultimate vendors-blocked pumps, aviation fuel dealers, LPG dealers, and consumers)
SMF-10 - Supplier's monthly report

January 27
Motor Fuel Tax
OMF-11 - Terminal operator's monthly report
Petroleum Products Gross Receipts Tax
PPT-40 - Quarterly return

January 30
Gross Income Tax (Employer)
NJ-927 or NJ-927W - Employer's quarterly report
NJ-927-H - Domestic employer's annual report
Motor Fuel Tax
TMF-10 - Transporter's monthly report

January 31
Domestic Security Fee
DSF-100 - Quarterly return

February 1
Real Property Tax
    Assessor shall notify by mail each taxpayer of current assessment and preceding year's taxes
    County Boards of Taxation meet on this date to equalize property assessments

February 18
Corporation Business Tax
CBT-100 - Annual return for accounting periods ending October 31
CBT-150 - Installment payment of estimated tax for 4th, 6th, 9th, or 12th month of current tax year
CBA-1 - Notice of Business Activities report by foreign corporations with periods ending October 31
Gross Income Tax (Employer)
NJ-500 - Employer's monthly remittance

February 20
Hotel/Motel Occupancy Fee
HM-100 - State occupancy fee and municipal occupancy tax monthly return
Sales and Use Tax
ST-51 - Monthly remittance
ST-250 - Combined Atlantic City luxury tax and State sales tax monthly return
ST-350 - Cape May County tourism sales tax and tourism assessment monthly return
ST-451 - Salem County sales and use tax monthly remittance
UZ-50 - Combined State sales and use tax/Urban Enterprise Zone/Urban Enterprise Zone Impacted Business District sales tax monthly return
Spill Compensation and Control Tax
SCC-5 - Monthly return
SCC-6 - Public storage terminal information return

February 24
Motor Fuel Tax
DMF-10 - Distributor's monthly return
RMF-10 - Combined motor fuel tax return (ultimate vendors-blocked pumps, aviation fuel dealers, LPG dealers, and consumers)
SMF-10 - Supplier's monthly report

February 25
Motor Fuel Tax
OMF-11 - Terminal operator's monthly report
Petroleum Products Gross Receipts Tax
PPT-41 - Monthly remittance

February 28
Gross Income Tax (Employer) NJ-W-3 - Employer's annual reconciliation
Motor Fuel Tax
TMF-10 - Transporter's monthly report

March 17
Corporation Business Tax
CBT-100 - Annual return for accounting periods ending November 30
CBT-150 - Installment payment of estimated tax for 4th, 6th, 9th, or 12th month of current tax year
CBA-1 - Notice of Business Activities report by foreign corporations with periods ending November 30
Gross Income Tax (Employer)
NJ-500 - Employer's monthly remittance
Litter Control Fee
LF-5 - Annual return

March 20
Hotel/Motel Occupancy Fee
HM-100 - State occupancy fee and municipal occupancy tax monthly return
Sales and Use Tax
ST-51 - Monthly remittance
ST-250 - Combined Atlantic City luxury tax and State sales tax monthly return
ST-350 - Cape May County tourism sales tax and tourism assessment monthly return
ST-451 - Salem County sales and use tax monthly remittance
UZ-50 - Combined State sales and use tax/Urban Enterprise Zone/Urban Enterprise Zone Impacted Business District sales tax monthly return
Spill Compensation and Control Tax
SCC-5 - Monthly return
SCC-6 - Public storage terminal information return

March 24
Motor Fuel Tax
DMF-10 - Distributor's monthly return
RMF-10 - Combined motor fuel tax return (ultimate vendors-blocked pumps, aviation fuel dealers, LPG dealers, and consumers)
SMF-10 - Supplier's monthly report

March 25
Motor Fuel Tax
OMF-11 - Terminal operator's monthly report
Petroleum Products Gross Receipts Tax
PPT-41 - Monthly remittance

March 31
Motor Fuel Tax
TMF-10 - Transporter's monthly report

April 1
Real Property Tax
On or before this date, petition may be filed with County Board of Taxation or complaint with Tax Court if assessment is greater than $1 million for review of property tax assessments

April 15
Corporation Business Tax
CBT-100 or CBT-100S - Annual return for accounting periods ending December 31
CBT-150 - Installment payment of estimated tax for 4th, 6th, 9th, or 12th month of current tax year
CBT-200-T - Tentative return and application for extension of time to file corporation business tax return for calendar year filers. Extension period is 6 months (5 months for banking and financial business corporations)
CBA-1 - Notice of Business Activities report by foreign corporations with periods ending December 31
Gross Income Tax (Individual)
NJ-1040 - Resident return
NJ-1040-H - Property tax credit application

NJ-1040NR - Nonresident return
NJ-1040-ES - Installment payment of estimated tax for first quarter of current tax year
NJ-1041 - Fiduciary return for calendar year filers
NJ-1080-C - Composite nonresident return
NJ-630 - Application for extension of time to file resident, nonresident, or fiduciary return. Extension period is 6 months for NJ-1040, NJ-1040NR, and NJ-1080C - 5 months for NJ-104P
Partnerships
NJ-1065 - Partnership return for calendar year filers
PART-200-T -Partnership tentative return and application for extension of time to file partnership return for certain calendar year filers (i.e., limited liability companies or limited partnerships that derive income from New Jersey sources and have corporate members or partners that do not consent to taxation). Extension period is 5 months

April 21
9-1-1 System and Emergency Response Fee
ERF-100 - Quarterly return
Cosmetic Medical Procedures Gross Receipts Tax
CMPT-100 - Quarterly return
Hotel/Motel Occupancy Fee
HM-100 - State occupancy fee and municipal occupancy tax monthly return
Motor Vehicle Tire Fee
TIR-100 - Quarterly return
Nursing Home Provider Assessment
NHA-100 - Quarterly return
Recycling Tax
RC-100 - Quarterly return

Sales and Use Tax
ST-50 - Quarterly return
ST-250 - Combined Atlantic City luxury tax and State sales tax monthly return
ST-350 - Cape May County tourism sales tax and tourism assessment monthly return
ST-450 - Salem County sales and use tax quarterly return
UZ-50 - Combined State sales and use tax/Urban Enterprise Zone/Urban Enterprise Zone Impacted Business District sales tax monthly return
Spill Compensation and Control Tax
SCC-5 - Monthly return
SCC-6 - Public storage terminal information return
Sports and Entertainment Facility Tax - Millville
SM-100 - Quarterly return

April 22
Motor Fuel Tax
DMF-10 - Distributor's monthly return
RMF-10 - Combined motor fuel tax return (ultimate vendors-blocked pumps, aviation fuel dealers, LPG dealers, and consumers)
SMF-10 - Supplier's monthly report

April 25
Motor Fuel Tax
OMF-11 - Terminal operator's monthly report
Petroleum Products Gross Receipts Tax
PPT-40 - Quarterly return

April 30
Domestic Security Fee
DSF-100 - Quarterly return
Gross Income Tax (Employer)
NJ-927 or NJ-927-W - Employer's quarterly report
Motor Fuel Tax
TMF-10 - Transporter's monthly report

May 1
Sales and Use Tax
ST-18B - Annual use tax return for qualified nonvendor businesses

May 15
Corporation Business Tax
CBT-100 - Annual return for accounting periods ending January 31
CBT-150 - Installment payment of estimated tax for 4th, 6th, 9th, or 12th month of current tax year
CBA-1 - Notice of Business Activities report by foreign corporations with periods ending January 31
Gross Income Tax (Employer)
NJ-500 - Employer's monthly remittance

May 20
Hotel/Motel Occupancy Fee
HM-100 - State occupancy fee and municipal occupancy tax monthly return
Sales and Use Tax
ST-51 - Monthly remittance
ST-250 - Combined Atlantic City luxury tax and State sales tax monthly return
ST-350 - Cape May County tourism sales tax and tourism assessment monthly return
ST-451 - Salem County sales and use tax monthly remittance
UZ-50 - Combined State sales and use tax/Urban Enterprise Zone/Urban Enterprise Zone Impacted Business District sales tax monthly return
Spill Compensation and Control Tax
SCC-5 - Monthly return
SCC-6 - Public storage terminal information return

May 22
Motor Fuel Tax
DMF-10 - Distributor's monthly return
RMF-10 - Combined motor fuel tax return (ultimate vendors-blocked pumps, aviation fuel dealers, LPG dealers, and consumers)
SMF-10 - Supplier's monthly report

May 27
Motor Fuel Tax
OMF-11 - Terminal operator's monthly report
Petroleum Products Gross Receipts Tax
PPT-41 - Monthly remittance

May 30
Motor Fuel Tax
TMF-10 - Transporter's monthly report

June 2
Property Tax Reimbursement (Senior Freeze)
PTR-1 or PTR-2 - Application for senior/disabled resident property tax "freeze"

June 16
Corporation Business Tax
CBT-100 - Annual return for accounting periods ending February 28
CBT-150 - Installment payment of estimated tax for 4th, 6th, 9th, or 12th month of current tax year
CBA-1 - Notice of Business Activities report by foreign corporations with periods ending February 28
Gross Income Tax (Employer)
NJ-500 - Employer's monthly remittance
Gross Income Tax (Individual)
NJ-1040-ES - Installment payment of estimated tax for second quarter of current tax year

June 20
Hotel/Motel Occupancy Fee
HM-100 - State occupancy fee and municipal occupancy tax monthly return
Sales and Use Tax
ST-51 - Monthly remittance
ST-250 - Combined Atlantic City luxury tax and State sales tax monthly return
ST-350 - Cape May County tourism sales tax and tourism assessment monthly return
ST-451 - Salem County sales and use tax monthly remittance

UZ-50 - Combined State sales and use tax/Urban Enterprise Zone/Urban Enterprise Zone Impacted Business District sales tax monthly return
Spill Compensation and Control Tax
SCC-5 - Monthly return
SCC-6 - Public storage terminal information return

June 23
Motor Fuel Tax
DMF-10 - Distributor's monthly return
RMF-10 - Combined motor fuel tax return (ultimate vendors-blocked pumps, aviation fuel dealers, LPG dealers, and consumers)
SMF-10 - Supplier's monthly report

June 25
Motor Fuel Tax
OMF-11 - Terminal operator's monthly report
Petroleum Products Gross Receipts Tax
PPT-41 - Monthly remittance

June 30
Motor Fuel Tax
TMF-10 - Transporter's monthly report

July 15
Corporation Business Tax
CBT-100 - Annual return for accounting periods ending March 31
CBT-150 - Installment payment of estimated tax for 4th, 6th, 9th, or 12th month of current tax year
CBA-1 - Notice of Business Activities report by foreign corporations with periods ending March 31

July 21
9-1-1 System and Emergency Response Fee
ERF-100 - Quarterly return
Cosmetic Medical Procedures Gross Receipts Tax
CMPT-100 - Quarterly return
Hotel/Motel Occupancy Fee
HM-100 - State occupancy fee and municipal occupancy tax monthly return
Motor Vehicle Tire Fee
TIR-100 - Quarterly return
Nursing Home Provider Assessment
NHA-100 - Quarterly return
Recycling Tax
RC-100 - Quarterly return
Sales and Use Tax
ST-50 - Quarterly return
ST-250 - Combined Atlantic City luxury tax and State sales tax monthly return
ST-350 - Cape May County tourism sales tax and tourism assessment monthly return
ST-450 - Salem County sales and use tax quarterly return
UZ-50 - Combined State sales and use tax/Urban Enterprise Zone/Urban Enterprise Zone Impacted Business District sales tax monthly return
Spill Compensation and Control Tax
SCC-5 - Monthly return
SCC-6 - Public storage terminal information return
Sports and Entertainment Facility Tax - Millville
SM-100 - Quarterly return

July 22
Motor Fuel Tax
DMF-10 - Distributor's monthly return
RMF-10 - Combined motor fuel tax return (ultimate vendors-blocked pumps, aviation fuel dealers, LPG dealers, and consumers)
SMF-10 - Supplier's monthly report

July 25
Motor Fuel Tax
OMF-11 - Terminal operator's monthly report
Petroleum Products Gross Receipts Tax
PPT-40 - Quarterly return

July 30
Gross Income Tax (Employer)
NJ-927 or *NJ-927-W* - Employer's quarterly report
Motor Fuel Tax
TMF-10 - Transporter's monthly report
Real Property Tax
  Application to have land valued as "farmland" due

July 31
Domestic Security Fee
DSF-100 - Quarterly return

August 15
Corporation Business Tax
CBT-100 - Annual return for accounting periods ending April 30
CBT-150 - Installment payment of estimated tax for 4th, 6th, 9th, or 12th month of current tax year
CBA-1 - Notice of Business Activities report by foreign corporations with periods ending April 30
Gross Income Tax (Employer)
NJ-500 - Employer's monthly remittance

August 20
Hotel/Motel Occupancy Fee
HM-100 - State occupancy fee and municipal occupancy tax monthly return
Sales and Use Tax
ST-51 - Monthly remittance
ST-250 - Combined Atlantic City luxury tax and State sales tax monthly return
ST-350 - Cape May County tourism sales tax and tourism assessment monthly return
ST-451 - Salem County sales and use tax monthly remittance
UZ-50 - Combined State sales and use tax/Urban Enterprise Zone/Urban Enterprise Zone Impacted Business District sales tax monthly return
Spill Compensation and Control Tax
SCC-5 - Monthly return
SCC-6 - Public storage terminal information return

August 22
Motor Fuel Tax
DMF-10 - Distributor's monthly return
RMF-10 - Combined motor fuel tax return (ultimate vendors-blocked pumps, aviation fuel dealers, LPG dealers, and consumers)
SMF-10 - Supplier's monthly report

August 25
Motor Fuel Tax
OMF-11 - Terminal operator's monthly report
Petroleum Products Gross Receipts Tax
PPT-41 - Monthly remittance

September 2
Motor Fuel Tax
TMF-10 - Transporter's monthly report

September 15
Corporation Business Tax
CBT-100 - Annual return for accounting periods ending May 31
CBT-150 - Installment payment of estimated tax for 4th, 6th, 9th, or 12th month of current tax year
CBA-1 - Notice of Business Activities report by foreign corporations with periods ending May 31
Gross Income Tax (Employer)
NJ-500 - Employer's monthly remittance
Gross Income Tax (Individual)
NJ-1041 - Fiduciary return for filers who requested a 5-month extension
NJ-1040-ES - Installment payment of estimated tax for third quarter of current tax year
Partnerships
NJ-1065 - Partnership return for calendar year filers who requested a 5-month extension

September 22
Hotel/Motel Occupancy Fee
HM-100 - State occupancy fee and municipal occupancy tax monthly return
Motor Fuel Tax
DMF-10 - Distributor's monthly return
RMF-10 - Combined motor fuel tax return (ultimate vendors-blocked pumps, aviation fuel dealers, LPG dealers, and consumers)
SMF-10 - Supplier's monthly report
Sales and Use Tax
ST-51 - Monthly remittance
ST-250 - Combined Atlantic City luxury tax and State sales tax monthly return
ST-350 - Combined Cape May County tourism sales tax and tourism assessment monthly return
ST-451 - Salem County sales and use tax monthly remittance
UZ-50 - Combined State sales and use tax/Urban Enterprise Zone/Urban Enterprise Zone Impacted Business District sales tax monthly return
Spill Compensation and Control Tax
SCC-5 - Monthly return
SCC-6 - Public storage terminal information return

September 25
Motor Fuel Tax
OMF-11 - Terminal operator's monthly report
Petroleum Products Gross Receipts Tax
PPT-41 - Monthly remittance

September 30
Motor Fuel Tax
TMF-10 - Transporter's monthly report

October 1
Real Property Tax
  Valuation date for real property

October 15
Corporation Business Tax
CBT-100 - Annual return for accounting periods ending June 30
CBT-100 or *CBT-100S* - Annual return for accounting periods ending December 31 for filers who requested a 6-month extension
CBT-150 - Installment payment of estimated tax for 4th, 6th, 9th, or 12th month of current tax year
CBA-1 - Notice of Business Activities report by foreign corporations with periods ending June 30
Gross Income Tax (Individual)
NJ-1040 - Resident return for filers who requested a 6-month extension
NJ-1040NR or *NJ-1080-C* - Nonresident return for filers who requested a 6-month extension

October 20
9-1-1 System and Emergency Response Fee
ERF-100 - Quarterly return
Cosmetic Medical Procedures Gross Receipts Tax
CMPT-100 - Quarterly return
Hotel/Motel Occupancy Fee
HM-100 - State occupancy fee and municipal occupancy tax monthly return
Motor Vehicle Tire Fee
TIR-100 - Quarterly return
Nursing Home Provider Assessment
NHA-100 - Quarterly return
Recycling Tax
RC-100 - Quarterly return
Sales and Use Tax
ST-50 - Quarterly return
ST-250 - Combined Atlantic City luxury tax and State sales tax monthly return
ST-350 - Cape May County tourism sales tax and tourism assessment monthly return
ST-450 - Salem County sales and use tax quarterly return

UZ-50 - Combined State sales and use tax/Urban Enterprise Zone/Urban Enterprise Zone Impacted Business District sales tax monthly return
Spill Compensation and Control Tax
SCC-5 - Monthly return
SCC-6 - Public storage terminal information return
Sports and Entertainment Facility Tax - Millville
SM-100 - Quarterly return

October 22
Motor Fuel Tax
DMF-10 - Distributor's monthly return
RMF-10 - Combined motor fuel tax return (ultimate vendors-blocked pumps, aviation fuel dealers, LPG dealers, and consumers)
SMF-10 - Supplier's monthly report

October 27
Motor Fuel Tax
OMF-11 - Terminal operator's monthly report
Petroleum Products Gross Receipts Tax
PPT-40 - Quarterly return

October 30
Gross Income Tax (Employer)
NJ-927 or NJ-927-W - Employer's quarterly report
Motor Fuel Tax
TMF-10 - Transporter's monthly report

October 31
Domestic Security Fee
DSF-100 - Quarterly return

November 1
Real Property Tax
   Taxes on added and omitted property assessments payable
   Initial statement for property tax exemption required to be filed by this date (further statements every 3 years)

November 17
Corporation Business Tax
CBT-100 - Annual return for accounting periods ending July 31
CBT-150 - Installment payment of estimated tax for 4th, 6th, 9th, or 12th month of current tax year
CBA-1 - Notice of Business Activities report by foreign corporations with periods ending July 31
Gross Income Tax (Employer)
NJ-500 - Employer's monthly remittance

November 20
Hotel/Motel Occupancy Fee
HM-100 - State occupancy fee and municipal occupancy tax monthly return
Sales and Use Tax
ST-51 - Monthly remittance
ST-250 - Combined Atlantic City luxury tax and State sales tax monthly return
ST-350 - Cape May County tourism sales tax and tourism assessment monthly return
ST-451 - Salem County sales and use tax monthly remittance
UZ-50 - Combined State sales and use tax/Urban Enterprise Zone/Urban Enterprise Zone Impacted Business District sales tax monthly return
Spill Compensation and Control Tax
SCC-5 - Monthly return
SCC-6 - Public storage terminal information return

November 24
Motor Fuel Tax
DMF-10 - Distributor's monthly return

RMF-10 - Combined motor fuel tax return (ultimate vendors-blocked pumps, aviation fuel dealers, LPG dealers, and consumers)
SMF-10 - Supplier's monthly report

November 25
Motor Fuel Tax
OMF-11 - Terminal operator's monthly report
Petroleum Products Gross Receipts Tax
PPT-41 - Monthly remittance

December 1
Real Property Tax
   On or before this date, petition may be filed with County Board of Taxation or complaint with Tax Court if assessment is greater than $1 million for review of added and omitted property tax assessments.
   Railroad property tax due and delinquent
Motor Fuel Tax
TMF-10 - Transporter's monthly report

December 15
Corporation Business Tax
CBT-100 - Annual return for accounting periods ending August 31
CBT-150 - Installment payment of estimated tax for 4th, 6th, 9th, or 12th month of current tax year
CBA-1 - Notice of Business Activities report by foreign corporations with periods ending August 31
Gross Income Tax (Employer)
NJ-500 - Employer's monthly remittance

December 22
Hotel/Motel Occupancy Fee
HM-100 - State occupancy fee and municipal occupancy tax monthly return
Motor Fuel Tax
DMF-10 - Distributor's monthly return
RMF-10 - Combined motor fuel tax return (ultimate vendors-blocked pumps, aviation fuel dealers, LPG dealers, and consumers)
SMF-10 - Supplier's monthly report
Sales and Use Tax
ST-51 - Monthly remittance
ST-250 - Combined Atlantic City luxury tax and State sales tax monthly return
ST-350 - Cape May County tourism sales tax and tourism assessment monthly return
ST-451 - Salem County sales and use tax monthly remittance
UZ-50 - Combined State sales and use tax/Urban Enterprise Zone/Urban Enterprise Zone Impacted Business District sales tax monthly return
Spill Compensation and Control Tax
SCC-5 - Monthly return
SCC-6 - Public storage terminal information return

December 26
Motor Fuel Tax
OMF-11 - Terminal operator's monthly report
Petroleum Products Gross Receipts Tax
PPT-41 - Monthly remittance

December 30
Motor Fuel Tax
TMF-10 - Transporter's monthly report
Real Property Tax
   Veterans or their widows must file application for property tax deduction on or before this date
   Senior citizen's application due for property tax deduction
Quarterly Recurring Dates
1st Feb., May, Aug., Nov. - General real property taxes due

PART I

TABLES

Tax Rates

¶ 1	Personal Income Tax
¶ 10	Corporation Business Tax
¶ 20	Sales and Use Taxes
¶ 25	Inheritance and Estate Taxes

Business Incentives and Credits

¶ 55	Corporation Business Tax
¶ 60	Sales and Use Taxes
¶ 65	Property Tax
¶ 70	Financial Incentives

TAX RATES

¶1 Personal Income Tax

Applicable to tax years beginning on or after January 1, 2010, the tax rates are as follows:

Married Filing Jointly—Head of Household (including nonresident aliens)—Surviving Spouse

Amount of Taxable Income	Amount of Tax
$20,000 or less	1.4% of taxable income
$20,001—50,000	$280 plus 1.75% of the excess over $20,000
$50,001—70,000	$805 plus 2.45% of the excess over $50,000
$70,001—80,000	$1,295.50 plus 3.5% of the excess over $70,000
$80,001—150,000	$1,645 plus 5.525% of the excess over $80,000
$150,001—500,000	$5,512.50 plus 6.37% of the excess over $150,000
$500,001 or more	$27,807.50 plus 8.97% of the excess over $500,000

Single—Married Filing Separately—Estates and Trusts

Amount of Taxable Income	Amount of Tax
$20,000 or less	1.4% of taxable income
$20,001—35,000	$280 plus 1.75% of the excess over $20,000
$35,001—40,000	$542.50 plus 3.5% of the excess over $35,000
$40,001—75,000	$717.50 plus 5.525% of the excess over $40,000
$75,001—500,000	$2,651.25 plus 6.37% of the excess over $75,000
$500,001 or more	$29,723.75 plus 8.97% of the excess over $500,000

See ¶ 112.

¶10 Corporation Business Tax

The tax is computed based upon the greater of a tax computed using entire net income allocated to New Jersey or an alternative minimum assessment imposed upon either New Jersey gross receipts or New Jersey gross profits. The entire net income component of the tax is imposed at the rate of 9% for corporations with an entire net income greater than $100,000; 7.5% for corporations with an entire net income of $100,000 or less but greater than $50,000; and 6.5% for corporations with an entire net income of $50,000 or less. The alternative minimum assessment component of the tax is computed at the following rates:

If New Jersey Gross Profits of:	Then AMA Equals:
Less than or equal to $1,000,000	No AMA is assessed
More than $1,000,000 but ≤ $10,000,000	.0025 × [the gross profits > $1,000,000]× 1.11111
More than $10,000,000 but ≤ $15,000,000	.0035 × the gross profits
More than $15,000,000 but ≤ $25,000,000	.0060 × the gross profits
More than $25,000,000 but ≤ $37,500,000	.0070 × the gross profits
More than $37,500,000	.0080 × the gross profits

If New Jersey Gross Receipts of:	Then AMA Equals:
Less than or equal to $2,000,000	No AMA is assessed
More than $2,000,000 but ≤ $20,000,000	.00125 × [the gross receipts > $2,000,000]× 1.11111
More than $20,000,000 but ≤ $30,000,000	.00175 × the gross receipts
More than $30,000,000 but ≤ $50,000,000	.00300 × the gross receipts
More than $50,000,000 but ≤ $75,000,000	.00350 × the gross receipts
More than $75,000,000	.00400 × the gross receipts

For tax periods beginning after June 30, 2006, the AMA rate is 0% except for corporate taxpayers that are otherwise protected against New Jersey income tax liability by P.L. 86-272.

Minimum tax: Beginning in calendar year 2006 and thereafter, the minimum tax for both domestic and foreign corporations (including S corporations) is based on the New Jersey gross receipts of the taxpayer, pursuant to the following schedule:

If New Jersey Gross Receipts of:	Then Minimum Tax Equals:
Less than $100,000	$500
$100,000 or more but less than $250,000	$750
$250,000 or more but less than $500,000	$1,000
$500,000 or more but less than $1,000,000	$1,500
$1,000,000 or more	$2,000

For tax periods beginning in calendar year 2012, the minimum tax for New Jersey S corporations is reduced as follows:

If New Jersey Gross Receipts of:	Then Minimum Tax Equals
Less than $100,000	$375
More than $100,000 but less than $250,000	$562.50
More than $250,000 but less than $500,000	$750
More than $500,000 but less than $1,000,000	$1,125
More than $1,000,000	$1,500

For each corporation (including S corporations) that is part of an affiliated or controlled group with total payroll of $5,000,000 or more, the minimum tax is $2,000.

For tax periods beginning on or after January 1, 2002 and ending before January 1, 2006, the minimum tax for a CBT taxpayer was $500; with the exception of a corporation that was part of an affiliated or controlled group with total payroll of $5,000,000 or more, in which case the minimum tax is $2,000.

Surcharge: A 4% corporation business tax surcharge applied to privilege periods ending on or after July 1, 2006 but before July 1, 2010. The surcharge lapsed for periods beginning on or after July 1, 2010.

RICs and REITs: The tax payable by a qualified regulated investment company (RIC) or a real estate investment trust (REIT) cannot be less than $250 (¶725).

¶20 Sales and Use Taxes

The tax is imposed at the rate of 7% (prior to July 15, 2006, the rate was 6%) (¶1213).

¶25 Inheritance and Estate Taxes

(Rates and exemptions applicable to estates of taxpayers dying on or after July 1, 1988.)
Spouse

There is no tax imposed on a transfer between a decedent and his or her spouse, domestic partner or, on or after February 19, 2007, civil union partners.

Parents; Grandparents; Children and Issue; Adopted Children

The transfer of property to a father, mother, grandparent, child or children of a decedent, or to any child or children adopted by the decedent in conformity with the laws of New Jersey or of any of the United States or of a foreign country, or the issue of any child or legally adopted child of a decedent, is not taxed.

Other Relatives

The transfer of property to a brother or sister of a decedent, wife or widow of a son of a decedent, or husband or widower of a daughter of a decedent is taxed at the following rates:

On any amount in excess of $25,000.00, up to $1,100,000.00 . . . . 11%
On any amount in excess of $1,100,000.00, up to $1,400,000.00 . . . . 13%
On any amount in excess of $1,400,000.00, up to $1,700,000.00 . . . . 14%
On any amount in excess of $1,700,000.00 . . . . 16%

Persons or Institutions Not Otherwise Classified

The transfer of property to every other transferee, distributee or beneficiary not classified above is taxed at the following rates:

On any amount up to $700,000.00 . . . . 15%
On any amount in excess of $700,000.00 . . . . 16%

The transfer of a share of less than $500 to persons or institutions not otherwise classified is not subject to tax (¶1504).

Estate Tax

The estate tax is equal to the maximum federal estate tax credit for state death taxes allowable under the Internal Revenue Code in effect on December 31, 2001.

BUSINESS INCENTIVES AND CREDITS

¶55 Corporation Business Tax

Corporation business tax credits may not exceed 50% of the total tax liability due or reduce the tax liability to less than the statutory minimum. For tax years beginning in 2002 and thereafter, these credits apply only against the entire net income component of the tax and not against the alternative minimum assessment component.

• *HMO assistance fund tax credit*

Credit available only to members of the Insolvent HMO Assistance Fund based upon their assessments paid to the fund for which a certificate of contribution is issued (¶721).

• *New jobs investment tax credit*

Corporation business tax credit for up to 20% of investment costs to business investments that create new jobs in New Jersey.

Credit percentage depends on the kind of investment and the number of jobs created (¶711).

• *Urban enterprise zone employee credit*

One-time corporation business tax credit of $1,500 (or $500) for each new full time permanent employee employed in the zone and meeting other criteria.

"Qualified businesses" must have certain level of active business in a designated zone (¶707).

• *Urban enterprise zone investment credit*

One-time corporation business tax credit of 8% of each new investment (with UEZ Authority approval) made by the qualifying business in the zone.

Only available to qualified businesses not entitled to the UEZ employee credit.

"Qualified businesses" must have certain level of active business in a designated zone (¶707).

- *Redevelopment authority project tax credit*

Corporation business tax credit of $1,500 for each new employee employed at least 6 months (and meeting other criteria) by a taxpaying business in a "project" location.

Businesses must be engaged at that location primarily in manufacturing or other business, but not in retail sales or warehousing (¶710).

- *Recycling equipment tax credit*

Expired December 31, 1996, but unused credits may still be carried forward.

- *Manufacturing equipment and employment investment tax credit*

Corporation business tax 2% credit for investments in certain manufacturing equipment, up to a maximum of $1,000,000. The credit is increased to 4% for certain small businesses.

Additional 3% credit (of investment amount) up to a maximum of $1,000 per new employee hired as a result of the investment (¶712).

- *Research activities credit*

Corporation business tax credit for "qualified research expenses" in New Jersey.

Credit is equal to 10% of the excess of the qualified research expense for the year over a base amount and 10% of the basic research payments, in accordance with the Internal Revenue Code.

Qualified research expenses in years beginning on or after July 1, 1998 and before June 30, 2001 may be carried over for 15 (instead of 7) years for certain high technology companies (¶713).

- *Employer-provided commuter transportation benefits*

Credit for cost of commuter transportation benefits to employees to be used against corporation business tax, savings institution tax, and various utility and insurance taxes.

For periods beginning on or after January 1, 1995 and ending not later than December 31, 2007, the credit is up to 10% of the cost of such benefits. Unused credits may be carried forward.

For 2007, the maximum allowable credit was $141 per employee (¶714).

- *High technology investment tax credit*

Corporation business tax 10% credit (up to $500,000) for "qualified investments" in small New Jersey based high-tech and biotech businesses.

Three-year test period for this credit ends for tax years beginning on and after July 1, 2001 (only includes investments made in tax years beginning on or after January 1, 1999), but 15-year carry forward may be available (¶715).

- *Neighborhood revitalization tax credit*

Credit for contributions to state-approved nonprofit corporations for the purpose of implementing approved neighborhood preservation and revitalization projects in low and moderate income neighborhoods. A certificate for the credit must be obtained from the Commissioner of Community Affairs. Credits can be awarded to qualified taxpayers for up to 100% of the contributed amounts (¶718). For tax years beginning in 2012, the credit may also be claimed against the gross income tax (¶ 117D).

¶55

• *Effluent treatment equipment credit*

A credit is available effective July 1, 2002 for up to 50% of the eligible cost of the qualified wastewater treatment equipment or conveyance equipment for use exclusively within New Jersey.

No more than 20% of the total credit may be used in one year. Equipment purchases must be certified by the Department of Environmental Protection (¶719).

• *Municipal rehabilitation and economic recovery credit*

Taxpayers locating or expanding their business in qualified municipalities that do not already receive a benefit under the Urban Enterprise Zones Act are eligible for a credit based upon new employees hired at that location.

Credit is equal to $2,500 per qualifying new full-time employee at the qualified location in the taxpayer's first eligible year and $1,250 per new employee in the second year (¶720).

• *Contaminated site remediation credit*

A credit was available in an amount equal to 100% of the eligible costs of the remediation of a contaminated site, as certified by the Department of Environmental Protection and the Division of Taxation, for remediation performed during tax periods beginning on or after January 1, 2004 and before January 1, 2007. Carryovers of the credit are available (¶723).

• *AMA tax credit*

Corporate business tax credits for the excess of the Alternative Minimum Assessment liability over the regular corporate business tax liability for a prior tax year. (¶724).

• *Business retention and relocation credit*

Corporation business tax credits for relocation of full-time jobs within New Jersey. Only available to businesses that have operated in New Jersey for at least ten years. Businesses must apply to the New Jersey Commerce and Economic Growth Commission to obtain the credit and must enter into a project agreement with respect to the relocation of full-time jobs (¶722). The amount of the credit is $1,500 times the number of retained full-time jobs times the applicable tier. The six tier system is based on the total number of employees retained or relocated. This credit is phased out by December 31, 2012 due to the New Jersey Economic Opportunity Act of 2013.

• *Sheltered workshop tax credit*

Corporation business tax credits for businesses that provide employment at an occupational training center or sheltered workshop for developmentally disabled clients. The credit is available in privilege periods beginning after January 12, 2006 and equals 20% of the salary and wages paid by the taxpayer during the privilege period for the employment of a qualified person, but not to exceed $1,000 for each qualified person for the privilege period (¶725).

• *Film production tax credit*

Corporation business tax credits equal to 20% of the qualified film production expenses incurred in New Jersey on or after January 12, 2006 in the production of a feature film, television series or television show for privilege periods and taxable years beginning on and after July 1, 2005 (¶716).

Temporarily suspended in fiscal year 2011.

• *Digital media content production expenses credit*

Corporation business tax credits for up to 20% of the qualified digital media content production expenses during a privilege period (¶717).

Temporarily suspended in fiscal year 2011.

• *Urban transit hub tax credit*

Corporation business tax credit for making a $50,000,000 qualified capital investment in a business facility located in an urban transit hub (¶708). This credit is phased out by December 31, 2013 due to the New Jersey Economic Opportunity Act of 2013.

• *Developer's credit*

Corporation business tax credit for a developer who makes a capital investment of at least $50,000,000 in a qualified residential project (¶709).

• *Wind Energy Facility Credit*

A business that makes or acquires a capital investment of at least $50 million in a qualified wind facility which employs at least 300 new, full-time employees, may qualify for a tax credit equal to 100% of its capital investment which is taken over a 10-year period (¶725A).

• *Jobs Tax Credit*

Corporation business tax credit of $5,000 per year (an additional $3,000 may be authorized) for a 10-year period for each new or retained full-time job for a business making a minimum $20 million in a qualified business facility and employing at least 100 full-time employees or creating at least 100 full-time jobs (¶725B).

• *Technology company transfer of unused R&D credits and NOL carryovers*

Qualified new or expanding technology/biotechnology businesses may sell unused corporation business tax net operating losses and R&D credits for at least 75% of value.

Effective for tax years beginning on or after January 1, 1999, applications are due to Economic Development Authority by June 30 and approvals are made in early fall.

$15,000,000 lifetime cap on transfers by selling companies (¶713).

• *Angel investor tax credit*

Beginning in 2012, a credit is allowed against the corporation business tax and the gross income tax for investments in New Jersey emerging technology businesses. The credit must be approved by the Economic Development Authority. (¶¶117E, 725C).

• *Taxes paid to other states*

If the allocation formula used to allocate a corporation's entire net income is unfair, the Division can provide relief by granting credit for taxes paid to other states (¶906).

¶60 Sales and Use Taxes

• *Urban enterprise zone rate reductions*

P.L. 2011, c.28, signed into law on March 1, 2011, applies to sales or services made or rendered on or after April 1, 2011. The law amends section 20 of P.L. 1983, c.303 (N.J.S.A. 52:27H-79) and allows all qualified urban enterprise zone (UEZ) businesses to be eligible to receive the sales tax exemption at the point of purchase regardless of annual gross receipts. Previously, P.L. 2006, c.34, (amended by P.L. 2007, c.328 and P.L. 2008, c.118) restricted the point-of-purchase exemption from sales and use tax on eligible purchases made by certain small qualified businesses for exclusive use or consumption of such business in the enterprise zone. Larger UEZ businesses had to pay sales tax at the time of purchase and then file for refunds.

- *Exemptions for particular products/services (See appropriate listed paragraphs)*

    In general (¶1301).

    Manufacturing and processing machinery, apparatus and equipment (¶1305).

    Machinery and equipment for utilities (¶1306).

    Machinery and equipment for broadcasting (¶1317).

    Materials used in research and development (¶1309).

    Postconsumer material manufacturing facility exemption (¶1320).

    Chemicals and catalysts used in processing (¶1311).

    Property used in producing film/video for sale (¶1302).

    Recycling equipment (¶1302).

    Effluent treatment equipment (¶1302).

    Imprinting services (¶1302).

    Components/property used for conversion into articles produced for sale (¶1303).

    Production/processing/printing services for property delivered outside the state (¶1302).

    Advertising materials delivered outside the state (¶1302).

    Advertising published in a newspaper (¶1302).

    Packaging (¶1302).

    Delivery/installation charges (¶1302).

    Energy/conservation equipment (¶1302).

    Various admissions charges (¶1313).

    Various meals and hotel occupancies (¶1314).

    Custom (not canned) software (¶1302).

    Ships and various marine terminal services/equipment (¶1316).

- *Various exempt transactions (See appropriate listed paragraphs)*

    In general (¶1303).

    Casual sales (¶1310).

- *Property/services used in farming*

    See (¶1307).

- *Fuels and utilities*

    See (¶1308).

- *Exempt organizations*

    See (¶1312).

- *Various use tax exemptions*

    See (¶1304).

- *Taxes paid to other states*

    New Jersey use tax is offset by sales and use taxes already paid to other states (¶1304).

¶60

¶65 Property Tax

• *Long term tax exemption law*

This law is construed in conjunction with Local Redevelopment and Housing Law. It provides for exemptions of improvements for up to 30 years. Payment in lieu of tax is made to the municipality based upon not less than 2% of project cost or not less than 10% of income for commercial projects.

• *Environmental opportunity zones*

Municipalities are authorized to grant 10-year exemptions for qualified real property requiring remediation located in environmental opportunity zones. Payment in lieu of tax made to municipality measured in terms of a percentage of tax otherwise due.

• *Tangible manufacturing machinery and equipment*

Machinery and equipment are exempt from local property tax to the extent they do not constitute real property.

• *Five year exemption and abatement law*

Municipalities may provide various exemptions or abatements for improvements to residential, commercial and industrial property.

• *Urban enterprise zone*

Abatements up to five years or thirty years for qualified property. Property in urban enterprise zone generally qualifies for abatements under Long Term Tax Exemption Law or Five-Year Tax Abatement Law.

• *Agricultural exemptions and deductions*

Land of at least 5 acres in an area actively devoted to agriculture or horticulture may be assessed at less than full market value.

• *Fire suppression system exemption*

Automatic fire suppression systems are exempt from property tax.

• *Pollution control facilities exemption*

Certified equipment, facilities or devices used primarily for the purpose of abating or preventing pollution are exempt.

• *Property owned and used for exempt purposes by certain types of exempt organizations*

See generally (¶1604).

• *Primary care physicians and dentists who practice in health enterprise zones*

Gross income tax and property tax incentives.

¶70 Financial Incentives

As a precondition to or as a component of the application process for awards of certain business assistance and incentive programs, the applicant must provide to the state a current tax clearance certificate issued by the Director of the Division of Taxation.

• *Grow New Jersey Assistance Program*

Effective September 18, 2013, the New Jersey Economic Opportunity Act of 2013 revised and expanded the Grow New Jersey Assistance Program. The Program offers qualified businesses, which satisfy certain capital investment in jobs-created or jobs-retained thresholds, a per employee tax credit that can be applied against the corporation business tax, the insurance premiums tax and to partnerships to pass down to their partners.

- *Economic Redevelopment and Growth Program*

Effective September 18, 2013, the New Jersey Economic Opportunity Act of 2013 revised and expanded the Economic and Redevelopment Growth Program. Developers who can demonstrate that their projects require a subsidy in order to close a project financing gap can apply for an incentive grant in an amount up to 75% of the annual incremental tax revenues generated by the project over a 20-year period. If the project is within a Garden State Growth Zone, 85% of the projected annual incremental revenues may be granted. The grant cannot exceed 20% of the total cost of the project and a developer must make a 20% equity investment.

- *Business employment incentive program*

Incentive grants of up to 80% of state income tax withholdings from new jobs created are available to companies when they relocate to New Jersey or expand their businesses in the state. This credit is phased out by December 31, 2013 due to the New Jersey Economic Opportunity Act of 2013.

- *Business relocation assistance grant program*

Grants are available through the New Jersey Commerce Commission for businesses that create new full-time jobs by relocating or expanding to New Jersey.

- *Small, minority/woman-owned business assistance*

The New Jersey Economic Development Authority (EDA) provides financial and technical support to small businesses (start-ups, micro-businesses), minority-owned and women-owned enterprises and individuals in New Jersey considering launching a new business.

- *Statewide Loan Pool*

The EDA can provide up to 50% of the financing subordinate to 50% bank participation in loans up to $1.25 million for fixed assets and up to $750,000 for working capital. The EDA may also guarantee up to 50% of the bank portion, up to a maximum of $1.5 million for fixed assets and up to $1.5 million for working capital.

- *SBA 504 Program*

The EDA arranges long-term financing up to $1,500,000 for certain real estate and fixed assets (loans less than 40% of project costs) for businesses with net worth under $7 million or average after-tax profits under $2.5 million for past two years.

- *EDA business loans/loan guarantees*

The EDA provides to credit-worthy businesses certain guarantees of conventional loans up to $2.5 million for working capital and $2.75 million for fixed assets.

EDA makes direct loans up to $750,000 for working capital and up to $1.25 million for fixed assets for up to 10 years to credit-worthy businesses unable to obtain sufficient credit on their own, through Statewide Loan Pool/SBA 504 Program, or with an EDA guarantee.

- *Film industry loan guarantees*

The EDA will guarantee a portion of loans for eligible film projects in New Jersey not in excess of 30% of the bank financing cost of the project, or $1.5 million, whichever is less.

- *Bond financing through EDA*

Taxable bond financing available for various established businesses. Tax-exempt bond financing available for qualified businesses.

• *Fund for community economic development*

EDA provides loans and loan guarantees to community development organizations for certain projects in urban areas.

• *Equipment/building loans for urban commercial/industrial projects*

EDA provides loans from $50,000 to $2 million for fixed assets such as buildings and equipment to applicants sponsored by their municipality.

• *Export financing*

EDA can provide one-year revolving lines of credit up to $1 million to businesses exporting goods or services produced in New Jersey.

• *Hazardous discharge site investigation/clean-up loan and grant program*

EDA provides loans up to $1 million for up to 10 years to companies involved in hazardous discharge investigation/clean-up.

• *Petroleum underground storage tax remediation/upgrade/closure program*

EDA provides loans and grants to businesses that own/operate less than 10 petroleum underground storage tanks in New Jersey, have net worth under $2 million and cannot obtain a commercial loan for costs of remediating, closing or upgrading underground storage tanks.

• *"Brownfields" hazardous waste site remediation reimbursement program*

Treasurer/Department of Commerce and Economic Development may enter into redevelopment agreements to reimburse a developer for up to 75% of remediation costs for hazardous waste sites.

• *Municipal solid waste landfill remediation program*

Treasurer/Department of Commerce and Economic Development may enter into redevelopment agreements to fund up to 75% of a developer's landfill closure/remediation costs.

• *Incentive utility rates*

Major utilities companies provide various incentives, including flex rates, energy credits, rate discounts/waivers for businesses that build/expand facilities to create jobs in New Jersey or utilize vacant commercial/industrial real property.

• *Real estate development loans*

The Real Estate Development Division of EDA offers loans and services to assist in the development of large-scale projects to produce significant economic benefits to the state.

• *New Jersey redevelopment low interest loans*

The Redevelopment Authority provides low and no-interest loans, loan guarantees, equity investments, and technical assistance to eligible businesses that further its mission of investing in neighborhood-based redevelopment projects in urban areas.

• *Sustainable development low interest loans*

The New Jersey Office of Sustainability has authority to provide low interest loan funds of up to $500,000 to "sustainable" businesses that meet the goal of encouraging economic development joined with environmental protection and social equity.

¶70

• *New Jersey Seed Capital Program*

Loans from $25,000 to $200,000 available to technology enterprises in New Jersey requiring seed capital to bring an established, emerging technology product to market.

• *New Jersey technology funding program*

Expansion capital loans from $100,000 to $3 million available for growing (second stage) technology-based companies (through local banks with EDA participation).

• *New Jersey Technology Council Venture Fund*

The Fund makes investments typically between $250,000 and $5 million in high-tech growth private companies in the seed, start-up and early stages, focusing on businesses with the potential to dominate a promising market niche.

• *Early State Enterprise Seed Investment Fund*

Very young technology enterprises may be eligible to receive investments ranging from $50,000 to $1.5 million.

• *Technology Centre of New Jersey*

High-tech tenants locating in this North Brunswick, NJ complex can obtain a tenant improvement allowance, as well as low-cost financing through EDA.

• *Jobs training programs*

Grants available for worker skills training, education and support.

• *Qualified municipality open for business rebate*

An eligible taxpayer may receive a corporation business tax rebate of up to 75% (or 100% in certain situations) of incentive payments it makes in a qualified municipality during the period that the municipality is under rehabilitation and economic recovery. Camden currently qualifies as such a municipality. (¶718).

• *Redevelopment incentive grant agreement*

Grants available for developers engaging in redevelopment projects in qualifying areas.

• *Developer's credit*

A credit is allowed to a developer who makes a capital investment of at least $50 million in a qualified residential project. The credit is equal to 20% of the capital improvement.

• *New Jersey Economic Stimulus Act of 2009*

Provides for financial incentives for public-private higher education construction and improvement projects. P.L. 2009, c. 90.

¶70

PART II

PERSONAL INCOME TAX

CHAPTER 1
IMPOSITION OF TAX, RATES, EXEMPTIONS, CREDITS

¶ 101	Overview
¶ 102	Persons Subject to Tax
¶ 103	Tax Base
¶ 104	Deductions—In General
¶ 105	Deductions—Personal Exemptions
¶ 106	Deductions—Medical Expenses
¶ 107	Deductions—Alimony and Separate Maintenance
¶ 108	Deductions—Conservation Contributions
¶ 109	Deductions—Health Enterprise Zones
¶ 110	Low-Income Exemption
¶ 111	Tax Rates
¶ 112	Credits Against Tax—In General
¶ 113	Credit Against Tax—Amounts Withheld
¶ 114	Credit for Taxes Paid to Other Jurisdictions
¶ 115	Credit Against Tax—Commuter Transportation Benefits
¶ 116	Credit Against Tax—Earned Income Credit
¶ 117	Credit Against Tax—Principal Residence
¶ 117A	Credit Against Tax—Employment of Disabled Persons
¶ 117B	Credit Against Tax—Film Production Expenses
¶ 117C	Credit Against Tax—Urban Transit Hub Tax Credit
¶ 117D	Credit Against Tax—Neighborhood Revitalization Tax Credit
¶ 117E	Credit Against Tax—Angel Investor Tax Credit
¶ 118	Accounting Periods and Methods
¶ 119	Decedents
¶ 120	Commuters' Taxes
¶ 121	Property Tax on Principal Residence

¶101 Overview

The New Jersey Gross Income Tax Act—the state's first broad-based personal income tax law—was enacted by Chapter 47, Laws 1976, as Title 54A of the New Jersey Statutes, applicable to income of resident and nonresident individuals, estates, and trusts (¶102) earned on and after July 1, 1976. Low-income taxpayers are exempt (¶110).

The personal income tax is imposed on the New Jersey gross income of every individual, estate, and trust (¶102). Only specified categories of income are subject to tax, as discussed in Chapter 2, and deductions are limited, as compared to federal income tax law (¶104). Tax rates range from 1.4% to 8.97% of taxable income (¶111).

Because of its central location on the Atlantic seaboard, taxation of nonresidents is an important element in the New Jersey tax picture. Definitions of residents and nonresidents are covered at ¶102, while the application of tax, as well as allocation and apportionment, are explained in Chapter 3.

Returns, payments, and withholding requirements are the subject of Chapter 4. The taxability of estates and trusts, partnerships, limited liability companies, and S corporation shareholders is discussed in Chapter 5.

The gross income tax is administered by the Department of the Treasury, Division of Taxation. Information on assessments, appeals, penalties, refunds, and compromises of tax liability are discussed in Chapter 6. See also Chapter 20, "State Tax Uniform Procedure Law."

¶102 Persons Subject to Tax

Law: R.S. 54A:1-2, 54A:2-1—54A:2-4, 54A:5-4 (CCH New Jersey Tax Reports ¶15-105—15-130; 15-155—15-185; 15-205; 16-505).

The New Jersey gross income tax is imposed at graduated rates (¶111) on the taxable income (¶201 and following) of resident and nonresident individuals, estates, and trusts. In the case of nonresidents, the tax applies only to income earned, received, or acquired from sources within New Jersey (¶301 and following). A nonresident with income from New Jersey sources must compute gross income tax liability as though the nonresident is a resident, then prorate the liability by the proportion of New Jersey source income to total income.

The only specific exemption provided is for taxpayers with low incomes (¶110). However, the Division of Taxation may enter into reciprocal agreements with the tax authorities of other states to exempt nonresidents from the tax with respect to compensation, and such an agreement is in effect with Pennsylvania (¶301).

Resident and nonresident individuals: A "resident taxpayer" is defined as an individual who

— is domiciled in New Jersey, unless the taxpayer maintains no permanent place of abode in the state, does maintain a permanent place of abode elsewhere, and spends an aggregate of no more than 30 days of the taxable year in the state, or

— is not domiciled in New Jersey, but maintains a permanent place of abode and spends an aggregate of more than 183 days of the taxable year in the state (unless the individual is in the U.S. Armed Forces).

CCH Tip: Legislation Determining Domicile

Legislation effective June 27, 2013, makes clear that for purposes of defining tax residency for gross income tax purposes, contributions to charities shall not be a factor in determining where a person is domiciled. P.L. 2013, c. 73.

A "nonresident" taxpayer is one who is not a resident.

Resident and nonresident estates or trusts: A resident estate is the estate of a decedent who was domiciled in New Jersey at the time of death.

A "resident trust" is defined as

— a trust, or portion of a trust, consisting of property transferred by will of a decedent who was domiciled in New Jersey at the time of death, or

— a trust, or portion of a trust, consisting of the property of the following: (1) a person domiciled in New Jersey at the time the property was transferred to the trust, if the trust or portion was then irrevocable, or if it was then revocable and has not subsequently become irrevocable; or (2) a person domiciled in the state at the time the trust or portion became irrevocable, if it was revocable when the property was transferred to the trust.

The tax does not apply to a charitable trust, a trust forming part of a pension or profit-sharing plan or a trust taxable as a corporation for federal purposes. A charitable lead trust exempt under the federal Internal Revenue Code does not qualify as a charitable trust under the New Jersey personal income tax (*Burke v. Director,* 11 N.J. Tax 29 (1990); CCH NEW JERSEY TAX REPORTS [1989—1994 Transfer Binder], ¶400-041). It is the Division of Taxation's position that a charitable remainder trust does not qualify as a charitable trust exempt from New Jersey income tax. *Technical Bulletin TB-64,* Division of Taxation, June 29, 2009.

A "nonresident estate or trust" is one that is not a resident under the above definitions.

Partnerships and associations: Except as described at ¶502, a partnership or association is not taxable, but an individual partner or member's distributive share of partnership income is subject to tax (¶212, ¶502).

Partnerships must file information returns (¶402).

S corporation shareholders: Shareholders of electing S corporations are subject to personal income tax on their pro rata share of S corporation income, dividends, and gain, whether or not actually distributed to the shareholder during the shareholder's taxable year. S corporation net operating losses can be carried forward in calculating the corporate income tax base. However, for purposes of the personal income tax, losses in one category of income cannot be used to offset income from another category (¶503).

Civil union partners: Beginning with the 2007 tax year, civil union partners may file joint income tax returns.

¶103 Tax Base

Law: R.S. 54A:2-1 (CCH NEW JERSEY TAX REPORTS ¶15-505).

The tax is imposed on specified categories of income, which make up New Jersey gross income, after allowance for personal exemptions and any other allowable deductions.

For the computation of taxable income, see Chapter 2. For deductions, see ¶104—109 below. For the low-income exemption, see ¶110.

¶104 Deductions—In General

Law: R.S. 54A:3-1 (CCH NEW JERSEY TAX REPORTS ¶15-540).

In contrast to the federal Internal Revenue Code, which provides for numerous itemized deductions (or a standard deduction) from gross income in determining taxable income, the New Jersey gross income tax law allows only the following deductions: personal exemptions and certain tuition expenses (¶105), medical expenses (¶106), alimony or separate maintenance payments (¶107), qualified conservation contributions (¶109), and property taxes paid on a resident taxpayer's principal residence (¶122).

For exclusions from gross income, see ¶218 and following. For credits against tax, see ¶112—¶117 below.

¶105 Deductions—Personal Exemptions

Law: R.S. 54A:3-1, 54A:3-1.1 (CCH NEW JERSEY TAX REPORTS ¶15-535).

Comparable Federal: Sec. 151.

The following personal exemptions are deducted from gross income:

Taxpayer: $1,000, plus $1,000 if age 65 or over at the close of the taxable year, plus $1,000 if blind or disabled.

Spouse: $1,000, plus additions as above for age, blindness or disability.

Dependent: $1,500 for each dependent qualified for federal income tax purposes. An additional $1,000 exemption is also allowed for each dependent under 22 who attends an accredited institution of higher education on a full-time basis, and for whom the taxpayer pays at least one-half of tuition costs and maintenance. The U.S. Supreme Court summarily affirmed a lower court decision (*Public Funds for Public Schools of New Jersey v. Byrne* (US SCt 1979) 442 US 907, 99 SCt 2818; CCH NEW JERSEY TAX REPORTS [1966—1979 Transfer Binder], ¶ 200-800) barring as unconstitutional a $1,000 personal income tax deduction for dependents attending private elementary or secondary schools.

The Domestic Partnership Act, effective July 10, 2004, established domestic partnerships for same sex and opposite sex unrelated partners. The meaning of "dependent" includes a qualified domestic partner. Consequently, taxpayers are able to claim an additional $1,000 personal exemption for a qualified domestic partner that does not file a separate income tax return.

Short taxable years: When a taxable year is less than a full year, the personal exemptions are reduced to a percentage equal to the number of months in the taxable year (taking 15 days or more as a month) divided by 12.

¶106 Deductions—Medical Expenses

Law: R.S. 54A:1-2, 54A:3-3, 54A:3-5 (CCH NEW JERSEY TAX REPORTS ¶ 15-755).

Comparable Federal: Sec. 213.

Medical expenses in excess of 2% of gross income are deductible when they were paid during the taxable year for the taxpayer, spouse or dependents. (For nonresidents, "gross income" means all gross income that would have been reported if they had been New Jersey residents during the entire taxable year.) Although certain adult non-dependent children may be covered by a taxpayer's medical insurance under federal law, the medical expense deduction on the New Jersey return is only allowed for an adult child who is considered a qualified dependent. For taxable years beginning on or after January 1, 2000, health insurance premiums paid by a self-employed individual are deductible in full, without regard to the 2% limitation.

"Medical expenses" are nonreimbursed payments for physicians' and dental and other medical fees, hospital care, nursing care, medicines and drugs, prosthetic devices, x-rays and other diagnostic services conducted or directed by a physician or dentist. The term may also include (1) transportation primarily for and essential to medical care, and (2) insurance covering medical care, including premiums paid under the supplementary medical insurance provisions of the Social Security Act. Amounts paid or distributed out of a medical savings account that are excluded from gross income are not qualified medical expenses.

Decedents: In the case of expenses for medical care of a taxpayer that are paid out of the taxpayer's estate after his death and allowed as a medical expense deduction for federal purposes, payments made within a year after death will be treated as paid by the taxpayer when they were incurred.

¶107 Deductions—Alimony and Separate Maintenance

Law: R.S. 54A:3-2 (CCH NEW JERSEY TAX REPORTS ¶ 15-610).

Comparable Federal: Sec. 215.

Alimony and separate maintenance payments made to a spouse or former spouse during the taxable period are deductible from gross income if the payments must be included in New Jersey gross income by the recipient (¶ 214), or would be included if the recipient were a resident.

¶108 Deductions—Conservation Contributions

Law: R.S. 54A:3-6 (CCH New Jersey Tax Reports ¶ 15-625).

Comparable Federal: Sec. 170(h).

For taxable years beginning on or after January 1, 2000, a deduction is allowed for a qualified conservation contribution as defined in IRC Sec. 170(h) of a qualified real property interest in property located in New Jersey to a qualified organization to be used exclusively for conservation purposes.

A "qualified organization" is any federal, state, or local governmental unit or nonprofit charitable organization that receives a substantial portion of its support from a governmental unit. Conservation purposes include (1) the preservation of land areas for outdoor recreation, (2) the protection of natural habitats, (3) the preservation of open space, and (4) the preservation of a historically important land area or a certified historic structure.

Deduction amount: The deduction is equal to the amount of the contribution allowed as a deduction in computing the taxpayer's taxable income for federal income tax purposes.

¶109 Deductions—Health Enterprise Zones

Law: R.S. 54A:3-7 and -8, 34:1B-189, 54:4-3.160 and -3.161; Reg. Sec. 18:35-2.7 (CCH New Jersey Tax Reports ¶ 16-350).

For tax years beginning after September 2, 2004, a doctor with a qualified practice who is providing primary care (as defined in N.J.S.A. 18A:71C-32) in or within five miles of a Health Enterprise Zone shall be allowed to deduct from gross income an amount equal to that proportion of the doctor's net income derived from the qualified practice that the qualified receipts of that practice for the tax year bear to the total amount received for services for the tax year.

The New Jersey Commissioner of Health and Senior Services will designate underserved areas as Health Enterprise Zones for purposes of this law. A "qualified practice" means a practice at which 50% or more of the total amount received for services at that practice for the tax year are qualified receipts and 50% or more of the patients whose services are compensated by qualified receipts reside in a Health Enterprise Zone. "Qualified receipts" means amounts received for services from the Medicaid program, including amounts received from managed care organizations under contract with the Medicaid program, the Family Care Health Coverage Program and the Children's Health Care Coverage Program, for providing health care services to eligible program recipients.

Beginning March 1, 2005, low interest loans, property tax exemptions and tenant rebates are also available to eligible medical practices located in or within five miles of a Health Enterprise Zone.

¶110 Low-Income Exemption

Law: R.S. 54A:2-4 (CCH New Jersey Tax Reports ¶ 15-535).

New Jersey gross (personal) income tax is not imposed on taxpayers whose gross income does not exceed the following amounts: (1) $10,000 for an unmarried individual or an estate or trust; (2) $20,000 for a married couple filing a joint return; and (3) $10,000 for a married person filing separately. These low-income exemptions apply to nonresidents only if they meet the test with respect to gross income determined as if they were residents.

Earned income credit: Taxpayers who qualify for the low-income exemption may also qualify for the refundable earned income credit (¶ 116).

¶111 Tax Rates

Law: R.S. 54A:2-1, 54A:8-2 (CCH NEW JERSEY TAX REPORTS ¶ 15-355).

Comparable Federal: Secs. 1, 3, 5.

The following rate tables are effective for taxable years beginning on or after January 1, 2010:

Married Filing Jointly—Head of Household (including nonresident aliens)—Surviving Spouse

Amount of Taxable Income	Amount of Tax
$20,000 or less	1.4% of taxable income
$20,001—50,000	$280 plus 1.75% of the excess over $20,000
$50,001—70,000	$805 plus 2.45% of the excess over $50,000
$70,001—80,000	$1,295.50 plus 3.5% of the excess over $70,000
$80,001—150,000	$1,645 plus 5.525% of the excess over $80,000
$150,001—500,000	$5,512.50 plus 6.37% of the excess over $150,000
$500,001 or more	$27,807.50 plus 8.97% of the excess over $500,000

Single—Married Filing Separately—Estates and Trusts

Amount of Taxable Income	Amount of Tax
$20,000 or less	1.4% of taxable income
$20,001—35,000	$280 plus 1.75% of the excess over $20,000
$35,001—40,000	$542.50 plus 3.5% of the excess over $35,000
$40,001—75,000	$717.50 plus 5.525% of the excess over $40,000
$75,001—500,000	$2,651.25 plus 6.37% of the excess over $75,000
$500,001 or more	$29,723.75 plus 8.97% of the excess over $500,000

The following rate tables were effective for taxable years beginning on or after January 1, 2009 but before January 1, 2010:

Married Filing Jointly—Head of Household (including nonresident aliens)—Surviving Spouse

Amount of Taxable Income	Amount of Tax
$20,000 or less	1.4% of taxable income
$20,001—50,000	$280 plus 1.75% of the excess over $20,000
$50,001—70,000	$805 plus 2.45% of the excess over $50,000
$70,001—80,000	$1,295.50 plus 3.5% of the excess over $70,000
$80,001—150,000	$1,645 plus 5.525% of the excess over $80,000
$150,001—400,000	$5,512.50 plus 6.37% of the excess over $150,000
$400,001—500,000	$21,437.50 plus 8.0% of the excess over $400,000
$500,001—1,000,000	$29,437.50 plus 10.25% of the excess over $500,000
$1,000,001 or more	$80,687.50 plus 10.75% of the excess over $1,000,000

Single—Married Filing Separately—Estates and Trusts

Amount of Taxable Income	Amount of Tax
$20,000 or less	1.4% of taxable income
$20,001—35,000	$280 plus 1.75% of the excess over $20,000
$35,001—40,000	$542.50 plus 3.5% of the excess over $35,000
$40,001—75,000	$717.50 plus 5.525% of the excess over $40,000
$75,001—400,000	$2,651.25 plus 6.37% of the excess over $75,000
$400,001—500,000	$23,353.75 plus 8.0% of the excess over $400,000
$500,001—1,000,000	$31,353.75 plus 10.25% of the excess over $500,000
$1,000,001 or more	$82,603.75 plus 10.75% of the excess over $1,000,000

Filing status must be the same as for federal income tax purposes, except that civil union partners may file joint income tax returns commencing with the 2007 tax year. However, any individual who would be eligible to file as a head of household for federal income tax purposes except for the fact that the taxpayer is a nonresident alien may use the tax rates specified for head of household for New Jersey income tax purposes.

The Director of the Division of Taxation is authorized to issue optional tax tables that may be used by individuals, provided that no amount of tax computed by use of the tables may differ by more than $5 from the tax due under the basic rate provision.

¶112 Credits Against Tax—In General

Law: R.S. 54A:4-1—54A:4-4 (CCH New Jersey Tax Reports ¶ 16-805—16-995).

The law provides for credits against the tax for amounts withheld from wages (¶ 113), for income or wage taxes paid to other jurisdictions (¶ 114), earned income (¶ 116), property taxes paid on a principal residence (¶ 121) and certain first-time home buyers (¶ 117).

The law also provides credits against the income tax for unincorporated businesses that provide commuter transportation benefits to their employees (¶ 115), the employment of developmentally disabled persons (¶ 117A), film production expenses (¶ 117B), qualified capital investments in an urban transit hub (¶ 117C), certain contributions for neighborhood preservation and revitalization (¶ 117D) and for "angel investors" in emerging technology businesses (¶ 117E).

There are no specific provisions concerning credits for payments of estimated tax, but a line is provided on Form NJ-1040 and Form NJ-1040NR for the payments to be credited against the taxpayer's tax liability for the year.

¶113 Credit Against Tax—Amounts Withheld

Law: R.S. 54A:4-2, 54A:4-4 (CCH New Jersey Tax Reports ¶ 15-826).

Any amount of tax actually deducted and withheld by an employer in any calendar year will be credited against the tax liability of the employee for the taxable year beginning in that calendar year. For a short taxable year, credit will be given as provided by regulation.

Employees may apply any excess unemployment and disability insurance contributions withheld during the year as a credit against the income tax, in lieu of a refund of the excess.

S corporations: S corporation shareholders may claim the credit to the extent of the amount of tax paid by an S corporation on behalf of the shareholder.

Partnerships: Any tax paid (withheld) by a partnership on a nonresident partner's share of partnership income apportioned to New Jersey is credited to the gross income tax account of the nonresident partner. For rules concerning partnerships, see ¶ 502.

¶114 Credit for Taxes Paid to Other Jurisdictions

Law: R.S. 54A:4-1 Reg. Sec. 18:35-4.1 (CCH New Jersey Tax Reports ¶ 15-825).

A resident taxpayer is allowed a credit against the New Jersey tax for any income tax or wage tax imposed by another state (or its political subdivisions) or the District of Columbia on the same income subject to tax by New Jersey. When computing the credit, a taxpayer may take into account all payments made with respect to a final tax liability for the taxable year, without regard to when the payments were made (*State Tax News*, Division of Taxation, Winter 1994; CCH New Jersey Tax Reports [1989—1994 Transfer Binder], ¶ 400-284).

Credit amount: The credit may not exceed a percentage of the New Jersey tax equal to the income subject to tax by the other jurisdiction divided by the taxpayer's entire New Jersey income.

Example: A New Jersey resident individual employed for part of the year in New York had New Jersey gross income of $20,000 (of which $19,000 was taxable income). $12,000 of the gross income was subject to New York State and City taxes. The New Jersey tax is $380, and the New York taxes on earnings total $470. The credit is computed as follows:

$$\frac{\$12{,}000 \text{ (subject to New York taxes)}}{\$20{,}000 \text{ (New Jersey gross income)}} \times \$380 \text{ (New Jersey tax before credit)} = \$228$$

Therefore, the maximum credit in these circumstances is $228. If the tax payment to the other jurisdiction is lower than the amount computed by the above formula, credit may be taken only for the actual amount of tax paid.

If the taxpayer is ultimately required to pay another jurisdiction a greater or smaller amount of tax than the amount for which credit was allowed, the taxpayer must notify the Director of the Division of Taxation. The tax will be redetermined for any years affected without regard to a limitation of time otherwise applicable.

Although generally a shareholder may not claim a credit for tax imposed by another jurisdiction on S corporation income that is allocated to New Jersey, in cases where an S corporation allocates 100% of its income to New Jersey and pays tax to New Jersey, but is still required to and pays tax to another state based on or measured by income, the corporate income which is subject to tax is considered to be S corporation income allocated outside of New Jersey. If the shareholder is required to file a personal income tax return in the other jurisdiction reporting the S corporation income, it is the Division's published position that for purposes of computing the shareholder's credit, only the S corporation income taxed on both the New Jersey CBT return and in the other jurisdiction is considered S corporation income allocated outside New Jersey. New Jersey TAM-10 (02/10/2011); Bulletin GIT-9S (12/07). See also N.J.A.C. 18:35-1.4.

However, in *Beljakovic v. Director*, 26 N.J. Tax 455 (2012), the Tax Court held that when S corporation income is sourced to another state and the shareholders file a non-resident individual income tax return and pay tax to that state, the limitation on credits for tax imposed by another jurisdiction on S corporation income does not supersede the scope and intent of the gross income tax credit provisions, which aims to relieve double taxation. Accordingly, the Tax Court concluded that resident shareholders were entitled to a gross income tax credit for taxes paid to another state on S corporation income which was required to be allocated 100 percent to New Jersey, but a portion of which was also subject to tax in the other state.

City taxes: The New Jersey Division of Taxation allows a credit for taxes paid to other jurisdictions with respect to all New Jersey resident taxpayers who earn income subject to the New York City unincorporated business tax or the net income portion of the Philadelphia business privilege tax.

¶115 Credit Against Tax—Commuter Transportation Benefits

Law: R.S. 27:26A-15 (CCH New Jersey Tax Reports ¶15-185).

Partners are allowed a credit against their tax liability for commuter transportation benefits provided to employees. The Smart Moves for Business Program tax credit does not apply at the partnership level. A partner is allowed a credit or benefit in the amount of 157% of commuter transportation benefits costs, not to exceed $2,230 per participating employee for 2007. The cap amount was $2,149 for 2006. The credit is not available for tax years ending later than December 31, 2007.

Individual taxpayers are allowed an exclusion from gross income tax for employer-provided commuter transportation benefits. For a discussion of this exclusion, see ¶221.

¶116 Earned Income Credit

Law: R.S. 54A:4-7 (CCH New Jersey Tax Reports ¶15-820).

Comparable Federal: Sec. 32.

For taxable years beginning on or after January 1, 2000, a refundable earned income credit (EIC) is available for certain low-income residents. The New Jersey credit is patterned after the federal EIC.

Qualifications: Resident individuals who meet the requirements to receive a federal EIC in the same taxable year may claim the New Jersey EIC.

Amount of credit: The New Jersey EIC is a percentage of the federal credit, as follows:

10% for taxable years beginning on or after January 1, 2000, but before January 1, 2001;

15% for taxable years beginning on or after January 1, 2001, but before January 1, 2002;

17.5% for taxable years beginning on or after January 1, 2002, but before January 1, 2003;

20% for taxable years beginning on or after January 1, 2003, but before January 1, 2008;

22.5% for taxable years beginning on or after January 1, 2008, but before January 1, 2009;

25% for taxable years beginning on or after January 1, 2009; and

20% for taxable years beginning on or after January 1, 2010.

Limitations and carryovers: For taxable years prior to 2007, the New Jersey EIC was limited to residents with gross income of $20,000 or less.

Any excess of the credit amount over the tax due is treated as an overpayment that is refunded to the taxpayer. Consequently, there is no provision for carryover of the credit.

Filing requirements: A New Jersey income tax return, including the Earned Income Credit Tax Schedule, must be filed to receive the credit, even if the person's income is below the minimum filing threshold (¶110). Part-year residents may qualify, but the credit is prorated based on the number of months of residence in New Jersey.

Notification: An employer is required to notify an employee in writing of the availability of the federal and New Jersey EIC if the employer knows or reasonably believes the employee may be eligible for the EIC based on wages reported.

¶117 Credit Against Tax—Principal Residence

Law: R.S. 52:27BBB-56(b) (CCH NEW JERSEY TAX REPORTS ¶16-890).

Beginning June 30, 2002, a taxpayer who purchases residential property within a qualified municipality for the purpose of occupying the property as a principal residence is allowed a credit against the tax not to exceed $5,000. The credit is allowed in the tax year of purchase and for four tax years thereafter. The taxpayer must not have previously owned (either singly or jointly) and occupied any residential property as a principal residence. A taxpayer who fails to occupy the property as a principal residence within one year after the date of purchase or who terminates occupation of the property as a principal residence within ten years after the later of the date of purchase or the date of occupation is liable for tax in an amount equal to the credit previously allowed.

¶117A Credit Against Tax—Employment of Disabled Persons

Law: R.S. 54A:4-11 (CCH NEW JERSEY TAX REPORTS ¶16-875).

For tax periods beginning after January 12, 2006, an income tax credit is available for businesses that provide employment at an occupational training center or sheltered workshop for developmentally disabled clients. A "sheltered workshop" is an occupation-oriented facility operated by a nonprofit agency with which the Division of Vocational Rehabilitation Services has entered into a contract to furnish extended employment programs to eligible individuals. The credit equals 20% of the salary and wages paid by the taxpayer during the tax period for the employment of a qualified person, but not to exceed $1,000 for each person for the tax period. The amount of credit applied against the income tax for a tax period, when taken together with any other credits allowed, may not exceed 50% of the tax liability for the year that bears the same proportional relationship to the total amount of such liability as the amount of the taxpayer's gross income from New Jersey sources and attributable to the business activity employing the qualified person bears to the taxpayer's entire gross income for the year. A partnership can pass the credit on to its partners in proportion to their ownership interests.

¶117B Credit Against Tax—Film Production Expenses

Law: R.S. 54A:4-12; Reg. Secs. 18:35-4.4, 18:7-3B.1—3B.7 (CCH New Jersey Tax Reports ¶16-950).

The film production tax credit provides income tax credits equal to 20% of the qualified film production expenses incurred in New Jersey on or after January 12, 2006 in the production of a feature film, television series, or television show for tax years beginning on and after July 1, 2005, provided that (1) at least 60% of the total production expenses, exclusive of post-production costs, of the taxpayer will be incurred for services performed and goods used or consumed in New Jersey, and (2) principal photography of the film commences within 150 days after the approval of the application for the credit by the Division of Taxation and the New Jersey Economic Development Authority. The amount of the film production credit for a tax year is applied against the tax otherwise due after all other credits and payments. If the credit exceeds the amount of tax due, the amount of the excess is considered a refundable overpayment of tax. A partnership can pass the credit on to its partners in proportion to their ownership interests. The credit expires with tax years first commencing after July 1, 2015.

A taxpayer may apply for a tax credit transfer certificate in lieu of the film production tax credit. The tax credit transfer certificate may be sold or assigned, in full or in part, to any other taxpayer that may have an income tax or a corporation business tax liability, in exchange for private financial assistance to be provided by the purchaser or assignee to the taxpayer.

Temporary Suspension—For the period July 1, 2010 through June 30, 2011, the gross income tax credit for qualified film production expenses was temporarily suspended, as the annual tax credit cap for such expenses was reduced to zero.

¶117C Credit Against Tax—Urban Transit Hub Tax Credit

Law: R.S. 34:1B-207-209 (CCH New Jersey Tax Reports ¶16-890).

Effective January 13, 2008 until July 28, 2009, a business that makes $75,000,000 of qualified capital investment in a business facility in an urban transit hub and employs at least 250 full-time employees at that facility may qualify for tax credits equal to 100% of the qualified capital investment that may be applied against New Jersey personal income tax. A tenant may also be eligible for the credit, if the tenant occupies space in a qualified business facility that proportionally represents at least $25,000,000 of the capital investment in the facility and employs at least 250 full-time employees in that facility. A business that is a partnership is not allowed a direct credit, but the amount of credit of a partner in the partnership is determined by allocating to each owner their proportion of the credit of the business. See ¶707A for definitions and more detailed discussion.

Effective July 28, 2009, the urban transit hub credit cannot be applied against the New Jersey personal income tax. An individual who is a holder of the credit may sell it under the tax credit transfer certificate program for consideration received by the business of not less than 75% of the transferred credit amount.

CCH Advisory: *New Jersey Economic Opportunity Act of 2013*

Effective September 18, 2013, the New Jersey Economic Opportunity Act of 2013 consolidates and expands the Grow New Jersey Assistance Program ("GrowNJ") as the primary job growth incentive program and the Economic Redevelopment and Growth Program ("ERG") as the sole economic redevelopment incentive program. Those two programs, administered by the Economic Development Authority ("EDA"), will incorporate aspects of the Urban Transit Hub Tax Credit Program, the Business Retention and Relocation Assistance Grant Program and the Business Employment Incentive Program, which will be phased out by December 31, 2013. The GrowNJ program offers qualified business entities that are partnerships, which satisfy certain capital investment and jobs-created or jobs-retained thresholds, a per employee tax credit that can be passed down to their partners. See ¶706 for a more detailed discussion of the New Jersey Economic Opportunity Act of 2013.

¶117D Credit Against Tax—Neighborhood Revitalization Tax Credit

Law: R.S. 52:27D-490, *et seq.*

For tax years beginning on or after January 1, 2012, the Neighborhood Revitalization Tax Credit may be claimed against the gross income tax to businesses that contribute to state-approved nonprofit corporations for the purpose of implementing approved neighborhood preservation and revitalization projects in low and moderate income neighborhoods. Taxpayers are issued certificates specifying the amount of the annual credit awarded to that business.

The credits can be awarded against other taxes as well, including the corporation business tax, the tax on marine insurance companies, the insurance premiums tax, sewer and water utility excise taxes, and the petroleum products gross receipts tax.

The Commissioner of Community Affairs issues the credit certificates, but may only do so if:

— The assistance is paid for a qualified neighborhood preservation and revitalization project;

— The payment is not less than $25,000 in each tax year for credit is sought;

— Neither the taxpayer nor any of its wholly owned subsidiaries has previously failed to make such payments after approval for the assistance had been granted (unless good cause for the prior failure is shown); and

— The total of all approved assistance amounts per project does not exceed $1 million.

• *Credit amount*

The available credit shall be a percentage of the taxpayer's gross income tax liability equal to the percentage of the taxpayer's gross income (before exclusions or deductions) attributable to the business through which the qualified project funding was provided. The credit may not exceed the taxpayer's total liability for that year.

• *Forms*

The neighborhood revitalization credit is calculated on Form 311, Neighborhood Revitalization State Tax Credit.

¶117E Credit Against Tax—Angel Investor Tax Credit

Law: R.S. 54A:4-13

For tax years beginning on or after January 1, 2012, the Angel Investor Tax Credit allows a credit against the gross income tax for individuals or entities investing in New Jersey emerging technology businesses. The taxpayer must apply to, and be approved by, the Economic Development Authority to be eligible for the credit.

• *Credit amount*

The credit is equal to 10% of the qualified investment made by the taxpayer in a New Jersey emerging technology business up to a maximum allowed credit of

$500,000 for the taxable year for each qualified investment. The amount of credits may not exceed a cumulative total of $25,000,000 in any calendar year.

• *New Jersey emerging technology business*

A New Jersey emerging technology business is a company with fewer than 225 employees (at least 75% of whom are filling a position in the State of New Jersey) that is doing business, employing or owning capital or property, or maintaining an office in the State, and that has qualified research expenses paid or incurred for research conducted in the State; conducts pilot scale manufacturing in the State or; conducts technology commercialization in the State in the fields of advanced computing, advanced materials, biotechnology, electronic device technology, information technology, life sciences, medical device technology, mobile communications technology or renewable energy technology.

• *Qualified investment*

Qualified investment means the nonrefundable transfer of cash to a New Jersey emerging technology business by a taxpayer that is not a related person of the New Jersey emerging technology business, the transfer of which is in connection with either (1) a transaction in exchange for stock, interests in partnerships or joint ventures, licenses (exclusive or nonexclusive), rights to use technology, marketing rights, warrants, options or any similar items, including but not limited to options or rights to acquire any of the items included above or (2) a purchase, production or research agreement.

• *Planning considerations*

For gross income tax purposes, the Angel Investor Tax Credit is a refundable tax credit. A partnership may not claim the credit directly, but may pass the credit through to its partners.

• *Forms*

At the time of publication, no form has been issued to claim the Angel Investor Tax Credit.

¶118 Accounting Periods and Methods

Law: R.S. 54A:8-3 (CCH NEW JERSEY TAX REPORTS ¶ 15-455—15-480).

Comparable Federal: Secs. 441—453, 481.

The taxable year and the method of accounting used for the New Jersey tax must be the same as those used by the taxpayer for federal income tax purposes. If either the year or the accounting method is changed in reporting the federal tax, the same change must be made for the state tax.

The adoption of federal accounting methods includes federal provisions for determination of gains, losses, deductions, credits, and the time of recognition or realization of gains or losses. For additional information, see ¶ 203.

Adjustments due to change of accounting methods: If a taxpayer changes from the accrual to the installment method of accounting, any additional tax for the year of change and any subsequent year, if attributable to the receipt of installment payments that had been properly accrued in a prior year, is to be reduced by the amount of tax paid in a prior year as a result of the accrual. The reduction is to be made in accordance with regulations.

¶118

If additional tax results from adjustments required because of any other change of accounting method, the additional tax is limited to the amount that would be imposed if the adjustments were ratably allocated and included for the year of change and the preceding tax year or years (not over two) during which the original accounting method was used.

¶119 Decedents

Law: R.S. 54A:5-1, 54A:8-3.1 (CCH NEW JERSEY TAX REPORTS ¶ 15-160).

Comparable Federal: Sec. 691.

The return for a decedent is made by the fiduciary or other person charged with the decedent's property (¶ 402). Continued income received by the estate of a decedent who was subject to the law's provisions is addressed by including "income in respect of a decedent" as a category of New Jersey gross income (¶ 210).

For special provisions concerning deductions for medical expenses, see ¶ 106.

¶120 Commuters' Taxes

Law: R.S. 54:8A-119, 54:8A-122, 54A:2-1.1, 54A:9-17 (CCH NEW JERSEY TAX REPORTS ¶ 16-615).

As a result of a reciprocal agreement with Pennsylvania, residents of that state are not subject to any New Jersey income tax on compensation paid in New Jersey, and New Jersey employers of such persons are to withhold Pennsylvania personal income tax from the employees' wages. Pennsylvanians are subject to the gross income tax on other income from New Jersey sources on the same basis as other nonresidents (Chapter 3).

The personal income tax imposed on nonresident taxpayers is first computed as if the nonresident were a resident, then multiplied by a fraction, the numerator of which is the taxpayer's income from sources within New Jersey and the denominator of which is the taxpayer's gross income for the tax year computed as if the taxpayer were a resident.

The New Jersey Attorney General is authorized to review the enactments of the state of New York to determine if New York's current method of taxation of the income from New York sources of taxpayers who are not New York residents has been repealed or superseded by subsequent enactment so as to restrict the computation of liability owed to New York to a method based only on the New York source income of the taxpayer.

The Division of Taxation is authorized to enter into agreements with the tax authorities of other states to provide for reciprocal exemptions from income taxes on the compensation of nonresidents (¶ 301).

¶121 Property Tax on Principal Residence

Law: R.S. 54A:3A-15—54A:3A-22 (CCH NEW JERSEY TAX REPORTS ¶ 15-540).

A deduction is allowed from gross income equal to the entire amount (up to $10,000) of property taxes due and paid in the taxable year on a resident taxpayer's homestead.

For the 2009 tax year only, the maximum property tax deduction was capped at $5,000 for taxpayers who have gross income of more than $150,000, but not exceeding $250,000 and are not 65 years of age or older or allowed a personal exemption as a blind or disabled individual. Also for 2009, taxpayers who have gross income of more than $250,000 were not eligible for any property tax deduction unless they were 65 years of age or older or allowed a personal exemption as a blind or disabled individual. The maximum deduction of $10,000 was restored for all taxpayers for 2010.

"Homestead" defined: The deduction is limited to property taxes paid on a taxpayer's "homestead," which is defined as the taxpayer's domicile that either is owned or rented, but must be used as the taxpayer's principal residence. A homestead includes condominiums, units in cooperatives, and continuing care retirement communities. Vacation homes or other secondary real property holdings do not qualify as principal residences.

Tenants: For tenants, property tax is calculated as 18% of rent paid. Rent paid for occupancy of a manufactured home installed in a mobile home park may qualify for the deduction. A rental unit in a rooming house, hotel, or motel may be considered a principal residence if the unit includes a kitchen and bathroom facilities.

Calculation of deduction: Homeowners are allowed to take the deduction in proportion to their ownership. The proportionate share of joint tenants or tenants in common is equal to that of all other individuals who hold title unless the conveyance under which title is held provides otherwise. Spouses who file separately and who both reside in the homestead and own the homestead as tenants by the entirety or are residential shareholders of a cooperative or mutual housing corporation, may each take one-half of the deduction.

When the homestead is a dwelling house consisting of more than one unit, the taxpayer may deduct only the property taxes assessed against the unit occupied by the taxpayer. When more than one tenant occupies the homestead, the deduction will be divided equally or in proportion to the rent actually paid by each. However, if a husband and wife file separate returns, the deduction must be equally divided.

A taxpayer who was a homeowner for part of the year and a tenant for the other part may deduct the taxes paid on the homestead for the part of the year that it was the taxpayer's homestead and may deduct 18% of rent paid for the part of the year the rental unit was occupied as the taxpayer's homestead.

In lieu of the deduction, taxpayers who are senior citizens or blind or disabled individuals may elect to claim a refundable credit. For additional property tax relief provided, see ¶1605.

CCH Tip: Deduction or Credit

Calculate taxes using the deduction and then using the credit to determine which method will provide the greater benefit.

PERSONAL INCOME TAX

CHAPTER 2
COMPUTATION OF TAXABLE INCOME

¶201	Taxable Income—In General
¶202	Remuneration for Services; Housing Furnished by Employer
¶203	Net Profits from Business
¶203A	Disallowance of Deductions for Certain Domestic Production Activities
¶204	Gains and Losses from Disposition of Property
¶205	Rents, Royalties, Patents, and Copyrights
¶206	Interest
¶207	Dividends
¶208	Gambling Winnings
¶209	Income from Estates and Trusts
¶210	Income in Respect of a Decedent
¶211	Pensions and Annuities
¶212	Income from Partnerships
¶213	Prizes and Awards
¶214	Alimony and Separate Maintenance
¶215	Gain from Criminal Acts
¶216	Environmental Fines or Penalties
¶217	S Corporation Shareholder's Pro Rata Share of Income
¶218	Exclusion of Gain from Sale of Principal Residence
¶219	Exclusion of Gain and Income from Certain Government Obligations
¶220	Excludable Retirement Income
¶221	Exclusion of Employer-Provided Commuter Transportation Benefits
¶222	Income Not Subject to Tax
¶223	Excludable Dividends of Qualified Investment Funds
¶224	Excludable Qualified Employee Benefits Under Cafeteria Plan

¶201 Taxable Income—In General

Law: R.S. 54A:2-1, 54A:2-1.1, 54A:5-2, 54A:5-3 (CCH NEW JERSEY TAX REPORTS ¶15-505, 16-505).

Comparable Federal: Sec. 61.

Taxable income is New Jersey gross income, as discussed in this chapter, minus allowable deductions (¶104—109). For the low-income exemption, see ¶110.

New Jersey gross income consists of the specified categories of income described at ¶202—217 below, after allowing for the exclusions noted at those paragraphs and at ¶218—224.

Losses: Losses within any category of income may be used to offset gross income in the same category during the taxable year. Except as provided in legislation adopted for tax years beginning in 2012 described below, a net loss in one category may not be applied to reduce gross income from any other category or categories of income.

CCH Advisory: Netting of Business Income and Loss Carryforwards Allowed

Effective for taxable years beginning on or after January 1, 2012, new legislation (P.L. 2011, c.60) establishes an "alternative business calculation" under the gross income tax to permit taxpayers who generate income from different types of business entities to offset gains from one type of business with losses from another, and permits taxpayers to carry forward business-related losses for a period of up to 20 taxable years. The Division of Taxation adopted a regulation implementing the statute. See Reg. Sec. 18:35-2.8.

Taxpayers may net gains and losses derived from one or more of the following business-related categories of gross income: net profits from business; net gains or net income derived from or in the form of rents, royalties, patents, and copyrights; distributive share of partnership income; and net pro rata share of S corporation income. A taxpayer who sustains a loss from a sole proprietorship may apply that loss against income derived from a partnership, subchapter S corporation, or rents and royalties, but is prohibited from applying those losses from those categories of income that are not related to the taxpayer's conduct of the taxpayer's own business, including salaries and wages, the disposition of property, and interest and dividends.

The law provides that net losses from the business-related categories of income may be carried forward and applied against income in future taxable years, however, these losses are limited to gains and losses from the same business-related categories of income from which the net loss is derived.

The alternative business calculation is done as follows:

The alternative business income or loss is first calculated by netting the loss in one or more of the net categories of gross income against any other gains or losses sustained in the categories of gross income and including any loss carry forward allowed. The next step is to subtract the alternative business income from regular business income in order to determine the business increment. Then, for purposes of calculating the taxpayer's gross income tax liability, the taxpayer's taxable income is adjusted pursuant to the following phase-in schedule:

For taxable years beginning in 2012, the taxpayer subtracts from taxable income 10% of the business increment;

For taxable years beginning in 2013, the taxpayer subtracts from taxable income 20% of the business increment;

For taxable years beginning in 2014, the taxpayer subtracts from taxable income 30% of the business increment;

For taxable years beginning in 2015, the taxpayer subtracts from taxable income 40% of the business increment;

For taxable years beginning in 2016 and thereafter, the taxpayer subtracts from taxable income 50% of the business increment.

CCH Tip: Choice of Entity

Consideration should still be given to choosing pass-through entities to conduct business in New Jersey. Unlike the pass-through entity netting which takes place on federal Schedule E, there still remain limitations on the netting of income, gains and losses from partnerships and S corporations under the gross income tax.

New Jersey does not allow losses to be carried back to other years, as otherwise provided by federal law.

A taxpayer may not claim a nonbusiness bad debt deduction as a loss for gross income tax purposes. Although a taxpayer may claim a worthless nonbusiness bad debt as a short-term capital loss, thereby offsetting short-term capital gains, on a federal return, the New Jersey Supreme Court held that there is no corresponding provision in the New Jersey gross income tax. N.J.S.A. 54A:5-1(c) does not integrate into the gross income tax every federal tax provision. Because the worthless nonbusiness debt of an unpaid loan was not a sale, exchange or other disposition of property under N.J.S.A. 54A:5-1(c), the taxpayer was not entitled to claim the loss. See *Waksal v. Director*, 215 N.J. 224 (2013).

Estates, trusts and beneficiaries: The taxable income of a resident estate or trust includes New Jersey gross income received and not distributed to beneficiaries (¶ 501).

For the taxation of beneficiaries, see ¶ 209 below.

CCH Advisory: Investment Theft Losses

The Division of Taxation has indicated in a public notice that it does not follow the Internal Revenue Service's announced treatment of Ponzi scheme and other investment theft losses. Unlike federal law, the New Jersey Gross Income Tax Act does not have a theft loss provision. New Jersey does, however, allow investment losses. Accordingly, individual taxpayers who have suffered investment theft losses may only claim an investment loss in the year of discovery pursuant to N.J.S.A. 54A:5-1.c, which governs net gains or income from the disposition of property. Any net loss in this category of income cannot be carried back or forward under the Gross Income Tax. Partnerships and/or S corporations that have suffered investment theft should net the investment theft losses against other business income or loss during the year of discovery in arriving at their New Jersey distributive share of partnership income or net pro rata share of S corporation income. The net income or loss flows out to the partners or shareholders who in turn report the income or loss on their returns in the category Net distributive share of partnership income or Net pro rata share of S corporation income.

Notwithstanding the foregoing, in an unpublished opinion in *Dalton v. Director*, New Jersey Tax Court Docket No. 020540-2010 (November 10, 2011), the Tax Court held that a taxpayer was entitled to amend his prior year returns with respect to capital gains and dividends originally reported as earned through Madoff Ponzi scheme investments. The court recognized that the taxpayer received no economic benefit from the income reported on his 2005, 2006 and 2007 gross income tax returns, but that he was nonetheless taxed on those amounts.

Nonresidents: Nonresident individuals, estates and trusts (see definitions at ¶ 102) are generally subject to tax on the same categories of income as residents, to the extent that the income is from New Jersey sources. A nonresident with income from New Jersey sources must compute gross income tax liability as though the nonresident is a resident, then prorate the liability by the proportion of New Jersey source income to total income. Income from intangibles is only taxable to nonresidents if the property is employed in a trade, profession, occupation, or business carried on in New Jersey. Pennsylvanians are not subject to tax on compensation paid in New Jersey. For details, see ¶ 120.

¶202 Remuneration for Services; Housing Furnished by Employer

Law: R.S. 54A:5-1; Reg. Secs. 18:35-1.2, 18:35-1.3, 18:35-1.23 (CCH NEW JERSEY TAX REPORTS ¶ 15-640, 15-705).

Comparable Federal: Sec. 61.

Salaries, wages, tips, fees, commissions, bonuses, and other remuneration for services rendered, whether received in the form of cash or property, make up the first category of New Jersey gross income subject to tax. Employee business expenses are not deductible.

See ¶224 for the treatment of benefits received by a taxpayer through a cafeteria plan, salary reduction agreements, such as flexible spending accounts and premium conversion options.

Individual retirement accounts: For treatment of Individual Retirement Account (IRA) contributions and withdrawals, see ¶211.

For the exclusion of certain armed forces payments, see ¶222.

The provisions of a separate, but related category require the inclusion of the rental value of a residence furnished by an employer, or a rental allowance paid by an employer to provide a home. The rental value of a residence provided for a clergyman by a church or congregation is excluded.

¶203 Net Profits from Business

Law: R.S. 54A:5-1, 54A:5-2; Reg. Sec. 18:35-1.1 (CCH New Jersey Tax Reports ¶15-770).

Comparable Federal: Sec. 61.

New Jersey gross income includes net income from the operation of a business, profession or other activity intended to produce income after provision for all costs and expenses incurred, other than taxes based on income, provided such activity qualifies for and reports as a trade or business for federal income tax purposes.

Business expenses: Net profits from business is determined by taking into account all ordinary costs and expenses incurred in the conduct of the business. No deduction is allowed with respect to any civil, civil administrative or criminal penalty or fine assessed and collected for violation of state or federal environmental laws (¶216). Only "ordinary" business costs and expenses are deductible. This is not the equivalent of the federal "ordinary and necessary" standard for deductibility (*Sabino,* New Jersey Tax Court, 17 N.J. Tax 29 (1997); CCH New Jersey Tax Reports ¶400-535).

Business costs and expenses are deductible if they are (1) incurred primarily and directly in the pursuit of business income, (2) incurred as common and accepted practice in that field of business, (3) required for and appropriate to the intended business purpose, and (4) reasonable in amount in relation to the intended business purpose.

CCH Tip: Federal Accounting Methods Applied

Recent cases have expanded the application by New Jersey of federal income tax methods of accounting, including federal provisions for determination of gains, losses, deductions, credits, and the time of recognition or realization (*Koch* (N.J. SCt 1999) 157 N.J. 1; CCH New Jersey Tax Reports ¶400-614).

¶203A Disallowance of Deductions for Certain Domestic Production Activities

Law: R.S. 54A:5-15 (CCH New Jersey Tax Reports ¶15-682).

Applicable to taxable years beginning after December 31, 2004, taxpayers computing the New Jersey gross income tax are not allowed a deduction for certain domestic production activities income that the taxpayer claimed as a deduction for federal income tax purposes under IRC Sec. 199. The federal deduction, which was enacted by the American Jobs Creation Act of 2004 (AJCA) (P.L. 108-357), allows businesses to claim a deduction equal to 3% of qualified production activities income for 2005. The percentage gradually increases in succeeding years, reaching 9% for 2010.

The New Jersey exclusion does not apply to amounts deducted for federal purposes that are exclusively based upon gross receipts derived from the lease, rental, license, sale, exchange, or other disposition of qualifying production property that was manufactured or produced by the taxpayer in whole or in significant part within the United States. The exception, which does not apply to qualified production property grown or extracted by the taxpayer, is limited to performance of an operation or series of operations which is intended to place items of tangible personal property in a different form, composition, or character. The change in form, composition, or character must be a substantial change, and result in a transformation of property into a different or substantially more usable product (R.S. 54A:5-15).

¶204 Gains and Losses from Disposition of Property

Law: R.S. 54A:5-1, 54A:5-14, 54A:6-14.1 (CCH New Jersey Tax Reports ¶ 15-710, 15-745).

Comparable Federal: Sec. 61.

Net gain or net income, less net losses, derived from the sale or exchange of any kind of property is to be included in New Jersey gross income. Deductions from gains or income from the disposition of property are disallowed for penalties, fines, economic benefits or treble damages paid for violations of environmental laws, ordinances or resolutions (¶ 216).

For New Jersey purposes, the method of accounting must be the same as for federal income tax purposes, and gain or income from transactions not recognized for the federal tax may be excluded from the state tax computation. Distributions paid by a qualified investment fund are also excluded from gross income to the extent attributable to interest or gain from obligations excluded from federal, state, or local taxes (¶ 223).

Mergers: The New Jersey statute contains provisions essentially the same as those of the Internal Revenue Code with respect to nonrecognition of gain or loss in connection with the exchange of securities in a corporate reorganization and the transfer of property to a corporation solely for its securities by persons who are in control of the corporation immediately after the exchange.

CCH Tip: New Jersey Basis May Differ from Federal

The cost basis of a taxpayer's partnership interest that was sold during the tax year for a net gain was not required to be reduced by partnership losses that were not deductible for gross income tax purposes, because only economic gain from a disposition of property is taxable and a return of capital is not taxable. Thus, the taxpayer was not required to use only the federal adjusted basis in calculating the gain from the sale of the partnership interest or to report the same amount of gain for New Jersey purposes as he reported for federal purposes (*Koch* (N.J. SCt 1999) 157 N.J. 1; CCH New Jersey Tax Reports ¶ 400-614).

The *Koch* case reversed a long-standing position that a New Jersey resident who disposes of a partnership interest must use the federal basis to calculate gain for New Jersey gross income tax purposes. The principle enunciated in *Koch* also applies to the sale or liquidation of a sole proprietorship, or the sale of rental property not held by a business entity (*State Tax News*, Division of Taxation, Summer 2001). In determining the taxable gain on the sale of rental property, basis is reduced by federal depreciation only to the extent a taxpayer used depreciation to offset income remaining after deduction of operating expenses (*Moroney*, N.J. Tax Court, 21 N.J. Tax 220 (2004), aff'd 376 N.J.Super 1 (App.Div. 2005); CCH New Jersey Tax Reports ¶ 400-958).

Stock options: The federal treatment of the recognition of income from a qualified incentive stock option plan is followed for New Jersey personal income tax purposes. The taxable event will be deemed to occur not when the option is granted or exercised, but when the stock is sold (*Letter from Acting Director*, Division of Taxation (1983); CCH NEW JERSEY TAX REPORTS [1979—1989 Transfer Binder], ¶ 201-083).

S corporation shareholders: The *Koch* case, discussed in the above "CCH Tip," may apply to the disposition of S corporation shares as well as partnership interests. Distributions by an S corporation to a resident shareholder are included in New Jersey gross income to the extent that the distribution is treated as a dividend or gain from the sale or exchange of property, as provided under IRC Sec. 1368.

¶205 Rents, Royalties, Patents, and Copyrights

Law: R.S. 54A:5-1 (CCH NEW JERSEY TAX REPORTS ¶ 15-790).

Comparable Federal: Sec. 61.

Net gains and net income derived from or in the form of rents, royalties, patents, and copyrights are included in gross income.

¶206 Interest

Law: R.S. 54A:5-1 (CCH NEW JERSEY TAX REPORTS ¶ 15-720).

Comparable Federal: Sec. 61.

Other than interest derived from exempt obligations (¶ 219), all interest received is includable in New Jersey taxable income.

¶207 Dividends

Law: R.S. 54A:5-1 (CCH NEW JERSEY TAX REPORTS ¶ 15-185, 15-645).

Comparable Federal: Sec. 61.

The provisions that make dividends a category of gross income define "dividends" essentially the same as in the Internal Revenue Code: the term means any distribution in cash or property made by an S corporation, C corporation, association or business trust out of accumulated earnings and profits or out of earnings and profits of the year in which payment is made. The term does not include exempt-interest distributions paid by a qualified investment fund (¶ 223).

Dividends received by a taxpayer on a paid-up life insurance policy are considered a return of premiums and are not taxable until they exceed the total premiums or other payments made on the policy. However, any interest paid on the dividends is subject to tax (*State Tax News*, Division of Taxation, Spring 1994; CCH NEW JERSEY TAX REPORTS ¶ 400-292).

¶208 Gambling Winnings

Law: R.S. 54A:5-1, 54A:6-11; Reg. Sec. 18:35-7.6 (CCH NEW JERSEY TAX REPORTS ¶ 15-780).

Gambling winnings are to be reported as an item of New Jersey gross income. Substantiated losses from gambling incurred during the same tax period as the winnings may be used to offset winnings. There are special rules for winnings from the New Jersey Lottery. For 2008 and prior tax years, New Jersey Lottery winnings were excluded from New Jersey gross income. For tax years beginning after 2008, New Jersey gross income includes New Jersey Lottery winnings from prize amounts exceeding $10,000. Lottery winnings in excess of $10,000 are subject to withholding at source. Any payment received for the assignment of lottery winnings is taxable; however, a lump sum received in exchange for future lottery installments, with the consent of the State and by judicial order, were found to be exempt lottery winnings (*McCauley*, N.J. Tax Court, 19 N.J. Tax 581 (2000); CCH NEW JERSEY TAX REPORTS ¶ 400-791).

¶209 Income from Estates and Trusts

Law: R.S. 54A:5-1, 54A:5-3 (CCH NEW JERSEY TAX REPORTS ¶ 15-215, 15-235).

Comparable Federal: Sec. 61.

Net gains or income derived through estates or trusts must be included in gross income.

Beneficiaries are subject to tax on that part of the income or gains received by the estate or trust for its taxable year ending in the beneficiary's taxable year, which is required to be distributed currently or actually paid or credited to the beneficiary.

Beneficiaries may exclude any income paid or credited to them (in the year it is paid or credited) if the estate or trust has already paid the New Jersey income tax on the income. For imposition of tax on an estate or trust, see ¶ 501.

Grantor Trusts: Income from a grantor trust retains its character, as reflected on the trust's Form NJ-1041, and is reportable by the grantor in the appropriate categories on the grantor's personal income tax return. *Notice,* Division of Taxation, Updated September 6, 2005.

¶210 Income in Respect of a Decedent

Law: R.S. 54A:5-1 (CCH NEW JERSEY TAX REPORTS ¶ 15-715).

Comparable Federal: Sec. 61.

Income in respect of a decedent is to be included as gross income in the return made for an estate subject to the gross income tax. (¶ 119).

¶211 Pensions and Annuities

Law: R.S. 54A:5-1, 54A:5-1.1, 54A:5-8, 54A:6-2, 54A:6-3, 54A:6-10, 54A:6-21, 54A:6-25, 54A:6-28 (CCH NEW JERSEY TAX REPORTS ¶ 15-800).

Comparable Federal: Secs. 61, 72, 402, 403.

The proceeds from public and private pensions and annuities must be included in New Jersey gross income to the extent that they exceed the exclusions noted below. However, New Jersey is prohibited by R.S. 54A:5-8 and federal law from taxing nonresidents on pension or annuity income derived from New Jersey sources.

Social Security and Railroad Retirement Act benefits: Payments received under the Social Security Act (including lump-sum death benefits) or the Railroad Retirement Act are excluded from New Jersey gross income.

For amounts of income excludable by persons not covered by the Social Security Act or Railroad Retirement Act, but who would be eligible for payments if they were covered, see ¶ 220.

Disability payments: Any amount received under a public or private plan because of permanent and total disability is excluded from gross income. For other exclusions of disability benefits, see ¶ 222.

Excludable annuity income: Gross income does not include that part of any amount received as an annuity under an annuity, endowment, or life insurance contract that bears the same ratio to such amount as the investment in the contract (as of the annuity starting date) bears to the expected return under the contract.

When (1) part of the consideration for an annuity, endowment, or life insurance contract is contributed by the employer, and (2) during the three-year period beginning on the date on which an amount is first received under the contract as an annuity, the aggregate amount receivable by the employee under the terms of the contract is equal to or greater than the consideration for the contract contributed by the employee, then all amounts received as an annuity under the contract will be excluded from gross income until the amount that has been excluded equals the consideration for the contract contributed by the employee.

Additional exclusion for persons age 62 or older or eligible for Social Security disability payments: Any person who is 62 years old or older, or who is (or would be) eligible to receive Social Security payments on the basis of disability, is permitted an additional exclusion from payments received as an annuity, endowment, or life insurance contract or as pension, disability, or retirement benefits. The excludable amounts are as follows: up to $20,000 for a married couple filing jointly; up to $10,000 for a married person filing separately; and up to $15,000 for a single taxpayer. For taxable years beginning on and after January 1, 2005, the additional exclusion is only available if the taxpayer has gross income for the taxable year of not more than $100,000.

The exclusions apply whether the payments are made under a public or a private plan, and whether contributions to the plan were made by the employee, the employer, or both.

For exclusions of other retirement income available to persons 62 years old or older who have limited income from remuneration, business profits, or partnerships, see ¶220. The maximum amounts noted above apply to total exclusions under both categories.

Rollovers: New Jersey provides an exclusion from gross income for distributions from a qualified employees' trust or annuity plan (except for any portion representing employee contributions) if they are eligible under federal provisions allowing exclusion of amounts rolled over into another investment vehicle. The New Jersey exclusion applies to the rollovers permitted by IRC Secs. 402(a)(5) and 403(a)(4), relating to distributions that constitute lump-sum distributions, as defined; payments upon termination of a plan; or amounts paid upon complete discontinuance of contributions to a profit-sharing or stock bonus plan.

Individual retirement account: As specified in the Instructions to Form NJ-1040, contributions to an IRA are not deductible in the year in which they are made. Such contributed amounts therefore, are not taxable when withdrawn from the account. Interest, dividends, and other earnings accumulated in the account, as well as amounts which were tax-free rollovers into the account, are not taxable until withdrawn.

A lump-sum distribution from an IRA or a qualified employee pension and annuity plan, which the recipient rolls over into an IRA, is excludable when such rollovers qualify for deferral for federal income tax purposes. As under federal law, any rollover must be made within the 60-day period after distribution.

If a lump-sum withdrawal from an IRA is received, the entire amount of accumulated earnings (any amount in excess of previously taxed contributions) must be reported in the year of the withdrawal. There is no provision in New Jersey for income averaging of a lump-sum distribution.

CCH Advisory: IRA Withdrawals for Charitable Gifts

Provisions in the Pension Protection Act of 2006 (P.L. 109-280) enable anyone 70½ or older to use as much as $100,000 a year from their tax-deferred IRA for charitable gifts, without paying federal income tax on the amount they use. For New Jersey income tax purposes, no similar legislation has been adopted. Therefore, there is no change to the New Jersey income tax treatment of distributions from an IRA account that corresponds to the federal income tax treatment and such distributions will be taxed in the same manner as any lump-sum withdrawal.

¶211

CCH Tip: Roth IRAs

New Jersey conforms to the federal treatment of Roth IRAs. Amounts rolled over from a traditional, non-Roth IRA to a Roth IRA are specifically included in New Jersey gross income in the same year as reported for federal income tax purposes. Thus, taxpayers interested in the advantages of a Roth IRA do not need to be concerned about state consequences differing from the federal treatment of Roth IRAs. With respect to distributions made before January 1, 1999, any amount required to be included in gross income under this provision is to be included ratably over the four-taxable-year period beginning with the taxable year in which the payment or distribution is made. (Technical Bulletin, TB-44R, February 9, 2010)

Roth IRAs: For taxable years beginning after December 31, 1997, a distribution from a Roth IRA is excluded from gross income if it is (1) made on or after an individual reaches age $59\frac{1}{2}$, (2) made to a beneficiary, or to an individual's estate, upon death of the individual, (3) attributable to an individual's being disabled, or (4) made for the purposes of purchasing a first home (up to $10,000 in expenses). However, a distribution will not be treated as qualified if it is made within the five-taxable-year period beginning with the first taxable year for which the individual made a contribution to a Roth IRA.

Education accounts: Gross income does not include the earnings on a qualified state tuition program account or an education IRA, as defined in IRC Sec. 530, until the earnings are distributed from the account. When the earnings are distributed from the account, they are includable in the gross income of the distributee unless the distribution is (1) a distribution from a qualified state tuition program account that is used for higher education expenses, as defined in IRC Sec. 529(e)(3), *i.e.,* tuition, fees, books, supplies, or equipment required for the enrollment or attendance of a designated beneficiary at an eligible institution of higher education or certain room and board expenses incurred by the designated beneficiary while attending such institution, (2) a rollover within 60 days from one qualified state tuition program account to another qualified state tuition program account, or from one education IRA to another education IRA, for the benefit of a member of the same family as the original beneficiary, or (3) a change in the designated beneficiary of an account to a member of the same family as the original beneficiary.

A "qualified state tuition program account" is an account established pursuant to the New Jersey Better Educational Savings Trust (NJBEST) Act or any other qualified state tuition program, as defined in IRC Sec. 529, or a tuition credit or certificate purchased pursuant to any such program. The portion of a distribution that is attributable to earnings must be determined in accordance with the principles of IRC Sec. 72 (annuities), as applied to IRC Secs. 529 and 530.

401(k) plans: An exclusion from gross income is provided for amounts contributed by an employer on behalf of and at the election of an employee to a trust which is part of a qualified cash or deferred arrangement. Amounts distributed or withdrawn from the trust are includable in gross income.

Simplified employee pension (SEP) plans: The Division of Taxation advised that employer and employee contributions to an employer-sponsored SEP are taxable at the time of contribution, but will be excluded from gross income upon withdrawal from the plan (*State Tax News*, Division of Taxation (1988); CCH NEW JERSEY TAX REPORTS [1979—1989 Transfer Binder], ¶ 201-422).

Withholding of tax: For voluntary withholding of state personal income tax from pension and annuity payments, see ¶ 408.

Compensation for injuries or sickness: See ¶ 222.

¶212 Income from Partnerships

Law: R.S. 42:1-15, 42:2B-69, 54A:5-1, 54A:5-4, 54A:8-6; Reg. Sec. 18:35-1.3 (CCH New Jersey Tax Reports ¶ 10-245, 15-185).

Comparable Federal: Sec. 61.

Partners, not partnerships, are subject to income taxation. A taxpayer's distributive share of partnership income is included as one of the gross income categories. The tax applies to the partner's share (whether or not distributed) of the income or gain received by the partnership for its taxable year ending within the partner's taxable year.

For definition of "partnership," see ¶ 502.

A partnership determines its partners' distributive shares of partnership income in the same manner a sole proprietorship determines "net profits from business." The partner's share of distributive income is taxed as a separate category of income without regard to character or category of income earned by the partnership.

Other entity level taxes can apply to partnerships, see ¶ 502.

• *Net profits from business*

A partner's share of distributive income includes net profits from business conducted by the partnership. Net profits from business are discussed at ¶ 203.

• *Deductibility of partnership expenses*

Expenses are deductible by a partner if they are "regular" or "ordinary" items paid or incurred in the conduct of the partnership's business. This test for deductibility of expenses differs from the federal standard of "ordinary and necessary" (¶ 203). Thus, unreimbursed travel and entertainment expenses incurred by a partner and charitable contributions made by the partnership were deductible by the partners, even though they may not have been deductible for federal income tax purposes (*Sabino* (N.J. SuperCt 1996) 296 N.J. Super. 269; CCH New Jersey Tax Reports ¶ 400-492).

Keogh plan contributions: Contributions by a partnership on behalf of a partner to a Keogh plan are not deductible in calculating the partner's share of partnership income (*Reck*, N.J. (Supreme Court) 175 N.J. 54 (2002) CCH New Jersey Tax Reports ¶ 400-873); 18 N.J. Tax 598 (2000); CCH New Jersey Tax Reports ¶ 400-678; 345 N.J. Super. 443 (App. Div. 2001), CCH New Jersey Tax Reports ¶ 400-785).

Interest on capital contributions: The interest on a loan used to pay a partner's capital contribution was deductible in calculating the partner's distributive share of partnership income. The loan was a legitimate business expense, and not a personal expense, because the capital contribution was required in order for the lawyer to derive his income from the practice of law in the partnership (*Dantzler*, 18 N.J. Tax 490 (1999); CCH New Jersey Tax Reports ¶ 400-664).

Limited liability partnerships (LLPs): New Jersey authorizes the creation of LLPs, which are treated as partnerships for tax purposes, but afford individual partners protection against liability for the acts or conduct of other partners or employees who are not under their direct supervision. Members of an LLP are liable for personal income tax in their separate or individual capacities. The income of LLPs is not taxed at the entity level, but LLPs are required to file annual information reports.

Limited liability companies (LLCs): New Jersey authorizes the creation of LLCs. LLCs are treated as partnerships for New Jersey gross income tax purposes, unless otherwise classified for federal income tax purposes. Members of LLCs are treated as partners in a partnership, and are taxed only in their separate or individual capacities.

¶212

An LLC with one member is disregarded as a separate entity from its owner unless classified differently for federal tax purposes.

¶213 Prizes and Awards

Law: R.S. 54A:5-1, 54A:6-8, 54A:6-11 (CCH New Jersey Tax Reports ¶ 15-780).

Comparable Federal: Sec. 74.

Gross income includes all prizes and awards, except New Jersey Lottery winnings where the amount of the prize does not exceed $10,000 (¶ 208) and any amount received as a scholarship at an educational institution or as a fellowship grant. The latter exclusion extends to amounts received for travel, research and equipment expenses incident to a scholarship or research grant to the extent that the recipient actually spends the money for those purposes.

¶214 Alimony and Separate Maintenance

Law: R.S. 54A:5-1 (CCH New Jersey Tax Reports ¶ 15-610).

Comparable Federal: Secs. 61, 71.

Alimony and separate maintenance payments received must be included in gross income to the extent that they are paid under a decree of divorce or separate maintenance. Payments received for support of minor children are not includable.

CCH Tip: Alimony Payments to Nonresidents

Alimony is not one of the categories of income that is sourced to New Jersey under R.S. 54A:5-8. Accordingly, alimony payments made by a New Jersey resident to a nonresident are not taxable by New Jersey (*State Tax News*, Division of Taxation, Fall 1998; CCH New Jersey Tax Reports ¶ 400-607).

¶215 Gain from Criminal Acts

Law: R.S. 54A:5-1 (CCH New Jersey Tax Reports ¶ 15-710).

Income, gain or profit from acts or omissions that are crimes or offenses are included in gross income.

¶216 Environmental Fines or Penalties

Law: R.S. 54A:5-1(b)(2), (3), 54A:5-1(c) (CCH New Jersey Tax Reports ¶ 15-770).

No deduction from gross income is allowed for the amount of any civil, civil administrative or criminal penalty or fine assessed and collected for a violation of a state or federal environmental law, an administrative consent order, or an environmental ordinance or resolution of a local governmental entity. In addition, any interest earned on the penalty or fine and any economic benefit having accrued to the violator as a result of the violation must be included when computing the tax.

No deduction from gross income is allowed for treble damages paid for clean-up costs.

Penalties or fines assessed in connection with violations resulting from fire, riot, sabotage or an act of God beyond the reasonable control of the violator, as well as those that result from violations caused by an act or omission of a person who was outside the reasonable control of the violator, may be excluded from entire net income.

¶217 S Corporation Shareholder's Pro Rata Share of Income

Law: R.S. 54A:5-1, 54A:5-9 (CCH New Jersey Tax Reports ¶ 15-185).

The taxpayer's net pro rata share of S corporation income must be included in gross income, whether or not actually distributed to the shareholder during the shareholder's taxable year. The treatment of S corporation income and S corporation shareholders is discussed at ¶ 503.

¶218 Exclusion of Gain from Sale of Principal Residence

Law: R.S. 54A:6-9.1, 54A:6-9.2 (CCH New Jersey Tax Reports ¶ 15-710).

Comparable Federal: Sec. 121.

New Jersey law conforms to federal treatment on sales of a residence by providing for the exclusion from gross income of all or part of the gain derived from the sale or exchange of a principal residence. The gain realized from the sale or exchange of a taxpayer's principal residence after May 6, 1997, is excludable from gross income up to a maximum of $250,000 for an individual or $500,000 for a husband and wife filing jointly.

To qualify for the exclusion, during the five-year period ending with the sale of the property, it must have been used by the taxpayer as the principal residence for periods aggregating two years. If the taxpayer fails to meet the two-year period of ownership and use due to a change in place of employment, health, or unforeseen circumstances, the taxpayer may still be able to prorate and exclude part of the gain from gross income. A similar exception and proration exists during a two-year period beginning on August 5, 1997, for taxpayers who held property on that date.

Also, if a taxpayer becomes physically or mentally incapable of self-care and owns and uses the property as his or her principal residence for a period of one year during the five years preceding the sale, the taxpayer shall be considered to have used the property as the principal residence during any period of residence in a nursing facility licensed by the state.

The destruction, theft, seizure, requisition, or condemnation of the property is treated as a sale.

¶219 Exclusion of Gain and Income from Certain Government Obligations

Law: R.S. 54A:5-1, 54A:6-14, 54A:6-15 (CCH New Jersey Tax Reports ¶ 15-710, 16-280).

Comparable Federal: Sec. 103.

Gross income does not include gains and income (¶ 204) or interest (¶ 206) derived from certain bonds and other obligations. The exempt obligations are as follows:

— Obligations of New Jersey or any of its political subdivisions, agencies, authorities, commissions, instrumentalities and public corporations (including such corporations created or existing under an interstate agreement or compact); and

— Obligations free from state or local taxation under any federal or New Jersey law.

Income from obligations of other states and foreign governments is to be included in New Jersey gross income.

Distributions paid by mutual funds are excluded from gross income to the extent the distributions are attributable to interest earned on United States securities and obligations (*Colonial Trust III,* 16 N.J. Tax 385 (1997); CCH New Jersey Tax Reports ¶ 400-503).

Distributions (income and gains) by a qualified investment fund, in which at least 80% of the underlying investments are obligations issued either directly by the federal government or by New Jersey or its political subdivisions, are excluded from gross income (¶223).

The U.S. Supreme Court, in *Nebraska Department of Revenue v. Loewenstein* (US SCt 1994) 115 SCt 557; CCH NEW JERSEY TAX REPORTS ¶400-343, has held that Nebraska's income tax on interest received by a taxpayer from ownership of shares in mutual funds that entered into repurchase agreements involving federal obligations was a valid tax on interest derived from loans rather than an invalid tax on interest from the federal obligations themselves. The Court found the exemption for federal obligations to be limited to (1) coupon interest that an investor receives as periodic payments from the U.S. government at the rate stated on the obligation, and (2) discount interest, which refers to an investor's acquisition of an obligation at a discount from the amount the government will redeem it for at maturity. The Court further held that Nebraska's income tax on interest from repurchase agreements did not violate the Supremacy Clause of the U.S. Constitution, since the tax did not impair the market in federal obligations or the borrowing ability of the federal government, nor did the state treat repurchase agreements involving federal obligations differently from repurchase agreements involving state obligations.

¶220 Excludable Retirement Income

Law: R.S. 54A:5-8, 54A:6-15, 54A:6-26 (CCH NEW JERSEY TAX REPORTS ¶15-800).

New Jersey is prohibited by R.S. 54A:5-8 from taxing nonresidents on pension or annuity income derived from New Jersey sources. Federal law also prohibits a state from imposing an income tax on any retirement income from a qualified plan or annuity received by an individual who is a nonresident (4 U.S.C. Sec. 114). In addition, the exclusions specifically applicable to pensions, annuities, Social Security benefits and similar items of income (¶211) are supplemented by the following exclusions of retirement income from other sources.

Certain taxpayers age 62 and over: Any person who is 62 years old or older, and who received no more than $3,000 in the tax year as remuneration for services (¶202), net profits from business (¶203), distributive share of partnership income (¶212), or net pro rata share of S corporation income (¶204), is entitled to an exclusion from gross income. Excludable amounts for tax years 2003 and later are as follows: up to $20,000 for a married couple filing jointly; up to $10,000 for a married person filing separately; and up to $15,000 for a single taxpayer. For years beginning on or after January 1, 2005, the exclusion is only available if the taxpayer has gross income for the taxable year of not more the $100,000.

CCH Tip: Younger Spouse

If a taxpayer and spouse file a joint return and only one of them is 62 years old, they may still claim the full exclusion.

The total exclusion under these provisions and the provisions permitting exclusion of income from pensions, annuities, etc. (¶211), may not exceed the limits noted above.

Persons not covered by Social Security Act or Railroad Retirement Act provisions: If a taxpayer is not covered by provisions of the Social Security Act or Railroad Retirement Act, but would be eligible for benefits if covered, $6,000 may be excluded from gross income by a married couple filing jointly, or $3,000 by a single person or married person filing separately. This exclusion is in addition to any others for which a taxpayer is eligible.

Military pension and survivor's benefits: For tax years beginning on or after January 1, 2001, U.S. military pension payments or military survivor's benefit payments paid to individuals with respect to service in the U.S. Armed Forces are not included in gross income. For years prior to 2001, this exclusion was limited to U.S. military pension payments or military survivor's benefit payments made to individuals age 62 or older or who, because of disability, were eligible to receive Social Security payments during the tax year. However, such payments may be considered income for purposes of determining eligibility for any state benefit or program.

¶221 Exclusion of Employer-Provided Commuter Transportation Benefits

Law: R.S. 54A:6-23; Reg. Sec. 18:35-7.8 (CCH New Jersey Tax Reports ¶15-705).

For tax years 1997 through 2001, employees were allowed an exemption from gross income for employer-provided commuter transportation benefits up to a maximum exemption amount of $1,000. The maximum exemption was adjusted annually for inflation by rounding down to the nearest $5 in proportion to the change in the average consumer price index for all urban consumers in the New York, northeast New Jersey, and Philadelphia areas. Beginning with the 2002 tax year, the exemption from gross income increased to $1,200, adjusted annually for inflation in parallel with the adjustment set forth in Section 132(f)(6) of the Internal Revenue Code. For the 2013 tax year, the adjusted limit is $2,940. The adjusted limit was also $2,880 for 2012.

The exemption only applies to benefits paid in addition to, and not in lieu of, any compensation otherwise payable to the employee. Amounts received in excess of the maximum exemption must be included in the taxpayer's gross income. Employees who receive advances of reimbursements are required to show proof (in the form of receipts, ticket stubs, etc.) to the employer that the monies were used for alternative means of commuting.

A written statement must be provided by the employer to the employee showing the cost of the commuter transportation benefits paid by the employer to the employee. This statement may be included on the W-2 form or other written benefit statement that shows the amount of the benefit.

Partners in a partnership are allowed a credit against tax for commuter transportation benefits provided to employees of the partnership. For details, see ¶115.

¶222 Income Not Subject to Tax

Law: R.S. 30:6D-40, 54A:6-4—54A:6-7, 54A:6-13, 9A:10-2.7 (CCH New Jersey Tax Reports ¶15-155, 15-175, 15-650, 15-655, 15-715, 15-780).

Comparable Federal: Secs. 101, 102, 104, 105, 112.

In addition to the exclusions from New Jersey gross income noted in the paragraphs above, the law provides the following specific exemptions from tax:

Death benefits: Reportable gross income does not include proceeds of life insurance contracts paid because of a death, or employees' death benefits paid by or on behalf of an employer because of the death of an employee.

Gifts and inheritances: The value of cash or property acquired by gift, bequest, devise or inheritance is excluded from gross income. However, the exclusion does not extend to income from such exempt property, or to income that itself constitutes the gift, bequest, devise or inheritance.

Discharge of indebtedness: Although not expressly excluded from income by the statute, income from the discharge of indebtedness is not a specifically enumerated category of income and thus, is not subject to the personal income tax. (*Weintraub*, N.J. Tax Court, 19 N.J. Tax 65 (2000); CCH New Jersey Tax Reports ¶400-717).

Employer provided accident/health insurance: The value of any employer-provided accident/health plan coverage or reimbursements, including coverage or reimbursements for an employee's child, that are excluded from the employee's income for federal income tax purposes are also excluded from the employee's income for gross income tax purposes. See New Jersey TAM-14 (04/20/2011).

Compensation for injuries or sickness: Payments as compensation for personal injuries or sickness are exempt from tax when they are

— amounts received under workmen's compensation acts,

— damages received as the result of a suit or agreement,

— amounts received through accident or health insurance (including amounts received from the state fund or a private plan under the Temporary Disability Benefits Law (*Formal Opinion of the Attorney General* (1979); CCH NEW JERSEY TAX REPORTS [1966—1979 Transfer Binder], ¶ 200-820), or

— payments as a pension, annuity or similar allowance for injuries or sickness resulting from active service in the U.S. Armed Forces, the Coast and Geodetic Survey, or the Public Health Service, or as a disability annuity under the Foreign Service Act of 1946.

However, sick pay and sick leave injury payments made to New Jersey state employees under N.J.S.A. 11A:6-8 are taxable. See New Jersey TAM-15 (05/11/2011).

Qualified disaster relief payments: Qualified disaster relief payments excluded under IRC Sec. 139 are not treated as taxable income for personal income tax purposes. Qualified disaster relief payments excluded under IRC Sec. 139 include amounts paid to cover reasonable and necessary personal, family, living or funeral expenses that were not covered by insurance, and reasonable and necessary expenses to repair or rehabilitate a personal residence or repair or replace its contents to the extent that they were not covered by insurance. Disaster-related payments for lost wage or business income, however, are subject to tax and must be reported for gross income tax purposes. (Notice, Division of Taxation, February 21, 2013.)

Clergy housing: The rental value of a residence provided to clergy by a church or congregation does not constitute income for the cleric. A housing allowance is considered a reimbursed business expense; however, if the amount of the allowance exceeds the expense of providing a home, the excess constitutes taxable self-employment income (*State Tax News,* Division of Taxation; CCH NEW JERSEY TAX REPORTS [1989—1994 Transfer Binder], ¶ 400-040).

Armed forces payments: Individuals who are not domiciled in New Jersey are not required to report compensation paid for service in the U.S. Armed Forces.

All taxpayers may exclude armed forces mustering-out payments. For tax years beginning on or after January 1, 2004, amounts received as housing and subsistence allowances by members of the active and reserve components of the U.S. Armed Forces and by members of the New Jersey National Guard while on active duty are excluded from income.

Unemployment insurance: All payments and benefits received under any unemployment insurance law are excludable.

Family support services: Benefits in the form of family support services, vouchers, or cash subsidies that are received by families that include members with a developmental disability are not subject to gross income tax.

Nazi Holocaust reparations: Reparations, including interest, to victims of the Nazi Holocaust are exempt for all tangible and intangible property received after October 20, 1998. Cash payments in lieu of property qualify for the exemption.

Medical savings accounts: Effective January 1, 1998, gross income does not include contributions to a taxpayer's medical savings account if the contributions are excluded from the taxpayer's federal gross income. The exclusion applies only to individuals qualifying under the limitation of IRC Sec. 220(i) and is subject to the numerical limits of IRC Sec. 220(j), as in effect on January 1, 1997.

September 11 Victims: Gross income does not include any income otherwise taxable of any individual who died as a result of the September 11, 2001 terrorist attacks. This exclusion applies to the 2000 and 2001 tax years. Refunds are available for taxes previously paid for these periods.

In addition, the New Jersey Division of Taxation has issued a notice that discusses the New Jersey gross (personal) income tax treatment for recipients of payments from the federal September 11th Victim Compensation Fund and the federal Victims of Terrorism Tax Relief Act of 2001. For New Jersey gross income tax purposes, payments are excludable from income to the extent they are excluded from federal income tax.

Social services student loan redemption payments: Gross income does not include amounts received as redemption for eligible student loan expenses under the Social Services Student Loan Redemption Program.

CCH Tip: Federally Exempt Income

New Jersey does *not* exempt the following income that is federally exempt:

— interest from obligations of states and their political subdivisions, other than New Jersey;

— income earned by a resident from foreign employment;

— certain contributions to pensions and tax-deferred annuities; and

— employee contributions to certain retirement plans other than 401(k) plans, such as SEPs and 403(b) plans.

¶223 Excludable Dividends of Qualified Investment Funds

Law : R.S. 54A:6-14.1, 54A:6-27 (CCH New Jersey Tax Reports ¶ 15-710).

Distributions paid by qualified investment funds are not included in gross income, to the extent attributable to interest or gain from obligations issued by New Jersey or its local government entities or obligations that are free from state or local taxation under New Jersey or federal law. Such distributions are, therefore, not subject to tax.

Qualified investment funds are investment companies or trusts registered with the Securities and Exchange Commission, or any series of an investment company or trust (*i.e.*, a segregated portfolio of assets whose beneficial interests are owned by the holders of a class or series of stock or shares of the investment company or trust, preferred over all other classes or series regarding the portfolio of assets), which for the calendar year in which distribution is made has no investments other than interest-bearing obligations, obligations issued at a discount, financial options, futures, forward contracts, or other similar financial instruments related to interest-bearing obligations, obligations issued at a discount or related bond indexes, and cash and cash items (including receivables). Also, not less than 80% of the aggregate principal amount of all the investments (excluding financial options, futures, forward contracts, or other similar financial instruments related to interest-bearing obligations, obligations issued at a discount or related bond indexes, cash and cash items, including receivables) must be in obligations exempt from federal, state, or local taxation.

¶224 Excludable Qualified Employee Benefits Under Cafeteria Plan

Law : R.S. 54A:6-24 (CCH New Jersey Tax Reports ¶ 15-705).

The value of an employee's qualified option under a cafeteria plan is excludable from gross income, provided the employee does not elect to receive cash and the value of the option is excludable from federal taxable income. Excludable benefits are group life insurance, group accident and health insurance, medical cost reimbursement, dependent care services, and cash or deferred arrangements. Salary reduction agreements, such as flexible spending accounts and premium conversion options, are not tax-exempt. See Division of Taxation Technical Bulletin TB-39(R) (03/03/2003).

In order for the exclusion to apply, the cafeteria plan must meet the requirements of IRC Sec. 125. The employees "qualified option" is defined as an option to receive cash in lieu of a qualified employer-provided benefit, which option may only be exercised if the employee derives a substantially similar benefit from a source other than the employer.

PERSONAL INCOME TAX

CHAPTER 3

ALLOCATION AND APPORTIONMENT

¶301   Taxation of Nonresidents
¶302   Allocation and Apportionment
¶303   Wages of Nonresidents
¶304   Estimated Tax on Sales of Real Property by Nonresidents

¶301 Taxation of Nonresidents

Law: R.S. 54:8A-122, 54A:2-1.1, 54A:2-4, 54A:3-3, 54A:5-6, 54A:5-8, 54A:5-9, 54A:5-10, 54A:5-13, 54A:9-17, Ch. 320, Laws 1993 (CCH NEW JERSEY TAX REPORTS ¶15-110, 15-115, 16-505, 16-615).

A nonresident individual, partner, S corporation shareholder, estate, or trust is subject to tax on the same kinds of income as a resident, to the extent that the income is earned, received, or acquired from sources within New Jersey in any of the following ways:

— By reason of ownership or disposition of any real or tangible personal property in New Jersey;

— In connection with a trade, profession, or occupation carried on or the rendition of personal services performed in the state (except as noted under "Reciprocal exemptions" below);

— As a distributive share of the income of an unincorporated business, profession, enterprise, undertaking, or other activity resulting from work done, services rendered, or other business activities conducted in New Jersey (except as allocated to another state pursuant to regulations);

— From intangible personal property employed in a trade, profession, occupation, or business carried on in the state;

— As a result of any lottery or wagering transactions in New Jersey other than excludable New Jersey lottery winnings; or

— As S corporation income allocated to New Jersey.

For definitions of resident and nonresident individuals, estates, and trusts, see ¶102. For gross income categories, see ¶201 and following. The taxability of estates and trusts is discussed at ¶501.

The New Jersey gross income tax due for each taxable year from a nonresident taxpayer will be equal to the tax computed as if the nonresident were a resident, multiplied by a fraction, the numerator of which is the taxpayer's income from sources within New Jersey and the denominator of which is the taxpayer's gross income for the taxable year computed as if the taxpayer were a resident.

The requirement that nonresident taxpayers prorate liability as though residents will be suspended if New York State eliminates that requirement for its taxpayers. The New Jersey Attorney General has the duty of reviewing New York laws to determine if New York's current method of taxation of income from New York sources of taxpayers who are not New York residents has been changed so as to restrict the computation of liability owed to New York to a method based only on the New York source income of the taxpayer. If the Attorney General determines that New York's method of taxation has been so changed, then no later than five days after the enactment of New York's new law, the Attorney General must certify to the

Director of the Division of Taxation the taxable years for which New York's fractional method of calculating liability for nonresident taxpayers has been repealed or superseded. For those years, the income of nonresident individuals will be limited to the individual's income derived from sources within New Jersey, except income derived from sources within New Jersey from pensions and annuities as set forth in R.S. 54A:5-1(j). Also, for those taxable years, nonresident taxpayers will be allowed the same deduction for personal exemptions as resident taxpayers. However, where the nonresident taxpayer's gross income subject to personal income tax is exceeded by more than $100, the gross income that the nonresident would be required to report if the taxpayer were a resident, then the deduction for personal exemptions is limited by the percentage that the nonresident's gross income subject to New Jersey personal income tax bears to the gross income that the nonresident would be required to report if he or she were a resident.

Pension and annuity income: Pension and annuity income received by nonresidents from sources within New Jersey is exempt from tax.

Limitations on deductions and low-income exemption: A deduction for medical expenses may be taken only to the extent that the expenses exceed the taxpayer's income from all sources (¶106).

The low-income exemption (¶110) applies to nonresidents only if they meet the test with respect to income determined as if they were residents.

Husband and wife: If a husband and wife who are both taxable nonresidents file separate returns, their income from New Jersey sources must be separately determined.

If one spouse is a resident and the other a nonresident, taxes must be computed on their separate incomes unless they elect to file a joint return as though they were both residents.

S corporation shareholders: Nonresident S corporation shareholders must allocate to New Jersey the portion of the S corporation income that is required to be allocated pursuant to corporate income tax allocation provisions (¶902—906). An S corporation shareholder that is both a resident and nonresident of New Jersey during the taxable year is required to prorate the pro rata share of allocable S corporation income between the shareholder's periods of residence and nonresidence during the taxable period.

Where the portion of the income from sources within New Jersey cannot readily or accurately be ascertained, the Director may, by regulation, prescribe uniform rules for apportionment or allocation of so much of the taxpayer's income as fairly and equitably represents income derived from sources within New Jersey and subject to New Jersey gross income tax.

Nonresident partners: Partnerships may have to pay (withhold) a tax at the rate of 6.37% on a nonresident noncorporate partner's share of partnership income apportioned to New Jersey. For rules concerning partnerships, see ¶502.

Reciprocal exemptions: The Division of Taxation may enter into an agreement with the taxing authorities of any other state imposing a tax on (or measured by) income, to provide for reciprocal exemption of nonresidents' compensation. Any such agreement may also provide for reciprocal requirements for employers to withhold tax on behalf of the other state, and may include arrangements for exchange of information and other forms of cooperation between the states.

Under a reciprocal agreement, Pennsylvania residents are not subject to the tax on their compensation paid in New Jersey, and are not required to file returns covering compensation. However, the reciprocal agreement between Pennsylvania and New Jersey does not apply to pension income that is derived by the residents of

¶301

each state as a result of employment in the other state. The gross income tax applies to other kinds of income from New Jersey sources.

Nonresident traders of commodities and securities: A nonresident taxpayer is not deemed to be carrying on a trade or business or rendering personal services in New Jersey solely as a result of the purchase, holding, and sale of commodities and securities if (1) the activities related to the commodities and securities are for the account of the trade or business, and (2) the trade or business does not hold the commodities and securities for sale to customers.

¶302 Allocation and Apportionment

Law: R.S. 54A:5-7, Reg. Sec. 18:35-1.1(e) (CCH NEW JERSEY TAX REPORTS ¶16-505).

If business activities are carried on both inside and outside New Jersey, business income may be allocated to determine the amount of income from New Jersey sources. Prior to 2013, carrying on business activities outside New Jersey means maintaining, operating or occupying a regular place of business outside New Jersey, such as an office, shop, store, warehouse, factory, agency or other place where the business affairs are systematically and regularly conducted. The business may not allocate income if it has only an occasional or isolated business transaction outside New Jersey.

CCH Advisory: *Regular Place of Business Not a Requirement for Allocation*

The Division of Taxation has announced that an unincorporated business is not required to maintain a regular place of business outside New Jersey in order to allocate its income. So long as the business carries on its business activities both inside and outside New Jersey, it may allocate its income on Form NJ-NR-A in order to determine the amount from New Jersey sources. Notice, Division of Taxation, March 13, 2013.

Business income is allocated using a three-fraction formula which measures the percentage of property, receipts and payroll in New Jersey over the property, receipts and payroll of the business everywhere. The three percentages are added together and divided by three. There is no double-weighting of the receipts fraction. The allocation of business income is set forth on the Business Allocation Schedule (Form NJ-NR-A) filed with the gross income tax return.

If the portion of a nonresident's income derived from or connected with New Jersey sources cannot be ascertained readily or accurately for any reason, the Director of the Division of Taxation may prescribe uniform rules for equitable allocation and apportionment of the income.

¶303 Wages of Nonresidents

Law: R.S. 54A:2-1.1, 54A:2-2.1, 54A:5-7 (CCH NEW JERSEY TAX REPORTS ¶16-570).

A nonresident individual, estate, or trust is subject to tax on income earned, received, or acquired from sources within New Jersey (except in the case of compensation income received by Pennsylvania residents; see ¶301 above). The New Jersey gross income tax due for each taxable year from a nonresident taxpayer will be equal to the tax computed as if the nonresident were a resident, multiplied by a fraction, the numerator of which is the taxpayer's income from sources within New Jersey and the denominator of which is the taxpayer's gross income for the taxable year computed as if the taxpayer were a resident (¶301).

The amount of compensation attributable to New Jersey services is a percentage of total compensation for services based on the ratio of the total number of working days employed within New Jersey to the total number of working days everywhere, exclusive of nonworking days.

Salespersons: In the case of a traveling salesperson or other employee whose compensation depends directly on the volume of business transacted, the amount of compensation attributable to New Jersey is a percentage of the compensation received based on the ratio of the volume of business transacted by the salesperson in the state to the total volume of business transacted by the salesperson everywhere.

See ¶ 408 with regard to withholding requirements.

¶304 Estimated Tax on Sales of Real Property by Nonresidents

Law: R.S. 54A:8–8–54A:8-10 (CCH New Jersey Tax Reports ¶ 15-610).

For sales or transfers of real property occurring on and after August 1, 2004, nonresident individuals, estates, and trusts who sell or transfer certain real property located within New Jersey are required to pay estimated gross income tax. The amount of the estimated gross income tax is determined by multiplying the amount of the gain, if any, from the sale or transfer of the real property recognized for federal income tax purposes by the highest applicable rate of New Jersey gross income tax in effect for the taxable year. The estimated tax payment may not be less than 2% of the consideration for the sale or transfer stated in the deed affecting the conveyance.

Nonresident sellers of real property must file the estimated tax form regardless of whether they have a gain on the sale or transfer. County recording officers are prohibited from recording or accepting for recording any deed for the sale or transfer of real property unless accompanied by an appropriate form. Nonresident transferors are entitled to a credit on their personal income tax returns for the estimated tax paid.

Exemptions: A nonresident transferor is exempt from the payment of estimated gross income tax if: (1) the real property being sold or transferred is used exclusively as the principal residence of the seller within the meaning of Section 121 of the Internal Revenue Code; (2) the seller is a mortgagor conveying the mortgaged property to a mortgagee in foreclosure or in a transfer in lieu of foreclosure with no additional consideration; or (3) the seller or transferor, or transferee is an agency or authority of the United States of America, an agency or authority of the State of New Jersey, the Federal National Mortgage Association, the Federal Home Loan Mortgage Corporation, the Government National Mortgage Association, or a private mortgage insurance company.

The New Jersey Division of Taxation has also issued Memoranda stipulating that sheriffs' sales and bankruptcy trustees' sales are not subject to the estimated tax requirements for sales of real property by nonresidents. In addition, the Division has indicated that nonresident sellers are exempt from the estimated tax requirements if gain from the sale will not be recognized for federal income tax purposes under Sections 721, 1031, 1033 of the Internal Revenue Code, if the real property is a cemetery plot, if the transfer is by an executor or administrator of a decedent to a devisee or heir to effect distribution of the decedent's estate in accordance with the provisions of the decedent's will or the intestate laws of New Jersey, and in the case of certain relocation transactions where an employee sells his property to a relocation company. In the case of a situation that is not covered by a specific exemption, but where the granting of a waiver would be appropriate, the Regulatory Services Branch of the Division of Taxation will consider other exemptions on a case by case basis. *Technical Bulletin TB-5*, Division of Taxation, September 26, 2005.

Filing Requirements: In order to have a deed recorded for the transfer of real property, one of the following forms (and payment, where applicable) needs to be completed and submitted to the County recorder: GIT/REP-1 (Nonresident Seller's Tax Declaration), GIT/REP-2 (Nonresident Seller's Tax Prepayment Receipt), GIT/REP-3 (Seller's Residency Certification Exemption) or GIT/REPa-4 (Waiver of Seller's Filing Requirement of GIT/REP Forms and Payment). In the case of the GIT/REP-1, the seller is required to provide the closing/settlement agent with the form at closing, along with payment. The form and payment are then filed with the deed by the closing/settlement agent. If a nonresident seller wishes to make his payment prior to closing, the GIT/REP-2 is completed by the nonresident at a Division of Taxation field office. GIT/REP-2 forms are not issued by the Division unless an estimated gross income tax payment is submitted.

PERSONAL INCOME TAX

CHAPTER 4
RETURNS, ESTIMATES, PAYMENT OF TAX, WITHHOLDING

¶401	Returns—Time and Place of Filing
¶402	Who Must File
¶403	Returns of Husband and Wife
¶404	Forms in Current Use
¶405	Extension of Time
¶406	Estimated Tax
¶407	Payment of Tax
¶408	Withholding of Tax—In General
¶409	Withholding—Tables and Methods
¶410	Withholding—Returns and Payment
¶411	Information at Source

¶401 Returns—Time and Place of Filing

Law: R.S. 54A:8-1, 54A:8-7, 54A:9-11 (CCH New Jersey Tax Reports ¶89-102).

Comparable Federal: Secs. 6072, 6091.

The New Jersey personal income tax return is due at the same time as the federal return: by the 15th day of the fourth month following the close of the taxpayer's fiscal year—April 15 in the case of calendar-year taxpayers.

When a due date falls on a Saturday, Sunday, or holiday, it is extended to the next business day.

The return is filed with the Division of Taxation, Trenton, NJ.

For declarations of estimated tax, see ¶406. For withholding requirements, see ¶408.

Report of federal changes: If a taxpayer's federal taxable income is changed or corrected, the taxpayer must report the change or correction to New Jersey within 90 days (or as otherwise required by the Director). The accuracy of the change or correction must be conceded or the taxpayer must state in what way it is erroneous.

A taxpayer who files an amended federal return must file an amended state return within 90 days thereafter.

The Director may make exceptions to these requirements by regulation.

¶402 Who Must File

Law: R.S. 54A:8-3.1, 54A:8-6; Reg. Secs. 18:35-5.2, 18:35-6.4 (CCH New Jersey Tax Reports ¶15-205—15-275, 89-102, 89-106).

Comparable Federal: Sec. 6012.

A return must be made by every individual, estate and trust with gross income in excess of the low-income exemption (¶110).

For return of husband and wife, see ¶403.

Nonresidents: Return requirements apply to nonresidents generally; however, residents of Pennsylvania are not required to file returns with respect to compensation received in New Jersey.

A filing entity may file a composite New Jersey Nonresident Gross Income Tax Return (Form NJ-1080-C) on behalf of its qualified nonresident individuals. A filing entity is a general or limited partnership, a limited liability partnership, a limited liability company, a New Jersey electing S corporation, an estate, a trust, or a professional athletic team doing business or conducting activities in New Jersey that files a composite return on behalf of its qualified nonresident individual partners, members, shareholders, or beneficiaries, respectively.

CCH Advisory: Composite Returns

The New Jersey Administrative Code requires income taxation on the composite return at the highest rate. However, for tax years prior to 2013, the Division of Taxation allows the use of two tax rates in order to encourage nonresident individuals to elect to participate in a composite return. For the tax year 2012, the two tax rates applied were 6.37% and 8.97%. The 6.37% rate was applied to participating individuals with New Jersey sourced income of less than $250,000, and the 8.97% rate was applied to participating individuals with New Jersey sourced income of $250,000 or more. For tax years beginning on or after January 1, 2013, all entity members or partners who elect to participate in the composite return filing will be required to pay tax at the highest 8.97% rate. Division of Taxation Notice, October 11, 2013.

Decedents: Returns for deceased individuals are to be made by their fiduciary or other person charged with their property.

Minors and other persons under disability: Returns for individuals who are unable to make a return because of age or a disability are to be made by their fiduciary or other person in charge of their person or property (except a receiver in possession of only a portion of the property), or by their authorized agent.

Partners and partnerships: Partnerships, including limited liability partnerships and limited liability companies, having income derived from New Jersey sources or having a partner or member who is a New Jersey resident, must file a Form NJ-1065 with the New Jersey Division of Taxation.

The Director of Taxation may prescribe a partnership return form that includes, at a minimum, the name and address of each partner. Every partnership that is required to file a return is required to furnish each partner, or person who holds an interest in the partnership as a nominee, with a copy of the information required to be shown on the return.

Electronic Filing: For the year 2006, any tax preparer who has prepared or filed 100 or more gross income tax returns for the preceding tax year must use electronic filing and payment methods, except for persons filing their own return and professionals preparing returns *pro bono.* For the year 2007 and later years, tax preparers who have prepared or filed more than 50 gross income tax returns for a prior tax year must use electronic filing and payment methods. For the year 2008 and later years, tax preparers who have prepared or filed 25 or more gross income tax returns for a prior tax year must use electronic filing and payment methods. For the year 2011 and later years, tax preparers who reasonably expect to prepare 11 or more individual gross income tax resident returns (including those filed for trusts and estates) during the tax year must use electronic methods for filing such returns and may pay the tax on behalf of the taxpayers in accordance with instructions published by the Director for all the individual gross income tax resident returns prepared or filed by the preparer. For each return for which a tax preparer fails to file electronically, there can be imposed a penalty of $50, in addition to any other penalty prescribed by law.

Information returns: See ¶411.

¶402

¶403 Returns of Husband and Wife

Law: R.S. 54A:5-6, 54A:8-3.1 (CCH New Jersey Tax Reports ¶ 15-125, 89-102).

Comparable Federal: Sec. 6013.

When a husband and wife are both residents or both nonresidents, they must file jointly or separately for New Jersey purposes in accordance with their filing status for federal purposes.

However, if one is a resident and one a nonresident for the entire year, or if both spouses are nonresidents but only one derives income from New Jersey sources, separate returns must be filed unless they elect to file a joint return.

Declarations of estimated tax: See ¶ 406.

¶404 Forms in Current Use

Law: R.S. 54A:8-6 (CCH New Jersey Tax Reports ¶ 89-070).

Forms may be obtained by calling the Taxpayer Services Branch of the Division of Taxation's automated number (800) 323-4400, 24 hours a day. Forms may be downloaded from the New Jersey Division of Taxation's website at http://www.state.nj.us/treasury/taxation/taxprnt.htm

Forms in current use include the following:

No.	Description
NJ-1040-ES	Declaration of Estimated Gross Income Tax
NJ-1040	Income Tax—Resident Return
NJ-1040NR	Gross Income Tax Nonresident Return
NJ-NR-A	Business Allocation Schedule
NJ-1040X	Amended Income Tax Return
NJ-1040-H	Property Tax Credit Application
NJ-1041	Gross Income Tax Fiduciary Return
NJ-1041SB	Gross Income Tax Fiduciary Return for Electing Small Business Trust
NJ-1041-V	Fiduciary Return Payment Voucher
NJ-1080C	Nonresident Composite Return
NJ-1080E	Election to Participate in Composite Return
NJ-1040-O	E-File Opt-Out Request Form
NJ-630	Application for Extension of Time to File New Jersey Gross Income Tax Return
NJ-2210	Underpayment of Estimated Tax
NJ-2440	Exclusions for Amounts Received for Personal Injury or Sickness
NJ-2450	Claim for Credit for Excess WD/HC and Disability Contributions
GIT-DEP	Depreciation Deduction Worksheet
GIT-317	Sheltered Workshop Credit
501-GIT	Domestic Production Activities Deduction
NJ-1065	Partnership Return
NJK-1	Partner's Share of Income
Part 100	Partnership Return Voucher
Part 160	Underpayment of Estimated Partnership Tax
Part 200-T	Partnership Tentative Return and Application for Extension of Time to File

¶405 Extension of Time

Law: R.S. 54A:8-1; Reg. Sec. 18:35-6.1 (CCH New Jersey Tax Reports ¶ 89-102).

Comparable Federal: Sec. 6081.

The Division of Taxation allows a six-month extension to taxpayers who have been granted a six-month extension for federal income tax purposes. A copy of the federal extension must be included with the New Jersey return. If a taxpayer must make a payment of New Jersey tax in connection with the New Jersey extension, then Form NJ-630 must be filed with the payment.

If a taxpayer has not obtained a federal extension, an automatic six-month extension may nevertheless be obtained by filing Form NJ-630, the application for extension of time to file the New Jersey Gross Income Tax Return. The form must be filed with payment of at least 80% of the tax liability by the original due date of the return.

Extension of time to file does not extend the time to pay tax. At least 80% of the tax liability must be paid in the form of withholdings, estimated or other payments by the original due date. Late payments of tax, even when an extension has been granted, are subject to a late payment penalty of 5% and interest at an annual rate of 3% above the prime rate imposed for each month (or fraction thereof) on the unpaid balance of tax.

Partnerships: A partnership may obtain a five-month extension to file its New Jersey partnership return by attaching a copy of the federal Form 7004 to the Form NJ-1065.

Military: New Jersey taxpayers who are members of the armed forces serving in or serving in support of the armed forces of the United States in a qualified hazardous duty area are granted an extension of time to file an income tax return, pay the tax, or meet any other deadlines.

¶406 Estimated Tax

Law: R.S. 54A:8-4, 54A:8-5, 54A:8-8—54A:8-10, 54A:9-6 (CCH New Jersey Tax Reports ¶89-104).

Comparable Federal: Sec. 6654.

Declarations and installment payments of estimated tax are required from all resident and nonresident individuals whose tax liability can reasonably be expected to exceed amounts withheld and other credits against the tax (¶¶112—117) by more than $400. These provisions are not further qualified, as they are in the Internal Revenue Code. A taxpayer may have to file declarations and make payments of New Jersey tax even though not required under federal law.

Declarations and installment payments are due by April 15, June 15, September 15, or January 15 for calendar-year taxpayers, depending on when the requirements are first met, with the number of installment payments varying according to when the declaration is first filed. Fiscal-year taxpayers substitute corresponding months of the fiscal year.

The declaration, on Form NJ-1040-ES, is filed with the New Jersey Division of Taxation.

In lieu of a declaration or amended declaration due by January 15, a final return accompanied by payment in full of the tax due may be filed by February 15 following the taxable year.

Estates and trusts: Estates and trusts are subject to the estimated tax provisions, except an estate or trust that meets the two-year limitation and other criteria of IRC Sec. 6654(l)(2).

Farmers: An individual whose estimated New Jersey income from farming (including oyster farming) is at least two-thirds of total estimated income for the taxable year may file a declaration by January 15 of the succeeding year, but must pay the entire estimated tax when the declaration is filed. New Jersey law does not include special estimated tax provisions, like those of the federal law, applicable to taxpayers whose income is principally derived from fishing.

Husband and wife: A husband and wife may make a joint declaration of estimated tax unless they have different taxable years or they are separated under a decree of divorce or separate maintenance. If they file separate annual returns, credit for payments of estimated tax may be divided between them as they elect.

Sale of real property by nonresidents: For sales or transfers of real property occurring on and after August 1, 2004, nonresident individuals, estates, and trusts who sell or transfer certain real property located within New Jersey are required to pay estimated gross income tax. The amount of the estimated gross income tax is determined by multiplying the amount of the gain, if any, from the sale or transfer of the real property recognized for federal income tax purposes by the highest applicable rate of New Jersey gross income tax in effect for the taxable year. The estimated tax payment may not be less than 2% of the consideration for the sale or transfer stated in the deed affecting the conveyance. For a discussion of exemptions and filing requirements see ¶304.

Underpayment of tax: An addition to tax at the rate set under the State Tax Uniform Procedure Law applies to any underpayment of tax for the period of underpayment. The rate is set at 3% above the prime rate as announced on the first day of the calendar quarter preceding the period for which interest is being computed (¶2010). For tax periods beginning on or after January 1, 1999, the amount of underpayment is the excess of the lesser of (1) the amount of the installment that would be required to be paid if the estimated tax were equal to 80% of the tax (66²/₃% in the case of farmers) shown on the return for the taxable year (or if no return is filed, 80% of the tax for the year), or (2) 100% of the tax shown on the taxpayer's return for the preceding taxable year. However, if a taxpayer's income after deductions for the preceding tax year exceeds $150,000 ($75,000 for married persons filing separately), the "safe harbor" provision referring to last year's tax requires payment of 110% of last year's tax, instead of 100%.

No underpayment exists with respect to due dates after a taxpayer's death.

¶407 Payment of Tax

Law: R.S. 54A:8-1, 54A:8-5 (CCH New Jersey Tax Reports ¶89-102, 89-108).

Comparable Federal: Sec. 6151.

Payment of the amount of tax shown due on the annual return must accompany the return (¶401). Estimated tax payments are made in equal installments with the declaration and by remaining due dates (¶406).

CCH Tip: Use Tax

Any use tax due may be reported and paid with the personal income tax return, if it is not reported using Form ST-18, Use Tax Remittance.

¶408 Withholding of Tax—In General

Law: R.S. 54A:7-1, 54A:7-1.1, 54A:9-17 (CCH New Jersey Tax Reports ¶16-605—16-665).

Comparable Federal: Sec. 3402.

New Jersey requires employers to withhold state personal income tax from the taxable wages of resident and nonresident employees.

Basically, any compensation regarded as "wages" for federal income tax withholding purposes is subject to the New Jersey requirements, except, in the case of nonresidents, the requirements apply only to wages for services performed in New Jersey. Because of provisions of federal law, tax is not withheld from the compensation of seamen engaged in foreign, coastwise, intercoastal, interstate, or noncontiguous trade or from interstate carrier employees who earn 50% or less of their wages in New Jersey, unless they do not earn more than 50% of their wages in any one state and are New Jersey residents.

CCH Tip: Employers of Household Workers

The reporting and payment of New Jersey gross (personal) income tax withholding, New Jersey unemployment compensation contributions, and New Jersey disability benefits contributions by individuals who employ only household workers is simplified, applicable to wages paid after 1999. For details, see ¶410.

Withholding exemptions: Generally, the number of withholding exemptions claimed by an employee on federal Form W-4 will be used for New Jersey withholding computation. However, a civil union partner must file NJ-W4 Employee's Withholding Allowance Certificate and check the *Married/Civil Union Couple Joint* or *Married/Civil Union Couple Separate* box for joint filing status for New Jersey withholding purposes.

An employer who has been furnished by an employee with federal Form W-4, showing no federal tax liability, is not required to withhold New Jersey tax from the employee's wages. However, the employer is required to furnish W-2 forms (¶410) to the employee.

Form NJ-W4-E, Employee's Withholding Exemption Form, is to be completed by employees who expect to have no income tax liability because their income will be less than the filing threshold (¶402).

Gambling winnings: The payor of gambling winnings must withhold New Jersey gross income tax on these winnings, other than a New Jersey Lottery prize not exceeding $10,000, at a rate of 3% in all instances where the payor is required to withhold for federal purposes under IRC Sec. 3402(q).

Pensions and annuities: Recipients of pensions and annuities may specify that the payor withhold state personal income tax from disability or retirement benefits. The amount to be withheld must be an even dollar amount (not less than $10 per pay period) stipulated by the recipient on a form specified by the Division of Taxation. The amount withheld may be changed or terminated upon request by the recipient.

Resident employees of employers required to withhold other state income taxes: All compensation paid to a New Jersey resident is subject to withholding even though the services were rendered outside of New Jersey. However, if a resident is employed wholly outside of New Jersey and is subject to withholding in the state where he or she is employed, an employer is required to withhold only any amount of New Jersey tax in excess of the amount withheld from the employee's wages on behalf of the other state. Special procedures apply if the tax authorities of another state have entered into a reciprocal agreement with New Jersey (see "Reciprocal agreements" below).

Nonresidents: An employer must deduct New Jersey income tax from all wages paid to a nonresident employee for services performed in New Jersey, except as noted under "Reciprocal agreements" below.

If a nonresident employee performs services partly within and partly outside of New Jersey, only compensation for the services within the state is subject to withholding (see ¶303 for methods of allocation). The allocation may be made on the basis of the preceding year's experience or on the basis of an estimate by employer or employee for the current year, subject to adjustment during the year. An employer must withhold tax from all compensation paid to such an employee unless the employer maintains adequate current records for accurate determination of the New Jersey compensation.

If it is expected that a nonresident employee will work only a short time in New Jersey and that total wages for services in the state will not exceed the employee's personal exemptions, the employer need not withhold the tax until the aggregate amount paid is in excess of the exemptions.

Sales of Real Property by Nonresidents: Nonresident individuals, estates and trusts are required to pay estimated gross income tax on the gain from the sale of New Jersey real estate. The estimated gross income tax is determined by multiplying the

¶408

gain recognized for federal income tax purposes by the highest applicable gross income tax rate and may not be less than 2% of the consideration stated in the deed. The estimated tax withholding requirements apply to sales occurring on or after August 1, 2004. For a more detailed discussion of the estimated tax withholding requirements, see ¶ 304.

Unregistered construction contractors: Beginning January 1, 2007, every person maintaining an office or transacting business in New Jersey (other than a governmental entity, homeowner or tenant) and making payments for services to unregistered, unincorporated construction contractors, must withhold New Jersey income tax at the rate of 7% from those payments. "Contractor" means a person entering into a contract for services to construct, improve, alter, or repair a building or structure, or improvement to real property and includes a subcontractor. "Unincorporated contractor" means an individual contractor or a contractor organized as a sole proprietorship, partnership, or any other business form not taxable as a corporation for federal tax purposes. Withholding on the payment is not required if the person making the payment has obtained from the contractor receiving the payment proof of the contractor's registration with the Division of Revenue, Department of Treasury.

CCH Tip: Classification of Construction Workers

Effective July 13, 2007, there is a statutory presumption that, for purposes of the New Jersey income tax, workers in the construction industry are deemed to be employees unless they meet a stringent three-prong test establishing them as independent contractors. Criminal penalties can be imposed for misclassification of the construction employee.

Reciprocal agreements: The Division of Taxation may enter into agreements with taxing authorities of other states to provide that the compensation of a nonresident employee is subject only to the personal income tax of the state of residence, and to require employers to withhold tax accordingly.

Under the terms of a reciprocal agreement with Pennsylvania, Pennsylvania residents are exempt from New Jersey tax on compensation paid in New Jersey, and New Jersey residents are similarly exempt from Pennsylvania tax on compensation paid in Pennsylvania (the agreement does not extend to Philadelphia taxes). The exemption applies only to compensation. Other kinds of taxable income are not affected (¶ 301).

When an employer in New Jersey or Pennsylvania is furnished with a certificate of nonresidence by an employee who resides in the other state, the employer is to withhold tax as required by the personal income tax law of the employee's state of residence.

¶409 Withholding—Tables and Methods

Law: R.S. 54A:7-1 (CCH NEW JERSEY TAX REPORTS ¶ 16-620).

Comparable Federal: Sec. 3402.

New Jersey tax is to be withheld from wages for each payroll period. Ordinarily, the tax to be withheld must be determined in accordance with the withholding tables or methods issued by the Division of Taxation. When a special situation exists, an employer may apply to the Director of the Division for permission to use another method. Additional amounts may be withheld if there is an agreement in writing to that effect between employer and employee.

To avoid double withholding, the amount of tax that would otherwise be withheld from the wages of a New Jersey resident should be reduced by any income tax withheld from the same wages pursuant to the laws of other states, their political subdivisions or the District of Columbia.

¶410 Withholding—Returns and Payment

Law: R.S. 54:8A-69, 54:48-4.1, 54A:7-2, 54A:7-4, 54A:7-7; Reg. Secs. 18:35-7.2, 18:35-7.3, 18:35-7.8 (CCH New Jersey Tax Reports ¶16-665).

Comparable Federal: Sec. 3403.

The following are the principal forms in current use in connection with withholding of tax:

No.	Description
NJ-165	Employee's Certificate of Nonresidence in New Jersey
NJ-927-H	Domestic Employer Tax Reporting
NJ-927/NJ-927W	Quarterly Employer Return Package
W-2	Wage and Tax Statement
NJ-W-4	Employee's Withholding Allowance Certificate
NJ-W-4P	Certificate of Voluntary Withholding from Pension and Annuity Payments
GIT/REP-1	Nonresident Seller's Tax Declaration
NJ-550	Monthly Return of Withholding from Unregistered Unincorporated Contractors
NJ-W-3-UNC	Annual Reconciliation of Withholding from Unregistered Unincorporated Contractors
NJ-W-3M	Reconciliation of Tax Withheld

Employers or payors of pensions or annuities required to deduct and withhold tax generally must file a withholding return and remit payment by the 15th of each month following the month in which tax was withheld. There are various exceptions, based on total amounts withheld, as noted below.

For calendar quarters after the quarter ending December 31, 2008, the following reports, including amendments, must be filed electronically by all employers and third-party processors: (1) Form WR-30, Employer Report of Wages Paid; (2) Form NJ-927, Employer's Quarterly Report; and (3) Form NJ-927H, Domestic Employer's Annual Report.

Regardless of the amount withheld, employers are allowed to file quarterly, and make payments on either a quarterly, monthly, or accelerated basis depending on the amount withheld. An employer who withholds $500 or more for either the first or second month of a calendar quarter is required to make a monthly payment for that particular month. If the amount withheld is less than $500, or if it is withheld during the third month of the quarter, the payment must be made with the quarterly return. An employer whose aggregate withholding during the prior tax year was at least $20,000 is termed an "accelerated payor" and must remit amounts withheld by the Wednesday following the week during which the tax was withheld.

When an employer is required to withhold and remit New Jersey gross income tax and the amount withheld in the prior year was $10,000 or more, the employer must remit withheld taxes using electronic funds transfer (EFT). EFT payments must be made on or before the Wednesday following the week of the payday on which the taxes were withheld. An employer who is required to make EFT payments of all taxes, other than the gross income tax, because of a prior year tax liability of $10,000 or more, must remit withheld gross income taxes on either a quarterly or monthly basis.

Household employees: According to a Technical Bulletin issued by the New Jersey Division of Taxation, a household worker (*i.e.,* a babysitter, nanny, health aide, nurse, maid, or yard worker) working at the private home of an employer may be considered to be a domestic employee. Employers are not required to withhold New Jersey gross income tax from wages paid to domestic employees if they are not required to withhold for federal income tax purposes. If federal withholdings are required, however, or if the employee elects to have federal income tax withheld, gross income tax also must be withheld.

¶410

CCH Tip: Employers of Household Workers

Beginning in 2000, if an employer is liable for withholding only with respect to remuneration for domestic service, returns reporting withheld taxes and contributions must be filed annually by January 31 following the close of the calendar year, and the withheld taxes and contributions must be paid to the Division of Taxation at that time. "Domestic service" includes employment as a babysitter, nanny, health aide, private nurse, maid, caretaker, yard worker, or the like. Previously, employers of household workers were subject to the same quarterly system of returns and payments as other employers.

If the employment of a household worker is terminated, an employer subject to the annual reporting and payment system must report to the Commissioner of the New Jersey Department of Labor, on a form prescribed by the Commissioner, all wage information for completed calendar quarters of employment not previously reported and such other separation information as may be required to correctly process an unemployment compensation claim.

Frequency of returns and payments: The Director may, by regulation, require withholding returns and payments to be made on a more frequent basis if the Director considers such action to be in the state's best interest. If the Director believes it necessary to protect revenues, the Director is authorized to require an employer to make a return and payment at any time.

Payments of withheld taxes by electronic funds transfer cannot be made more frequently than once a week.

Annual requirement: Every employer and payor of a pension or annuity required to deduct and withhold tax must, on or before February 15, furnish each employee and pension or annuity recipient with written statements prescribed by the Division of Taxation, specifying the amount of wages, pension, or annuity payments paid and the amount deducted and withheld as tax. If employment or the pension or annuity is terminated prior to the close of the year, the written statements must be provided within 30 days of the date on which the last payment was made. The employer must also furnish information as to the employee's unemployment and disability insurance contributions and the cost of both commuter transportation benefits that are excludable and those which are not excludable by the employee.

By February 15 an employer must file NJ-W-3, the annual Reconciliation Statement, with the Division of Taxation along with Copy 1 of all W-2's and a totaled listing of all tax withheld. An employer that goes out of business or permanently stops paying wages must furnish the foregoing material within 30 days from the date of the last payment of wages, along with Form NJ-500, marked "Final Return."

Employer provided commuter transportation benefits: An employer must provide an employee with a written statement showing the cost of commuter transportation benefits paid by the employer to the employee. The written statement, specifying the taxable benefits includable in gross income, may be shown on the W-2 or other written information statement.

¶411 Information at Source

Law: R.S. 54A:8-6; Reg. Sec. 18:35-8.1 (CCH New Jersey Tax Reports ¶16-655).

Comparable Federal: Sec. 6041.

Information as to individuals' income is furnished in withholding statements (¶410) and in returns by partnerships, estates, and trusts (¶402), all of which are required by law. In addition, the Director is authorized to require information returns to be filed by February 15 with respect to payments of $100 or more to any taxpayer during the preceding calendar year. Under current regulations, however, the information must be furnished only as to payments of $1,000 or more.

Information return requirements apply to banks, savings associations, and other payers of interest and dividends, limited liability partnerships, and to any person (including a lessee or mortgagor of property) having control, receipt, custody, disposal, or payment of interest, rents, salaries, wages, premiums, annuities, compensation, remuneration, emoluments, or other fixed or determinable gains, profits, or income, except interest coupons payable to bearer.

The requirements may be satisfied by providing copies of federal Form 1099 (or alternative forms) or copies of magnetic tape submitted to the Internal Revenue Service.

PERSONAL INCOME TAX

CHAPTER 5
ESTATES AND TRUSTS, PARTNERSHIPS, S CORPORATIONS

¶501	Estates and Trusts
¶502	Partnerships and Limited Liability Companies
¶503	S Corporations

¶501 Estates and Trusts

Law: R.S. 54A:1-2, 54A:2-1, 54A:2-1.1, 54A:3-1, 54A:5-3, 54A:5-8 (CCH New Jersey Tax Reports ¶15-205—15-240).

Comparable Federal: Secs. 641—662.

A resident or nonresident estate or trust, as defined at ¶102, must file a return and may be subject to tax unless it meets the low-income test (¶110). Estates and trusts are required to file declarations of estimated tax, other than estates and trusts that meet the criteria of IRC Sec. 6654(l)(2) (¶406).

A resident estate or trust is subject to tax on any of the applicable items of income or gain (discussed at ¶201 and following) received by the estate or trust and not distributed or credited to beneficiaries. A nonresident estate or trust is similarly subject to the extent that the items of income or gain are derived from New Jersey sources, determined by the same standards that apply to the income of nonresident individuals (¶301).

The New Jersey gross income tax due for each taxable year from a nonresident estate or trust will be equal to the tax computed as if the estate or trust were a resident, multiplied by a fraction, the numerator of which is all income from sources within New Jersey and the denominator of which is gross income for the taxable year computed as if the estate or trust were a resident.

An estate or trust is included in the general definition of "taxpayer" and, therefore, is entitled to a personal exemption (¶105).

For the imposition of tax on beneficiaries, see ¶209.

¶502 Partnerships and Limited Liability Companies

Law: R.S. 42:2B-69, 54A:1-2, 54A:2-2, 54A:5-4, 54A:8-6 (CCH New Jersey Tax Reports ¶15-185).

Comparable Federal: Secs. 701-761, 7701.

A partnership or association, as such, is not subject to the gross income tax, but partners and members of associations are subject to tax as individuals.

Limited liability companies (LLCs) are classified as partnerships for New Jersey personal income tax purposes, unless otherwise classified for federal income tax purposes. New Jersey also authorizes the creation of limited liability partnerships (LLPs), which are treated as partnerships for tax purposes. Thus, members of LLCs and LLPs are treated as partners and are liable for tax in their individual capacities (¶212).

"Partnership" is defined to include a syndicate, group, pool, joint venture, or other unincorporated organization through or by means of which any business, financial operation, or venture is carried on (but the term does not include a trust, estate, or corporation). "Partner" includes a member in any such entity. Federal partnership adjustments, such as the IRC Sec. 174 election, are permitted for New Jersey income tax purposes. New Jersey TAM-8 (02/09/2011).

Partnership filing fees: Every domestic and foreign partnership (including limited liability companies or other entities treated as partnerships for federal tax purposes) with more than two owners which has New Jersey source income must pay a fee of $150 per partner/member, up to a maximum of $250,000, for taxable years beginning in 2002 and thereafter. The fee must be paid by the original due date of the partnership return and there is no extension for payment of the filing fee, even if the partnership has an extension for the filing of the partnership return. (*Technical Bulletin,* TB-55(R), April 3, 2009). Unless the partnership indicates that it is filing a "Final Return," the partnership must make an additional installment payment of 50% of its current year's fee toward the following year's filing fee with its New Jersey return. The partnership filing fee is remitted with Form PART-100 or with PART-200-T if the partnership files the NJ-1065 on extension. Where nonresident partners have no "physical nexus" to New Jersey, their $150 fees may be apportioned based on the partnership's allocation factor (double-weighted receipts, but single-weighted payroll and property). Investment clubs are exempt from the filing fee requirement if they have less than $60,000 in shared capital assets. Investment clubs are partnerships that (1) are classified as partnerships for federal purposes; (2) have only individual owners; (3) hold only securities, cash or cash equivalents, the market value of which must not exceed the lesser of $43,000 per owner or $306,600 (for tax year 2011, with amounts adjusted for inflation annually); and (4) are not required to register with the federal Securities and Exchange Commission.

Nonresident partner withholding: For tax years beginning in 2002, a partnership (including limited liability companies or other entities treated as partnerships for federal tax purposes) must pay a tax at the rate of (1) 6.37% on a nonresident noncorporate partner's share of partnership income apportioned to New Jersey; and (2) 9% on a nonresident corporate partner's share of partnership income apportioned to New Jersey. A nonresident noncorporate partner is a partner that is an individual, estate or trust that is a resident taxpayer subject to taxation under the gross income tax. A partnership which carries on its business activities both inside and outside New Jersey allocates and reports its business income on Form NJ-NR-A to determine the amount from New Jersey sources.

The tax paid by the partnership is credited to the gross income tax account of the nonresident partner, although for tax periods prior to 2007 the nonresident partner could not take into account the payment of the tax by the partnership in determining the nonresident partner's own estimated tax obligations. The tax is due on or before the 15th day of the fourth month following the close of the partnership's tax period. The tax is remitted with Form PART-100 or with Form PART-200-T if the partnership files the NJ-1065 on extension. If the partnership files a composite return and makes timely quarterly estimated tax payment on behalf of its nonresident, noncorporate partners, then the partnership itself will not be required to remit the tax after the close of its tax year.

For tax periods beginning on or after January 1, 2007, the tax paid by the partnership is amended to provide that the tax must be made in four installments on or before the 15th day of each of the fourth, sixth and ninth months of the tax period and on or before the 15th day of the first month succeeding the close of the tax period. The tax must be paid electronically through the Division of Taxation's Online Partnership Service at www.state.nj.us/treasury/taxation. The tax installments paid by a partnership are credited to the accounts of each nonresident partner in proportion to each nonresident partner's share of allocated income and may be taken into account in determining the nonresident partner's quarterly estimated tax obligations.

Qualified investment partnerships, investment clubs (described above) and partnerships listed on a United States national stock exchange are not subject to the tax. A "qualified investment partnership" has more than 10 members or partners, with no member or partner owning more than a 50% interest in the entity, and derives at least 90% of its gross income from dividends, interest, payments with respect to securities, loans, and gains from the sale or other disposition of stocks, securities, foreign currencies or commodities or other similar income derived with respect to its business of investing or trading in such stock, securities, currencies or commodities. A "qualified investment partnership" does not include a dealer in securities.

¶503 S Corporations

Law: R.S. 54A:5-9, 54A:5-10, 54A:5-12; Reg. Sec. 18:35-1.5 (CCH New Jersey Tax Reports ¶15-185).

S corporation shareholders are subject to tax to the extent of the shareholder's net pro rata share of S corporation income, whether or not actually distributed to the shareholder during the shareholder's taxable year. Although the applicable statute provides that the character of any S corporation item taken into account by an S corporation shareholder is determined as if such items were received or incurred by the S corporation and not its shareholder, regulations provide that the income, gain or loss earned by an S corporation does not maintain its separate character when passed through to the individual shareholders. The S corporation's income, gain or loss is aggregated and netted at the corporate level and reported by the S corporation shareholders as a separate category of net pro rata share of S corporation income, regardless of where the income is allocated. A nonresident shareholder of a New Jersey S corporation is taxed only on the portion of his net pro rata share of S corporation income allocated to New Jersey. A resident shareholder of a New Jersey S corporation reports the entire pro rata share of the corporation's income, regardless of where it is allocated.

If a federal S corporation does not make the election to be treated as an S corporation for New Jersey purposes, then a resident shareholder's net pro rata share of S corporation income is limited to his pro rata share of the S corporation's income that is not allocated to New Jersey. A nonresident shareholder would not be subject to tax on any portion of the nonelecting S corporation's income, even if the income is allocated to New Jersey.

Taxable S corporation income: The following items of S corporation income must be included in the shareholder's taxable pro rata share: (1) any dividend exclusion or deduction allowed under R.S. 54-10A-4(k); (2) taxes paid to the United States, its territories and possessions, states and their political subdivisions, or the District of Columbia that are measured by profits, income, or the business presence or activity of the corporation; (3) income taxes paid to the United States, its territories and possessions, states and their political subdivisions, or the District of Columbia, that are paid on behalf of, or in satisfaction of, the liabilities of S corporation shareholders; (4) interest income on obligations of any state other than New Jersey, or of the federal government; and (5) interest on indebtedness incurred or continued, and expenses paid and incurred to produce or manage, and expenses of collection of the income or gains from obligations the income or gain from which is deductible for New Jersey income tax purposes.

Gain from liquidating assets: Capital gain from an S corporation's sale of all of its assets should be aggregated with and into the category of pro rata share of S corporation income (*Miller,* 352 N.J. Super. 98 (App. Div. 2002); CCH New Jersey Tax Reports ¶400-821; reversing and remanding New Jersey Tax Court, 19 N.J. Tax 522 (2001); CCH New Jersey Tax Reports ¶400-775). However, 2007 regulations provide that the income or loss from an S corporation's sale or deemed sale, exchange, distribution or other disposition of all of its assets when in conjunction with the sale, exchange or disposition of all of the S corporation's stock must be reported by the shareholder in the category, net gains or income from the disposition of property.

Deductions: S corporation shareholders may deduct the following items from S corporation income: (1) gains, income, and interest from obligations of New Jersey, its political subdivisions, or agencies, and obligations that are statutorily exempt from state or local taxation pursuant to any state or federal law; and (2) gains or income from securities that evidence ownership in a qualified investment fund, and distributions paid by qualified investment funds, to the extent attributable to interest or gain from obligations issued by New Jersey or its local governmental entities or that are exempt from state or local taxation under New Jersey or federal law.

Deduction limitations: The aggregate amount of S corporation losses or deductions allowed to an S corporation shareholder may not exceed his or her combined adjusted basis in the stock of the S corporation and any indebtedness of the S corporation to the shareholder. Losses or deductions that are disallowed for any taxable period may not, with respect to that shareholder, be treated as incurred by the corporation in succeeding taxable periods.

S corporation net operating losses can be carried forward in calculating the corporation's income tax base under the Corporation Business Tax. However, for purposes of the personal income tax, and except as allowed under the alternative business calculation (see ¶201), losses in one category of income cannot be used to offset other income from another category. An allowable loss can offset the pro rata share of income from another S corporation, provided that the income and loss occur in the same tax year. Losses which cannot be used in the current year are allowed as an adjustment to the shareholder's basis in that S corporation upon the disposition of stock by the shareholder. A shareholder may only use the pro rata share of loss from an S corporation to the extent that it does not exceed the shareholder's New Jersey adjusted basis in that S corporation.

Basis: A resident shareholder of S corporation stock who held the stock on the first day of the first taxable year following July 7, 1993, has an initial basis in the stock and any indebtedness of the S corporation equal to the basis of the stock determined as though it were stock of a non-S corporation plus any indebtedness of the S corporation to the shareholder. In such instances, initial basis is determined as of the first day of the first taxable year following July 7, 1993.

For resident shareholders of S corporation stock who did not hold the stock on the first day of the first taxable year following July 7, 1993, their initial basis in the stock of the S corporation and any indebtedness of the S corporation is as determined pursuant to the IRC. In such instances, initial basis is determined as of the date following which is the latest to occur: (1) the date on which the shareholder last became a New Jersey resident; (2) the date on which the shareholder acquired the stock of the corporation; or (3) the effective date of the corporation's most recent S election under the IRC.

For a nonresident shareholder, the initial basis in the stock and indebtedness of the S corporation is zero on whichever is the latest to occur: (1) the date on which the shareholder last became a nonresident of New Jersey; (2) the date on which the shareholder acquired the stock of the S corporation; or (3) the date of the corporation's most recent New Jersey S corporation election.

¶503

PERSONAL INCOME TAX

CHAPTER 6
ADMINISTRATION, DEFICIENCIES, PENALTIES, REFUNDS, APPEALS

¶601	Administration—In General
¶602	Assessment
¶603	Petition for Redetermination—Appeals
¶604	Jeopardy Assessments
¶605	Transferee Liability
¶606	Statute of Limitations on Assessment
¶607	Penalties and Interest
¶608	Refunds
¶609	Closing Agreements and Compromises

¶601 Administration—In General

Law: R.S. 54A:9-1, 54A:9-17 (CCH NEW JERSEY TAX REPORTS ¶ 15-015).

The personal income tax is administered by the Director of the Division of Taxation, Department of the Treasury.

The State Tax Uniform Procedure Law (Chapter 26) supplements the provisions discussed below.

¶602 Assessment

Law: R.S. 54A:9-2, 54A:9-3 (CCH NEW JERSEY TAX REPORTS ¶ 89-164).

Comparable Federal: Secs. 6201—6212.

The personal income tax is generally self-assessed through the filing of returns by the taxpayer. However, when the Director determines that there has been a deficiency of tax, he or she is authorized to mail a notice of deficiency to the taxpayer stating the amount, including any applicable interest, additions and penalties.

The notice becomes an assessment of the specified amount after 90 days from the date of mailing (150 days if it was addressed to a person outside of the United States), except as to any amount concerning which the taxpayer has filed a petition with the Director during the period.

If a taxpayer has failed to comply with provisions requiring a report of change or correction of federal taxable income, a notice by the Director of additional tax due is not considered a notice of deficiency with respect to certain limitations. The amount of deficiency is deemed to be assessed at the time the notice is mailed unless the taxpayer, within 30 days thereafter, files the required report or return concerning the federal change with a statement showing that the determination of additional tax is erroneous.

A notice of additional tax due that results from a mathematical error by the taxpayer is not treated as a notice of deficiency. The additional tax is deemed to be assessed as though it had been properly reported on the date the return was filed.

¶603 Petition for Redetermination—Appeals

Law: R.S. 54A:9-9, 54A:9-10 (CCH New Jersey Tax Reports ¶ 89-228).

Comparable Federal: Secs. 6213, 6532, 7422.

A taxpayer may file a petition (protest) with the Director for a redetermination of the claimed deficiency within 90 days after the mailing of the notice of deficiency (150 days after mailing if the notice was addressed to a person outside of the United States). Provision is made for hearing upon reasonable notice. The Director's decision must be made as quickly as practicable, and the taxpayer is to be notified of the decision promptly.

Within 90 days after the decision of the Director, the taxpayer may appeal to the Tax Court of New Jersey. For appeal procedure, see ¶ 2005. For gross income tax purposes only, if a taxpayer does not file a protest seeking a redetermination of the claimed deficiency within 90 days, the second 90-day period to appeal to the Tax Court begins to run automatically after the first 90 days (*Lunin*, N.J. Tax Court, 19 N.J. Tax 277 (2001), CCH New Jersey Tax Reports ¶ 400-737).

¶604 Jeopardy Assessments

Law: R.S. 54A:9-14 (CCH New Jersey Tax Reports ¶ 89-168).

Comparable Federal: Secs. 6851, 6861.

If the Director believes the assessment or collection of a deficiency will be jeopardized by delay, he may make an immediate assessment and demand for payment. The Director is also authorized to declare a taxpayer's taxable period terminated at any time, and to demand immediate payment of tax, if it appears that collection would be in doubt under normal procedures. Collection of any tax assessed under these provisions will be stayed if the taxpayer files a bond to cover the amount assessed.

¶605 Transferee Liability

Law: R.S. 54A:9-13 (CCH New Jersey Tax Reports ¶ 89-166).

Comparable Federal: Sec. 6901.

The New Jersey personal income tax law contains provisions similar to those of the Internal Revenue Code concerning the liability of a transferee (such as a donee, heir, or distributee) for any tax, penalty, or interest on the same basis that would have applied to the transferor, except that the limitation for assessment is extended by one year for every transfer, to a maximum of three years.

¶606 Statute of Limitations on Assessment

Law: R.S. 54A:9-4 (CCH New Jersey Tax Reports ¶ 89-164).

Comparable Federal: Sec. 6501.

Generally, no assessment of tax may be made more than three years after the due date for the applicable return, or, if later, the date when the return was actually filed. In the case of a withholding return filed before April 15 of the succeeding year, the limitation period begins to run from the April 15 date.

If more than 25% of includable income is omitted from the amount reported in a return, and the omission is not disclosed, the tax may be assessed within six years after the return is filed. A deficiency arising out of an erroneous refund (regarded as an underpayment of tax) may be assessed within three years from the making of the refund, or within five years if it appears that fraud or misrepresentation was involved.

When a taxpayer reports a change or correction in federal income, the assessment may be made within two years after the report or amended return is filed.

There is no time limit on assessment if (1) no return is filed, (2) a false or fraudulent return is filed with intent to evade tax, or (3) the taxpayer fails to report a change or correction in federal income.

Any limitation period may be extended by agreement between the taxpayer and the Director.

¶607 Penalties and Interest

Law: R.S. 54:49-3, 54:52-6, 54:52-8, 54:52-14, 54:52-15, 54A:9-5, 54A:9-6 (CCH NEW JERSEY TAX REPORTS ¶ 89-202—89-210).

Comparable Federal: Secs. 6601, 6602, 6651—6652, 6654, 6672, 6674, 6677, 7201—7207.

Interest: Interest is imposed on any unpaid tax, including tax withheld, from the original due date for payment (whether or not an extension was granted) to the date paid. The rate of interest is set under the State Tax Uniform Procedure Law (¶ 2010).

Additions to tax and civil penalties: A taxpayer who fails, without reasonable cause, to file a return by the due date (or extended date) is subject to an addition to the tax as provided by the State Tax Uniform Procedure Law (¶ 2010). The same provisions apply to the nonwillful failure of an employer to make return and payment of tax withheld.

If any deficiency is due to negligence or to intentional disregard of the law or administrative provisions, but without intent to defraud, a 10% penalty will be added to the amount of deficiency. If the deficiency is due to fraud, 50% is added.

If a taxpayer fails to file a declaration or pay all or part of an installment of estimated tax, interest, in the amount set under the State Tax Uniform Procedure Law, is added to the taxpayer's tax for the period of underpayment, but not beyond the due date for the annual return. Internal Revenue Code provisions are followed in the determination of underpayment and in exceptions to the imposition of additional tax, except that New Jersey does not make special provision for fishermen.

Any employer who willfully fails to withhold or pay over tax as required is liable for a penalty of 100% of the amount due.

For failure to furnish statements required by provisions concerning information at the source, the penalty is $2 for each statement not filed, to a maximum of $2,000 in the year.

An additional penalty of up to $5,000 may be imposed for any failure, with fraudulent intent, to comply with requirements as to returns, declarations, payment, withholding or supplying information.

Criminal penalties: Criminal penalties, including fine and imprisonment, are provided for attempts to evade tax and for willful failure to withhold or to pay over withheld taxes.

¶608 Refunds

Law: R.S. 54A:9-7—54A:9-9 (CCH NEW JERSEY TAX REPORTS ¶ 89-224).

Comparable Federal: Secs. 6401—6407.

Provision is made for credit and refund of any overpayment of tax as shown on a return or established by the taxpayer in a claim for credit or refund.

A claim must be filed within three years from the time the return was filed or two years from the time the tax was paid, whichever is later. In the case of such a claim in connection with a report or amended return resulting from a change in federal taxable income, the claim must be filed within two years from the time the report or amended return was required to be filed.

A petition concerning a claimed refund may be filed with the Director within two years after: (1) the Director has mailed a notice of disallowance of the claim, or (2) six months have passed since the claim was filed.

Interest will be paid on overpayments that have not been refunded six months and one day after the later of (1) the last date prescribed for filing a return or permitted pursuant to an approved application for extension of time to file, or (2) the date the return (whether original or amended) requesting the refund is actually filed. Interest on overpayments is allowed at the rate determined by the Director to be the prime rate.

A New Jersey hospital had the right, under R.S. 22:2H-18:4 *et seq.*, to request the Division of Taxation to withhold income tax refunds of patients or responsible parties in order to recover the amount owing on the patient's account (*State Tax News*, Division of Taxation, November 1, 1990; CCH New Jersey Tax Reports [1989—1994 Transfer Binder], ¶ 400-106).

¶609 Closing Agreements and Compromises

Law: R.S. 54:53-1, 54:53-7 (CCH New Jersey Tax Reports ¶ 89-186).

The Director is authorized to make closing agreements and compromises under provision of the State Tax Uniform Procedure Law (¶ 2014).

PART III

CORPORATION BUSINESS TAX

CHAPTER 7
IMPOSITION OF TAX, RATES, EXEMPTIONS, CREDITS

¶701	Overview
¶702	Corporations Subject to Tax
¶703	Exempt Corporations
¶704	Tax Base—In General
¶705	Tax Rate
¶706	Tax Credits
¶707	Credit Against Tax—Urban Enterprise Zones
¶708	Credit Against Tax—Urban Transit Hub
¶709	Credit Against Tax—Developer's Credit
¶710	Credit Against Tax—Redevelopment Authority Project Tax Credit
¶711	Credit Against Tax—New Jobs Investment
¶712	Credit Against Tax—Manufacturing Equipment and Employment Investment Tax Credit
¶713	Credit Against Tax—Research and Development
¶714	Credit Against Tax—Employer-Provided Commuter Transportation Benefits
¶715	Credit Against Tax—High Technology
¶716	Credit Against Tax—Film Production
¶717	Credit Against Tax—Digital Media Content Production Expenses
¶718	Credit Against Tax—Neighborhood Revitalization Tax Credit
¶719	Credit Against Tax—Effluent Treatment Equipment Credit
¶720	Credit Against Tax—Municipal Rehabilitation and Economic Recovery Credit
¶721	Credit Against Tax—HMO Assistance Fund Tax Credit
¶722	Credit Against Tax—Business Retention and Relocation Credit
¶723	Credit Against Tax—Contaminated Site Remediation Credit
¶724	Credit Against Tax—AMA Tax Credit
¶725	Credit Against Tax—Sheltered Workshop Tax Credit
¶725A	Credit Against Tax—Wind Energy Facility Credit
¶725B	Credit Against Tax—Jobs Tax Credit
¶725C	Credit Against Tax—Angel Investor Tax Credit
¶726	Domestic Corporations Ceasing to Possess a Franchise
¶727	Foreign Corporations Ceasing to Have a Taxable Status in New Jersey
¶728	Investment Companies, Regulated Investment Companies, and Real Estate Investment Trusts
¶729	Merger, Consolidation, or Reorganization
¶730	Corporations Doing Business Within and Without the State
¶731	S Corporations
¶732	Corporate Partners

¶733   Accounting Periods and Methods
¶734   When Period Covered Differs for New Jersey and Federal
                  Returns
¶735   Short Accounting Periods

¶701 Overview

New Jersey has imposed a franchise tax on domestic corporations since 1884 and on foreign corporations since 1937. The Corporation Business Tax Act, which is the basis of the present law, came into effect in 1946.

Legislation enacted in 1975 imposed the franchise tax on banking corporations and incorporated financial businesses, in place of the special levies to which those entities had been subject. For corporate financial businesses, the corporation business tax was made applicable to calendar and fiscal periods ending after December 31, 1974. The tax was imposed on banking corporations beginning with 1975 net income and net worth as of December 31, 1975. Effective January 1, 2002 and concurrent with the repeal of the Savings Institution Tax (Law 2002, c. 40, sec. 23), savings institutions also became subject to the corporation business tax. The repeal of the savings institution tax does not affect any obligation, lien or duty to pay taxes which were accrued or may accrue for periods prior to its repeal.

The tax is imposed on domestic corporations for the privilege of existing as a corporation under New Jersey law, and on foreign corporations for the privilege of having or exercising a corporate franchise, deriving receipts from sources, engaging in contacts, doing business, employing or owning capital or property, or maintaining an office in New Jersey. Generally, the tax applies to each privilege period, that is, the taxpayer's fiscal or calendar year, and the annual return and final payment are due by the 15th day of the fourth month following the end of the year, along with a prepayment for the current year. In the case of banking corporations, the privilege period is specified as the calendar year, with the annual return and final payment due by April 15 of the privilege year, based on the preceding year's income. Since a prepayment for the following period is also required, the effect of the special provisions is essentially the same as that of the general provisions with respect to calendar years.

Until June 30, 1986, the tax was imposed on net worth and net income allocated to New Jersey. Federal taxable income is the starting point for computing net income. The net worth portion of the tax was phased out by means of a gradual reduction in rates, applicable to privilege periods beginning on or after April 1, 1983. The net worth portion of the tax has been completely eliminated with respect to periods beginning after June 30, 1986. For tax periods beginning on or after January 1, 2002, the tax is imposed based upon the greater of the tax computed on net income allocated to New Jersey or an alternative minimum assessment based upon either New Jersey gross receipts or New Jersey gross profits.

Prior to January 1, 2002, New Jersey also imposed a corporation income tax, a direct tax on income derived from New Jersey sources by corporations that were not subject to the corporation business tax. Due to expanded subjectivity under the corporation business tax, very few corporations paid the corporation income tax. Effective for tax years beginning on or after January 1, 2002, the corporation income tax was repealed (Law 2002, c. 40, sec. 23) and any corporation previously subject to the corporation income tax became subject to the corporation business tax. The repeal of the corporation income tax did not affect any obligation, lien or duty to pay taxes which were accrued or may accrue from periods prior to its repeal.

The tax base is discussed at Chapter 10. Allocation is discussed at Chapter 11. Exempt corporations are discussed at ¶703. Tax rate is discussed at ¶705.

¶701

¶702 Corporations Subject to Tax

Law: R.S. 54:10A-2, 54:10A-4, 54:10A-5, 54:10A-5a, 54:10A-34, 54:10B-2(b); Reg. Secs. 18:7-1.6, 18:7-1.7, 18:7-1.8, 18:7-1.9, 18:7-1.14.

All domestic corporations and all foreign corporations having a taxable status, not specifically exempt, are subject to the corporation business tax. Exempt corporations are discussed at ¶703.

Joint-stock companies or associations and business trusts are treated as corporations. Limited partnership associations organized under R.S. 42:3-1 by September 21, 1998, are included by regulation, the validity of which was upheld by the Superior Court of New Jersey, Appellate Division, in *Thomas Ltd. v. State of New Jersey* 121 NJ Super 577, 298 A2d 285 (1972) (CCH New Jersey Tax Reports [1966—1979 Transfer Binder], ¶200-576) petition for certification denied by the New Jersey Supreme Court, 62 NJ 429 (1973).

Limited liability companies (LLCs) and limited liability partnerships (LLPs) are treated as partnerships for tax purposes, unless otherwise classified for federal income tax purposes. As partnerships, LLCs and LLPs are not subject to the franchise tax. Rather, members of LLCs and partners of LLPs are taxed in their corporate or individual capacities. Corporate partners and LLC members are subject to the franchise tax to the extent the partnership or LLC is organized under New Jersey law or does business in New Jersey. Any entity treated as a partnership for federal tax purposes may be required to pay tax, creditable to the account of the relevant partner(s), for any nonresident corporate partner based upon 9% of that partner's share of partnership entire net income allocated to New Jersey. For discussion of corporate partners, see ¶732. For discussion of LLCs and LLPs, see ¶212 and ¶502.

Financial business corporations, New Jersey banking corporations (including national banks), and savings institutions (including savings banks and building and loan or savings and loan associations) are also subject to the franchise tax. Financial business corporations are enterprises that are in substantial competition with the business of national banks and that employ moneyed capital with the object of making profit by its use as money. Foreign banks and foreign national banks are, under certain conditions, subject to corporation business tax.

Domestic corporations: A corporation organized under the laws of New Jersey, unless specifically exempt, is subject to tax throughout its existence. Consequently, tax liability is incurred even if a corporation does not own property or capital, does not maintain an office or is totally inactive. For the same reason, the tax applies even if the corporation carries on all of its business activities outside of New Jersey.

Foreign corporations: A foreign corporation with sufficient business activity in New Jersey to give the state jurisdiction to impose tax under the Constitution and federal law is subject to tax in New Jersey if:

— it holds a certificate of authority to do business issued by the Division of Revenue,

— it holds a certificate, license, or other authorization from any other New Jersey department or agency permitting it to carry on any corporate activity in the state,

— it derives receipts from sources in New Jersey,

— it engages in contacts in New Jersey,

— it does business in New Jersey,

— it employs or owns capital in New Jersey,

— it employs or owns property in New Jersey, or

— it maintains an office in the state.

A foreign corporation is not deemed to be doing business, or employing or owning capital or property in New Jersey by reason of

— the maintenance of cash balances with banks or trust companies in New Jersey;

— the ownership of stock or securities kept in New Jersey in a safe deposit box, safe, vault or other receptacle rented for the purpose, or pledged as collateral security, or deposited with one or more banks or trust companies, or brokers who are members of a recognized security exchange, in safekeeping or custody accounts;

— the taking of any action by any such bank or trust company or broker, which is incidental to the rendering of safekeeping or custodian service to the corporation; or

— any combination of the foregoing activities.

The following examples, taken from Reg. Sec. 18:7-1.8, illustrate the circumstances under which a foreign corporation is subject to tax:

Example 1: A foreign manufacturing corporation has its factory outside New Jersey. Its only activity in New Jersey is the maintenance of an office within the state. The orders are forwarded to its home office outside the state for acceptance, and the merchandise is shipped from the factory direct to the purchasers. The corporation is subject to tax, because it maintains an office within the state.

Example 2: A foreign corporation that operates several retail stores outside New Jersey leases an office in New Jersey for the convenience of its buyers when they come to New Jersey. It has several employees permanently assigned to such office. Salesmen call at the office to solicit orders from the buyers, and the merchandise is shipped to such office by the sellers. Upon receipt, the merchandise is examined, separated and ticketed by the corporation's employees and then shipped by them to the various stores of the corporation outside New Jersey. The corporation is subject to tax because it maintains an office, is regularly doing business through its constituted representatives, and owns property in New Jersey.

Note: Examples 1 and 2 illustrate conditions giving rise to subjection to the tax, without regard to whether or not the corporation holds a general or special certificate of authority to do business in New Jersey.

Example 3: A foreign corporation has applied for and has received a certificate of authority to do business in New Jersey by the Secretary of State, but does not actually do any business in New Jersey, nor does it have any office or property or any employees in New Jersey nor does it own or employ capital in New Jersey. The corporation has sought and received the privilege of exercising its corporate franchise in New Jersey and is therefore subject to the tax and must file a return and pay the minimum tax.

CCH Advisory: *Corporations Providing Interstate Transportation Services*

Legislation adopted for tax years beginning on or after January 1, 2013, provides that a corporation operating automobiles or buses over public roads for the carriage of passengers in transit from a location outside New Jersey to a destination in New Jersey or for the carriage of passengers in transit from a location in New Jersey to a location outside New Jersey shall not be deemed to be doing business in New Jersey for purposes of the corporation business tax. (P.L. 2013, c.98).

CCH Tip: *Website in New Jersey May Create Nexus*

According to the Division of Taxation, the maintenance of a website on a computer server located within New Jersey creates substantial nexus with the state for income tax purposes if (1) the taxpayer also has some physical presence in New Jersey connected with the construction, maintenance, or operation of the website; (2) the computer server and the technicians that keep it functioning are located in New Jersey; and (3) the website is accessible in New Jersey by downloading it into computers located in New Jersey. As such, the out-of-state seller is considered to have the intention to "exploit the market" in New Jersey. Any minimal physical presence of the taxpayer in New Jersey in connection with this scenario would be considered doing business in New Jersey and would cause the taxpayer to have nexus in this state (R.S. 54:10A-2; Reg. Secs. 18:7-1.6(a)2.iii, 18:7-1.9(a) and (b)). In addition the taxpayer is considered to be "employing" or maintaining tangible personal property in the state, which also would give rise to nexus (Reg. Sec. 18:7-1.6(a)2.v) (*Response to CCH Internet/Electronic Commerce Survey*, Division of Taxation, September 22, 1999; CCH NEW JERSEY TAX REPORTS ¶ 400-665).

Federal restrictions: Federal legislation (P.L. 86-272, also known as the Interstate Income Law) prohibits a state from imposing a tax on net income derived by a foreign corporation from interstate commerce, provided the business activities within the state are limited to the solicitation of orders for sales of tangible personal property by employees or other representatives, orders are sent outside the state for approval, and orders are filled by shipment or delivery from a point outside the state. The prohibition against the imposition of the tax also protects a foreign corporation that sells through a sales office maintained within the state by independent contractors whose activities consist solely of making sales or soliciting orders. P.L. 86-272 does not protect foreign corporations from the minimum tax (see ¶ 705) (*Home Impressions* 21 NJ Tax 448 (2004); CCH NEW JERSEY TAX REPORTS, ¶ 400-987). Furthermore, New Jersey takes the position that P.L. 86-272 does not apply to or restrict its imposition of the alternative minimum assessment component of the corporation business tax, because it is computed on the basis of gross receipts or gross profits (rather than net income).

Business activities by employees extending beyond mere solicitation of orders will subject a corporation to tax (*Clairol Incorporated* 57 NJ 199 (1970); CCH NEW JERSEY TAX REPORTS [1966—1979 Transfer Binder], ¶ 200-483; affirming 109 NJ Super 22; appeal dismissed U.S. Supreme Court, April 19, 1971).

New Jersey has adopted the Multistate Tax Commission's Statement of Information Under P.L. 86-272. As a signatory to the Statement of Information, New Jersey indicates its intention to impose the net income tax, subject to state and federal legislative limitations, to the fullest extent constitutionally permissible. Although the corporation business tax statute does not provide for a "throwback" rule, pursuant to the Statement, if any sales are made in a state that is precluded by P.L. 86-272 from taxing the income of the seller, these sales would remain subject to throwback to the appropriate state that has jurisdiction to impose its net income tax on the income derived from those sales. For tax years beginning on or after January 1, 2002, New Jersey enacted a throwout rule for the net income tax component of the corporation business tax which is repealed for tax years beginning on or after July 1, 2010.

According to the Statement, for in-state activity to be immune under the solicitation of orders standard, it must be limited solely to (1) speech or conduct that explicitly or implicitly invites an order; and (2) activities that neither explicitly nor implicitly invite an order, but are entirely ancillary to requests for an order. Activities that seek to promote sales are not ancillary. P.L. 86-272 protects only ancillary activities that facilitate the request for an order. The exemption from net income tax afforded by P.L. 86-272 is lost if the activities do not fall within the definition of "solicitation," unless the disqualifying activities, taken together, are *de minimis*, so as to establish only a trivial additional connection with the taxing state. An activity regularly conducted within a taxing state pursuant to a company policy or on a continuous basis should not normally be considered trivial.

Prior to 1995, New Jersey's exception to the Statement of Information provided that corporate ownership of an automobile registered in New Jersey for New Jersey resident sales personnel would subject the corporation to taxation in New Jersey, and therefore, would not be an immune activity. However, Reg. Sec. 18:7-1.9 was amended in 1995 to conform with the U.S. Supreme Court's holding in *Wisconsin Dept. of Revenue v. William Wrigley* (US SCt 1992) 112 SCt 2247; CCH NEW JERSEY TAX REPORTS [1989—1994 Transfer Binder], ¶400-176. Under the regulation, a corporation's provision of automobiles, owned or leased, registered or not registered in New Jersey, to sales personnel for their use in conducting protected activities is a corporate activity immune from taxation.

In *Pomco Graphics, Inc. v. Director, Division of Taxation* 13 NJ Tax 578 (1993); CCH NEW JERSEY TAX REPORTS [1989—1994 Transfer Binder], ¶400-260, the New Jersey Tax Court ruled that a Pennsylvania corporation that provided commercial printed materials to customers in New Jersey was immune from net income tax because all of its business activities in New Jersey were protected from state taxation under P.L. 86-272, which prohibits a state from imposing a net income tax on a foreign corporation whose in-state activity is limited to protected forms of solicitation. Reg. Sec. 18:7-1.8, which conforms with *Pomco Graphics*, as well as Reg. Secs. 18:7-1.6, 1.9, and 1.10 specify the circumstances under which a foreign corporation that is soliciting business in New Jersey may be considered either (1) a minimum taxpayer under the Corporation Business Tax Act, and not subject to the tax measured by income by virtue of the provisions of P.L. 86-272; or (2) a corporation subject to the tax based on income. In *Chester A. Asher, Inc. v. Director, Division of Taxation*, 22 N.J. Tax 582 (2006); CCH ¶401-135, the New Jersey Tax Court held that the activities of picking up damaged goods and collecting payments, which were conducted by a Pennsylvania corporation's delivery drivers, exceeded the solicitation of orders. The New Jersey Tax Court has upheld the Division of Taxation's position that P.L. 86-272 does not protect foreign corporations from the minimum tax under the Corporation Business Tax since the minimum tax is not based on net income. *Home Impressions, Inc. v. Director, Division of Taxation*, 21 N.J. Tax 448 (2004); see CCH NEW JERSEY TAX REPORTS ¶400-987.

Licensing agreements: A foreign corporation that holds trademarks and receives fees as a result of licensing those trademarks to New Jersey companies for use in New Jersey, is subject to the tax on its apportioned income. The Division similarly contends that a foreign corporation, represented in New Jersey by a foreign independent contractor that receives fees for licensing its software to New Jersey businesses is subject to corporation business tax on its apportioned income. On October 12, 2006, the Supreme Court of New Jersey held in *Lanco, Inc. v. Director, Division of Taxation*, 188 N.J. 380 (2006); CCH NEW JERSEY TAX REPORTS ¶401-221, aff'g 379 N.J. Super. 562 (2005), rev'g 21 N.J. Tax 200 (2003), that physical presence is not a necessary element of Commerce Clause nexus for subjecting a foreign intangibles holding company that licensed trademarks and trade names to its affiliate in New Jersey to the CBT. On June 18, 2007, the United States Supreme Court denied the taxpayer's petition for certiorari in *Lanco*.

CCH Practice Tip: Subjectivity of Foreign Affiliated Licensees

In addressing claimed deductions for intangible expenses and costs between affiliated corporations where the recipient or payee affiliate is not a United States taxpayer, the Division of Taxation has expressed a "policy of restraint" with respect to the tax subjectivity of the foreign affiliate or parent if the domestic payor affiliate cooperates in an audit to determine whether the domestic affiliate's intangible expense deductions meet the arm's length standards of IRC Sec. 482 and N.J.A.C. 18:7-5.10. New Jersey TAM 2011-22 (12/07/2011).

Banks and credit card companies: A financial business corporation, banking corporation, credit card company or similar business with a commercial domicile in another state is subject to the CBT if during any year it obtains or solicits business or receives gross receipts from sources within New Jersey. Reg Sec. 18:7-1.8(b); New Jersey TAM-6 (01/10/2011).

¶702

Software sales: On August 13, 2009, the Tax Court of New Jersey held that a corporation domiciled out of state did not have sufficient nexus with New Jersey through its sales of computer software to be subject to the CBT. *AccuZIP, Inc. v. Director, Division of Taxation,* 25 N.J. Tax 158 (2009). AccuZIP, Inc. (AccuZIP) was a Nevada corporation with offices in California that sold prewritten software on CD-ROM to customers in New Jersey. AccuZIP solicited sales by placing advertisements in national trade magazines and maintaining a web page. Its customers placed orders for products by telephone, email, or fax with employees in California. AccuZIP had no agents, officers, or employees in New Jersey. The Tax Court determined that AccuZIP was a seller of tangible property (rather than a licensor of intangible property) and that its activities in New Jersey were de minimis and insufficient to create substantial nexus with New Jersey under the Commerce Clause.

Limited partner nexus: On August 23, 2011 the Appellate Division of the Superior Court of New Jersey held that a limited partner investment company was not subject to the CBT because it had insufficient nexus with the state. *BIS LP, Inc. v. Division of Taxation,* 29 N.J. Tax 489 (App. Div. 2011); CCH NEW JERSEY TAX REPORTS ¶ 401-594, affg 25 N.J. Tax 88 (2009). Pursuant to the limited partnership agreement, the taxpayer limited partner did not have the right or obligation to participate directly or indirectly in the active management of the limited partnership nor was it authorized to perform any act in the name of, or on behalf of, the limited partnership. The limited partner had no place of business, employees, agents, representatives, or property in New Jersey. Moreover, the limited partner was not in the same line of business as the limited partnership nor was it part of a unitary business with the limited partnership. On remand from the Appellate Division on the issue of the right to a refund, the Tax Court held that the limited partner, not the limited partnership, was entitled to a refund of corporation business tax withheld on its behalf.

Telecommuting employees: A Delaware corporation with offices in Maryland was subject to the CBT because the corporation's employee who telecommuted from her New Jersey residence was sufficient to give the corporation nexus with the state. *Telebright Corporation, Inc. v. Division of Taxation,* 25 N.J. Tax 333 (2010), aff'd, 424 N.J. Super. 384 (App. Div. 2012). The corporation's employee was expected to report for work, regularly received and carried out assignments, was supervised by the corporation, began and ended her work day and delivered her finished work product in New Jersey. Moreover, until the employee purchased her own computer, the corporation had provided a laptop to the employee for the purpose of performing her work assignments and was therefore employing property in the state.

Interstate commerce: A foreign corporation that falls within any of the categories creating a taxable status is subject to tax, notwithstanding that its business is wholly or partly in interstate commerce, and must measure its tax by entire net income allocable to New Jersey or its gross receipts assignable to New Jersey, including that portion derived from or used in interstate commerce.

S corporations: S corporations are allowed limited pass-through treatment, although the corporate level tax (¶ 731) was fully phased-out for tax periods ending after July 1, 2007, except for the minimum tax. S corporations are and will remain subject to tax on the portion of entire net income that is subject to federal income tax.

Professional corporations: Corporations organized as professional corporations under N.J.S.A. 14A:17-5 with two or more licensed professionals and with New Jersey receipts must pay an annual filing fee of $150 per professional for tax years beginning in 2002 and thereafter.

Foreign sales corporations: Foreign sales corporations (FSCs) generally replaced domestic international sales corporations (DISCs) beginning with 1985. An FSC is subject to the tax if it acquires a taxable status under the criteria applicable to foreign corporations. No special treatment of FSCs is allowed under state statutes.

For the net income tax component of the corporation business tax, entire net income includes total net income from all sources, whether within or without the United States, but any deemed paid distribution may be excluded in arriving at entire net income of a shareholder. The usual New Jersey dividend exclusions apply: 100% if a corporate shareholder of the FSC holds 80% or more of the FSC's capital stock, 50% if the corporate shareholder holds less than 80% but at least 50%, and no exclusion for corporate shareholders holding less than 50%. For tax years beginning in 2002 and thereafter, taxes on or measured by profits or income, or business presence or business activity that are paid to any foreign jurisdiction may not be excluded or deducted from entire net income.

Period when subject to tax: Domestic corporations become subject to tax upon incorporation; foreign corporations become subject to tax when they acquire a taxable status. The tax is imposed for all or any part of a calendar or fiscal year during which a domestic corporation holds a franchise or during which a foreign corporation has a taxable status.

For treatment of corporations ceasing to be subject to tax, see ¶726 and ¶727.

¶703 Exempt Corporations

Law: R.S. 54:10A-3, Ch. 162, Laws 1997.

Comparable Federal: Sec. 501.

The following corporations are exempt from the corporation business tax:

— Corporations subject to a tax assessed on the basis of gross receipts, other than the alternative minimum assessment component of the corporation business tax or the Retail Gross Receipts Tax Act. Beginning January 1, 1998, gas and electric public utilities became subject to the New Jersey corporate business (income) tax. The exemption for corporations subject to the franchise and gross receipts tax on utilities continues to apply to (1) sewerage and water corporations and (2) municipal electric corporations or utilities that were in existence as of January 1, 1995, and were exempt from the utilities tax. Gas, electric, gas and electric, and telecommunications and municipal electric corporations that were subject to a New Jersey public utilities tax (franchise and gross receipts taxes) as of December 31, 1996, are required to pay estimated corporate business (income) taxes during the calendar year they are first subject to the taxes. Taxes on utilities are discussed at ¶1807.

— Corporations subject to a tax on insurance premiums collected. Taxes on insurance companies are discussed at ¶1802.

— Railroads, canal corporations, production credit associations organized under the Farm Credit Act of 1933, and agricultural cooperative associations exempt from tax under IRC Sec. 521. Building and loan or savings and loan associations and savings banks became subject to the corporation business tax for tax periods beginning on or after January 1, 2002.

— Nonprofit cemetery corporations.

— Qualified nonprofit corporations.

— Certain utility corporations using the public streets.

— Non-stock cooperative housing corporations.

— Nonprofit retirement community organizations.

— Insurance companies licensed under the laws of another state, including surplus lines insurers declared eligible by the Commissioner of Insurance to insure risks within New Jersey.

— Municipal electric corporations or utilities in existence as of January 1, 1995, provided that all of the corporations' or utilities' income is from sales, exchanges, or deliveries of electricity to customers using the electricity within the corporations' municipal boundaries or the utilities' franchise area existing as of January 1, 1995.

The following corporations are exempt from the alternative minimum assessment component of the corporation business tax, but otherwise remain subject to the entire net income component of the tax:

— New Jersey S corporations (that have made a valid New Jersey S election).

— Investment companies, as defined under New Jersey law (¶728).

— Professional corporations organized under New Jersey law or similar for-profit corporations organized under the laws of another state for the purpose of rendering professional service.

— Persons operating on a cooperative basis under Part I of Subchapter T of the federal Internal Revenue Code of 1986 (26 U.S.C. Sec. 1381 et seq.).

¶704 Tax Base—In General

Law: R.S. 54:10A-5, 54:10A-5a.

Comparable Federal: Sec. 63.

The New Jersey corporation business tax is imposed based upon the greater of a tax computed using entire net income allocated to New Jersey or an alternative minimum assessment computed using New Jersey gross receipts or New Jersey gross profits. "Entire net income" is federal taxable income with modifications (¶801).

The base for the alternative minimum assessment component of the corporation business tax is either New Jersey gross receipts or New Jersey gross profits. The taxpayer elects whether to use the gross receipts or gross profits computation and is bound by that election for the next four tax periods. "New Jersey gross receipts" include essentially the same categories of receipts that make up the numerator of the allocation formula for the entire net income component of the tax, with the exception that intercompany dividends are not specifically excluded:

— Receipts from sales of tangible personal property where shipment is made to a point within New Jersey;

— Receipts from services performed within New Jersey;

— Receipts from rentals of property situated within New Jersey;

— Royalties from the use of patents or copyrights within New Jersey; and

— All other business receipts earned within New Jersey (with no exception made for intercompany dividends).

"New Jersey gross profits" are New Jersey gross receipts less cost of goods sold. A taxpayer's "cost of goods sold" means the cost of goods sold determined for purposes of computing the taxpayer's federal income tax multiplied, at the taxpayer's election, by either the receipts fraction of the business allocation factor or the full business allocation factor (if any) used by the taxpayer in allocating its entire net income (¶902), or some other measure of input or expenditures that is determined by the Director of Taxation to equitably reflect business activity.

Special rules apply to investment companies, regulated investment companies and real estate investment trusts (¶728).

S corporation losses can be used by shareholders to offset certain categories of other business income on their personal income tax returns.

¶705 Tax Rate

Law: R.S. 54:10A-5, 54:10A-5.1, 54:10A-5.2. 54:10A-5.40; Reg. Sec. 18:7-3.6 (CCH NEW JERSEY TAX REPORTS ¶ 10-380, 10-385).

The New Jersey corporation business tax is computed based upon the greater of a tax computed using entire net income allocated to New Jersey, or an alternative minimum assessment (AMA) imposed upon either New Jersey gross receipts or New Jersey gross profits. The entire net income portion of the tax is imposed at the rate of 9% for corporations with an entire net income greater than $100,000; 7.5% for corporations with an entire net income of $100,000 or less but greater than $50,000; and 6.5% for corporations with an entire net income of $50,000 or less.

The AMA portion of the corporation business tax is computed at the following rates:

If New Jersey Gross Profits of:	Then AMA Equals:
Less than or equal to $1,000,000	No AMA is assessed
More than $1,000,000 but ≤ $10,000,000	.0025 × [the gross profits > $1,000,000]× 1.11111
More than $10,000,000 but ≤ $15,000,000	.0035 × the gross profits
More than $15,000,000 but ≤ $25,000,000	.0060 × the gross profits
More than $25,000,000 but ≤ $37,500,000	.0070 × the gross profits
More than $37,500,000	.0080 × the gross profits

If New Jersey Gross Receipts of:	Then AMA Equals:
Less than or equal to $2,000,000	No AMA is assessed
More than $2,000,000 but ≤ $20,000,000	.00125 × [the gross receipts > $2,000,000]× 1.11111
More than $20,000,000 but ≤ $30,000,000	.00175 × the gross receipts
More than $30,000,000 but ≤ $50,000,000	.00300 × the gross receipts
More than $50,000,000 but ≤ $75,000,000	.00350 × the gross receipts
More than $75,000,000	.00400 × the gross receipts

For tax periods beginning after June 30, 2006, the AMA rate becomes 0% except for corporate taxpayers that are otherwise protected against New Jersey tax liability by P.L. 86-272. Those taxpayers are subject to the AMA indefinitely, unless they consent to be subject to the entire net income component of the tax (effectively waiving their P.L. 86-272 protection) for tax periods beginning after December 31, 2006.

The AMA liability for a group of five or more affiliated corporations is capped at $20,000,000, with the entire net income tax paid by members of the group also counting toward the $20,000,000 AMA cap. However, the sum of "untaxed" amounts for all members of a group may not exceed $5 million of gross profits or $10 million of gross receipts (or a combination thereof, when members of the group are using both the gross receipts and the gross profits methods).

Minimum tax: Beginning in calendar year 2006 and thereafter, the minimum tax for both domestic and foreign corporations is based on the New Jersey gross receipts of the taxpayer, pursuant to the following schedule:

If New Jersey Gross Receipts of:	Then Minimum Tax Equals:
Less then $100,000	$500
$100,00 or more but less then $250,000	$750
$250,000 or more but less then $500,000	$1,000
$500,000 or more but less then $1,000,000	$1,500
$1,000,000 or more	$2,000

Beginning in calendar year 2002 and thereafter, each corporation that is part of an affiliated or controlled group (under Section 1504 or 1563 of the federal Internal Revenue Code) with total payroll of $5,000,000 or more, is subject to a minimum tax of $2,000.

For calendar years 2002 through 2005, the minimum tax was $500 (except with respect to taxpayers that were part of an affiliated or controlled group and were subject to the $2,000 minimum tax described above).

The minimum tax applies to S corporations as well, whether or not they elect New Jersey S corporation status. For tax years beginning in 2001, the minimum tax was $210. For tax years 1997 to 2000, the minimum tax was $200. RICs and REITs pay a minimum tax of $250 for the entire net income component of the corporation business tax, but may also be subject to the alternative minimum assessment component of the tax.

Surtax: A 4% corporation business tax surcharge applied to tax periods ending on or after July 1, 2006 and before July 1, 2010. The surtax applied to the liability remaining after application of any credits allowed against that liability other than credits for installment payments, estimated payments made with a request for an extension of time for filing a return, or overpayments from prior privilege periods.

Regulated investment companies: A qualified regulated investment company pays a flat tax of $250 for the entire net income component of the corporation business tax, but may also be subject to the alternative minimum assessment component of the tax.

• *S corporations*

S corporation income has been allowed limited pass-through treatment for taxable years beginning after July 7, 1993, provided the S corporation has elected to be treated as a New Jersey S corporation by filing Form CBT-2553. Effective for privilege periods ending on or after July 1, 1998, a 2% tax rate is imposed on entire net income not subject to federal corporate income tax. However, certain built-in gains and excess passive investment income, which are subject to federal corporate income tax (IRC Secs. 1374, 1375), are taxable at the maximum corporation business tax rate.

The 2% tax rate imposed on the entire net income of S corporations with annual income over $100,000 has been phased out to zero as follows: for taxable years ending on or after July 1, 1998 but prior to July 1, 2001, at the rate of 2% on entire net income allocable to New Jersey (and not subject to federal tax); for taxable years ending on or after July 1, 2001, at a rate of 1.33%; for taxable years ending on or after July 1, 2006, at a rate of 0.67%; and 0% for periods ending on or after July 1, 2007.

"Small business" S corporations, with annual incomes of less than $100,000, are taxed at reduced rates noted below.

S corporations are subject to the minimum corporate tax. But for tax periods beginning in calendar year 2012, the minimum tax for New Jersey S corporations is reduced as follows:

If New Jersey Gross Receipts of:	Then Minimum Tax Equals:
Less then $100,000	$375
More than $100,000 but less than $250,000	$562.50
More than $250,000 but less than $500,000	$750
More than $500,000 but less than $1,000,000	$1,125
More than $1,000,000	$1,500

The minimum tax on New Jersey subchapter S corporations with total payrolls of $5,000,000 or more remains $2,000 annually.

• *Small businesses*

Small businesses are subject to tax at lower rates. Corporations, other than S corporations, with entire net incomes of $100,000 or less for a 12-month privilege period are taxed at 7.5% for the privilege period, and corporations with entire net income of $50,000 or less are taxed at 6.5% for that privilege period.

S corporations that have an entire net income of $100,000 or less in a 12-month privilege period ending before July 1, 2001 were taxed at the rate of 0.5% on income that was not subject to federal taxation. Effective for tax periods ending on or after July 1, 2001, S corporations with annual income of $100,000 or less pay no corporation business tax on entire net income not subject to federal taxation. Small S corporations will continue to be taxed on income that is subject to federal tax, such as excessive passive investment income.

If the accounting period for the corporation or S corporation is less than 12 months, the reduced rate only applies if the taxpayer's entire net income, when prorated, does not exceed $8,333 per month.

¶706 Tax Credits

Law: R.S. 54:10A-15; Reg. Sec. 18:7-3.17 (CCH New Jersey Tax Reports ¶12-001—12-150).

Estimated tax payments may be taken as a credit against liability for the corporation business tax.

Credit for tax improperly paid: The corporation income tax has been repealed for tax periods beginning on or after January 1, 2002. For earlier periods, however, a taxpayer that paid corporation income tax for a calendar or fiscal year for which it was not properly subject to tax could offset the amount of tax paid against the corporation business tax due. A similar credit could be taken for improperly paid corporation business tax, to be applied against the taxpayer's corporation income tax liability.

Coordination of tax credits providing economic incentives: There are several corporate business tax economic incentive credits and carryovers of expired credits available to offset the tax computed on entire net income. For those taxpayers paying the alternative minimum assessment component of the corporation business tax (because that component exceeds their tax liability as computed based on entire net income), these credits are not available. When a taxpayer is entitled to more than one of the corporate business tax economic incentive credits, the credits may be applied against the corporation business tax in the following sequence:

(1) HMO assistance fund credit (¶721);

(2) new jobs investment credit (¶711);

(3) urban enterprise zone credit (¶707);

(4) redevelopment authority project tax credit (¶710);

(5) manufacturing equipment and employment investment tax credit (¶712);

(6) research and development credit (¶713);

(7) employer-provided commuter transportation benefits credit (¶714);

(8) high technology credit (¶715);

(9) neighborhood revitalization credit (¶718);

(10) effluent treatment equipment credit (¶719);

(11) economic recovery credit (¶720);

(12) contaminated site remediation credit (¶723);

(13) AMA tax credit (¶724);

(14) business retention and relocation credit (¶722);

(15) sheltered workshop tax credit (¶725);

(16) film production tax credit (¶716);

(17) digital media content production expenses credit (¶717);

(18) urban transit hub tax credit (¶708);

(19) developer's credit (¶709);

¶706

(20) wind energy facility credit (¶725A);

(21) jobs tax credit (¶725B); and

(22) Angel Investor Tax Credit (¶725C).

These credits cannot reduce a taxpayer's tax liability in any one year by more than 50% of the tax otherwise due, and cannot be used to reduce tax liability below the minimum tax.

Credit carryovers are to be calculated according to the individual statute granting each credit. Carryovers are calculated with regard to the priority sequence, and where the individual credit statute does not specify carryover, no carryover is allowed.

Carryforward credit for alternative minimum assessment paid: Taxpayers that pay the alternative minimum assessment (which is only paid when that assessment amount exceeds the taxpayer's tax liability as computed based on entire net income, subject to other limitations) will receive a credit for the amount by which the alternative minimum assessment paid exceeds what its liability would have been as computed based upon entire net income. The credit may be carried forward to future years (without any limitation on the number of years) to offset liability for the entire net income component of the corporation business tax, in years when the taxpayer's entire net income tax liability exceeds its alternative minimum assessment liability. The credit cannot reduce the entire net income tax liability by more than 50% or below the alternative minimum assessment liability or the corporate minimum tax.

Air carrier credit against the alternative minimum assessment. For taxpayers that qualify as "air carriers" pursuant to 49 U.S.C. Sec. 40102, any air carrier that contributes more than 25% of the total amortization for capital improvement projects at Newark International Airport paid by air carriers to the Port Authority of New York and New Jersey is allowed a credit against the alternative minimum assessment otherwise imposed in an amount equal to 50% of such payments made by the air carrier. The credit cannot exceed 50% of the alternative minimum assessment otherwise due and cannot reduce the alternative minimum assessment below the statutory minimum.

CCH Advisory: New Jersey Economic Opportunity Act of 2013

Effective September 18, 2013, the New Jersey Economic Opportunity Act of 2013 consolidates and expands five tax incentive programs into two programs and extends the two programs to July 1, 2019.

The Act expands the Grow New Jersey Assistance Program ("GrowNJ") as the primary job growth incentive program and the Economic Redevelopment and Growth Program ("ERG") as the sole economic redevelopment incentive program. Those two programs, administered by the Economic Development Authority ("EDA"), will incorporate aspects of the Urban Transit Hub Tax Credit Program, the Business Retention and Relocation Assistance Grant Program and the Business Employment Incentive Program, which will be phased out by December 31, 2013.

The Act is designed to extend eligibility to more businesses within greater geographical boundaries and to lower eligibility thresholds in order to encourage job growth and substantial capital investment in priority areas across the State, particularly in the State's four poorest cities: Camden, Trenton, Passaic City and Paterson, called "Garden State Growth Zones"; in the State's Urban Transit Hubs and; in eight of the State's counties: Atlantic, Burlington, Camden, Cape May, Cumberland, Gloucester, Ocean and Salem.

• *GrowNJ*

The GrowNJ program offers qualified businesses, which satisfy certain capital investment and jobs-created or jobs-retained thresholds, a per employee tax credit that can be applied toward the business's corporation business tax obligation annually for up to ten years. Credits are also available against the insurance premiums tax and to partnerships to pass down to their partners.

The Act lowers the amount of previously-required capital investment and newly-created or retained jobs thresholds based upon the type of premises, the type of industry and the location of the business. Those thresholds are further lowered for businesses located in Garden State Growth Zones, Urban Transit Hubs and Atlantic, Burlington, Camden, Cape May, Cumberland, Gloucester, Ocean and Salem counties, and for businesses in the technology startup, manufacturing, transportation, defense, logistics, life sciences, health and finance fields.

The base tax credit ranges from $500 to $5,000 per job, per year. Additional tax credits can be awarded for particular project types and project locations, which may increase the total tax credit to as much as $15,000 per job, per year.

• *ERG*

The ERG program allows developers, who can demonstrate that their projects require a subsidy in order to close a project financing gap, to apply for an incentive grant in an amount up to 75% of the annual incremental tax revenues generated by the project over a twenty year period. If the project is within a Garden State Growth Zone, 85% of the projected annual incremental revenues may be granted. The grant, however, cannot exceed 20% of the total cost of the project and a developer must make a 20% equity investment.

The Act authorizes eligible businesses a bonus incentive of up to 10% of project costs, thereby permitting an award of up to 30% of total cost. Projects that are eligible for that bonus include those involving: supermarkets in distressed municipalities; health care facilities in distressed municipalities; projects in distressed municipalities pursuant to federal contracts; transit projects; residential projects with a 10% set aside for moderate income housing; projects in highland development areas; projects in Garden State Growth Zones; disaster recovery projects; aviation projects; tourism destination projects and; projects involving substantial rehabilitation of existing structures.

For those residential redevelopment projects that have already applied for the urban transit hub tax credit, a qualified residential project can receive a tax credit of up to 35% of its capital investment or up to 40% of its capital investment in Garden State Growth Zones.

In the case of a qualified residential project where the state revenues from the project are inadequate to fully fund the grant, the EDA may convert the grant award into tax credits equal to the full amount of the incentive grant.

• *Planning considerations*

The Act establishes no cap on the cumulative value of tax credits that may be awarded under the GrowNJ program nor does it cap incentives for nonresidential ERG projects. For residential ERG projects, tax credits are capped at $600 million.

Tax credits applies dollar-for-dollar against the corporation business tax and other taxes, including the premiums tax on domestic and foreign insurers. Business entities that are partnerships may pass down credits to their partners. Certain credits can be transferred or can be sold or assigned, either fully or partially.

The deadline to apply for incentives or tax credits under the GrowNJ or ERG programs is June 30, 2019.

¶707 Credit Against Tax—Urban Enterprise Zones

Law: R.S. 52:27H-77, 52:27H-78, 52:27H-86; Reg. Secs. 18:7-3.17, 18:7-3A.2—18:7-3A.5 (CCH New Jersey Tax Reports ¶ 12-060).

Under the New Jersey Urban Enterprise Zones Act, a "qualified business" may be entitled to a corporation business tax credit against the entire net income component of the tax for either hiring new employees or making new investments in a state designated enterprise zone. Basic eligibility requirements for either credit are as follows:

— The taxpayer must be authorized to do business in the state;

— The taxpayer must be engaged within an enterprise zone in the active conduct of a trade or business that consists primarily of manufacturing or some activity other than retail sales or warehousing;

— If the business was started within an enterprise zone after the zone was designated, at least 25% of the taxpayer's full-time employees at its business location within the zone must be (a) residents of an enterprise zone or of a "qualifying municipality" (*i.e.*, a municipality experiencing high unemployment), (b) individuals who during the six months prior to their hiring were unemployed or public assistance recipients, or (c) individuals who are deemed economically disadvantaged under the federal Jobs Training Partnership Act;

— The taxpayer annually must be certified as qualifying for the credit by the Department of Commerce, Energy, and Economic Development; and

— The taxpayer must satisfy specified new employment or minimum new investment requirements.

• *New employees credit*

The new employees credit is available to an otherwise qualified taxpayer whose total number of full-time, permanent employees employed in the enterprise zone during the calendar year in which the new employees are hired exceeds the total number of such employees employed at any time during any prior year during the period of the zone's designation. However, the credit is determined only with respect to new full-time, permanent employees who

— are residents of a qualifying municipality located within any enterprise zone,

— are employed for at least six continuous months during the tax year for which the credit is claimed, and

— immediately prior to being employed by the taxpayer were unemployed, dependent upon public assistance as their primary source of income, or employed at a location outside of the municipality in which the taxpayer's business is located.

Credit amount: The credit is allowed in the tax year immediately following the tax year in which the qualifying new employees are first employed. The credit amount is $1,500 for each qualifying new employee who, prior to being employed, was unemployed for at least 90 days or was dependent upon public assistance, and $500 for each other qualifying new employee.

CCH Example: Calculation of New Employees Credit

ABC Company, a calendar-year taxpayer, is a qualified business that has operated within an enterprise zone since the zone was designated in 1990. Through 2007, ABC's highest number of full-time, permanent employees as of any given date was 100. On June 1, 2008, ABC hires five new employees, each of whom are qualifying employees for purposes of the new employees credit. On February 1, 2009, ABC terminates three of those new employees. On March 1, 2009, ABC hires one new qualifying employee. The two non-terminated employees hired on June 1, 2008, and the employee hired on March 1, 2009, remain with ABC through 2010. Assuming no other changes in employees during 2008 through 2010, then

— for its 2009 tax year, ABC can claim the new employees credit only with respect to the two non-terminated employees hired on June 1, 2008. The credit is not available for the other three employees hired on June 1, 2008, who worked for the company for a total of eight months, because they were not continuously employed by ABC for at least six months during 2009 (*i.e.*, the year for which the credit is claimed);

— for its 2010 tax year, ABC is not entitled to the new employees credit for the employee hired on March 1, 2009. Because ABC's highest level of employment during 2009 (103 employees as of March 1) is less than its highest level of employment at any point in a prior calendar year (105 employees in 2008), the individual hired on March 1, 2009, is deemed not to be a new employee for purposes of the credit.

- *Investment tax credit*

An otherwise qualified taxpayer that is not entitled to the new employees tax credit may claim an investment credit if the taxpayer

— was engaged in the active conduct of a trade or business in the zone for at least one year prior to the zone's designation,

— employs fewer than 50 employees, and

— enters into (with the qualifying municipality in which the enterprise zone is located) a written investment agreement that is approved by the state Urban Enterprise Zone Authority.

Credit amount: The credit equals 8% of each new investment made during the tax year pursuant to the approved agreement.

Investment requirements: The investment agreement must provide for investments in the zone that will contribute substantially to the economic attractiveness of the zone. The types of investment contemplated include those directed toward permanent improvements of the exterior appearance or customer facilities of the taxpayer's property in the zone and those taking the form of monetary contributions to the municipality for use in increasing the general safety and attractiveness of the zone.

A taxpayer employing 10 or fewer employees must commit to making investments that total at least $5,000. For other taxpayers, the minimum commitment increases by $500 for each additional employee.

- *Planning considerations*

Designated enterprise zones: Urban enterprise zones have been designated in the state that fall within the following municipalities: Asbury Park/Long Branch, Bayonne, Bridgeton, Camden, Carteret, East Orange, Elizabeth, Gloucester City, Guttenberg, Hillside, Irvington, New Brunswick, Jersey City, Kearny, Lakewood, Millville/Vineland, Mount Holly, Newark, North Bergen, Orange, Passaic, Paterson, Pemberton, Perth Amboy, Phillipsburg, Plainfield, Pleasantville, Roselle, Trenton, Union City, West New York, and a joint zone consisting of North Wildwood City, Wildwood City, Wildwood Crest Borough and West Wildwood Borough.

Credits mutually exclusive: A qualified business may not claim both the new employees credit and the investment credit in the same tax year, even if one of the credits is earned for the tax year and the other merely is carried forward from a prior year.

Limitations and carryforwards: Both credits apply only to the entire net income component of the corporation business tax. The credit may not, alone or in conjunction with any other allowable credits, reduce a taxpayer's corporation business tax liability in any tax year by more than 50% of the tax otherwise due or to an amount that is less than the statutory minimum tax. Nor may the credits be used to decrease the tax due under the alternative minimum assessment. Any unused credit may be carried forward to the next succeeding tax year, subject to limitations. For the priority in which the enterprise zone credits are claimed and the limitations applied vis-a-vis other available credits, see ¶706.

¶707

• *Forms*

The allowable credit and carryforward are calculated on Form 300, Urban Enterprise Zone Employees Tax Credit and Credit Carryforward, or Form 301, Urban Enterprise Zone Investment Tax Credit and Credit Carryforward.

¶708 Credit Against Tax—Urban Transit Hub

Law: R.S. 34:1B-207—209

Effective July 28, 2009, a business that makes $50,000,000 of qualified capital investment in a business facility in an urban transit hub and employs at least 250 full-time employees at that facility may qualify for tax credits equal to 100% of the qualified capital investment that may be applied against New Jersey CBT. A tenant may also be eligible for the credit, if the tenant occupies space in a qualified business facility that proportionally represents at least $17,500,000 of the capital investment in the facility and employs at least 250 full-time employees in that facility. Prior to July 28, 2009, the capital investment required for the credit was $75,000,000 and the minimum investment threshold for tenants was $25,000,000. A business that is a partnership is not allowed a direct credit, but the amount of credit of an owner of the partnership is determined by allocating to each owner their proportion of the credit of the business.

To be eligible for the Urban Transit Hub tax credit, a business must demonstrate, at the time of its application, that the State's financial support of the proposed capital investment in a qualified business facility will yield a net positive benefit to both the State and the eligible municipality.

• *Urban transit hub*

"Urban transit hub" means (1) property located within a $1/2$ mile radius surrounding the mid point of a New Jersey Transit Corporation, Port Authority Transit Corporation or Port Authority Trans-Hudson Corporation rail station platform area, including all light rail stations, and property located within a one mile radius of the mid point of the platform area of such a rail station if the property is in a qualified municipality under the Municipal Rehabilitation and Economic Recovery Act or in an area that is the subject of a Choice Neighborhoods Transformation Plan funded by the federal government; (2) the site of the campus of an acute care medical facility or a closed hospital located within a one-mile radius of the midpoint of the platform area of such a rail station; (3) property located within a $1/2$ mile radius surrounding the midpoint of any light rail station platform area other than a station that is in a qualified municipality under the Municipal Rehabilitation and Economic Recovery Act; (4) property located within a $1/2$ mile radius surrounding the mid point of one of up to two underground light rail stations' platform areas that are most proximate to an interstate rail station; and (5) property adjacent to, or connected by rail spur to, a freight rail line if the business utilizes that freight line at any rail spur located adjacent to or within a one mile radius surrounding the entrance to the property for loading and unloading freight cars on trains; which property shall have been specifically delineated by the New Jersey Economic Development Authority. Currently, the hubs include rail stations in nine urban municipalities—Camden, East Orange, Elizabeth, Hoboken, Jersey City, Newark, New Brunswick, Paterson, and Trenton. Property which is partially included within the radius is only considered to be part of the hub if over 50 percent of its land area falls within the radius.

• *Qualified business facility*

"Qualified business facility" means any building, complex of buildings or structural components of buildings, and all machinery and equipment located within a designated urban transit hub in an eligible municipality, used in connection with the operation of a business.

- *Qualified capital investment*

"Qualified capital investment" refers to expenses incurred after, but before the end of the eighth year after, January 13, 2008 for: (i) the site preparation and construction, repair, renovation, improvement, equipping, or furnishing of a building, structure, facility or improvement to real property; and (ii) obtaining and installing furnishings and machinery, apparatus or equipment for the operation of a business in a building, structure, facility or improvement to real property.

- *Full-time employee*

"Full-time employee" means a person employed by the taxpayer for at least 35 hours a week, or who renders any other service generally accepted as full-time employment, or a person who is employed by a professional employer organization pursuant to an employee leasing agreement between the business and the professional employer or organization for at least 35 hours a week, or who renders any other standard of service generally accepted by custom or practice as full-time employment, and whose wages are subject to New Jersey gross income tax withholding. "Full-time employee" includes a partner of an eligible partnership whose distributive share of income, gain, loss, or deduction, or whose guaranteed payments, or any combination thereof, is subject to the payment of estimated New Jersey gross income taxes, but does not include any person who works for the taxpayer as an independent contractor or on a consulting basis.

- *Credit amount*

The total credit is equal to 100% of a business' capital investment. Beginning with the tax period in which the business is first approved by the New Jersey Economic Development Authority as having met the investment capital and employment qualifications, the taxpayer may claim 10% of the credit per tax period over a 10-year period. The credit amount that may be taken for a tax period of the business that exceeds the final liabilities of the business for the tax period may be carried forward for use by the business in the next 20 successive tax periods, and shall expire thereafter. However, if, in any tax period, fewer than 200 full-time employees of the business at the qualified business facility are employed in new full-time positions, the amount of the credit will be reduced by 20% for that tax period and each subsequent tax period until the business can prove that the 200 full-time positions have been restored; provided, however, that for businesses applying before January 1, 2010, there shall be no reduction if a business relocates to an urban transit hub from another location or other locations in the same municipality. Also, if the business reduces its statewide workforce by more than 20%, the credit will be forfeited until the business can prove restoration of the workforce. The value of all credits approved may not exceed $1,750,000,000.

- *Planning considerations*

Application for credit.—A business must apply for the credit prior to July 1, 2014 and must submit its documentation for approval of the credit amount no later than July 28, 2017.

If the qualified business facility is sold in whole or in part during the 10-year eligibility period the new owner does not acquire the capital investment of the seller and the seller forfeits all credits for the tax period in which the sale occurs and all subsequent tax periods, provided however that any credits of tenants remain unaffected. If a tenant subleases its tenancy in whole or in part during the 10-year eligibility period the new tenant does not acquire the credit of the sublessor, and the sublessor tenant forfeits all credits for the tax period of its sublease and all subsequent tax periods.

A business is not allowed Urban Transit Hub tax credits if the business participates in a business employment incentive grant relating to the same capital and employees that qualify the business for the Urban Transit Hub tax credit, or if the business receives assistance pursuant to the Business Retention and Relocation Assistance Act. A business that is allowed an Urban Transit Hub tax credit is also not eligible for incentives offered under the Municipal Rehabilitation and Economic Recovery Act. Moreover, a business shall not qualify for the Urban Transit Hub credit based upon capital investment and employment of full-time employees if that capital investment or employment was the basis for which a grant was provided to the business pursuant to the Invest NJ Business Grant Program Act.

CCH Practice Alert: Phase-Out of Urban Transit Hub Credit

The New Jersey Economic Opportunity Act of 2013 (effective September 13, 2013), incorporates aspects of and phases out the Urban Transit Hub Credit by December 31, 2013. (L.2013, c.161).

¶709 Credit Against Tax—Developer's Credit

Law: P.L. 2009, c. 90, sec. 35

Effective July 28, 2009, a credit is allowed to a developer who makes a capital investment of at least $50,000,000 in a qualified residential project. The total credit is equal to 20% of the capital investment. A developer shall apply for the credit within five years after, and must submit its documentation for approval of its credit amount within eight years after July 28, 2009.

¶710 Credit Against Tax—Redevelopment Authority Project Tax Credit

Law: R.S. 55:19-3, 55:19-13, 55:19-23; Reg. Secs. 18:7-3.17, 18:7-3.28 (CCH NEW JERSEY TAX REPORTS ¶ 12-070a).

Under provisions of the New Jersey Urban Development Corporation Act, a taxpayer conducting business within a project location under an agreement with the New Jersey Redevelopment Authority may claim a corporation business tax credit against the entire net income component of the tax for hiring new employees.

Eligibility requirements are as follows:

— The taxpayer must be actively conducting business at a location within a project;

— The business conducted at the location must consist primarily of manufacturing or other business that is not retail sales or warehousing oriented;

— New employees hired by the business must be employed at that location, residents of the qualified municipality, and either unemployed at least 90 days immediately prior to employment or public assistance recipients.

Project qualifications: Any specific work or improvement, including lands, buildings, improvements, and real and personal property, that is owned, constructed, or improved by the New Jersey Redevelopment Authority, a subsidiary, or other business entity under agreement with the NJRA constitutes a "project" for purposes of the credit. The project may be

— industrial,

— land-use improvement,

— civic,

— utility,

— mixed-use or multipurpose, and

— must be located in a qualified municipality (*i.e.,* an economically depressed municipality receiving state aid).

• *Credit amount*

The credit is $1,500 per year for each new employee who was employed by the taxpayer for at least six consecutive months in the year of qualification. The credit is taken during the tax year following the year of qualification and may be continued into a second tax year if the taxpayer remains qualified.

• *Planning considerations*

Limitations and carryforwards: The credit applies only against the entire net income component of the corporation business tax. The credit may not, alone or in conjunction with any other allowable credits, reduce a taxpayer's corporation business tax liability in any tax year by more than 50% of the tax otherwise due or to an amount that is less than the statutory minimum tax. Nor may the credit be used to decrease the tax due under the alternative minimum assessment. Any unused credit may be carried forward to the next succeeding tax year, subject to the same 50% minimum tax limitation. Unused credit after the second year is forfeited. For the priority in which the redevelopment authority project credit is claimed and the limitations are applied with respect to other available credits, see ¶706.

• *Forms*

The credit is claimed on Form 302, Redevelopment Authority Project Tax Credit.

¶711 Credit Against Tax—New Jobs Investment

Law: R.S. 54:10A-5.4—54:10A-5.15; Reg. Secs. 18:7-3.17, 18:7-3.22 (CCH New Jersey Tax Reports ¶12-070).

A corporation business tax credit is allowed against the entire net income component of the tax to taxpayers making qualified investments in new or expanded business facilities in New Jersey that result in new jobs. The credit is allowed against the portion of corporation business tax attributable to, and a direct consequence of, the investment.

The investment must be in real or personal property purchased for expansion or relocation, and consequently must constitute capital investment in a new or expanded business facility. Qualifying investments include the following:

— improvements to real property placed in service during tax years beginning after July 7, 1993;

— tangible personal property with allowable depreciation or amortization that has a remaining recovery period of three or more years; or

— tangible personal property moved into New Jersey if it has a remaining recovery period of three or more years.

Nonqualifying property: Property purchased for business relocation or expansion does not include the following:

— property purchased by the taxpayer and leased to another party;

— property purchased from a related person, unless it was acquired for fair market value and the acquisition was not tax-motivated;

— repair costs and materials used in repair, unless these costs must be capitalized, not expensed, for federal income tax purposes;

— airplanes;

— property primarily used outside New Jersey, based on the amount of time the property is actually used within and outside the state;

— property acquired incident to the purchase of stock or assets of the seller, unless the Division of Taxation waives this disqualification for good cause shown;

— property for which the cost or consideration cannot be quantified with any reasonable degree of certainty at the time it is placed into service (however, if a contract to purchase specifies a minimum purchase price, that price may be used); or

— property that qualifies for the manufacturing equipment and employment investment tax credit (¶712).

Jobs requirement: The investment by small or mid-size business taxpayers must create at least five jobs. For other taxpayers, the investment must create at least 50 jobs. The resulting new jobs must have a minimum median annual compensation. At the time of publication the number for 2013 had not been made available. The minimum median annual compensation was $43,150 in 2012. This minimum salary requirement is adjusted for inflation each year.

A position of employment is directly attributable to the qualified investment if

— the employee's service is performed or the employee's base of operations is at the new or expanded business facility in New Jersey;

— the position did not exist prior to construction, renovation, expansion, or acquisition of the business facility and making the qualified investment; and

— the position would not have existed except for the qualified investment.

Small or mid-size business taxpayers: In order to qualify as a small or mid-size business taxpayer, a cap is set on payroll and gross receipts that are both adjusted for inflation each year. For 2012, they are as follows:

— payroll: $6,403,500 or less; and

— gross receipts: $12,807,100 or less.

• *Determination of credit amount*

The credit is computed by multiplying the amount of the taxpayer's qualified investment in property purchased for business relocation or expansion by the taxpayer's new jobs factor.

A taxpayer's qualified investment is determined on the basis of all or a portion of the cost of the property placed into service, depending on the recovery period for the property under IRC Sec. 168, as follows:

Recovery Period	Qualified Investment
3 years	35% of cost
5 years	70% of cost
7 years or more	100% of cost

New jobs factor: A taxpayer's new jobs factor is determined on the basis of the number of new jobs created in New Jersey directly attributable to the qualified investment. The new jobs factor is equal to 0.01 for small or mid-size business taxpayers that create and fill five new jobs during the taxable year. The new jobs factor increases by 0.01 for each additional five new jobs that result, up to a maximum new jobs factor of 0.20 for 100 new jobs.

The new jobs factor for other taxpayers is equal to 0.005 for 50 new jobs created and filled during the taxable year, increased by 0.005 for each additional 50 new jobs, up to a maximum of 0.1 for 1,000 new jobs.

The new jobs factor is redetermined in each subsequent year in which the credit is allowed.

Criteria for new employees: To be included in the determination of the new jobs factor, new employees must

— reside in and be domiciled in New Jersey, and

— be employed on a regular full-time or part-time and permanent basis.

Full-time employees must be employed for at least 140 hours per month. Part-time employees must customarily perform their duties at least 20 hours per week for at least six months of the year. The hours of part-time employees are aggregated for the purpose of determining the new jobs factor.

The following individuals do not qualify as new employees:

— related individuals as defined in IRC Sec. 51;

— individuals who own 10% or more of the business as determined under IRC Sec. 267;

— individuals who worked for the taxpayer during the six-month period ending on the date the taxpayer's qualified investment is placed in service or use and are rehired during the six-month period beginning on the date the taxpayer's qualified investment is placed in service or use in New Jersey; and

— employees for whom the taxpayer receives an enterprise zone employer tax credit (¶707) or a credit for businesses in redevelopment authority projects hiring employees who formerly received public assistance (¶710).

CCH Example: Computation of Credit

The taxpayer qualifies as a small or mid-size business in New Jersey and purchases a newly-constructed building for $1 million and equipment for $150,000 that is placed in service with a five-year life. The taxpayer currently has 10 full-time employees with a median salary of $50,000 and hires five new full-time employees with a median salary of $35,000. Corporation business tax liability for the year is $25,000 and is composed of the entire net income component of the tax rather than the alternative minimum assessment.

New building for $1 million × 1.00	= $1,000,000
Cost of equipment placed in service with five year life $150,000 × 0.07	= 105,000
Investment base =	$1,105,000
Five new annual jobs = 0.01 new jobs factor	
$1,105,000 × 0.01 new jobs factor × 0.02	
maximum allowable credit=	$221
Aggregate annual credit=	$2,210
$35,000 annual median compensation × 5 new employees	=$175,000
$50,000 annual median compensation × 10 existing employees	= $500,000
$\dfrac{175,000}{500,000}$ = 0.35	
$25,000 CBT liability × 0.35	= $8,750
$8,750 × 0.50 maximum credit allowed	= $4,375

The lessor amount of $2,210 and $4,375 is $2,210, which is the amount of the credit.

- *Planning considerations*

Application for credit: A taxpayer must make written application to the Division of Taxation and receive written acknowledgement of receipt of the application before claiming the new jobs investment credit. Application for the credit is considered timely if filed no later than the final due date of the corporation business tax return, without extensions, for the tax year in which the property is placed in service.

Penalty for failure to timely file: Failure to timely file for the credit results in a forfeiture of 50% of the credit allowance. The penalty applies annually until a proper application is filed.

Claiming the credit: The credit is taken over a five-year period, at the rate of one-fifth of the total credit each year, beginning with the year in which the property was placed in service. The aggregate annual credit allowed for a tax year is the sum of one-fifth of the credit for qualified investment placed into service or use during a prior tax year and one-fifth of the credit for qualified investment placed into service or use during the current tax year.

¶711

Property tax offset: Some or all of the credit remaining after application against corporation business tax may be refunded to the taxpayer as a partial offset against property taxes. The excess credit is refunded to the taxpayer to the extent it does not exceed 50% of the sum of

— the property taxes the taxpayer actually paid, and

— the taxpayers implicit property taxes (equal to 15% of rent or lease payments for property subject to property tax).

Limitations and carryforwards: The credit applies only against the entire net income component of the corporation business tax. The credit may not, alone or in conjunction with any other allowable credits, reduce tax liability by more than 50% of the tax otherwise due or to an amount that is less than the minimum tax. Nor may the credit be used to decrease the tax due under the alternative minimum assessment. For the priority in which the new jobs investment credit is claimed and limitations are applied vis-a-vis other available credits see ¶706.

No carryforward or carryback is allowed for any unused credit that remains after the allowable application against corporation business tax and property tax. Any remaining amount is forfeited.

Any allowable urban enterprise zone credit (¶707) or redevelopment authority project credit (¶710) is required to be applied against and reduce the amount of the entire net income component of the corporation business tax not apportioned to the qualified investment of the new jobs investment tax credit. Any excess of those credits may be applied against the amount of corporation business tax apportioned to the qualified investment that is not offset by the amount of annual new jobs investment credit for the tax year.

• *Forms*

The allowable credit is calculated on Form 304, New Jobs Investment Tax Credit.

¶712 Credit Against Tax—Manufacturing Equipment and Employment Investment Tax Credit

Law: R.S. 54:10A-5.16—54:10A-5.21; Reg. Sec. 18:7-3.17 (CCH New Jersey Tax Reports ¶12-055).

A corporation business tax credit is allowed against the entire net income component of the tax for investment in qualified manufacturing equipment. In addition, taxpayers qualifying for the credit are allowed an additional credit against tax determined on the basis of the increase in employment by the taxpayer in the two tax years following the investment.

• *Amount of credit—Manufacturing equipment*

The credit is equal to 2% of the investment credit base, which is the cost of qualified equipment acquired by purchase and placed in service in the tax year, up to a maximum credit of $1 million. For qualified equipment placed in service during tax years beginning on and after July 1, 2004, the credit is increased to 4% of the investment credit base for taxpayers with 50 or fewer employees and entire net income of less than $5,000,000 for the tax year.

For purposes of computing the credit, the cost of the equipment does not include the value of equipment given in trade or exchange for equipment purchased for business relocation or expansion. Similarly excluded are insurance proceeds received in compensation for the loss of damaged or destroyed equipment and used in the purchase of replacement equipment. The cost of self-constructed equipment (equipment constructed by the taxpayer) is the amount chargeable to the taxpayer's capital account for depreciation for federal income tax purposes. The cost of equipment acquired by written lease is the minimum amount required to be paid by the terms of the lease, provided the minimum amount does not include any amount required to be paid after the expiration of the useful life of the equipment.

• *Amount of credit—Employment credit*

Taxpayers electing the manufacturing equipment credit are allowed an additional credit equal to 3% of the investment credit base upon which the manufacturing equipment credit was calculated, applicable to the two succeeding tax years for which the manufacturing equipment credit was taken. The credit is limited to $1,000 multiplied by the number of new employees hired as a result of the manufacturing investment. The number of new employees is the increase in the average number of full-time employees and full-time employee equivalents residing and domiciled in New Jersey employed at work locations in New Jersey from the tax year immediately preceding the tax year in which the manufacturing equipment credit was allowed (or the year in which the credit was allowed if the taxpayer was not previously subject to tax), to the year immediately following the tax year in which the credit was allowed. The hours of part-time employees are aggregated to determine the number of full-time employee equivalents. "Full-time employees" are employees working for the taxpayer for at least 140 hours per month at a wage not less than the state or federal minimum wage, if applicable to the business, not including temporary or seasonal employment. "Part-time employees" are employees working for the taxpayer for at least 20 hours per week for at least six months during the tax year.

• *Qualified equipment*

Equipment qualifying for the manufacturing investment credit is machinery, apparatus, or other equipment acquired by purchase for use or consumption by the taxpayer directly and primarily in the production of tangible personal property by means of manufacturing, processing, assembling, or refining. For tax years beginning in 2002, qualified equipment also includes machinery, apparatus or other equipment acquired by purchase for use or consumption directly and primarily in the generation of electricity to the point of connection to the grid or in the generation of thermal energy. Qualified equipment must have a useful life of four or more years and be placed in service in New Jersey. Property that the taxpayer contracts or agrees to lease or rent to another person or licenses to another person to use does not qualify for the investment tax credit.

CCH Tip: Equipment Moved from Outside New Jersey

If a corporation moves equipment that otherwise would qualify for the credit from a location outside New Jersey to a location within New Jersey, the equipment would be eligible for the credit. Depreciation that started when the property was originally placed in service outside the state would continue. The equipment is not disqualified from the credit by the fact that its depreciation did not first begin in New Jersey (*State Tax News*, Division of Taxation, Winter 1999; CCH New Jersey Tax Reports ¶ 400-673).

• *Limitations and carryovers;*

Application of credits: Before application of the manufacturing equipment investment tax credit, the entire net income component of the corporation business tax must first be reduced by any enterprise zone employee tax credit, any credit for new employment at a business within an urban development project, and any recycling equipment credit. The manufacturing equipment credit is applied first against the corporation business tax; the employment credit is applied against the amount of corporation business tax liability remaining after application of the manufacturing equipment credit. Manufacturing credits are applied in the order of the credits' tax years. Employment credits are applied in the order of the manufacturing equipment credits to which they relate. The credits may not, alone or in conjunction with any other allowable credits, reduce tax liability by more than 50% of the tax otherwise due or to an amount that is less than the statutory minimum. Nor may the credits be used to decrease the tax due under the alternative minimum assessment.

Unused credit may be carried forward to the seven tax years following the credit's tax year. However, credit carryover is not allowed in a tax year that the taxpayer was a target corporation in a corporate acquisition or, in some instances, party to a merger or consolidation.

• *Forms*

The credit and carryover are calculated on Form 305, Manufacturing Equipment and Employment Investment Tax Credit.

¶713 Credit Against Tax—Research and Development

Law: R.S. 34:1B-7.42, 54:10A-4.3, 54:10A-5.24; Reg. Secs. 18:7-3.17, 18:7-3.23 (CCH New Jersey Tax Reports ¶ 12-065).

Comparable Federal: Sec. 41.

A credit against corporation business tax is allowed against the entire net income component of the tax for qualifying increased research activities for which qualified research expenses and basic research payments are made. The credit is limited to expenditures made in New Jersey.

"Qualified research expenses" include

— in-house research expenses, and

— contract research expenses.

Qualified research is limited to scientific experimentation or engineering activities designed to aid in the development of a new or improved product, process, technique, formula, invention, or computer software program held for sale, lease, or license, or used by the taxpayer in a trade or business.

For in-house research expenses, the trade or business requirement will be met if the principal purpose of the research is to use the results in the active conduct of a future trade or business.

Exclusions: The following types of activities do not qualify for credit eligibility:

— research conducted after the commencement of commercial production of a business component;

— research for adapting existing business components to a particular customer's needs;

— duplication of an existing business component;

— studies or surveys;

— research on computer software developed for a customer's internal use;

— research conducted outside of New Jersey;

— research in the social sciences, arts, or humanities; or

— funded research by another person or governmental agency.

• *Credit amount*

The credit is equal to 10% of the excess of the qualified research expenses for the tax year over the base amount, plus 10% of basic research payments, as determined under IRC Sec. 41.

The base amount cannot be less than 50% of the current year research expenses and is determined by multiplying a fixed-based percentage by the average gross receipts of the taxpayer for the four taxable years preceding the tax year for which the credit is being determined. The fixed-based percentage cannot exceed 16%.

• *Planning considerations*

Disallowances: The new jobs investment tax credit (¶711), or manufacturing equipment and employment investment tax credits (¶712) are not allowed for any property for which the research and development credit is allowed or that is included in the calculation of the research and development credit.

Limitations and carryforwards: For tax periods beginning before January 1, 2012, the amount of the credits applied under this section against the tax imposed for the privilege period shall not exceed 50% of the tax liability otherwise due and shall not reduce the tax liability to an amount less than the statutory minimum. For tax periods beginning on or after January 1, 2012, the amount of the credits applied against the tax imposed for the privilege period shall not reduce the tax liability to an amount less than the statutory minimum.

Excess credit may be carried over to the seven accounting years following the credit's tax year or 15 years for certain high technology companies.

CCH Tip: Carryforward for High Technology Companies

High technology companies that have incurred expenses for certain research conducted in New Jersey may carry over the amount of the research and development tax credit and net operating losses for 15 years rather than the seven-year period permitted for other taxpayers (although note the two-year suspension of net operating loss carryforwards for 2002 and 2003, discussed separately). This applies to expenses incurred beginning on or after July 1, 1998, but before July 1, 2001, for research conducted in the following fields:

— advanced computing;

— advanced materials;

— biotechnology;

— electronics device technology;

— environmental technology; and

— medical device technology.

Tax benefit transfers: Beginning in 1999, new or expanding emerging technology and biotechnology companies in New Jersey with unused research and development tax credits and unused net operating loss carryovers (otherwise allowable but which cannot be applied due to statutory limitations) may surrender those tax benefits to other New Jersey corporate taxpayers for use against the entire net income component of the corporation business tax in exchange for private financial assistance. Neither the total suspension of net operating loss carryforward deductions for 2002 and 2003, nor the partial suspension in 2004 and 2005, impacted this transfer program.

In order to qualify, new or expanding emerging technology and biotechnology companies must

— employ fewer than 225 people, of which at least 75% work in New Jersey,

— meet certain income requirements, and

— not be directly or indirectly owned or controlled by another corporation.

Effective July 28, 2009, an application for a corporation business tax benefit transfer certificate shall not be approved for a new or expanding emerging technology or biotechnology company that (1) has demonstrated positive net operating income in any of the two previous full years of ongoing operations or (2) is directly or indirectly at least 50% owned or controlled by another corporation that has demonstrated positive net operating income in any of the two previous full years of ongoing operations.

¶713

A company surrendering benefits is limited to $250,000 per year, with a lifetime limit of $15,000,000. For state fiscal year 2011, the State is authorized to approve no more than $30,000,000 of tax benefits. The transfer cap for fiscal years 2005 through 2010 was $60,000,000.

• *Forms*

The allowable credit and carryover are calculated on Form 306, Research and Development Tax Credit.

¶714 Credit Against Tax—Employer-Provided Commuter Transportation Benefits

Law: R.S. 27:26A-15; Reg. Secs. 18:7-3.17, 18:7-3.19 (CCH New Jersey Tax Reports ¶ 12-125).

The Smart Moves for Business Program allows corporate taxpayers a credit for commuter transportation benefits provided to employees. The credit can be applied against the entire net income component of the corporation business tax, insurance premiums taxes, public utility taxes, and the gross income tax liability of partnerships.

• *Credit amount*

For tax years beginning on or after January 1, 1995, the credit amount was 10% of commuter transportation benefits provided, up to a maximum ceiling amount. The credit ceiling was adjusted annually for inflation and could be claimed during accounting or privilege periods ending not later than December 31, 2007. For 2007, the maximum credit was $141 per employee.

The Smart Moves for Business Program credit is not available in privilege periods ending later than December 31, 2007.

• *Forms*

The credit was calculated on Form 307, Smart Moves for Business Program Tax Credit.

¶715 Credit Against Tax—High Technology

Law: R.S. 54:10A-4.3, 54:10A-5.24b, 54:10A-5.29, 54:10A-5.30; Reg. Sec. 18:3-7.17 (CCH New Jersey Tax Reports ¶ 12-150).

Comparable Federal: Sec. 41.

A credit may be taken against the entire net income component of the corporation business tax by taxpayers who make qualified investments in certain small New Jersey-based high technology businesses.

A "qualified investment" is a nonrefundable cash investment at risk in a small New Jersey-based high technology business that is transferred to the small New Jersey-based high technology business by a taxpayer that is not a related person of that business.

The cash transfer must be in connection with a transaction in exchange for the following:

    — stock;

    — interests in partnerships or joint ventures;

    — licenses (exclusive or nonexclusive);

    — rights to use technology;

    — marketing rights;

    — warrants; or

    — options or rights to acquire any of the above.

To qualify as a small New Jersey-based high technology business, the corporation must

— have gross receipts from start-up activities of under $1 million;

— be doing business, employing, or owning capital or property, or maintaining an office in New Jersey;

— employ fewer than 225 employees, of which 75% are New Jersey-based employees working in the state; and

— have qualified research expenses incurred for research conducted in New Jersey or conduct pilot scale manufacturing in New Jersey.

"Qualified research expenses" are as defined in IRC Sec. 41, in the fields of

— advanced computing;

— advanced materials;

— biotechnology;

— electronic device technology;

— environmental technology; or

— medical device technology.

• *Credit amount*

The credit is equal to 10% of the qualified investment during each of the three taxable years beginning on or after January 1, 1999, with a maximum credit amount of $500,000 allowed for a tax year for each qualified investment. This credit expired for tax years beginning on and after July 1, 2001.

• *Planning considerations*

Limitations and carryforwards: The research and development credit (¶713) will not be allowed for expenses paid from funds for which this credit is allowed or which are includable in the calculation of this credit.

The credit applies only against the entire net income component of the corporation business tax. The credit may not, alone or in conjunction with any other allowable credits, exceed 50% of the tax liability due in any year and cannot reduce tax liability to an amount less than the statutory minimum tax. Nor may the credit be used to decrease the tax due under the alternative minimum assessment.

The credit may be carried forward 15 years, subject to the same 50% minimum tax and $500,000 per year limitation. However, credit carryover is not allowed in a tax year that the taxpayer is a target corporation in a corporate acquisition or, in some instances, party to a merger or consolidation.

• *Forms*

The allowable credit and carryforward are calculated on Form 308, Small New Jersey-Based High-Technology Investment Tax Credit.

¶716 Credit Against Tax—Film Production

Law: R.S. 54:10A-5.39; Reg. Secs. 18:7-3B.1—3B.7.

The film production tax credit provides CBT credits equal to 20% of the qualified film production expenses incurred in New Jersey on or after January 12, 2006 in the production of a feature film, television series or television show for tax years beginning on and after July 1, 2005, provided that (1) at least 60% of the total production expenses, exclusive of post-production costs, of the taxpayer will be incurred for services performed and goods used or consumed in New Jersey, and (2) principal photography of the film commences within 150 days after the approval of the application for the credit by Division of Taxation and the New Jersey Economic Development Authority. The amount of the film production credit for a tax period, when taken together with any other credits may not exceed 50% of the tax liability otherwise due and may not reduce the tax liability to an amount less than the statutory minimum. The credit expires with tax years first commencing after July 1, 2015. The credit is claimed on Form 318.

A taxpayer may apply for a tax credit transfer certificate in lieu of the film production tax credit. The tax credit transfer certificate may be sold or assigned, in full or in part, to any other taxpayer that may have a CBT or gross income tax liability, in exchange for private financial assistance to be provided by the purchaser or assignee to the taxpayer.

For the period July 1, 2010 through June 30, 2011, the film production tax credit was temporarily suspended, as the annual tax credit cap for film production was reduced to zero.

¶717 Credit Against Tax—Digital Media Content Production Expenses

> *Law:* R.S. 54:10A-5.39; Reg. Secs. 18:7-3B.1-3

The digital media content production expenses credit, enacted on January 11, 2008, provides CBT credits for up to 20% of the qualified digital media content production expenses of the taxpayer during a privilege period, provided that at least $2,000,000 of the total digital media content production expenses of the taxpayer will be incurred for services performed and goods used or consumed in New Jersey and at least a significant percentage, as determined by the New Jersey Economic Development Authority, of the qualified digital media content production expenses will include wages and salaries paid to one or more new full-time employees in New Jersey. The Division of Taxation and the New Jersey Economic Development Authority has determined that at least $1,000,000 of the total digital media content production expenses must consist of wages and salaries for full-time digital media employees in New Jersey. The amount of the digital media content production expenses credit for a tax period, when taken together with any other credits may not exceed 50% of the tax liability otherwise due and may not reduce the tax liability to an amount less than the statutory minimum. The credit expires with tax years first commencing after July 1, 2015. The credit is claimed on Form 318.

A taxpayer may apply for a tax credit transfer certificate in lieu of the digital media content production expenses credit. The tax credit transfer certificate may be sold or assigned, in full or in part, to any other taxpayer that may have a CBT liability, in exchange for private financial assistance to be provided by the purchaser or assignee to the taxpayer.

For the period July 1, 2010 through June 30, 2011, the digital media content production expenses credit was temporarily suspended, as the annual tax credit cap for digital media content was reduced to zero.

¶718 Credit Against Tax—Neighborhood Revitalization Tax Credit

> *Law:* R.S. 52:27D-490, et seq.; Reg. Secs. 5:47-1.1—5:47-10.3, 18:7-3.17, 18:7-3.27 (CCH NEW JERSEY TAX REPORTS ¶12-085).

Effective July 1, 2002, a credit is available against the entire net income component of the corporation business tax to businesses that contribute to state-approved nonprofit corporations for the purpose of implementing approved neighborhood preservation and revitalization projects in low and moderate income neighborhoods.

Taxpayers are issued certificates specifying the amount of the annual credit awarded to that business.

The credits can be awarded against other business taxes as well, including the tax on marine insurance companies, the insurance premiums tax, sewer and water utility excise taxes, and the petroleum products gross receipts tax.

The Commissioner of Community Affairs issues the credit certificates, but may only do so if:

— The assistance is paid for a qualified neighborhood preservation and revitalization project;

— The payment is not less than $25,000 in each tax year for which credit is sought;

— Neither the taxpayer nor any of its wholly owned subsidiaries has previously failed to make such payments after approval for the assistance had been granted (unless good cause for the prior failure is shown); and

— The total of all approved assistance amounts per project does not exceed $1 million.

• *Credit amount*

The credit applies only against the entire net income component of the corporation business tax. Prior to May 6, 2007, the credit amount was up to 50% of the assistance provided. Effective May 6, 2007, the credit amount may be in an amount up to 100% of the assistance provided. The credit is awarded only for assistance provided in the same year that the certificate was issued or, if more than one year of assistance was approved, within the year in which payment was scheduled and made. No more than $10,000,000 in total tax credits may be certified in any fiscal year.

Prior to May 6, 2007, an entity's credit could not exceed the lesser of $500,000 or the total tax liability of the entity for the tax year. Effective May 6, 2007, an entity's credit may not exceed $1,000,000 or the total tax liability otherwise payable for the tax year. Notwithstanding the foregoing, the Division of Taxation also takes the position that the credit may not, alone or in conjunction with other allowable credits, exceed 50% of the tax liability otherwise due or reduce liability below the statutory minimum. Nor may the credit be used to decrease the tax due under the alternative minimum assessment. The credit is disallowed for activities for which the taxpayer is already receiving credit.

• *Forms*

The neighborhood revitalization credit is calculated on Form 311, Neighborhood Revitalization State Tax Credit.

¶719 Credit Against Tax—Effluent Treatment Equipment Credit

Law: R.S. 54:10A-5.31, et seq.; Reg. Secs. 18:7-3.17, 18:7-3.24 (CCH New Jersey Tax Reports ¶ 12-080).

Taxpayers purchasing wastewater treatment equipment or conveyance equipment for use exclusively within New Jersey and with Department of Environmental Protection approval are eligible for corporation business tax credit against the entire net income component of the tax, effective July 1, 2002. The equipment must be used in the treatment of effluent for reuse in an industrial process, exclusively in New Jersey.

• *Credit amount*

The credit is allowed for 50% of the eligible cost of the qualified equipment, less the amount of any loan received and excluding any applicable sales and use tax.

The credit is applied only against the entire net income component of the corporation business tax. No more than 20% of the total credit may be used in one year and the credit cannot (with any other credits allowed) exceed 50% of the tax liability otherwise due or reduce liability below the statutory minimum. Nor may the credit be used to decrease the tax due under the alternative minimum assessment. Unused credit amounts may be carried forward to future tax periods.

- *Forms*

The effluent equipment credit is calculated on Form 312, Effluent Equipment Tax Credit. A copy of the Department of Environmental Protection's approval must be filed with an affidavit certifying that the equipment will be used exclusively in New Jersey.

¶720 Credit Against Tax—Municipal Rehabilitation and Economic Recovery Credit

Law: R.S. 52:27BBB-54, 52:27BBB-55; Reg. Secs. 18:7-3.17, 18:7-3.25 (CCH New Jersey Tax Reports ¶ 12-085a).

Taxpayers conducting business in qualified municipalities that do not already receive a benefit under the Urban Enterprise Zones Act may apply for an economic recovery tax credit against the entire net income component of the corporation business tax. The credit is available based upon new employees hired by the taxpayer at that location.

- *Credit amount*

The credit applies only against the entire net income component of the corporation business tax. Credit may be claimed in amounts of $2,500 per new full-time employee at the qualified location in "credit year one" and $1,250 for each qualifying new employee in "credit year two." Credit year one is the first twelve calendar months following the taxpayer's initial or expanded operations at its location in the qualified municipality, and credit year two is the following twelve months. No taxpayer is allowed more than a single two-year continuous period in which credit is allowed for activity at a location in a qualified municipality.

Unused credits may be refundable following credit year two, to the extent of the unused credit multiplied by a ratio of the taxpayer's new full-time positions in credit year two over its new full-time positions in credit year one (not to exceed 1). If not refundable, credits may be carried forward for up to five tax periods following the period for which the credit is allowed.

The credit may not, alone or in conjunction with any other allowable credits, be used to reduce tax liability by more than 50% of the tax due or to an amount that is less than the minimum tax. Nor may the credit be used to decrease the tax due under the alternative minimum assessment.

- *Forms*

The municipal rehabilitation credit is calculated on Form 313, Economic Recovery Tax Credit.

- *Tax rebate-qualified municipality open for business incentive program*

As a means to foster business investment in qualified municipalities, businesses that locate or expand in a qualified municipality during the period that the municipality is under rehabilitation and economic recovery are eligible to receive a rebate of corporation business tax. Camden currently qualifies as such a municipality. Effective June 30, 2002, an eligible taxpayer may receive a rebate of up to 75% of the "incentive payment" it has made. If a taxpayer can establish that a particular business relocation or expansion will more effectively contribute to the rehabilitation and recovery of a qualified municipality, the taxpayer may receive a rebate of up to 100% of the incentive payment it has made. Taxpayers must apply for the rebate within two years of the deposit of their incentive payments and must establish that the taxpayer will utilize the money for business relocation or business expansion property.

¶721 Credit Against Tax—HMO Assistance Fund Tax Credit

Law: R.S. 17B:32B-12; Reg. Secs. 18:7-3.17, 18:7-3.26 (CCH New Jersey Tax Reports ¶12-127).

A member organization of the Insolvent HMO Assistance Fund is allowed a credit against the entire net income tax component of the corporation business tax of up to 50% of an assessment for which a certificate of contribution has been issued.

• *Credit amount*

Member organizations obtain a credit of up to 10% of any assessment for each of the five tax periods beginning on or after the third calendar year beginning after the assessment was paid. This computation is based upon credit for 50% of the member's assessment, 20% of which may be applied against the entire net income tax component of the corporation business tax for each of those five tax periods. However, no member organization may reduce its tax liability by more than 20% of the amount (determined without regard to any other credits) otherwise due.

In the event that an assessment is later refunded to a member organization, those amounts are deemed to be assessment amounts for which a credit was already allowed. If the member organization has already used the credit, then 50% of the amount of any refund must be paid by the member organization to the State as the Division of Taxation requires until the amounts paid equal the amounts applied as credit.

• *Forms*

The HMO assistance fund credit is calculated on Form 310, HMO Assistance Fund Tax Credit.

¶722 Credit Against Tax—Business Retention and Relocation Credit

Law: R.S. 34:1B-113 *et seq.* (CCH New Jersey Tax Reports ¶12-070d).

Effective July 1, 2004, taxpayers that have operated in New Jersey for at least ten years may obtain grants of corporation business tax credits if they enter into a project agreement to relocate or maintain a minimum number of full-time jobs from one or more locations within the state to a new business location in the state. Effective January 13, 2008, the minimum number of full-time jobs is 50. Prior to that date, the minimum number of full-time jobs was 250. By relocating more than 2,000 full-time employees from one or more locations outside of a designated urban center to a designated urban center, a taxpayer can qualify for an additional bonus award equal to 50% of the amount of the original tax credit. Businesses that consist solely of point-of-final-purchase retail facilities are not eligible for a grant of tax credits.

To be considered a full-time employee, a person must be employed for at least thirty-five hours a week and must receive wages that are subject to withholding. Independent contractors or consultants are not considered full-time employees.

To qualify for a grant of credits, the taxpayer must demonstrate that the receipt of the tax credits will be a material factor in the decision not to relocate outside of New Jersey. A taxpayer that relocates 1,500 or more retained full-time jobs from outside of a designated urban center to one or more new locations within a designated urban center is not required to make such a demonstration if the taxpayer applies for a grant of tax credits within six months of signing its lease or purchase agreement.

• *Amount and Timing of Credit*

The amount of the credit is based upon the "total allowable relocation costs," which is defined as $1,500 times the number of retained full-time jobs. However, amendments taking effect January 2011 have created six tiers of retained or relocated employees. Tier 1 ranges from 50 to 250 employees; Tier 2 ranges from 251 to 400 employees; Tier 3 ranges from 401 to 600 employees; Tier 4 ranges from 601 to 800 employees; Tier 5 ranges from 801 to 1,000 employees; and Tier 6 includes 1,001 or more retained employees.

The incentive to retain or relocate additional employees is established in the six tier system. Tier 1 allows a grant of tax credits at $1,500 times each relocated or maintained employee, plus any applicable bonus awards, and this credit may be applied against the liability in the tax period in which the credit is issued. Tier 2 allows a grant of tax credits at twice the yearly tax credit amount plus any applicable bonus awards, and this credit may be applied against the liability in the tax period in which the credit is issued and the next tax period for one-half of the total grant per period. Tier 3 allows a grant of tax credits at three times the yearly tax credit amount plus any applicable bonus awards, and this credit may be applied against the liability in the tax period in which the credit is issued and the next two tax periods for one-third of the total grant per period and the next tax period for one-half of the total grant per period. Tier 4 allows a grant of tax credits at four times the yearly tax credit amount plus any applicable bonus awards, and this credit may be applied against the liability in the tax period in which the credit is issued and the next three tax periods for one-fourth of the total grant per period. Tier 5 allows a grant of tax credits at five times the yearly tax credit amount plus any applicable bonus awards, and this credit may be applied against the liability in the tax period in which the credit is issued and the next four tax periods for one-fifth of the total grant per period. Tier 6 allows a grant of tax credits at six times the yearly tax credit amount plus any applicable bonus awards, and this credit may be applied against the liability in the tax period in which the credit is issued and the next five tax periods for one-fifth of the total grant per period.

• *Planning considerations*

Application for credit: At least 45 days prior to moving to the new business location, the taxpayer seeking the credit must submit an application for approval of the relocation project to the New Jersey Commerce Commission. However, a business relocating 1,500 or more retained full-time jobs to one or more new locations within a designated urban center need only submit an application within six months of executing its lease. The application must include the following:

— employment projections;

— terms of lease or purchase agreements existing or proposed;

— estimated retained State tax revenues;

— description of the type of contribution the business can make to the long-term growth of the State's economy;

— description of the potential impact on the State's economy if the jobs are not retained;

— evidence that the business has been operating in the State for at least ten years;

— evidence of alternative relocation plans;

— evidence that the State will realize a net positive benefit from the grant of tax credits and resultant retention of full-time jobs and any capital investment.

¶722

Limitations: A taxpayer that is receiving a business employment incentive grant or other State grant is not eligible to receive the credit with respect to a job that is the subject of the grant. Furthermore, a taxpayer must submit, no later than March 1st of each year, from the first year the credits are granted through the commitment duration, a certification of compliance that indicates that the business continues to maintain the number of retained full-time jobs as specified in the project agreement. The credit is subject to recapture if a taxpayer fails to maintain the full-time jobs level required by the program for five years or fails to meet or comply with any condition or requirement under the project agreement. Pursuant to a credit transfer program, grant recipients can sell their unused credits to other taxpayers. The total value of grants of tax credits that New Jersey employers collectively may apply against their tax liabilities is capped at an aggregate annual limit of $20 million; and the total value of the grant of tax credits that any single New Jersey employer may apply against its tax liability is capped at an aggregate annual limit of $10 million.

CCH Practice Alert: Phase-Out of Business Retention and Relocation Credit

The New Jersey Economnic Opportunity Act of 2013 (effective September 13, 2013), incorporates aspects of and phases out the Business Retention and Relocation Credit by December 31, 2013. (L.2013, c.161).

¶723 Credit Against Tax—Contaminated Site Remediation Credit

Law: R.S. 54:10A-5.33 (CCH New Jersey Tax Reports ¶ 12-081).

A credit was available in an amount equal to 100% of the eligible costs of the remediation of a contaminated site, as certified by the Department of Environmental Protection and the Division of Taxation, for remediation performed during tax periods beginning on or after January 1, 2004 and before January 1, 2007.

The Department had to certify the eligible costs of the remediation if the Department found that:

— the taxpayer entered into an agreement with the Commissioner of Environmental Protection for the remediation of the contaminated site and the taxpayer was in compliance with the agreement;

— the taxpayer was not liable for the contamination of the site; and

— the costs of the remediation were actually and reasonably incurred.

In addition, the Division of Taxation had to certify that:

— the remediated site was within an area designated as Planning Area 1 (Metropolitan) or Planning Area 2 (Suburban);

— the subsequent business activity at the site represented new corporation business tax, or sales and use tax or gross income tax receipts;

— there was a high probability that the estimated new tax receipts derived from business activity at the remediated site, within a three-year period from the inception of the business activity, equaled or exceeded the value of tax credits issued; and

— if the subsequent business activity at the remediated site was as a result of a relocation of an existing business from within the State, then the tax credit would have been equal to the difference in aggregate value of tax receipts from the corporation business tax, the sales and use tax and the gross income tax generated by the business activity in the tax period immediately following the business relocation less the aggregate value of such tax receipts generated in the tax period immediately prior to relocation, up to 100% of the eligible costs. If the difference in aggregate value was zero or less, no credit was awarded.

• *Planning considerations*

Application for credit: To qualify for the credit a taxpayer submitted an application to the Department of Environmental Protection for review and certification of the eligible costs.

Limitations: The priority of the credit was determined by the Division of Taxation. The amount of the credit could not exceed 50% of the tax liability otherwise due and could not reduce the tax liability to an amount less than the statutory minimum. The amount of credit otherwise allowable which was not applied for the tax year due to the preceding limitations could be carried over to the next five tax periods. However, a taxpayer could not carry over the credit to a tax period during which a corporate acquisition with respect to which the taxpayer was a target corporation occurred. In no event could the credit, when taken together with the property tax exemption received pursuant to the Environmental Opportunity Zone Act or any other tax incentive or grant to remediate a site, exceed 100% of the total cost of remediation. Pursuant to a credit transfer program, taxpayers could sell their unused credits to other taxpayers.

¶724 Credit Against Tax—AMA Tax Credit

Law: R.S. 54:10A-5a, Schedule A-3 of the Corporation Business Tax Return (Form CBT-100).

For taxable periods beginning on or after January 1, 2002, if a taxpayer incurs an Alternative Minimum Assessment (AMA) liability in excess of the regular corporation business tax (CBT) liability the excess may be carried over to subsequent years and used as a credit against the regular CBT liability. The carryovers never expire. There are, however, limitations as to how much credit can be taken on any single return. The credit taken must not reduce the taxpayer's CBT liability to less than the AMA, nor to below 50% of the regular CBT liability otherwise due, nor to below the minimum tax due ($500 or $2,000). In addition, all other credits available to the taxpayer per Schedule A-3 of the Corporation Business Tax Return (Form CBT-100) must be used before taking the AMA tax credit. If a key corporation is remitting AMA for a controlled group, only the key corporation may take the AMA tax credit.

¶725 Credit Against Tax—Sheltered Workshop Tax Credit

Law: R.S. 54:10A-5.38.

For tax periods beginning after January 12, 2006, New Jersey enacted a CBT credit for business that provide employment at an occupational training center or sheltered workshop for developmentally disabled clients. A "sheltered workshop" is an occupation-oriented facility operated by a nonprofit agency with which the Division of Vocational Rehabilitation Services has entered into a contract to furnish extended employment programs to eligible individuals. The credit equals 20% of the salary and wages paid by the taxpayer during the tax period for the employment of a qualified person, but not to exceed $1,000 for each qualified person for the tax period. The amount of credit applied against the CBT for a tax period, when taken together with any other credits allowed may not exceed 50% of the tax liability otherwise due and may not reduce the tax liability to an amount less then the statutory minimum. The credit is claimed on Form 317.

¶725A Credit Against Tax—Wind Energy Facility Credit

Law: R.S. 34:18-209.4.

Effective August 19, 2010, a business that makes or acquires a capital investment of at least $50,000,000 in a qualified wind facility, at which the business, including tenants at the qualified wind energy facility, employs at least 300 new, full-time employees, may qualify for a tax credit equal to 100% of its capital investment. A tenant may also be eligible for the credit if the tenant occupies a leased area of the qualified wind energy facility that represents at least $17,500,000 of the capital investment in the qualified wind energy facility.

To be eligible for the wind energy facility credit, a business must demonstrate at the time of its application that the State's financial support of the proposed capital investment in the qualified wind energy facility will yield a net positive benefit to the State.

The wind energy facility credit shall be administered in the same manner as tax credits are administered under the Urban Transit Hub Tax Act.

• *Credit amount*

The total credit is equal to 100% of a business' capital investment (or the capital investment represented by the business' leased area). The credit shall be taken over a 10-year period at the rate of one-tenth of the total amount of the business' credit for each tax accounting or privilege period of the business beginning with the tax period in which the business is approved as having satisfied the investment capital and employment qualifications. The value of all credits approved may be up to $100,000,000, except as may be increased by the New Jersey Economic Development Authority pursuant to statutory limitations.

• *Planning considerations*

A business must apply for the wind energy facility credit within five years after, and must submit its documentation for approval of the credit amount within eight years after, January 13, 2008.

A business is not allowed a wind energy facility credit if it participates in a business employment incentive grant relating to the same capital and employees that qualify the business for the wind energy facility credit or if the business receives assistance pursuant to the Business Retention and Relocation Assistance Act. A business that is allowed a wind energy facility credit is not eligible for incentives authorized pursuant to the Municipal Rehabilitation and Economic Recovery Act.

¶725B Credit Against Tax—Jobs Tax Credit

Law: R.S. 34:1B-242-249 (CCH New Jersey Tax Reports ¶12-070f).

Effective January 5, 2012, the Jobs Tax Credit under "Grow New Jersey Assistance Act" allows a credit against the corporation business tax and taxes imposed on insurance companies for the creation and retention of jobs within New Jersey. The program is administered by the Economic Development Authority (EDA). To be eligible, the business must make a minimum of a $20 million investment in a qualified business facility and employ at least 100 full-time employees or create at least 100 full-time jobs in an industry identified by the EDA as desirable. The business must also show that the capital investment will yield a benefit to the state and that the credit is a material factor in the decision to create or retain jobs. Point of final purchase retail facilities are not eligible for the credit. The business must also provide health care benefits.

• *Credit amount*

The amount of the credit equals $5,000 per year per qualified full-time position for a period of 10 years. An additional $3,000 per year per qualified full-time position for a period of 10 years may be awarded as a bonus. The amount of tax credit available is limited to the lesser of 1/10 of the capital investment or $4 million. Businesses must apply for the tax credit prior to July 1, 2014.

¶725B

• *Planning considerations*

While partnerships are not allowed the credit directly, the credit is allowed based on each corporate partner's share of the total distributive income or gain of the partnership for its tax period ending with or within the partner's tax period, or based on that proportion that is allocated by an agreement among the owners of the partnership.

The amount of the tax credit that exceeds the business's tax liability for the tax period can be carried forward for a period of 20 years, provided the total value of all credits awarded by the EDA does not exceed the yearly limit of $200 million or $1.5 million in the course of 10 years. A business which receives the tax credit can also apply for a benefit transfer certificate covering tax years over one or more years in lieu of using the credits. The transfer certificate can be sold to another business that has corporation business tax liabilities for consideration equal to at least 75% of the value of the tax credit transferred. The tax credit transfer certificate used and applied by a purchaser or assignee shall be subject to the same limitations and conditions that apply to the use of the credit by the business that originally received the credit.

¶725C Credit Against Tax—Angel Investor Tax Credit

Law: R.S. 54:10A-5.28, 54:10A-5.29, 54:10A-5.30.

For tax years beginning on or after January 1, 2012, the Angel Investor Tax Credit allows a credit against the corporation business tax for individuals or entities investing in New Jersey emerging technology businesses. The taxpayer must apply to, and be approved by, the Economic Development Authority to be eligible for the credit.

• *Credit amount*

The credit is equal to 10% of the qualified investment made by the taxpayer in a New Jersey emerging technology business up to a maximum allowed credit of $500,000 for the taxable year for each qualified investment. The amount of credits may not exceed a cumulative total of $25,000,000 in any calendar year.

• *New Jersey emerging technology business*

A New Jersey emerging technology business is a company with fewer than 225 employees (at least 75% of whom are filling a position in the State of New Jersey) that is doing business, employing or owning capital or property, or maintaining an office in the State, and that has qualified research expenses paid or incurred for research conducted in the State; conducts pilot scale manufacturing in the State or; conducts technology commercialization in the State in the fields of advanced computing, advanced materials, biotechnology, electronic device technology, information technology, life sciences, medical device technology, mobile communications technology or renewable energy technology.

• *Qualified investment*

Qualified investment means the nonrefundable transfer of cash to a New Jersey emerging technology business by a taxpayer that is not a related person of the New Jersey emerging technology business, the transfer of which is in connection with either (1) a transaction in exchange for stock, interests in partnerships or joint ventures, licenses (exclusive or nonexclusive), rights to use technology, marketing rights, warrants, options or any similar items, including but not limited to options or rights to acquire any of the items included above or (2) a purchase, production or research agreement.

• *Planning considerations*

For corporation business (franchise) tax purposes, a business taxpayer may choose between a refund and a 15-year carryforward credit. However, credit carryover is not allowed in a tax year that the taxpayer was a target corporation in a corporate acquisition or, in some instances, party to a merger or consolidation. A taxpayer who claims the Angel Investor Tax Credit against the corporation business (franchise) tax may not claim a research and development credit for the same expenditures.

• *Forms*

At the time of publication, no form has been issued to claim the Angel Investor Tax Credit.

¶726 Domestic Corporations Ceasing to Possess a Franchise

Law: R.S. 54:10A-2, 54:50-13, 54:50-14, 54:50-15.

The New Jersey corporation business tax is imposed for all or any part of each calendar or fiscal year for which the corporation possesses a franchise. A domestic corporation is required to pay the franchise tax until it ceases to possess a franchise because of its dissolution, merger or consolidation, or because of the surrender, revocation, or annulment of its charter.

Payment of all state taxes must be made, or assured, prior to dissolution, withdrawal, surrender, merger or consolidation, as provided by the State Tax Uniform Procedure Law (¶2008). A tax clearance certificate must be obtained from the Director of the Division of Taxation, except in the case of a merger or consolidation in which the survivor is a domestic or authorized foreign corporation.

When application for a tax clearance certificate is made, all taxes that were due for prior periods must be paid. In addition, an estimated tax return and payment are generally required for the period between the last regular due date and the date of the proposed dissolution or other action. The estimated tax requirements do not apply in specified cases when payment is guaranteed by certain corporations meeting the standards provided in the Uniform Procedure Law (¶2008).

For short period returns, see ¶735.

¶727 Foreign Corporations Ceasing to Have a Taxable Status in New Jersey

Law: R.S. 54:10A-2, 54:50-13, 54:50-14, 54:50-15.

A foreign corporation ceasing to have a taxable status in New Jersey is subject to corporation business tax for the portion of the calendar or fiscal year during which it had a taxable status. The tax requirements applicable to a foreign corporation withdrawing from New Jersey are provided by the State Tax Uniform Procedure Law (¶2008); in general, the requirements are the same as those that apply to a domestic corporation ceasing to possess a franchise (¶726), and tax liability is determined in the same manner. However, special rules apply if the foreign corporation's short year does not coincide with its federal accounting period (¶735).

¶728 Investment Companies, Regulated Investment Companies, and Real Estate Investment Trusts

Law: R.S. 54:10A-4(f), (*l*), 54:10A-5(d) (CCH New Jersey Tax Reports ¶10-355, 10-360, 10-525).

Investment companies and real estate investment trusts may elect to be taxed on a reduced base for the entire net income component of the corporation business tax, but without allocation. The regular tax rate applicable to entire income (¶705) applies to the reduced base.

Minimum tax: The total tax may not be less than $250.

Investment companies: In the case of investment companies, the tax is imposed on 40% of entire net income. Investment companies are expressly excluded from the alternative minimum assessment component of the tax.

"Investment company" defined: An "investment company" is a corporation, at least 90% of whose business during the period covered by its report consisted of holding, investing and reinvesting in stocks, bonds, notes, mortgages, debentures, patents, patent rights, and other securities for its own account; but *not* any corporation

— that is a merchant or dealer in securities, regularly engaged in buying stocks, bonds, and other securities and selling the same to customers; or

— that had less than 90% of its average gross assets in New Jersey, during the period covered by the return, at cost, either invested in stocks, bonds, debentures, mortgages, notes, patents, patent rights, and effective August 7, 2006, publicly traded limited partnership or limited liability company interests, or other securities or consisting of cash on deposit; or

— that is a banking corporation or financial business corporation for franchise tax purposes.

Regulated investment companies: RICs that satisfy the requirements of IRC Sec. 852(a) pay a flat tax of $250 per year. Unless otherwise qualified as an "investment company" (see above), RICs may also be subject to the alternative minimum assessment component of the tax.

Real estate investment trusts: In the case of REITs, the tax is imposed on 4% of entire net income and they are subject to the alternative minimum assessment component of the tax.

"Real estate investment trust" defined: A "real estate investment trust" is a corporation, trust, or association qualifying and electing to be taxed as a real estate investment trust under federal law.

¶729 Merger, Consolidation, or Reorganization

Law: R.S. 54:10A-34, 54:50-14.

The Treasurer's Office cannot (1) accept a certificate of dissolution of a domestic corporation for filing; (2) issue a certificate of withdrawal of a foreign corporation (unless the withdrawal is effected by its merger or consolidation into a domestic or foreign corporation authorized to transact business in New Jersey); (3) accept for filing a certificate of merger or consolidation of a domestic corporation into a foreign corporation not authorized to transact business in New Jersey; or (4) accept for filing a certificate of merger or consolidation of any business entity into any other business entity (other than a domestic or foreign corporation authorized to transact business in New Jersey), unless the business entity files a certificate issued by the Director of the Division of Taxation dated not earlier than 45 days prior to the effective date of the business entity's action evidencing that the business entity's taxes have been paid or provided for. See ¶726 for domestic corporations and ¶727 for foreign corporations.

Banking corporations: When a banking corporation merges or consolidates with another such corporation, the survivor must include the income of the merged bank in taxable income for the privilege period.

¶730 Corporations Doing Business Within and Without the State

Law: R.S. 54:10A-6.

Corporations doing business both within and without New Jersey are entitled to allocate net income. For tax years beginning prior to July 1, 2010, a corporation doing business within and without the state is entitled to allocate net income only if it maintains a regular place of business outside the state. For tax years beginning on or after July 1, 2010, the "regular place of business" requirement has been repealed. A taxpayer will no longer need to show that a regular place of business exists outside New Jersey in order to allocate less than 100% of its net income to the State.

For full discussion of the allocation of net income, see Chapter 8.

¶731 S Corporations

Law: R.S. 54:10A-5(c), 54:10A-5.22, 54A:5-1(c); Reg. Secs. 18-7-20.1, 18:7-20.2, 18:7-20.3.

Comparable Federal: Secs. 1371—1377.

For all tax years beginning after July 7, 1993, New Jersey recognizes S corporations and imposes the corporation business tax at a reduced rate on the portion of the S corporation's entire net income that is not subject to federal income tax. Beginning in 2001, New Jersey started the process of phasing out the corporate level tax on S corporations. For tax years ending on or after July 1, 2007, the tax rate on an S corporation's entire net income is reduced to 0%. New Jersey S corporations are subject to the same minimum tax payment obligations as C corporations, but are not subject to the Alternative Minimum Assessment.

Rate of tax on S corporations: See ¶705.

A "New Jersey S corporation" is a corporation that is a federal S corporation and that has made a valid election to be a New Jersey S corporation on Form CBT-2253. In order to make a New Jersey S corporation election, the electing corporation and each of its shareholders must consent to the election. The New Jersey S corporation election must be filed within one calendar month of the time at which a federal S corporation election would be required.

Regulations provide a procedure for a federal S corporation that failed to file a timely New Jersey S corporation election to make a retroactive election to be recognized as a New Jersey S corporation if certain conditions are satisfied.

A federal S corporation is permitted to own a Qualified Subchapter S Subsidiary (QSSS) and effectively to treat the subsidiary as if it were a division. New Jersey will recognize a New Jersey QSSS if certain requirements relating to the qualification of the parent company as a New Jersey S corporation, the consent to New Jersey's taxation of the QSSS's income, and the filing of a form CBT-2553 are satisfied. For corporation business tax purposes, the assets, liabilities, and items of income, deduction, and credit of the QSSS flow through to the parent S corporation retaining the same character. Notwithstanding a corporation's qualification as a NJ-QSSS, every qualified NJ-QSSS must file a CBT-100S and pay the applicable minimum tax.

¶732 Corporate Partners

Law: R.S. 54:10A-15.6 through -15.10.

As the result of legislation effective for tax periods beginning on or after January 1, 2002, which replaced foreign corporate partner legislation enacted in 2001, partnerships with nonresident corporate or individual partners are subject to a new tax that, when paid, is credited to the nonresident partner. Any entity treated as a partnership for federal tax purposes must pay tax at 9% on all nonresident corporate partners' shares of partnership income apportioned to New Jersey, based upon the partnership's apportionment factor. The "tax" paid by the partnership is credited to the accounts of the nonresident partners based upon the share of tax paid on each such partner's behalf. Tax must also be paid on all nonresident noncorporate partners' shares of partnership income apportioned to New Jersey, but at a rate of 6.37%. This partnership-level tax is due on or before the 15th day of the fourth month following the close of the partnership's tax period. Although the partnership-level tax is credited to the accounts of its nonresident partners, the full tax must be paid regardless of any estimated tax payments that were already made by the nonresident partner for the relevant tax period. Similarly, for tax periods beginning prior to January 1, 2007, a nonresident partner cannot take into account the payment of the partnership-level tax in determining the nonresident partner's own estimated tax obligations.

For tax periods beginning on or after January 1, 2007, the partnership-level tax is amended to provide that the tax must be made in 25% installments on or before the 15th day of each of the fourth, sixth and ninth months of the tax period and on or before the 15th day of the first month succeeding the close of the tax period. The partnership-level tax installments paid by a partnerships are credited to the accounts of each nonresident partner in proportion to each nonresident partner's share of allocated income and may be taken in to account in determining the nonresident partner's own estimated tax obligations.

Qualified investment partnerships and partnerships listed on a United States national stock exchange are not subject to the tax. A "qualified investment partnership" has more than 10 members or partners with no member or partner owning more than a 50% interest in the entity and derives at least 90% of its gross income from dividends; interest; payments with respect to securities loans; and gains from the sale or other disposition of stocks, securities, foreign currencies, commodities; or other similar income derived with respect to its business of investing or trading in those stocks, securities, currencies or commodities. A "qualified investment partnership" does not include a dealer in securities.

Under legislation enacted in 2001 that is now superseded, and which applied only to tax years beginning in 2001, all corporations with ownership interests in a limited partnership ("LP") or limited liability company ("LLC") doing business in New Jersey are now themselves subject to the corporation business tax (P.L. 2001, ch. 136). Foreign corporations, who may not have paid tax under prior New Jersey authority that considered such ownership interests alone to be insufficient to subject a foreign corporation to New Jersey tax, became (and are still considered to be) subject to tax.

Under the 2001 law, an LP or LLC could obtain the consent of each of its corporate owners that New Jersey has the right and jurisdiction to tax the corporate owner's income derived from the activities of the limited partnership or limited liability company in New Jersey. If the LP or LLC did not obtain such consent from all of its corporate owners, then the entity was required to pay the corporation business tax liability on behalf of its nonconsenting owners for their shares of the business' New Jersey income. The 2001 law provided two alternative formulae for determining a corporate owner's share of New Jersey income, depending on whether the corporation's relationship with the LP or LLC is unitary. LPs and LLCs listed on a national exchange or that met the test for a "qualified investment partnership" (as defined above) were exempt from the 2001 law's requirements, although the foreign corporation was still subject to tax.

¶733 Accounting Periods and Methods

Law: R.S. 54:10A-4, 54:10A-15; Reg. Secs. 18:7-2.3, 18:7-2.4.

A corporation subject to New Jersey corporation business tax is required to use the same accounting period and method for state tax purposes as it uses for federal income tax purposes.

CCH Tip: Tax Year

While the ending month of the accounting period must be the same for federal and state returns, the tax year for return filing may differ. The 2012 federal Form 1120 is used for taxpayers with a tax year beginning in 2012. The 2013 New Jersey Form CBT-100 is used for taxpayers with taxable years ending on or after July 31, 2013 through June 30, 2014. So a taxpayer with a taxable year beginning October 1, 2012 and ending September 30, 2013, files its return on a 2012 federal Form 1120 and a 2013 New Jersey Form CBT-100.

Within 90 days after becoming subject to tax, a corporation must submit to the Division of Taxation proof of the accounting period adopted for federal purposes. A 52-53 week accounting period is permitted if it is used for federal returns.

The Director may determine the year or period in which any item of income or deduction is to be included without regard to the method of accounting used by the taxpayer in order to properly reflect the entire net income of the taxpayer.

¶734 When Period Covered Differs for New Jersey and Federal Returns

Law: Reg. Secs. 18:7-12.1—18:7-12.3.

The period covered by a taxpayer's New Jersey corporation business franchise tax return will be different from the period covered by its federal income tax return when it is a foreign corporation that commences to do (or ceases to do) business in New Jersey during its federal taxable year. In this case, entire net income is determined for the period covered by the federal return. Then this item is divided by the number of calendar months or parts of months covered by the federal return, and the result is multiplied by the number of calendar months or parts of months covered by the New Jersey return. See ¶735 for short accounting periods and ¶729 for merger, consolidation, or reorganization.

¶735 Short Accounting Periods

Law: R.S. 54:10A-17; Reg. Secs. 18:7-12.1—18:7-12.3.

The Director may determine the net income of a taxpayer who is required to file a return for a period of less than 12 months.

For adjustment when New Jersey and federal periods differ, see ¶734.

For rules relating to merger, consolidation, withdrawal, or surrender, see ¶729.

CORPORATION BUSINESS TAX

CHAPTER 8
BASIS OF TAX—ENTIRE NET INCOME

¶801	In General
¶802	Inclusions in Entire Net Income (Additions to Federal Taxable Income)
¶803	Exclusions from Entire Net Income (Deductions from Federal Taxable Income)
¶804	Interest and Dividends
¶805	Net Operating Losses
¶806	Taxes
¶807	Deduction for Net Income of International Banking Facility
¶808	Other Adjustments to Entire Net Income
¶809	Allocation of Entire Net Income

¶801 In General

Law: R.S. 54:10A-4, 54:10A-5; Reg. Sec. 18:7-5.2.

The corporation business tax currently consists of two components, one of which is based upon the taxpayer's entire net income. The alternative minimum assessment (AMA) component of the tax is computed based on New Jersey gross receipts or gross profits (¶704). The taxpayer pays the higher of the two components of the tax. However, for tax periods beginning after June 30, 2006, the AMA rate became 0% for all taxpayers other than corporations that are otherwise protected against New Jersey taxation by P.L. 86-272. Those taxpayers continue to be subject to the AMA.

Entire net income is the federal taxable income that the corporation is required to report for the taxable year with certain additions, exclusions and modifications. New Jersey generally adopts federal income tax treatment of items of gross income and deductions. However, New Jersey entire net income includes income within or without the United States. Therefore, income of alien corporations from foreign sources not subject to federal taxation is subject to New Jersey tax.

S corporations: S corporations are currently subject to a reduced corporate business tax rate imposed on the amount of entire net income of the S corporation that is *not* subject to federal income taxation, although the tax on such income will be phased out for tax periods ending on or after July 1, 2007 (¶705). S corporation net operating losses can be carried forward in calculating the corporate income tax base, subject to the same rules and limitations applicable to C corporations (including the suspension and limited use of net operating loss carryforward deductions from 2002 through 2005).

¶802 Inclusions in Entire Net Income (Additions to Federal Taxable Income)

Law: R.S. 54:10A-4; Reg. Sec. 18:7-5.2.

The starting point for computing New Jersey entire net income is federal taxable income before any net operating loss deduction or special deductions. The following items are included in New Jersey entire net income and must be added to federal taxable income:

— The amount of any specific exemption or credit allowed by any U.S. law imposing a tax on or measured by the income of corporations;

— Interest and dividend income, less interest expense incurred to carry such investments, from federal, state and municipal obligations. Interest from New Jersey state and local government bonds as well as interest from federal obligation must be included because the corporation business tax is considered to be a franchise tax rather than an income tax;

— Taxes paid or accrued to the U.S. or its possessions or territories, individual states and their political subdivisions, or the District of Columbia, or to any foreign country, state, province, territory or subdivision thereof, on or measured by profits or income, or business presence or business activity, or the corporation business tax, or any tax paid or accrued with respect to subsidiary dividends excluded from entire net income must be included in the entire net income base (¶806);

— Any amounts deducted in the federal computation that represent: (i) any additional "bonus" depreciation claimed as a federal deduction for tax years beginning in 2002 under IRC Sections 168(k) and 1400L, pursuant to the federal Job Creation and Worker Assistance Act of 2002, (30% bonus depreciation for property acquired after September 10, 2001 and before May 6, 2003), the Jobs and Growth Tax Relief Reconciliation Act of 2003 (50% bonus depreciation for property acquired after May 5, 2003 and placed in service before January 1, 2005), the Gulf Opportunity Zone Act of 2005 (50% bonus depreciation for GOZA property placed in service on or after August 28, 2005, and before January 1, 2008, the Economic Stimulus Act of 2008 (50% bonus depreciation for property placed in service after December 31, 2007 and before January 1, 2009), and the Small Business Jobs Act of 2010 (50% bonus depreciation for property placed in service before December 31, 2010 or December 31, 2011); (ii) additional depreciation under the accelerated cost recovery system (ACRS) provisions of the federal Economic Recovery Tax Act of 1981, applicable to property placed in service on or after January 1, 1981, and prior to the taxpayer's fiscal or calendar accounting year beginning on or after July 7, 1993; or (iii) deductions allowable under the federal safe-harbor leasing provisions (except in connection with leases of qualified mass commuting vehicles). For property placed in service in the taxpayer's accounting years beginning on or after July 7, 1993, corporations are permitted, for New Jersey corporation business tax purposes, to use the federal modified ACRS for depreciation of property, subject to the limitations described in part (i) above;

— For property placed in service on and after January 1, 2004, amounts deducted in the federal computation under IRC Section 179 in excess of $25,000;

— Amounts deducted under IRC Section 199, except with respect to amounts deducted pursuant to that section that are exclusively based upon domestic production gross receipts of the taxpayer which are derived only from lease, rental, license, sale, exchange, or other disposition of qualifying production property which the taxpayer demonstrates was manufactured or produced by the taxpayer in whole or in significant part within the United States, but not qualified production property that was grown or extracted by the taxpayer;

— Interest deducted in the federal computation that was paid to a "related member" cannot be deducted from entire net income unless the taxpayer meets one of four alternative tests: (1) the recipient was taxed on the interest payment in New Jersey or in another state or country at an effective tax rate not less than 3% under New Jersey's effective tax rate (taking into account the apportionment or allocation percentages in both states), and the taxpayer shows by clear and convincing evidence that the debt was at arm's length and did not have a "principal purpose" to avoid New Jersey tax; (2) the taxpayer shows with clear and convincing evidence that the disallowance of the deduction is unreasonable; (3) the Division of Taxation agrees in writing to an alternative method; or (4) the taxpayer shows by a preponderance of the evidence that the interest was paid either to a related member in a foreign country that has in force a comprehensive income tax treaty with the United States (as disclosed on the taxpayer's return) or to an independent lender (even indirectly) when the taxpayer guarantees the debt on which the interest is paid. The term "related member" includes: (1) a related entity; (2) a component member of a controlled group of corporations under IRC Section 1563; (3) a person to or from whom there is attribution of stock ownership under IRC Section 1563; or (4) a person or entity, regardless of form of organization, that bears the same relationship to the taxpayer corporation as a party described in items (1) through (3). The definition of a "related entity" generally refers to the attribution rules of IRC Section 318. This includes: (1) an individual stockholder and the members of the stockholder's family if the stockholder and the members of the stockholder's family own directly or indirectly, beneficially or constructively, in the aggregate, at least 50% of the taxpayer corporation's outstanding stock; and (2) a stockholder, or a stockholder's partnership, limited liability company, estate, trust or corporation, if the stockholder and the stockholder's entities own directly or indirectly, beneficially or constructively, in the aggregate, at least 50% of the value of the taxpayer corporation's outstanding stock (see New Jersey TAM-13 (02/24/2011));

— Certain federally deductible costs that are related to intangible property (i.e., patents, trademarks, copyrights), including but not limited to interest expense, if paid to or incurred for (directly or indirectly) one or more "related members" (as defined in the immediately preceding paragraph). Royalty, patent and copyright fees, licensing fees, and losses related to factoring or discounting transactions must also be added back. However, the taxpayer need not add back these costs to entire net income if one of four alternative tests is met: (1) the related member is in a foreign country that has a comprehensive income tax treaty in force with the United States; (2) the taxpayer shows by clear and convincing evidence that the "add back" is unreasonable; (3) the Division of Taxation agrees in writing to an alternative method; or (4) the taxpayer shows by a preponderance of the evidence that the related party paid the same funds over to an unrelated third party in the same year in a transaction that did not have a principal purpose of avoiding New Jersey tax;

— No deduction is allowed for research and experimental expenditures that constitute qualified research expenses or basic research payments for which a credit is claimed under N.J.S.A. 54:10A-5.24, unless those same expenditures are also used to compute a federal credit under former IRC Sec. 41 (the federal credit expired December 31, 2005);

— The amount of any civil, civil administrative, or criminal penalty or fine assessed and collected for a violation of a state or federal environmental law, an administrative consent order, or an environmental ordinance or resolution of a local governmental entity. In addition, any interest earned on the penalty or fine and any economic benefit having accrued to the violator as a result of the violation must be included when computing the tax. Penalties or fines assessed in connection with violations resulting from fire, riot, sabotage or an act of God beyond the reasonable control of the violator, as well as those which result from violations caused by an act or omission of a person who was outside the reasonable control of the violator, may be excluded from entire net income. Also, the amount of treble damages paid to the Department of Environmental Protection for costs incurred in removing, or arranging for the removal of, an unauthorized discharge upon failure of the discharger to comply with a department directive to do so is to be added back;

— All income from sources outside the United States that has not been included in computing federal taxable income less all allowable deductions to the extent that such allowable deductions were not taken in computing federal taxable income; and

— For privilege periods beginning after December 31, 2008, and before January 1, 2011, the amount of discharge of indebtedness income excluded for federal income tax purposes pursuant to IRC Section 108(i) (P.L. 2009, c. 72).

Income from property classified as "operational" in prior privilege periods, and later demonstrated to have not been serving an operational function, must be added back to entire net income. Income that the taxpayer establishes as non-operational may be subject to specific allocation to New Jersey if New Jersey is the principal place from which the taxpayer directs or manages its trade or business.

Since the starting point for computing New Jersey entire net income is federal taxable income before special deductions and any net operating loss deduction, it is unnecessary to adjust for some federal reductions that are not allowed by New Jersey. Examples of differences would include deductions for dividends received and net operating losses. While New Jersey allows deductions, it does not adopt the federal treatment (¶803 and ¶805 for New Jersey deductions). New Jersey does not adopt nor have a similar provision for the investment credit, but again no adjustment is required.

CCH Tip: Solar Grants and Credits

The American Recovery and Reinvestment Act of 2009, P.L. 111-5 ("ARRA"), signed into law February 17, 2009 provides for cash grants and credits for certain energy properties. IRC Sec. 48(d)(3) excludes these ARRA grants from income and reduces the basis of the property by 50% of the cash grant. For CBT purposes, the ARRA grant is not taxable as income and the basis of the property must be reduced in the same manner as the federal reduction.

The 30% energy credit available under IRC Sec. 48 is not available to CBT taxpayers. Where the taxpayer took the 30% energy credit for federal purposes, the corporation is required to report only the reduced expenses claimed for federal purposes and the reduced federal basis on its CBT return. (New Jersey TAM-11 (02/10/2011).

Banking corporations: Since a banking corporation must include the income of any other such corporation that was merged or consolidated during a privilege period (¶729), an adjustment may be required to the extent that the income was not included for federal purposes.

S corporations: New Jersey S corporations must include in New Jersey gross income the value of the fringe benefits paid for 2% shareholders. Federal S corporations that have not made the S election in New Jersey continue to exclude the value of fringe benefits paid for 2% shareholders from New Jersey gross income (*Technical Bulletin* 36, Division of Taxation (1994)).

¶803 Exclusions from Entire Net Income (Deductions from Federal Taxable Income)

Law: R.S. 54:10A-4, 54:10A-9; Reg. Secs. 18:7-5.2, 18:7-5.3, 18:7-5.11.

The following are deducted from federal taxable income in computing New Jersey entire net income:

— One hundred percent of subsidiary dividends included in computing federal taxable income, with a "subsidiary" being a corporation in which a taxpayer owns at least 80% of the total combined voting power of all classes of stock entitled to vote and at least 80% of all other classes except nonvoting stock, which is limited and preferred as to dividends. The investment is determined with reference only to capital stock, exclusive of loans and advances to subsidiaries. For tax years beginning on or after January 1, 2002, a taxpayer may deduct 50% of dividends paid by a corporation in which it has such an ownership interest of less than 80% but at least 50%, with no deduction allowed for dividends paid by corporations in which the taxpayer has ownership interest under 50%. In years prior to 2002, taxpayers could deduct 50% of any dividend paid by a non-subsidiary corporation. With respect to dividend distributions after February 6, 2006, the deduction for subsidiary dividends is no longer available for dividends received from a REIT;

— The net operating loss carryover to the taxable year subject to the suspension of carryover deductions for 2002 and 2003 and the 50% partial suspension for 2004 and 2005 (¶805);

— Income, war-profits, and excess profits taxes imposed by foreign countries or U.S. possessions, which are utilized as a foreign tax credit, instead of a deduction for federal purposes are to be deducted from federal taxable income (¶806);

— Income received solely as the result of federal safe-harbor leasing provisions (except with respect to qualified mass commuting vehicle leases), the benefits of which are disallowed for New Jersey purposes (¶802);

— Depreciation determined under IRC Sec. 167, as in effect on December 31, 1980, for property placed in service after 1980 and before the taxpayer's accounting year beginning on or after July 7, 1993. For property placed into service during the taxpayer's accounting years beginning on or after July 7, 1993, New Jersey generally follows federal depreciation rules except with respect to amendments to federal depreciation under the Job Creation and Worker Assistance Act of 2002 and the Jobs and Growth Tax Relief Reconciliation Act of 2003 (see ¶1002);

— For purposes of determining gain or loss upon the physical disposal of recovery property, any excess of depreciation disallowed over depreciation claimed;

— Effective retroactively to January 1, 1998, the income from the international operation of ships or aircraft derived by a corporation organized in a foreign country is exempt if the income is also exempt from federal taxation under IRC Sec. 883; and

— Income derived by a foreign corporation from investing or trading in stock, securities, or commodities for its own account if the corporation's activities in New Jersey are limited to these investments. However, if the corporation receives additional income from infrequent, extraordinary, or nonrecurring activities, including the sale of tangible property, that income is taxable but investment and trading income remains nontaxable.

Corporate expenses related to nonoperational income not assigned to New Jersey are not deductible from the federal taxable income when computing entire net income.

The Division of Taxation takes the position that expenditures incurred to make a business accessible to disabled individuals which were taken as a credit under IRC Sec. 44 disabled access credit on the federal return may not be deducted in computing New Jersey entire net income (*State Tax News*, Division of Taxation, Fall 2000).

Caution

The Division of Taxation has reversed a long-standing position which allowed the portion of wages paid equal to the federal jobs credit to be deducted in computing entire net income. Now, if a federal deduction for wages is reduced because the taxpayer elects to take a federal jobs or employment credit, an adjustment cannot be made to entire net income to increase the deduction to what it would have been if the federal credit had not been elected by the taxpayer. (*State Tax News*, Division of Taxation, Spring 2006)

¶804 Interest and Dividends

Law: R.S. 54:10A-4.

Interest and dividends that are not included in federal taxable income must be added in determining New Jersey entire net income.

Interest from New Jersey State and local government bonds and from bonds of other state and local governments is included even though exempt for federal purposes. The New Jersey corporation business tax is measured by and not imposed upon entire net income; consequently, federal bond interest may be included (*Werner Machine Co., Inc. v. Director* (US SCt 1956) 350 US 492; CCH NEW JERSEY TAX REPORTS [1954 - 1957 Transfer Binder], ¶200-008, ¶200-033).

The inclusion of the principal and interest of federal, as well as state obligations, in the taxpayer's net income base has been held to be permissible by the New Jersey Supreme Court in *Garfield Trust Co. v. Director*, 508 A.2d 1104 (1986); CCH NEW JERSEY TAX REPORTS [1979—1989 Transfer Binder], ¶201-310. The U.S. Supreme Court dismissed an appeal of this decision (Docket No. 86-261, November 3, 1986).

New Jersey prohibits the deduction of interest paid to related parties unless one of several tests can be met (¶802), although interest should be imputed and charged on loans or advances made by one related party to another from the day after the debt arises until the debt is satisfied (Reg. Sec. 18:7-5.10(a)(5); *Metro Touch v. Director, Division of Taxation*, 21 NJ Tax 312 (2004); CCH NEW JERSEY TAX REPORTS ¶400-982.

Federal dividend deductions (70% of dividends from domestic corporations and dividends on certain preferred stock of public utilities) are not allowed for New Jersey franchise tax purposes. (Since the federal taxable income used to start the computation of entire net income for New Jersey franchise tax purposes does not reflect this dividend deduction, no adjustment is required on the return.) However, New Jersey allows its own deduction for dividends (¶803).

¶805 Net Operating Losses

Law: R.S. 54:10A-4, 54:10A-4.3; Reg. Sec. 18:7-5.17.

Net operating losses currently may be carried forward to each of the 20 years following the year of loss. Net operating losses incurred in tax periods ending prior to June 30, 2009 could only be carried forward to each of the seven years following the year of loss, and net operating losses incurred by certain high technology companies could be carried forward for 15 years (¶713).

For tax periods beginning in calendar years 2002 and 2003, net operating loss carryforward deductions were suspended entirely. For tax periods beginning in calendar years 2004 and 2005, the net operating loss carryforward deduction was limited to 50% of a taxpayer's pre-apportionment entire net income. Although some or all of a net operating loss carryover deduction was not permitted for these years, the date on which those carryforwards that could not be deducted normally would expire may be extended for a period equal to the period of suspension in certain circumstances. Generally, the carryover must be carried to the earliest year in which it may be used.

The deduction is reduced in each succeeding year by the amount of the entire net income in the prior year before the following:

— the net operating loss deduction;

— the exclusion for international banking facilities; or

— the exclusion for dividends.

Net operating losses may not be carried back to any year preceding the year of loss.

CCH Practice Tip: Operation of Net Operating Loss
Suspension and Extension Provisions

Effective September 4, 2007, the Division issued regulations which provide that any net operating deduction that was disallowed by the suspension provisions that applied to 2002 and 2003, and would have expired, is extended for two years. Any net operating loss deduction that was disallowed by the suspension provisions that applied to 2004 and 2005, and would have expired, is extended for one return period for each return period that it was disallowed. While the statute does not contain a requirement that a net operating loss must have expired in a suspension year in order for its expiration to be extended, it is the Division's interpretation that extension of the expiration date is only available if the net operating loss would have expired in a suspension year.

Mergers, acquisitions: Net operating losses may be carried over only by the corporation that sustained the losses, including the surviving corporation of a statutory merger. If there is a change in 50% or more of the ownership of a corporation because of redemption or sale of stock and the corporation changes the trade or business giving rise to the loss, no net operating loss sustained before the changes may be carried over to be deducted from income earned after the changes. A 2002 statutory amendment that was made retroactive to tax periods ending after June 30, 1984, specifically noted that net operating loss carryovers may be lost as the result of federally qualified reorganizations under IRC Sec. 368(a)(1)(A), (C), (D), (F) or (G), and that net operating losses may not be carried over by a taxpayer that changes its state of incorporation. In addition, the Director of the Division of Taxation may disallow a carryover under other circumstances where the primary purpose of an acquisition was to obtain the net operating loss carryover.

S corporations: Subject to the two-year suspension for 2002 and 2003 and 50% suspension for 2004 and 2005 described above, S corporation net operating losses can be carried forward in calculating the S corporation's income tax base taxable at the entity level.

Tax benefit transfer program: New or expanding emerging companies in New Jersey with unused net operating losses and unused research and development tax credits may surrender those tax benefits to other New Jersey taxpayers in exchange for private financial assistance under a corporation business tax benefit certificate transfer program (¶713). The two-year suspension of net operating loss carryforward deductions described above does not restrict this program.

¶806 Taxes

Law: R.S. 54:10A-4; Reg. Secs. 18:7-5.2, 18:7-5.3.

In computing entire net income for New Jersey corporation business tax purposes, taxpayers must add back to federal taxable income any taxes paid or accrued to the United States, its possessions or territories, individual states and their political subdivisions, or the District of Columbia, or any foreign country, state, province, territory or subdivision thereof, on or measured by income or profits, or business presence or business activity, or the corporation business tax, or taxes imposed with respect to subsidiary dividends excluded from entire net income.

Since New Jersey corporation business tax deducted for federal purposes must be added back, any corporation business tax refund or credit included in federal taxable income is deducted in determining entire net income.

CCH Tip: Deductible Taxes

In *Ross Fogg Fuel Oil Co. v. Director, Division of Taxation,* 22 NJ Tax 372 (2005); CCH New Jersey Tax Reports ¶ 401-108, the Tax Court of New Jersey held that the provision requiring an addback of taxes was not intended to include taxes paid to New Jersey, other than the CBT and was not intended to apply to excise taxes or taxes not measured by profits or income or business presence or business activity.

¶807 Deduction for Net Income of International Banking Facility

Law: R.S. 54:10A-4.

A deduction from entire net income is allowed for the eligible net income (gross income minus expenses) of an international banking facility.

"International banking facility" defined: An "international banking facility" is a set of asset and liability accounts segregated on the books and records of a depository institution, U. S. branch or agency of a foreign bank, or an Edge or Agreement Corporation that includes only international banking facility time deposits and international banking facility extensions of credit as defined in the regulations of the Board of Governors of the Federal Reserve System.

Eligible gross income: Eligible gross income includes, but is not limited to, gross income derived from the following: (1) making, arranging for, placing or carrying loans to foreign persons, provided that, in the case of a foreign individual, or a foreign branch of a domestic corporation (other than a bank) or a foreign corporation or foreign partnership that is controlled by one or more domestic corporations (other than banks), domestic partnerships, or resident individuals, all the proceeds of the loan are for use outside of the United States; (2) making or placing deposits with foreign banks or foreign branches of banks (including foreign subsidiaries) or foreign branches of the taxpayers or with other international banking facilities; (3) entering into foreign exchange trading or hedging transactions related to any of the above transactions; and (4) such other activities in which the international banking facility may, from time to time, be authorized to engage. The expenses applicable include expenses and deductions which are directly or indirectly attributable to eligible gross income.

¶808 Other Adjustments to Entire Net Income

Law: R.S. 54:10A-4, 54:10A-8, 54:10A-10.

The Director has broad power to redetermine a taxpayer's entire net income if he or she finds the corporate books do not properly reflect the same. Among other things, the Director may determine the accounting period in which any item of income or deduction should be included. The Director is not limited to the accounting method used by the taxpayer, and may also adjust the allocation factor. In making an adjustment, the Director must abide by sound accounting principles. The Director may even, under certain circumstances, force a taxpayer to file returns on a consolidated basis (¶ 1004).

When the Division determines the true earnings of the taxpayer on its business carried on in New Jersey are not accurately reported, the Director may make adjustments to any tax return as may be necessary to make a fair and reasonable determination of the amount of corporation business tax payable. The term "fair and reasonable tax" is defined as the tax that would be payable by a taxpayer reporting the same transaction(s) on a separate entity basis where the parties to the transaction(s) have independent economic interests. The analysis of determining a "fair and reasonable tax" is similar to the arm's length pricing requirements under IRC Sec. 482.

CCH Practice Tip: Intercompany Pricing

Technical Advisory Memorandum 2012-01 (02/16/2012) (replacing TAM 2011-17) provides that, in most cases, when arriving at a fair and reasonable tax, the Division will utilize IRC Sec. 482 standards and will "accept an APA or third-party pricing study between a taxpayer and the Internal Revenue Service as proper documentation and evidence in the evaluation of intercompany transfer pricing." However, TAM 2012-01 also notes that the Division has the authority to examine these agreements and challenge their underlying assumptions and interpretations if the true earnings of the taxpayer on its business carried on in New Jersey are not reflected by the terms of the APA or advanced pricing study at issue.

¶809 Allocation of Entire Net Income

Law: R.S. 54:10A-6.

For tax years beginning prior to July 1, 2010, net income may be allocated outside of New Jersey only if the taxpayer maintains a regular place of business (other than a statutory office) outside of New Jersey. For tax years beginning on or after July 1, 2010, net income may be allocated outside of New Jersey regardless of whether the taxpayer maintains a regular place of business outside of New Jersey. In general, a three-factor (property, receipts, payroll) formula is used to allocate net income. However, for tax periods beginning on or after January 1, 2012, use of the property and payroll factors will begin to phase out. For tax periods beginning on or after January 1, 2014, the allocation formula will be based exclusively on the receipts factor. (¶902).

A decision of the U.S. Supreme Court, that a multistate corporation domiciled outside of New Jersey was not required to include the gains realized on the sale of a minority stock interest in a second corporation in its apportionable tax base, rejected New Jersey's contention that all income of a corporation doing any business in a state is, by virtue of common ownership, part of the corporation's unitary business and apportionable (*Allied-Signal, Inc. (Bendix Corp.) v. Director, Division of Taxation* (US SCt 1992) 504 US 768; CCH New Jersey Tax Reports [1989—1994 Transfer Binder], ¶400-172).

For discussion of net income allocation, see Chapter 9.

CORPORATION BUSINESS TAX

CHAPTER 9
ALLOCATION OF INCOME

¶901   In General
¶902   Business Allocation Factor
¶903   Property Fraction
¶904   Receipts Fraction
¶905   Payroll Fraction
¶906   Adjustment of Allocation Factor

¶901 In General

Law: R.S. 54:10A-5, 54:10A-5a, 54:10A-6, 54:10A-17; Reg. Secs. 18:7-7.2, 18:7-12.3.

For the alternative minimum assessment component of the corporation business tax, apportionment is accomplished by taxing those receipts that constitute gross receipts (or gross profits), which are derived from New Jersey. (See ¶704). New Jersey gross profits are determined by subtracting from New Jersey gross receipts the taxpayer's cost of goods sold multiplied, at the taxpayer's election, by either the receipts fraction of the business allocation factor or the full business allocation factor (¶902).

With regard to the income tax component of the corporation business tax, for tax years beginning prior to July 1, 2010, only those corporations maintaining a regular place of business outside of New Jersey pay tax on only those portions of their entire net income allocable to New Jersey. For tax years beginning on or after July 1, 2010, all corporations doing business within and without the state pay tax on only those portions of their entire net income allocable to New Jersey. Apportionment for the income tax component of the corporation business tax is accomplished by the use of a business allocation factor (¶902).

Regular place of business: A regular place of business is any bona fide office (other than a statutory office), factory, warehouse, or other identifiable space of the taxpayer that is regularly maintained, occupied, and used by the taxpayer in carrying on its business and in which one or more regular employees are in attendance. The taxpayer must be directly responsible for the expenses incurred in maintaining the regular place of business and must either own or rent the facility in its own name and not through a related person or entity. The regular place of business must be occupied and used by one or more regular, full-time employee who is in attendance during normal working hours. Independent contractors and members of the taxpayer's board of directors are not considered regular employees of the taxpayer.

When, even if in the regular course of business, property of the taxpayer is stored by it in a public warehouse in another state until it is shipped to customers, the warehouse is not a regular place of business of the taxpayer. Also, when, even if in the regular course of business, raw materials or partially finished goods of a taxpayer are delivered to an independent contractor in another state to be converted, processed, finished, or improved, and the finished goods remain in the possession of the independent contractor until shipped to customers, the plant of the independent contractor is not a regular place of business of the taxpayer.

A taxpayer does not acquire a regular place of business outside New Jersey solely by consigning goods to an independent factor outside New Jersey for sale at the direction of either the consignor or consignee. A home office maintained by a sales employee usually does not qualify as a regular place of business outside New Jersey.

CCH Practice Alert: "Regular Place of Business" Requirement Repealed

The statutory rule that net income may be allocated outside of New Jersey only if the taxpayer maintains a regular place of business outside the state was repealed on December 19, 2008. Applicable to tax years beginning on or after July 1, 2010, a taxpayer is no longer required to show that a regular place of business exists outside the state in order to allocate less than 100% of net income to New Jersey (L.2008, c.120).

Short period returns: Taxpayers filing short period returns may reflect in the allocation fractions only that activity taking place during the period covered by the return. The resulting allocation factor is applied to prorated net income (¶735).

Adjustment of allocation factor: Adjustment of the business allocation factor is discussed at ¶906.

Investment companies and regulated investment companies: For purposes of the entire net income component of the corporation business (franchise) tax, taxpayers eligible and electing to report as investment companies or regulated investment companies (¶728) pay tax on a specified portion of net income without further allocation.

Banking corporations: In the case of a banking corporation that maintains a regular place of business outside of New Jersey other than a statutory office, and that elects to take the deduction from entire net income for the eligible net income of an international banking facility, the numerator and the denominator of the allocation percentage must include all amounts attributable, directly or indirectly, to the production of the eligible net income of an international banking facility, whether or not the amounts are otherwise attributable to New Jersey.

¶902 Business Allocation Factor

Law: R.S. 54:10A-6, 54:10A-8; Reg. Secs. 18:7-8.1, 18:7-8.2.

The business allocation factor is a three-fraction (property, receipts, payroll) formula similar to that used in many other states for the apportionment of income of corporations doing business within and without the taxing state. One significant difference from most states, however, is that the receipts fraction employs a throwout rule for tax periods beginning in 2002 but before July 1, 2010 (¶904). In New Jersey, for tax periods beginning prior to July 1, 2010, the business allocation factor is used only if the taxpayer has a regular place of business outside New Jersey (¶901).

For tax years beginning on or after July 1, 1996, the business allocation factor is computed by adding together the percentages of the property fraction (¶903), the payroll fraction (¶905), and twice the receipts fraction (¶904), and dividing the total by four.

If the receipts fraction is missing, the other two percentages are added and the sum is divided by two. If both the receipts fraction and one other fraction are missing, the remaining percentage may be used as the business allocation factor. If the receipts fraction is present and either of the other fractions is absent, then the percentages represented by the two fractions present are added together and divided by three. A fraction is not missing merely because the numerator is zero; it is, however, considered to be missing if both the numerator and the denominator are zero.

When the business allocation percentage computed on the three-factor basis does not properly reflect the activity, business, capital, or income of the taxpayer in New Jersey, the Director may adjust the percentage (¶906).

In computing allocation percentages, division must be carried to six decimal places.

CCH Practice Alert: Phase-In of Single Sales Factor

Pursuant to Public Law 2011, Chapter 59, the CBT formula used to determine the income of the corporation subject to tax in New Jersey will change from the three factor formula described above to a single sales factor formula. Instead of a weighted average of the corporation's property, sales, and payroll in the state and elsewhere, the new law will, over a period of three years, phase out the payroll and property factors. For tax periods beginning on or before January 1, 2012 but before January 1, 2013, 15% of the property fraction plus 70% of the sales fraction plus 15% of the payroll fraction will be used. For tax periods beginning on or after January 1, 2013 but before January 1, 2014, 5% of the property fraction plus 90% of the sales fraction plus 5% of the payroll fraction will be used. For tax periods beginning on or after January 1, 2014, 100% of the sales fraction will be used.

• *International banking facility*

When a banking corporation takes an international banking facility exclusion or deduction in determining net income, the corporation must include all amounts attributable to production of the international banking facility's eligible net income in the numerator and denominator of the business allocation factor fractions. The requirement applies to amounts that would not otherwise be attributable to New Jersey.

• *Operational and nonoperational income*

Generally, activities of a multi-jurisdictional corporation which are "operational" in nature are apportioned to New Jersey using the three factor business allocation formula. Activities that are deemed to be nonoperational are not apportioned by the general formula but are specifically assigned to New Jersey or another state where the nonoperational activity has nexus. Income from tangible and intangible property is deemed to be "operational" in nature if the acquisition, management, and disposition of the property constitute integral parts of the taxpayer's regular trade or business operations, and includes investment income serving an operational function. Income that the taxpayer demonstrates is nonoperational income is not allocated to New Jersey for taxpayers whose principal place of business is not in New Jersey. Taxpayers for which New Jersey is the principal place from which they direct or manage their trade or business must allocate 100% of their nonoperational income to New Jersey.

The Division of Taxation has issued a nonoperational activity packet, CBT-100-O, containing a three part schedule that must be filed as part of the Corporation Business Tax Return by taxpayers seeking to treat income, expenses, or assets as nonoperational and not subject to apportionment.

All the activities of a separate corporate entity are presumed to be operational in nature. The taxpayer has the burden to overcome this presumption with clear and convincing evidence. The Division of Taxation will consider activities as operational to the maximum extent permitted by the U.S. Constitution.

Classification tests: Income will be classified as operational if it meets any of the following three tests: the transactional test, functional test, or operational test. The transactional test treats income as operational if the acquisition, management, use, or disposition of property is in the regular course of the taxpayer's business, or if it is reasonable to conclude that such activity is customary for the kind of business conducted by the taxpayer. The functional test treats income from property or activities that do not constitute a trade or business as operational if the property (tangible or intangible) from which income and expenses are derived is or was an integral or functional component to, or a part of, the taxpayer's regular trade or business operations. The operational test is applied to intangible property to determine whether, based on the objective characteristics of the intangible property's acquisition and use and the relation to the taxpayer's overall activities, the intangible property served an operational, rather than an investment, function. It treats as operational income all other income or gain that New Jersey is not prohibited from taxing by the U.S. Constitution.

CCH Practice Alert: Nonoperational Income

In *McKesson Water Products Company v. Division of Taxation*, 23 N.J. Tax 449 (2007), the New Jersey Tax Court held that gain from the sale of a corporation's stock was not subject to the corporation business tax because it resulted from a deemed sale of assets under IRC Sec. 338(h)(10), which was nonoperational income allocable to its principal state of business, California. On July 16, 2009, the Appellate Division of the Superior Court of New Jersey affirmed the Tax Court's decision.

¶903 Property Fraction

Law: R.S. 54:10A-6; Reg. Secs. 18:7-8.4—18:7-8.6.

The property fraction of the business allocation factor is as follows:

$$\frac{\text{Average Value of Real and Tangible Personal Property in New Jersey}}{\text{Average Value of Real and Tangible Personal Property Everywhere}}$$

Average value: Reg. Sec. 18:7-8.6 provides that average value is normally computed (without deduction of any encumbrance) on a quarterly basis. At the option of the taxpayer, or Director, a more frequent basis may be used. Where the taxpayer's usual accounting practice does not permit quarterly valuation, a semi-annual or annual basis may be used if there is no distortion of value.

Average value is to be determined without consideration of additional amounts of depreciation allowed for federal purposes in computing income under the accelerated cost recovery system (ACRS), but disallowed for New Jersey income computation (¶802).

Property included: The property allocation factor includes property owned, leased, rented, or used by the taxpayer during the period covered by the return. The value at which it is to be included is book value or, for leased or rented property, eight times the annual rent, including amounts, such as taxes, paid or accrued in addition to, or in lieu of, rent.

Tangible personal property: Tangible personal property is within New Jersey if and so long as it is physically situated in the state even though it may be stored in a bonded warehouse, or held by an agent, consignee, or factor.

Property in transit between points in New Jersey is considered situated in New Jersey. Similarly, property in transit between points outside New Jersey is considered situated outside of the state. Property in transit from a point outside of New Jersey to a point within the state, or property in transit from a point inside of New Jersey to a point without the state is not considered within or without New Jersey. Consequently, it is not included in either the numerator or denominator of the property fraction. Property is no longer in transit when it is delivered to the owner at the point of destination.

¶904 Receipts Fraction

Law: R.S. 54:10A-6, 54:10A-6B; Reg. Secs. 18:7-8.7—18:7-8.12.

The receipts fraction of the business allocation factor is as follows for tax periods beginning in 2002 but before July 1, 2010:

Receipts from Sales of Tangible Personal
Property, Services, Rentals, Royalties and
Other Business Receipts Attributable to New Jersey

Receipts from Sales, etc. Everywhere Less Receipts
Thrown Out

The receipts fraction is double weighted, so it is included twice in the computation of the allocation factor. For tax periods beginning prior to 2002, the "throwout" provision did not limit the denominator of the receipts fraction.

The following receipts are allocable to New Jersey:

— *Sales:* Receipts from sales of tangible personal property where shipments are made to points within New Jersey.

— *Compensation for services performed within New Jersey:* Receipts for services performed within New Jersey are allocable to New Jersey. It is immaterial whether the services were performed by employees or agents of the taxpayer, by subcontractors or other persons, and where the amounts for such services were payable or paid.

Commissions received by the taxpayer are attributable to New Jersey if paid for services performed in New Jersey. Commissions received for services performed by salesmen attached to or working out of a New Jersey office of the taxpayer will be deemed to be performed in New Jersey.

Lump-sum payments for services performed within and without New Jersey are to be apportioned on the basis of time or by other reasonable method that reflects the trade or business practice and economic realities underlying the generation of the compensation for services.

— *Rents and royalties:* Receipts from rentals of real and personal property situated in New Jersey and royalties from the use of patents or copyrights within New Jersey, are allocable to New Jersey. A patent or copyright is used in New Jersey to the extent that activities thereunder are carried on in New Jersey. Receipts from royalties derived from trademark license agreements, which wholly or in part authorize the licensee to sell or market products or services, are sourced to New Jersey in the same ratio as the licensee recognizes in its sales fraction receipts from sales related to the trade marked items or services.

— *Other business receipts:* Other business receipts earned within New Jersey are allocable to New Jersey. Sales of capital assets (property not held by the taxpayer for sale to customers in the regular course of business) are not business receipts. Also excluded from business receipts is the total amount of dividends excluded from the computation of entire net income (¶803) and any payment for gas or electric energy sold to a public utility subject to gross receipts tax for resale by the utility to rate payers.

CCH Tip: Drop Shipments

A manufacturer's receipts from drop-shipment sales to out-of-state customers of the manufacturer's wholly owned New Jersey subsidiary were allocated to New Jersey and included in the numerator of the receipts fraction of the allocation and apportionment formula because the receipts were earned in New Jersey. The manufacturer received orders for merchandise from its New Jersey-based subsidiary and shipped the merchandise from New Jersey directly to the subsidiary's in-state and out-of-state customers, but payment for the merchandise was received from the subsidiary. The applicable statute (R.S. 54:10A-6B) provides, in part, that (1) receipts from sales of property shipped to points within New Jersey, and (2) all other receipts earned in New Jersey are included in the numerator of the receipts fraction of the allocation and apportionment formula. Although the out-of-state shipments did not satisfy the first element because

¶904

the actual physical transfer of the merchandise took place outside New Jersey, the shipments were nonetheless included in the numerator of the receipts fraction under the second element because the subsidiary was located in New Jersey and ordered and made payment for the merchandise in New Jersey. The transactions generating the manufacturer's receipts were New Jersey transactions; thus, the receipts were earned in New Jersey. The court also noted that the holding would have been different if the New Jersey subsidiary had instead been a division of the manufacturer (*Stryker Corporation,* New Jersey Supreme Court, 168 N.J. 138 (2001); CCH NEW JERSEY TAX REPORTS ¶ 400-647).

CCH Tip: Dock Sales

Under the New Jersey "dock sales" rule, when goods are shipped to a non-New Jersey customer and possession is transferred in New Jersey, the receipts therefrom are allocable to the numerator of the New Jersey receipts fraction. Reg. Secs. 18:7-8.8(a)1ii. However, it is the Division's position that if a buyer, either directly or via a common carrier that the buyer engaged, picks up inventory from the seller at a site outside New Jersey and then transports the goods into New Jersey, such sale would be considered a non-New Jersey sale and the receipts therefrom would be included in the numerator of the receipts fraction. (*State Tax News,* Division of Taxation, Winter 2004).

Intangibles: Intangible income not otherwise apportioned is included in the numerator of the receipts fraction if the taxable situs of the intangible is in New Jersey. The taxable situs of an intangible is the commercial domicile of the owner or creditor unless the intangible has been integrated with a business carried on in another state. However, even if the commercial domicile is outside New Jersey, the taxable situs of an intangible is in New Jersey to the extent that the intangible has been integrated with a business carried on in New Jersey.

CCH Tip: Digitized Products

According to the Division of Taxation, the sale of software or digitized products over the Internet by an out-of-state vendor is sourced the same for income tax receipts factor purposes as the sale of the same products delivered on a storage medium, such as tape or disk (Reg. Secs. 18:7-8.8(a)1 and (a)5). For example, if canned software is sent to or shipped to a destination in New Jersey, the destination of the sale, not the medium of transmission, governs the sourcing of the receipt (*Response to CCH Internet/Electronic Commerce Survey,* Division of Taxation, September 22, 1999; NEW JERSEY TAX REPORTS ¶ 400-665).

Throwout rule: The receipts fraction also employs a throwout rule for all tax periods beginning on or after January 1, 2002, but before July 1, 2010. Receipts assigned to a state, the District of Columbia, a territory of the United States or any foreign country in which the taxpayer is not subject to a tax on or measured by profits or income or business presence or business activity are excluded from the denominator of the receipts fraction. Applicable taxes would include net worth taxes, gross receipts taxes and the single business tax, but not property taxes, excise taxes, payroll taxes or sales taxes.

The throwout rule applies to any receipts, not merely receipts from the sale of goods. As interpreted by the Division of Taxation, sales that are "thrown back" to another state (under that other state's law) are still thrown out of the New Jersey denominator. The standard is not whether there is nexus in any other state, but whether there is actual tax subjectivity in another state. The throwout rule applies to receipts sourced to single entity taxing jurisdictions as well as "postapportionment" combination states. Receipts sourced to "preapportionment" combination states are not thrown out if they create a potential tax in another state.

¶904

For affiliated or controlled groups, the throwout provision cannot increase the aggregate liability of all of the members of the group by more than $5 million over what the liability would be without the throwout provision.

In *Pfizer, Inc. v. Director, Div. of Taxation,* 24 N.J. Tax 116 (2008), the New Jersey Tax Court upheld the facial constitutionality of the throwout rule. The Tax Court's decision was affirmed by the Appellate Division. The issue was further appealed and heard before the Supreme Court in *Whirlpool Properties, Inc. v. Director, Division of Taxation,* 208 N.J. 141 (2011). The Supreme Court found that the throwout rule was constitutional with respect to untaxed receipts from states lacking jurisdiction to tax a taxpayer due to: (1) an insufficient connection with the taxpayer; or (2) Congressional action, such as P.L. 86-272. However, the court also held that the throwout rule cannot apply to receipts that are untaxed because a state chooses not to impose an income tax.

CCH Practice Alert: Throwout Rule Repealed

On December 19, 2008, the throwout rule was repealed for tax periods beginning on or after July 1, 2010 (L. 2008, c. 120).

¶905 Payroll Fraction

Law: R.S. 54:10A-6, 54:10A-7; Reg. Secs. 18:7-8.13, 18:7-8.15.

The wage and salary fraction of the business allocation factor is as follows:

$$\frac{\text{Total Wages, Salaries and Other Personal Service Compensation of Employees and Officers within New Jersey}}{\text{Total Wages, Salaries and Other Personal Service Compensation of Employees and Officers Everywhere}}$$

Wages, salaries, and other personal service compensation are computed on the cash or accrual basis in accordance with the method of accounting used for computing net income for federal purposes during the same taxable period.

Included in the fraction are salaries and compensation paid to every individual with whom there is an employee-employer relationship. This may include general officers, but not directors in their capacity as directors. In general, an employee-employer relationship exists if the taxpayer has the right to control the individual not only as to the result to be accomplished, but also as to the means to be used to accomplish the result.

Payroll attributable to New Jersey: The numerator of the payroll fraction includes the full amount of wages, salaries, and other personal service compensation paid to an employee for services performed in New Jersey. In certain circumstances, it also includes the full amount of an employee's pay even if part of the work is performed outside of New Jersey. In general, a taxpayer who reports to the New Jersey Division of Employment Security allocates to New Jersey (includes in the numerator) all pay reportable to the Division, including in individual cases the portion thereof in excess of reportable wages.

¶906 Adjustment of Allocation Factor

Law: R.S. 54:10A-8, 54:10A-10; Reg. Sec. 18:7-8.3.

The Director may, on the Director's own initiative or at the request of a taxpayer, adjust a business allocation factor that does not properly reflect the activity of a taxpayer reasonably attributable to New Jersey.

Permissible adjustments include the following:

— excluding one or more of the property, receipts, or payroll fractions;

— including one or more other elements, such as expenses, purchases, or contract values (minus subcontract values);

— excluding one or more assets in computing an allocation factor; or

— applying any other similar or different method calculated to effect a fair and proper allocation of the entire net income reasonably attributable to New Jersey.

In addition, the factor may be adjusted by reducing the New Jersey tax to reflect income tax of another state where the allocation factor is 100%. This situation could occur for tax periods prior to July 1, 2010, when a taxpayer does not maintain a regular place of business outside of New Jersey (other than a statutory office), but still has income from sources outside the state. For example, a reduction may be allowed where a firm that does not maintain a regular place of business outside New Jersey, sells property located in another state, and pays tax on proceeds from the sale. The reduction is allowed only where the taxpayer acquired a taxable status in the foreign state by reference to at least one of the criteria that subjects a corporation to state taxation as if the New Jersey Corporation Business Tax Act were the laws of the foreign state (¶702).

The Director also has broad powers to adjust an allocation factor where necessary in order to prevent undue avoidance of taxes.

CORPORATION BUSINESS TAX

CHAPTER 10
RETURNS, ESTIMATES, PAYMENT OF TAX

¶1001	Returns—Time and Place of Filing
¶1002	Forms in Current Use
¶1003	Extension of Time
¶1004	Consolidated Returns
¶1005	Payment of Tax
¶1006	Prepayment and Estimated Payments for Current Year

¶1001 Returns—Time and Place of Filing

Law: R.S. 54:10A-13, 54:10A-15, 54:10A-18, 54:10A-19; Reg. Secs. 18:7-11.2, 18:7-11.4, 18:7-11.6, 18:7-11.7, 18:7-11.8.

Comparable Federal: Sec. 6072.

Corporations subject to tax are required to file an annual return within three and one-half months after the close of the fiscal year (April 15 for calendar-year corporations). As a practical matter, the return must be prepared in conjunction with the federal return that is due one month earlier.

A return is filed on time if received by the Division of Taxation by the due date. When a due date falls on a Saturday, Sunday, or state holiday, it is extended to the next business day.

Returns are filed with the Division at the address designated on the return.

Returns may be signed by one officer: the president, vice-president, comptroller, secretary, treasurer, assistant treasurer, accounting officer, or any other officer of the corporation authorized to perform this act.

S corporation returns: S corporation returns must also include the following information: (1) the name, address, and federal taxpayer identification number of each shareholder; (2) information regarding whether the shareholder is a resident or nonresident; (3) whether the shareholder has consented to jurisdictional requirements allowing taxation of shareholder income; (4) the S corporation allocation factor; (5) the amount of any distribution made to each shareholder; (6) the balance of the taxpayer's accumulated earnings and profits account; (7) the balance of the taxpayer's accumulated adjustments account; and (8) any other information the Director of Taxation may prescribe by regulation.

Tentative returns are required only in connection with requests for extensions of time (¶1003). Estimated payments are required (¶1006).

Amended federal return: A taxpayer filing an amended federal return is required to file an amended New Jersey return within 90 days thereafter. Also, if any change or correction is made in taxable income by federal authorities, or where income is changed by renegotiation of government contracts or subcontracts, the taxpayer is required to report such change or correction within 90 days of the final determination or on its next franchise tax report. The taxpayer is required to concede the accuracy of the federal determination or to state wherein it is erroneous. In case of failure to file a report of the federal changes, an assessment may be made at any time.

Notice of Business Activities Report: A foreign corporation that disclaims liability for the corporation business tax and any obligation to obtain a certificate of authority to do business in New Jersey is required to file a Notice of Business Activities Report if it is deriving income from sources within New Jersey or is engaged in any type of activity or interrelationship within New Jersey. A foreign corporation is exempt from the requirement of filing a Notice of Business Activities Report if by the end of its accounting period for the preceding calendar or fiscal year it had received a certificate of authority to do business in New Jersey or files a timely corporation business tax or corporation income tax return for such calendar or fiscal year.

¶1002 Forms in Current Use

Law: R.S. 54:10A-18; Reg. Sec. 18:7-11.8.

The following forms are in current use:

Form No.	Description
CBT-100	Corporation Business Tax Return
CBT-100-V	Corporation Business Tax Payment Voucher
CBT-150	Estimated Tax Vouchers
CBT-160-A	Underpayment of Estimated Corporation Business Tax (Taxpayers with less than $50 million gross receipts)
CBT-160-B	Underpayment of Estimated Corporation Business Tax (Taxpayers with more than $50 million gross receipts)
CBT-200-T	Tentative Return and Application for Extension of Time to File Corporation Business Tax Return
CBT-100S	New Jersey S Corporation Business Tax Return
CBT-100S-V	Corporation Business Tax Payment Voucher
CBT-2553	New Jersey S Corporation Election
CBT-2553-R	Retroactive S Election Application
BFC-1	Corporation Business Tax Return for Banking and Financial Corporations
CBA-1	Notice of Business Activities Report by a Foreign Corporation
CITT-1	Controlling Interest Transfer Tax
CITT-1E	Statement of Waiver of Transfer Tax
300	UEZ Employees Tax Credit and Credit Carry Forward
301	UEZ Investment Tax Credit and Credit Carry Forward
302	Redevelopment Authority Project Tax Credit
303	Recycling Equipment Tax Credit
304	New Jobs Investment Tax Credit
305	Manufacturing Equipment and Employment Investment Tax Credit
306	Research and Development Tax Credit
308	Small NJ-Based High-Tech Business Investment Tax Credit
310	HMO Assistance Fund Tax Credit
311	Neighborhood Revitalization State Tax Credit
312	Effluent Equipment Tax Credit
313	Economic Recovery Tax Credit
314	Remediation Tax Credit
315	AMA Tax Credit
316	Business Retention and Relocation Tax Credit
317	Sheltered Workshop Tax Credit
318	Film Production Tax Credit
319	Urban Transit Hub Tax Credit
400	New Jersey Receipts Factor Throw Out
401	Key Corporation and Affiliates Claiming AMA Threshold Limit
500	Net Operating Loss Deduction
501	Domestic Production Activities Deduction
Schedule G-2	Claim for Exceptions to Disallowed Interest and Intangible Expenses
Schedule N	Nexus-Immune Activity Declaration
Schedule O	Nonoperational Activity Declaration and Tax Computation

Form CBT-100 is furnished to the taxpayer with the corporate name and address imprinted, together with a serial number. The pre-stenciled form should be used by the taxpayer; if not, the serial number should be exactly duplicated.

CCH Advisory: Annual Reports for Corporations

Beginning with the tax year 2005, the Annual Report Form CAR-100 is eliminated. Annual reports must now be filed and paid electronically by all business entities including but not limited to corporations, limited liability companies, limited liability partnerships, limited partnerships and non-profit entities. The formation or registration date is the due date for the annual report. To file and pay electronically, visit the Division of Revenue's website as http://www.state.nj.us/njbgs.

Reproduction of forms is permitted provided they meet standards set by the Division. Among other things, the size, weight, and texture of paper must be substantially the same as that used by the Division.

Forms may be obtained by calling the Taxpayer Services Branch of the Division of Taxation automated number (800) 323-4400, 24 hours a day.

Forms may be downloaded from the New Jersey Division of Taxation's website at http://www.state.nj.us/treasury/taxation/taxprnt.htm

¶1003 Extension of Time

Law: R.S. 54:10A-19; Reg. Sec. 18:7-11.12.

Comparable Federal: Sec. 6081.

The Division of Taxation may grant a reasonable extension of time for the filing of returns and/or the payment of tax. Application for an extension must be received by the Division of Taxation prior to the due date of the return.

Tentative return: For business corporations generally, an automatic six-month extension is granted if Form CBT-200-T is filed and estimated tax for the current year and any installment payment otherwise due is paid on or before the due date of the return.

Banks: In the case of banking and financial corporations, extension requests are to be made on page 1 of Form BFC-1, accompanied by Schedule L, a copy of any federal extension request, and tentative tax payment. The New Jersey extension will generally be made for a maximum of five months. If no federal extension has been obtained but sufficient cause is shown, a two-month extension will be granted.

Interest: When any extension is granted, interest applies to any unpaid portion of the tax at the rate set under the State Tax Uniform Procedure Law (¶2010). Interest accrues from the time the return was originally required to be filed, to the date of actual payment under the extension. If the unpaid portion of the tax is not paid within the time fixed under the extension, the interest on the unpaid portion is computed at the rate provided in the State Tax Uniform Procedure Law from the date the tax was originally due to the date of actual payment.

Penalty: The taxpayer will be liable for a 5% monthly penalty, up to a maximum of 25%, on the amount of underpayment, in addition to interest charges, if the amounts paid, up to and including the time of the filing of the tentative return, total less than the lesser of

— 90% of the amount due; or

— for a taxpayer that had a preceding 12-month fiscal or calendar accounting year and filed a return for that year showing a tax liability, an amount equal to the tax computed at the rates applicable to the current fiscal or calendar accounting year, but otherwise on the basis of the facts shown on the taxpayer's return for, and the law applicable to, the preceding fiscal or calendar accounting year.

¶1004 Consolidated Returns

Law: R.S. 54:10A-10 Reg. Sec. 18:7-11.15.

Comparable Federal: Secs. 1501—1504.

Regulation 18:7-11.15 entitled "Consolidated Returns" specifies that consolidated returns are not permitted, although any business conducted by an entity holding a license pursuant to the Casino Control Act is required to file a consolidated return. Beginning in 2002, certain air carriers, as defined under 49 U.S.C. Sec. 40102, may elect to file a consolidated return.

A taxpayer filing a consolidated federal return must (for New Jersey tax purposes) reflect its net income as if it had filed a separate federal return. However, a copy of the Affiliations Schedule must be filed.

Even though taxpayers cannot elect to file consolidated returns in New Jersey, for tax years beginning in 2002 and thereafter, the Director of the Division of Taxation has statutory discretion to require combined reporting. Combination may be required without regard to whether other members of the taxpayer's affiliated or controlled group are exercising their own franchises in New Jersey. When demanded, the taxpayer bears the burden to prove, with clear and convincing evidence, that separate reporting discloses the taxpayer's true earnings in New Jersey.

Taxpayers that are forced to combine must file a consolidated return within 60 days after it has been demanded by the Director. Members of an affiliated or controlled group filing separate returns also must supply any additional information that the Director requires for the return regarding their entire net income. Any subsequent demands for further information by the Director must be satisfied within 30 days.

If requested by the Director of Taxation, taxpayers that are members of a federal affiliated or controlled group must disclose in their returns all "inter-member costs or expenses," including management fees, rents, purchased goods, and other services. The Director must give 90 days' notice of such a request. A taxpayer that fails to comply will be deemed to have filed an incomplete tax return.

¶1005 Payment of Tax

Law: R.S. 54:10A-15, 54:48-4.1; Reg. Sec. 18:7-3.13.

Comparable Federal: Secs. 6151, 6161.

Any tax not paid prior to the time the annual return is due (¶1001) must be remitted with the return. Credit is allowed for prepayments and installments of estimated tax (¶1006), for payment made with a tentative return (¶1003), and for payments of tax made by a partnership on behalf of a taxpayer that is a nonresident corporate partner (¶732).

Extensions of time for payment may be granted (¶1003).

Taxpayers with an annual tax liability for the prior tax year of $10,000 or more are required to pay by electronic funds transfer.

¶1006 Prepayment and Estimated Payments for Current Year

Law: R.S. 54:10A-15—54:10A-15.4; Reg. Sec. 18:7-3.13.

A corporation with a tax liability of less than $500 may make a single installment payment of 50% of the total tax due for that year, due by the original due date for filing a return.

In the case of a taxpayer with a liability of $500 or more, payments are due in the following year so that total estimated tax will be paid currently during that year. Generally, 25% of estimated tax must be paid as installments on or before the fifteenth day of the fourth, sixth, ninth and twelfth months of the tax year. For the current year, 25% of estimated tax must be paid by April 15, June 15, and September 15; on December 15, the balance of estimated tax is due. Notwithstanding this general rule, for tax periods beginning in 2003 and thereafter, taxpayers with gross receipts of $50 million or more for the prior period must make a 50% payment in the sixth month of the year, with the balance due in the twelfth month (accelerating the third quarter's payment into the second quarter).

A corporation may apply to the Director of the Division of Taxation for relief from the above percentage requirements if (1) it is in bankruptcy or receivership; (2) it has a nonrecurring, extraordinary gain that would distort the installment amount; or (3) it estimates that the business will be operated at a loss in the current year.

Credits and refunds: When the annual return is filed, prepayments and installment payments are credited against total tax liability for the year (¶1005). If the payments were greater than the tax actually due for the year, the excess will be refunded.

Underpayment of installments: An addition to tax at the rate set pursuant to the State Tax Uniform Procedure Law (¶2010) will be added to the amount of underpayment of any installment from the date when the installment was due to the date the deficiency is paid, or the date when the annual return is due, whichever is earlier.

Applicable to return years beginning on or after January 1, 1999, an underpayment is the lesser of (1) 90% of the tax shown on the return, or if no return was filed, 90% of the tax due; or (2) 100% of the tax shown on the taxpayer's return for the preceding taxable year. However, notwithstanding these exceptions, a taxpayer must pay the full 25% of its estimated tax liability for the tax period beginning in calendar year 2002, based upon the facts and the law applicable to that period as its fourth quarter installment payment in that tax year. Formerly, an underpayment was considered to be the difference between the amount paid and the amount that would be due if total installment payments were equal to 90% of the tax shown on the annual return (or 90% of the actual tax if no return is filed). Interest was not imposed if installments paid were at least equal to (1) the tax that would have been due on the basis of the current year's rates applied to the facts on the preceding year's return under provisions in effect in that year; or (2) 90% of the amount that would have been due if taxable income were annualized for applicable portions of the year preceding the installment dates.

CORPORATION BUSINESS TAX

CHAPTER 11
ADMINISTRATION, DEFICIENCIES, PENALTIES, REFUNDS, APPEALS

¶1101	Administration of Tax—In General
¶1102	Deficiencies—Procedure
¶1103	Deficiencies—Review
¶1104	Jeopardy Assessment
¶1105	Bankruptcy and Receivership
¶1106	Statute of Limitations on Assessments
¶1107	Penalties and Interest
¶1108	Refunds
¶1109	Closing Agreements and Compromises

¶1101 Administration of Tax—In General

Law: R.S. 54:10A-23, 54:50-1.

The corporation business tax is administered by the Director of the Division of Taxation, Department of Treasury.

The State Tax Uniform Procedure Law (Chapter 20) supplements the assessment and collection provisions discussed below.

¶1102 Deficiencies—Procedure

Law: R.S. 54:10A-17, 54:10A-19.1, 54:49-5, 54:49-7, 54:49-11.

Returns are examined and additional taxes, penalties, and interest assessed in accordance with the State Tax Uniform Procedure Law.

Any taxpayer who fails to file a return when due or to pay any tax when due is subject to the penalties and interest provided in the State Tax Uniform Procedure Law. The Director may abate or remit any penalty, in whole or in part, if the Director is satisfied that the failure to comply was excusable. Statutory penalties imposed where a taxpayer failed to resolve certain tax liabilities during an available tax amnesty program may be waivable only under limited circumstances. See *United Parcel Service General Services Co. v. Director*, 430 N.J. Super. 1 (App. Div. 2013) (appeal pending in New Jersey Supreme Court).

Jeopardy assessment: If the assessment or collection of a deficiency will be jeopardized by delay, the Director may make a jeopardy assessment (¶1104).

¶1103 Deficiencies—Review

Law: R.S. 54:10A-19.2, 54:49-18.

Protest: A taxpayer aggrieved by a finding or assessment of the Director may file a written protest, under oath and specifying the reasons, with the Director. A taxpayer has 90 days in which to file a protest. At the time the protest is filed, the taxpayer may request a hearing. If a hearing is requested, the time to appeal the assessment or finding is tolled.

Appeals: An appeal from any decision, assessment, order, finding, or action of the Director must be taken to the Tax Court of New Jersey within 90 days. For appeal procedure, see ¶2005.

Filing of a protest or an appeal stays the collection or enforcement of tax unless security is required but not paid.

¶1104　Jeopardy Assessment

Law: R.S. 54:49-7.

Comparable Federal: Secs. 6851, 6861.

Upon finding the assessment or collection of tax is in jeopardy, the Director may make an arbitrary assessment and proceed to collect the tax or compel security thereof. The Director then gives notice to the taxpayer and demands a return and the tax due.

¶1105　Bankruptcy and Receivership

Law: R.S. 54:10A-11.

Comparable Federal: Sec. 6012.

New Jersey law specifically provides that receivers, referees, trustees, assignees, or other fiduciaries conducting the business or conserving the assets of a corporation are subject to the corporation business (franchise) tax. There are no sections comparable to the federal provisions authorizing immediate assessment of tax.

¶1106　Statute of Limitations on Assessments

Law: R.S. 54:10A-13, 54:10A-19.1, 54:10A-31, 54:49-6; Reg. Sec. 18:7-13.1.

Comparable Federal: Secs. 6501—6504.

Generally, no assessment of additional tax may be made after more than four years from the date on which the tax liability or claim accrued. However, the statute of limitations with regard to any "contested issue" for any tax disputed by a taxpayer in New Jersey Tax Court is tolled for later years that are not part of the litigation.

With respect to false or fraudulent returns with intent to evade tax, and failure to file returns, the tax may be assessed at any time. If a shorter time for assessment of additional tax is fixed by the law imposing the tax, the shorter time governs. Prior to the expiration of the prescribed assessment period, a taxpayer may give written consent to extend the time for assessment. In such case, the amount of additional tax due may be determined at any time within the extended period. The time period for assessment may be further extended by subsequent written consent made before the expiration of the extended period.

In the case of a change in taxable income by the Internal Revenue Service, the four-year statute of limitations for deficiency assessments runs from the date of the filing of the report change or correction, or an amended return. The additional period of limitation will only be applicable to the increase or decrease in tax attributable to the adjustments in the changed or corrected taxable income.

In addition to the general limitation period, there is a 10-year limitation on the assessment or collection of tax where a return has been filed. The period runs from the filing of the return but does not prevent collection under recorded certificates of debt, decrees or judgments, nor does it bar collection under bonds or other agreements securing the payment of tax.

¶1107　Penalties and Interest

Law: R.S. 54:10A-15.4, 54:10A-17, 54:10A-19.1, 54:10A-21, 54:10A-22, 54:52-1 *et seq.*

The Corporation Business Tax Act provides for the imposition of interest and penalties in accordance with the State Tax Uniform Procedure Law for delinquency in filing returns or paying the tax or estimated tax payments, and for fraud and other misdemeanors (¶2010, ¶2011).

Under franchise tax law provisions, a corporation is also subject to forfeiture of its franchise or its authority to do business for failing to pay tax.

¶1108 Refunds

Law: R.S. 54:10A-13, 54:10A-19.2, 54:49-14; Reg. Sec. 18:7-13.8.

While there are no specific provisions for refund procedures under the Corporation Business Tax Act, there are refund provisions under the State Tax Uniform Procedure Law (¶2006) and corporation business tax regulations. There is a four-year statute of limitations period for filing a claim for refund that commences to run from the later of (1) the payment of tax for the taxable year; or (2) the filing of the final return for the taxable year.

A claim for a refund is considered filed on the date it is received by the Division of Taxation. The same statute of limitations applies to a claim for refund relating to an amended return (additional self-assessment) and commences to run from the later of (1) the payment of the additional self-assessment; or (2) the filing of an amended return reflecting the additional self-assessment.

The period of limitation to file a claim for refund will commence to run for an additional four-year period from the date that taxable income is finally changed or corrected by the Commissioner of Internal Revenue, provided the federal change or correction which gives rise to the refund is reported to New Jersey within 90 days of the change or correction by federal authorities. In such instances, the additional period of limitation will only be applicable to the increase or decrease in tax attributable to the adjustments in the changed or corrected taxable income.

When the Director has made a determination on a refund claim, the Director's determination must be protested or appealed to the Tax Court of New Jersey within 90 days (¶1103).

CCH Tip: Refund Recovered After Limitations Period Expired

The Division of Taxation could recover corporation business tax refunded after the statute of limitations had passed on the taxpayer's right to seek a refund because the recovery of the refund was not to correct an error in judgment, but rather to correct a clerical mistake that led to the mailing of a refund check to which the taxpayer was not entitled. The Division, however, did not have unlimited inherent authority to correct and revise erroneous tax determinations once made (*Playmates Toys, Inc.,* New Jersey Supreme Court, No. A-70-98, December 21, 1999; CCH NEW JERSEY TAX REPORTS ¶400-659).

¶1109 Closing Agreements and Compromises

Law: R.S. 54:53-4, 54:53-7.

Comparable Federal: Secs. 7121, 7122.

The Director is authorized to enter into closing agreements that may not be reopened except in cases of fraud, malfeasance, or misrepresentation of a material fact.

The Director may compromise criminal and civil liabilities arising under tax laws. The grounds for making a compromise of any taxpayer liability are limited. Only cases in which there is doubt as to the liability of the taxpayer or the collectibility of the tax can be compromised. All civil and criminal penalties generally can be reduced or eliminated, unless the matter has already been referred to the Attorney General for further action. Statutory penalties imposed where a taxpayer failed to resolve certain tax liabilities during an available tax amnesty program may not be waivable.

PART IV

SALES AND USE TAXES

CHAPTER 12
IMPOSITION OF TAX, BASIS, RATE

¶1201	Overview
¶1202	Transactions Subject to Sales Tax—In General
¶1203	Retail Sales of Tangible Personal Property or Digital Property
¶1204	Services
¶1205	Restaurant Meals, Catered Meals, Meals for Off-Premises Consumption, Vending Machine Sales of Food and Beverages
¶1206	Hotel Room Occupancy
¶1207	Admission Charges
¶1208	Transactions Subject to Use Tax
¶1209	Basis of Tax
¶1210	Basis of Tax—Use Tax on Property Used Out of State and Later Brought Into New Jersey
¶1211	Basis of Tax—Use Tax on Manufacturer's Use of Own Product
¶1212	Basis of Tax—Installment and Credit Sales
¶1213	Rate of Tax and Bracket Collection Schedule
¶1214	Building and Construction Trades—Related Activities
¶1215	Lease and Rental Transactions
¶1216	Alcoholic Beverages
¶1217	Sourcing Rules

¶1201 Overview

The New Jersey Sales and Use Tax was enacted in 1966. The tax is imposed by Chapter 32B Title 54 of the New Jersey Revised Statutes (N.J.S.A. 54:32B-1 *et seq.*) at a rate of 7% on (1) sales of tangible personal property or digital property unless exempt, (2) sales of certain enumerated services, (3) use of taxable tangible personal property or digital property and services, (4) occupancies of hotel and motel rooms, (5) food and beverages sold by restaurants and caterers, (6) certain admission charges, (7) initiation fees, membership fees or dues for a health and fitness, athletic, sporting or shopping club or organization in New Jersey, however, membership fees for a club or organization whose members are predominantly age 18 or under are exempt from tax, and (8) parking services, including any charges for parking, storing or garaging a motor vehicle, however, charges for residential parking, employee parking and municipal metered parking are not subject to tax.

The Sales and Use Tax Act exempts from sales tax membership fees or dues for access to facilities of a health and fitness, athletic, sporting or shopping club or organization when the charges are made by qualified exempt organizations or New Jersey state or local government entities. All other charges for initiation fees, membership fees or dues for access to facilities of a health and fitness, athletic, sporting or shopping club or organization remain subject to sales tax. (Ch. 105, Laws 2007).

The Sales and Use Tax Act was amended to exempt charges for parking, storing and garaging a motor vehicle when made by a municipality or county parking authority. All other charges for parking, storing or garaging a motor vehicle, other than residential and employee parking, remain subject to tax. The amendment also eliminates the imposition of sales tax on the $3 parking fee at Atlantic City casino hotels. (Ch. 105, Laws 2007).

The tax on sales of tangible personal property or digital property is general in nature (¶1202). On the other hand, the tax on services is selective, in that taxable services are enumerated, all others being exempt (¶1204). The use tax, in general, is complementary to the sales tax (¶1208). In general, the exemptions that apply to the sales tax also apply to the use tax.

Sales tax is imposed on the sales price of taxable items and the charge for any taxable service (¶1209). Use tax is imposed on the purchase price of property purchased outside New Jersey and brought into the state (¶1210). Use tax is also imposed on a manufacturer's use of its own products (¶1211).

Exemptions are discussed in Chapter 19. Information on returns, payment, and administration, including dealer registration requirements, is presented in Chapter 20.

• *Streamlined Sales and Use Tax Agreement*

The purpose of the Streamlined Sales and Use Tax (SSUTA) Agreement is to simplify and modernize sales and use tax administration in the member states to substantially reduce the burden of tax compliance. The Agreement was developed by representatives of state governments, with input from local governments and the private sector. The Agreement is in effect as of October 1, 2005, with a Governing Board made up of member states.

New Jersey is a full member of the Agreement with a seat on the Governing Board. It has enacted all of the provisions necessary to comply with the Agreement's requirements and these provisions currently are in effect. (N.J.S.A. 54:32B-44, et seq.) As a full member, it may vote on amendments to or interpretations of the Agreement, and sellers registering under the SSUTA system must collect and remit tax on sales into the state.

As a result of P.L. 2008, c.123, effective January 1, 2009, the New Jersey Sales and Use Tax Act was again amended to conform with SSUTA.

A state that wishes to become a member of the Agreement must certify that its laws, rules, regulations, and policies are substantially compliant with each of the requirements of the Agreement. The requirements of the Agreement include the following:

— a central online registration system for all member states;

— an amnesty for uncollected or unpaid tax for sellers that register to collect tax, so long as they were not previously registered in the state;

— the use of new technology models for tax collection, including certified service providers (CSPs);

— a monetary allowance for CSPs;

— relief from liability for collecting the incorrect amount of tax as a result of relying on data that each member state must provide in the form of a taxability matrix;

— state level administration of local sales and use taxes;

— a single state and local tax base in each state;

— adequate notice to sellers of changes in tax rates, the tax base, and jurisdictional boundaries;

— a single tax rate per taxing jurisdiction, with the exception that a state (but not a locality) may have a second rate on food and drugs;

— uniform, destination-based sourcing rules (origin-based sourcing allowed under certain circumstances);

— direct pay authority for holders of permits;

— limitations on exemptions to make them simpler to administer;

— uniform returns and remittances;

— uniform rules for bad debt deductions; -- limitations on sales tax holidays;

— elimination of most caps and thresholds;

— a uniform rounding rule;

— customer refund procedures that limit a purchaser's ability to sue for a return of over-collected tax from the seller;

— uniform definitions, including uniform product definitions; and

— a "books-and-records" standard for certain bundled transactions.

The most significant new definitions are noted throughout Chapters 18, 19 and 20.

Sourcing: The Agreement requires that sales be sourced generally to the destination of the product sold, with a default to origin-based sourcing in the absence of that information. New Jersey has adopted the destination-based sourcing requirements, effective October 1, 2005. (N.J.S.A. 54:32B-3.1) (See ¶1817)

Effective January 1, 2009, by repealing N.J.S.A. 54:32B-3.2, the law repeals the MPU sourcing provision which was repealed in the SSUTA. Computer software and related services are sourced according to the Streamlined Sales Tax Governing Board's Rules and Procedures (amended June 18, 2008).

Taxability matrix: States that are members of the Agreement must provide a taxability matrix indicating the state's tax treatment for clothing and clothing-related items, computer-related products, delivery and installation charges, food and food products, and healthcare products under the Agreement. New Jersey's taxability matrix can be found at http://www.streamlinedsalestax.org/compliance/New%20Jersey/2008/New%20Jersey%20Taxability_Matrix%208-1-08.pdf. A seller or certified service provider is not liable for having charged and collected an incorrect amount of sales or use tax resulting from their reliance on erroneous data provided in the taxability matrix. (N.J.S.A., Sec. 54:32B-14(f), (g))

Certificate of compliance: States must file certificates of compliance with the Streamlined Sales Tax Governing Board in order to become members of the Agreement. The purpose of the certificate is to document compliance with the provisions of the Agreement and cite applicable statutes, rules, regulations, or other authorities evidencing that compliance. Topics covered in the certificate include definitions (see above), sourcing, exemption certificates, bad debts, amnesty, and tax remittance.

Registration: To register under the Agreement, sellers must go to https://www.sstregister.org/sellers. Sellers can also update previously submitted registration information at this website. The information provided will be sent to all of the full member states and to associate members for which the seller chooses to collect. When a seller registers under the Agreement, it must select the certified technology model it will be using (or it must select "Other" if it will not be using one of the certified models). The models are the following:

— Certified Service Provider (CSP), an agent certified under the Agreement to perform all the seller's sales and use tax functions.

— Certified Automated System (CAS), software certified under the Agreement to calculate the appropriate tax (for which the seller retains responsibility for remitting).

— Certified System (CS), a proprietary automated sales tax system certified under the Agreement.

Uniform Exemption Certificate: The SST Governing Board has approved a uniform exemption certificate. Although full member states may continue to use their pre-existing exemption certificates, they must also accept the uniform certificate. Associate member and nonmember states may, but are not required to, accept the certificate. As a full member state, New Jersey is required to accept the certificate.

Digital property: P.L. 2011, c.49, was signed into law on April 8, 2011, and became effective immediately, except for sections 1 through 15, that became operative on May 1, 2011. The law makes various technical changes in sales tax law to maintain compliance with the Streamlined Sales and Use Tax Agreement (SSUTA), which was adopted by New Jersey in 2005. For purposes of compliance, the bill removes the current definition of, and eliminates references to, "digital property" under sales tax law and replaces it with "specified digital product," the defined term for electronically transferred digital products under the SSUTA. This change technically modifies but does not substantively affect the taxability of digitally downloaded music, movies, books, and certain other goods currently subject to sales and use tax. To conform the State's current tax treatment of digital goods within the parameters of the defined term under the Agreement, the law makes certain other ancillary changes that were required in addition to the adoption of the new SSUTA definition. Specifically, it (1) revises the definition of "retail sale" to reiterate that sales of specified digital products are only taxable to end users (sales for resale are excluded from tax); (2) specifies that a digital code which provides a purchaser the right to obtain the product is treated as a specified digital product for purposes of taxation; (3) stipulates that specified digital products are subject to tax regardless of whether the sale of the product is for permanent or less than permanent use and regardless of whether continued payment for the product is required; and (4) carves out a specific statutory exemption for all video programming services, including video-on-demand television services, and broadcasting services, including content to provide such services, to ensure that sales of those services are not taxable as specified digital products. The former digital property definition excluded these services; therefore, this exemption is necessary to maintain treatment under prior law. The law also provides a separate statutory exemption for specified digital products that are accessed but not delivered electronically to the consumer. Previously, New Jersey excluded from tax digital property that was temporarily streamed or uploaded to a consumer to access certain digital content. However, "specified digital products" includes electronically transferred digital audio-visual works, digital audio works, and digital books, where "transferred electronically" means obtained by the purchaser by means other than tangible storage media. Since "transferred electronically" includes instances where specified digital products are streamed or uploaded, the exemption ensures that access alone is not used to determine the taxability of specified digital products. This exemption is necessary to maintain treatment under prior law.

Seller liability: P.L. 2011, c.49, also makes changes to seller liability rules. New compliance provisions incorporate SSUTA provisions that relieve certain sellers from liability due to changes in the sales and use tax rate. The Director of the Division of Taxation may not hold a seller liable for failure to collect tax that may be due at a new tax rate if the director provides less than 30 days between the date a change in rate is enacted and the date that change takes effect. However, the relief from liability is limited and further described in the new statute.

Definitions: P.L. 2011, c.49, makes technical changes and clarifications to the tax by removing remaining references to the previously defined term "vendor," replacing them with "seller," and removing charges for installation as part of the enumerated charges included in the definition of "sales price." The elimination of installation charges from the definition of "sales price" clarifies the imposition of tax on charges

¶1201

for installation. A separate statutory provision specifies that installation charges are an enumerated service subject to the sales and use tax regardless of how "sales price" is defined. This revision is necessary to clarify treatment of installation charges, which have always been statutorily subject to tax.

¶1202 Transactions Subject to Sales Tax—In General

Law: R.S. 54:32B-3 (CCH New Jersey Tax Reports ¶60-020).

A sales tax is imposed on receipts from the following:

— Retail sales of tangible personal property or digital property, including leases or rentals of such property (¶1203);

— Sales of enumerated services (¶1204);

— Sales of food and drink (except alcoholic beverages) by restaurants, taverns, vending machines or other establishments and caterers (¶1205);

— Occupancies of hotel and motel rooms (¶1206); and

— Admission and cabaret charges (¶1207).

¶1203 Retail Sales of Tangible Personal Property or Digital Property

Law: R.S. 54:4-1.7, 54:32B-2, 54:32B-3, 54:32B-7.1; Reg. Secs. 18:24-7.15, 18:24-15.2, 18:24-15.5, 18:24-25.1, 18:24-25.2 (CCH New Jersey Tax Reports ¶60-020, ¶60-260, ¶60-310, ¶60-330, ¶60-460).

Retail sales of tangible personal property are taxable (for exemptions, see Chapter 19).

The sales and use tax base has been expanded to include digital property. Digital property is defined as electronically delivered music, ringtones, movies, books and audio and video works where the customer is granted a right or license to use, retain or make a copy of such item. Video programming services, including video on demand television services and broadcasting services, including the content to provide such services, are not included in the definition of digital products and thus are not subject to sales and use tax.

P.L. 2011, c.49, was signed into law on April 8, 2011, and became effective immediately, except for sections 1 through 15, that became operative on May 1, 2011. The law makes various technical changes in sales tax law to maintain compliance with the Streamlined Sales and Use Tax Agreement (SSUTA), which was adopted by New Jersey in 2005. For purposes of compliance, the bill removes the current definition of, and eliminates references to, "digital property" under sales tax law and replaces it with "specified digital product," the defined term for electronically transferred digital products under the SSUTA. This change technically modifies but does not substantively affect the taxability of digitally downloaded music, movies, books, and certain other goods currently subject to sales and use tax. To conform the State's current tax treatment of digital goods within the parameters of the defined term under the Agreement, the law makes certain other ancillary changes that were required in addition to the adoption of the new SSUTA definition. Specifically, it (1) revises the definition of "retail sale" to reiterate that sales of specified digital products are only taxable to end users (sales for resale are excluded from tax); (2) specifies that a digital code which provides a purchaser the right to obtain the product is treated as a specified digital product for purposes of taxation; (3) stipulates that specified digital products are subject to tax regardless of whether the sale of the product is for permanent or less than permanent use and regardless of whether continued payment for the product is required; and (4) carves out a specific statutory exemption for all video programming services, including video-on-demand television services, and broadcasting services, including content to provide such services, to ensure that sales of those services are not taxable as specified digital products. The former digital property definition excluded these services; therefore, this exemption is necessary to maintain treatment under prior law. The law also provides a separate statutory exemption for specified digital products that are accessed but not delivered electronically to the consumer. Previously, New Jersey excluded from tax digital property that was temporarily streamed or uploaded to a consumer to access certain digital content. However, "specified digital products" includes electronically transferred digital audio-visual works, digital audio works, and digital books, where "transferred electronically" means obtained by the purchaser by means other than tangible storage media. Since "transferred electronically" includes instances where specified digital products are streamed or uploaded, the exemption ensures that access alone is not used to determine the taxability of specified digital products. This exemption is necessary to maintain treatment under prior law.

"Retail sale" is defined as any sale, lease, or rental for any purpose, other than for resale, sublease, or subrent. The term includes sales of tangible personal property to all contractors, subcontractors or repairmen of materials and supplies for use by them in erecting structures for others, or building on, or otherwise improving, altering, or repairing real property.

"Tangible personal property" is defined broadly as "corporeal personal property of any nature." Thus, the sales tax applies generally to all tangible personal property, unless specifically exempted. "Tangible personal property" includes electricity, water, gas, steam, and prewritten computer software. Prewritten electronically delivered computer software is subject to tax unless it is used directly and exclusively in the conduct of the purchaser's business, trade or occupation. See ¶1302.

The rental, lease, or license to use tangible personal property or digital property is subject to tax since such transactions are included in the definition of "sale" (¶1215). Sales or rentals of real property are not subject to tax.

Under SSUTA the words "lease" and "rental" are used interchangeably in the law. They defined as any transfer of possession or control of tangible personal property for a fixed or indeterminate term for consideration. Sales tax on a lease or rental for a term of more than six months is paid by the lessee either on the original purchase price of the leased property or on the total of the periodic payments required under the lease agreement.

Sales to contractors, subcontractors, fabricators, and repair persons: See ¶1214.

Sales of alcoholic beverages to retailers: See ¶1216.

Automobile and truck rentals: The tax applies to the total charge for rental of a motor vehicle unless nontaxable charges for such items as registration and license fees, insurance and gasoline are separately stated. See ¶1215 regarding leases and rentals. See ¶1302 for the treatment of commercial trucks and motor vehicles.

Manufactured homes: The tax applies to the manufacturer's invoice price of a manufactured or mobile home upon the first sale of that home. The sale of a used manufactured or mobile home is exempt from sales and use tax, whether or not the home is installed in a mobile home park.

Race horses: The purchase of a race horse delivered to a person within New Jersey is subject to sales tax. A sale of a race horse is deemed to have occurred when it is claimed in a claiming race within New Jersey. However, race horses sold through claiming races within New Jersey are subject to tax only on the excess of the purchase price over the highest of any prior purchase price paid for the same horse within the state during the same calendar year. When no previous purchases have been made within the calendar year, the full purchase price is taxable.

Computers, software, and related services: The sale or lease of computer hardware is taxable, unless purchased with the intention of reselling or subleasing. Equipment

¶1203

that is subleased is taxable to the sublessee on the charges made to the sublessee. Incidental use of the equipment made by the lessee is subject to use tax, on the basis of the same rate charges as those charged to a sublessee.

The sale or lease of a terminal device is taxable. It is not essential for a transfer of possession to include the right to move the tangible personal property that is the subject of a rental, lease, or license to use. Use of a computer through a remote terminal device is not deemed to be a taxable transfer of possession of the computer. See ¶ 1302 for the sales tax treatment of software.

The processing of data by a service bureau constitutes a nontaxable service, whether or not the customer supplies the medium (¶ 1204).

Databases: The sale of databases in the form of tangible property such as CD-ROM, magnetic tape, or microfilm is subject to tax. However, the sale of databases delivered electronically or via the Internet is not taxable because it is not the sale of tangible personal property. If customers subscribe to a taxable database rather than purchase it, the subscription is considered a license to use, which is subject to use tax (*State Tax News*, Division of Taxation, Summer 1996; CCH New Jersey Tax Reports, ¶ 400-456). Also see information services at ¶ 1203 below and ¶ 1204.

Information services: Information services which are defined as the furnishing of information of any kind, which has been collected, compiled, or analyzed by the seller, and provided through any means or method, other than personal or individual information which is not incorporated into reports furnished to other people, are subject to tax.

¶ 1204 Services

Law: R.S. 54:4-11.1, 54:32B-2, 54:32B-3, 54:32B-4, 54:32B-4.6; Reg. Secs. 18:24-25.1, 18:24-25.2 (CCH New Jersey Tax Reports ¶ 60-240, ¶ 60-310, ¶ 60-645, ¶ 60-665, ¶ 60-720).

Sales, except for resale, of specified services are taxable. Services not specifically taxed by law are not subject to tax. Wages, salaries, and other compensation paid by an employer to an employee for rendering services otherwise taxable are not subject to tax.

• *Telecommunications services*

The sales tax is imposed on receipts from sales of telecommunication services. Effective January 1, 2009, the law adds a revised definition of "telecommunications service". "Telecommunications service" means the electronic transmission, conveyance, or routing of voice, data, audio, video, or any other information or signals to a point, or between or among points. "Telecommunications service" shall include such transmission, conveyance, or routing in which computer processing applications are used to act on the form, code, or protocol of the content for purposes of transmission, conveyance, or routing without regard to whether such service is referred to as voice over Internet protocol services or is classified by the Federal Communications Commission as enhanced or value added. N.J.S.A. 54:32B-2(cc).

Since 1990, New Jersey imposes tax on telephone answering services and radio subscription services pursuant to the prior definition of telecommunications. However, since the SSUTA telecommunications definition excludes these services, tax must be separately imposed. Telephone answering services (N.J.S.A. 54:32B-3(b)(14)) and radio subscription services (N.J.S.A. 54:32B- 3(b)(15)) thus remain taxable.

The law provides a new definition of "ancillary services" which includes many services that New Jersey has always taxed as telecommunications services (*e.g.,* directory assistance, vertical service, voice mail, conference bridging service). Since the SSUTA distinguishes between ancillary services and telecommunications services, the tax must be separately imposed. See N.J.S.A. 54:32B-3(f)(1). Language was added to source these ancillary services to the place of primary use which is the street address where the customer's use of the telecommunications service primarily occurs, which is the residential street address or the primary business street address of the customer. N.J.S.A. 54:32B-3.4(d); N.J.S.A. 54:32B-3(f)(1); N.J.S.A. 54:32B-3.4(c)(5).

The law provides definitions of "conference bridging service", "detailed telecommunications billing service", "directory assistance", "vertical service", and "voice mail service". N.J.S.A. 54:32B-2(cc). The taxability of these services has not changed.

The law provides an expanded exemption for all telephone calls paid by inserting coins in a coin operated telecommunications device, rather than only those calls subject to the local calling rate.

"In house" use of telecommunications services provided by a user or by the user's subsidiary, not in the business of providing telecommunications to the public, was excluded from the prior definition of telecommunications. The SSUTA definition of telecommunications does not provide an exception for "in house" use of telecommunications. Thus in order to retain this treatment, the new law provides a specific exemption for this service.

The law revises definitions of "intrastate telecommunications", "interstate telecommunications", and "international telecommunications". N.J.S.A. 54:32B-2(dd). This does not result in a change of taxability from previous law.

The law revises the definition of "pre-paid calling service" N.J.S.A. 54:32B-2(ll); N.J.S.A. 54:32B-3.4(d). This does not result in a change of taxability from previous law.

The law revises the definition of "mobile telecommunications service" N.J.S.A. 54:32B-2(mm). This does not result in a change of taxability from previous law.

Resale of telecommunications – the law moves the telecommunications resale language from the telecommunications definition to the resale provision. N.J.S.A. 54:32B-2(e)(1). This does not result in a change of taxability from previous law; the resale of telecommunications services for use as a component part of telecommunications services provided to an end-user remains not taxable.

• *Processing and printing services*

The tax applies to the services of producing, fabricating, processing, printing or imprinting tangible personal property for a person who directly or indirectly furnishes the tangible personal property (not purchased for resale) upon which the services are performed.

The tax does not apply to services on property delivered outside of New Jersey for use outside of the state.

• *Installation and maintenance services*

The tax is imposed on the services of installing tangible personal property or digital property or maintaining, servicing or repairing tangible personal property or digital property not held for sale in the regular course of business. The tax does not apply to services on property which is delivered outside of New Jersey for use outside of the State. N.J.S.A. 54:32B-3(b)(2). Not taxed are laundering, dry cleaning, tailoring, weaving or pressing clothing and shoe repairing and shoe shining. Also not taxed are services rendered with respect to installing property which, when installed, will constitute an addition or capital improvement to real property, property or land, other than landscaping services and other than installing carpeting and other flooring.

The services of an individual who works for a private home owner or lessee at their residence, but is not in a regular trade or business of offering such services to the public, are not taxable.

¶1204

Contractors: Installation of property that becomes an addition or capital improvement to real property when installed is exempt. For example, a charge for removing the stucco exterior of a house and installing aluminum siding in its place would not be taxable since this constitutes a capital improvement. The materials would be subject to use tax (payable by the contractor).

For further discussion of taxability of contractors, see ¶ 1214.

• *Real estate maintenance or repair*

In general, maintaining, servicing, or repairing real property inside or outside of a building, are taxable. However, the services of adding to or improving real property by a capital improvement are not taxable (¶ 1214).

Capital improvement does not include landscaping services such as seeding, sodding or grass plugging of new lawns, planting trees, shrubs, hedges, plants and clearing or filling land.

• *Storage and safe deposit rentals*

The storing of tangible personal property not held for sale in the regular course of business and the rental of safe deposit boxes or similar space are taxable services.

Taxed are self storage services which are defined as the furnishing of space for storage of tangible personal property. However, the lease or rental of an entire building, such as a warehouse or airplane hangar is not subject to tax.

• *Advertising services*

Advertising services are not subject to tax. Direct-mail advertising processing services in connection with the distribution of advertising or promotional material to in-state recipients are taxable. Such services related to out-of-state recipients are not taxable. SSUTA defines "direct mail" as "printed advertising" material delivered or distributed by U.S. Mail or other delivery service to a mass audience or to addresses on a mailing list, including items of tangible property supplied by the purchaser and included in the packaging. Direct mail does not include multiple items of printed material delivered to a single address, *e.g.*, a shipment of flyers in bulk to the purchaser. (R.S. 54:32B-2(ss)).

Under prior law, both the printed material and the direct mail processing service were subject to tax when the material was delivered to New Jersey recipients. Both remain subject to tax under the new law. Promotional items sent with printed material remain exempt but are taxed if not sent with printed material. Under prior law, "direct mail" included all promotional material, whether sent with promotional material or not. A multi-state Certificate of Exemption is available for use by the purchaser of direct mail. The law also contains specific sourcing rules for direct mail.

Outdoor advertising signs: Applicable to receipts from July 1, 2003, through June 30, 2006, a 6% tax is imposed on the gross amounts collected by a retail seller for advertising space on an outdoor advertising sign. The gross amounts collected include amounts collected from contracts to place advertising on outdoor advertising signs located in New Jersey, regardless of the advertiser's location.

This tax has been extended to June 30, 2007. However for the period from July 1, 2006 through June 30, 2007 the fee was reduced to 4% (Ch. 42, Laws 2004). Beginning July 1, 2007, there is no fee.

CCH Tip: Advertising Services and the Internet

Charges for creating and designing a website for advertising or promotional purposes are subject to tax as advertising services through October 1, 1998, just as designing a brochure or other form of advertising would be. Effective November 1, 1998 advertising services are no longer subject to tax.

Charges for housing a website are exempt from tax as a charge for advertising space (*State Tax News*, Division of Taxation, Spring 1998; CCH NEW JERSEY TAX REPORTS, ¶ 400-568).

Computer-related information services: Information services which are defined as the furnishing of information of any kind, which has been collected, compiled, or analyzed by the seller, and provided through any means or method, other than personal or individual information which is not incorporated into reports furnished to other people, are subject to tax.

• *Utility services*

The sale of utility services provided to persons in New Jersey is taxable. For further details, see ¶ 1308.

• *Tanning services*

Tanning services are subject to tax, including the application of a temporary tan, by any means are taxable.

• *Massage, bodywork or somatic services*

Massage, bodywork or somatic services, except such services provided pursuant to a doctor's prescription, are subject to tax. The taxability of the services does not depend upon the type of facility where the services are performed.

• *Tattooing services*

Tattooing services, including all permanent body art and permanent cosmetic make-up applications, are subject to tax.

• *Investigation and security services*

The New Jersey Division of Taxation has issued a publication (ANJ-28) discussing the imposition of sales tax on the sale of investigation and security services that are sourced to New Jersey. "Investigation and security services" means investigation and detective services, including detective agencies and private investigators; and fingerprint, polygraph, missing person tracing, and skip tracing services; security guard and patrol services, including bodyguard and personal protection, guard dog, guard, patrol, and security services; armored car services; and security systems services, including security, burglar, and fire alarm installation, repair, and monitoring services. (ANJ-28)

Investigation and detective services are sourced to the location where the customer makes first use of the service. First use is deemed to be where the investigative report is delivered. A license to perform such activities is not required in order for the service to be taxable. The tax is imposed regardless of who performs the service. The amount of the receipt subject to sales tax includes the fee charged for the investigation and security service, as well as the cost of materials used, labor or service, interest, losses, all costs of transportation to the seller, all taxes imposed on the seller, any other expense of the seller, and charges by the seller for any services necessary to complete the sale. Charges for such items as travel time, meals, tolls, and mileage billed by a service provider are considered inseparable from the taxable service and are part of the receipt. Because the service provider is providing a taxable service, all expenses incurred by the seller in providing that service (i.e., overhead costs passed on to the client) are also subject to tax regardless of how they are billed.

Security guard and patrol services are sourced based upon where the customer makes first use of the service. Since security guard and patrol services are specific to an actual location, they are sourced based on the location of the property being guarded. Thus, security guard and patrol services performed at a location in New Jersey are subject to tax.

¶1204

Armored car services that are performed entirely within New Jersey are subject to sales tax. If the service is not performed entirely within New Jersey, then the service is sourced to the customer's location. Thus, if the customer's location is in New Jersey, regardless of whether goods are picked up or delivered to that location, the service is subject to sales tax. An armored car company may charge separately for armored car services and cash management services. The cash management services are not taxable if they are separately stated from the taxable armored car services. It is presumed that the separate charges for cash management services and armored car services are reasonable in relation to prevailing market prices.

Charges for the installation and monitoring of security systems are subject to tax. Installation is taxable whether it results in a capital improvement to real property or not. Thus, the installation of hard-wired security systems, where the wires are placed within the walls, is subject to sales tax. The installation of mobile or portable alarm systems, closed circuit television systems (cameras, monitors, recorders), and alarm systems that are rented or leased is also subject to tax. Sales of security systems are taxable whether they are sold to individual property owners, other sellers, or contractors. The customer may install the system himself or hire an outside contractor to install the system. Either way, the customer must pay sales tax on the purchase of the equipment.

• *Transportation services*

Transportation services originating in New Jersey state and provided by a limousine operator, except such services provided in connection with funeral services, are subject to tax.

• *Parking services*

Parking services, including a charge for parking, storing or garaging a motor vehicle, are subject to tax. However, charges for residential parking, employee parking, and municipal parking are not subject to tax.

The Sales and Use Tax Act was amended to exempt charges for parking, storing and garaging a motor vehicle when made by a municipality or county parking authority. All other charges for parking, storing or garaging a motor vehicle, other than residential and employee parking, remain subject to tax. The amendment also eliminates the imposition of sales tax on the $3 parking fee at Atlantic City casino hotels. (Ch. 105, Laws 2007).

• *Delivery services*

Delivery services for taxable tangible personal property are subject to tax, even if the delivery charge is separately stated on the invoice or purchase order.

• *Initiation fees*

Initiation fees, membership fees or dues for a health and fitness, athletic, sporting or shopping club or organization in New Jersey are subject to tax. However, membership fees for a club or organization whose members are predominantly age 18 or under are exempt from tax.

The Sales and Use Tax Act was amended to exempt from sales tax membership fees or dues for access to facilities of a health and fitness, athletic, sporting or shopping club or organization when the charges are made by qualified exempt organizations or New Jersey state or local government entities. All other charges for initiation fees, membership fees or dues for access to facilities of a health and fitness, athletic, sporting or shopping club or organization remain subject to sales tax. (Ch. 105, Laws 2007).

¶1204

• *Employee leasing services*

P.L. 2011, c.118, clarifies that the prospective imposition of sales tax on employee leasing services provided by an employee leasing company to a client company will apply after August 19, 2012. The tax will be imposed only on receipts that reflect the amounts charged to client companies for employee leasing services and not on receipts that represent the amounts charged for the payment of wages, salaries, benefits, worker's compensation costs, withholding taxes, or other assessments paid to or on behalf of a covered employee by the employee leasing company under an employee leasing agreement. The law also provides that for purposes of implementing the sales and use tax law, any taxes due for services performed by covered employees must be paid by the client company and not the employee leasing company. Ch. 118 (S.B. 2164), Laws 2011, effective August 19, 2012.

¶1205 Restaurant Meals, Catered Meals, Meals for Off-Premises Consumption, Vending Machine Sales of Food and Beverages

Law: R.S. 54:32B-3, 54:32B-8.3; Reg. Secs. 18:24-12.3, 18:24-12.5, 18:24-12.7 (CCH NEW JERSEY TAX REPORTS ¶ 60-390, ¶ 60-760).

Sales of restaurant meals, catered meals, and take-out food are subject to tax. Taxable receipts include cover, minimum, entertainment, or other charges, but do not include separately stated charges designated on the bill as a gratuity where all the money is paid over in total to employees. For provisions pertaining to the taxability of purchases made with restaurant discount coupons, see ¶ 1209.

Alcoholic beverages: Special rules apply to alcoholic beverages (¶ 1216, ¶ 1804).

On-premises consumption: The tax applies to sales of food and drink (other than alcoholic beverages) for consumption on the premises of restaurants, taverns, and other establishments.

Off-premises catering: The sale of food and beverages (other than alcoholic beverages) by caterers for off-premises consumption is taxable if the vendor (or any person whose services are arranged for by the vendor) serves, cooks, heats, or provides other services with respect to the food or drink after delivery.

Take-out food: The tax applies to sales of food for off-premises consumption that constitute a meal, or of food prepared and ready to be eaten (including sandwiches and other food or drink) unless sold in an unheated state and in the same form and condition commonly used by food stores not principally engaged in selling foods prepared and ready to be eaten. For example, if potato salad and hot pastrami are sold by the pound, the salad is exempt but the pastrami is taxable.

Vending machines: Sales of food and beverages (except milk) through coin-operated vending machines are subject to tax at their "wholesale price," which is defined as 70% of the retail vending machine price.

Exemptions: Sales of food and drink to an airline for consumption in flight are exempt, as are certain meals sold to students, and meals sold in a cafeteria used exclusively by hospital employees. Charges for meals that are included in the total charges made to residents of rest homes, nursing homes, and similar facilities licensed by the Departments of Health, Human Services, or Community Affairs, are exempt.

Exempt organizations: See ¶ 1312.

Meals for elderly or disabled persons: See ¶ 1302.

See ¶ 1302 for SSUTA changes effective October 1, 2005.

¶1205

¶1206 Hotel Room Occupancy

Law: R.S. 54:32B-2, 54:32B-3, 54:32B-9, 54:32D-1; Reg. Sec. 18:24-3.2 (CCH New Jersey Tax Reports ¶60-480).

Hotel room occupancy is subject to 7% sales tax in addition to the New Jersey hotel and motel occupancy tax. See ¶1903 for hotel and motel occupancy tax fee. The New Jersey hotel and motel occupancy tax is 5%. An optional municipal hotel and motel occupancy tax may also be imposed. The combined rates of these taxes plus state and local sales and use taxes must not exceed 14%.

The tax applies to hotel occupancies including occupancy in an apartment hotel, motel, boarding house, or club, whether or not meals are served. However, the tax applies to a boarding house only if it contains at least eight units. Occupancies at a rental of $2 or less per day are exempt, as are rents paid by permanent residents.

Rental of a hotel room for use as a place of assembly is exempt.

Exemptions applicable to occupancies by certain exempt organizations and occupancies in a hotel operated on the premises of certain nonprofit organizations in furtherance of their activities are discussed at ¶1312.

Any city imposing a hotel use or occupancy tax is authorized to collect both the real property tax and the hotel use or occupancy tax on hotels located in those cities.

See ¶1903 for a discussion of the state hotel and motel occupancy fee that became effective in 2003.

¶1207 Admission Charges

Law: R.S. 54:32B-2, 54:32B-3 (CCH New Jersey Tax Reports ¶60-230).

Admission charges to any place of amusement in New Jersey are taxable if the charge is in excess of 75¢, except as noted at ¶1313.

Taxable admission charges include charges for admission to race tracks, baseball, football, basketball games or exhibitions, motion picture theaters, and dramatic, choreographic, and musical arts performances. Charges imposed for the use of rides at an amusement pier are taxable as admission charges, even when the pier is open to the public and there is no general admission charge for entering the amusement pier's facilities (*Mariner's Landing, Inc. v. Director,* December 19, 1989, 11 NJ Tax 215; CCH New Jersey Tax Reports [1989—1994 Transfer Binder], ¶400-029).

Tax applies to initiation fees, membership fees or dues for access to or use of the property or facilities of a health and fitness, athltetic, sporting or shopping club or organization. However, tax does not apply for membership in a club or organization whose members are predominantly age 18 or under.

Roof garden, cabaret, or other similar place: The tax is payable on any amount paid as charges to the extent not included in the tax on restaurant meals (¶1205).

¶1208 Transactions Subject to Use Tax

Law: R.S. 54:32B-2, 54:32B-6 (CCH New Jersey Tax Reports ¶60-020).

The compensating use tax is imposed, unless the property or service has already been subject to the sales tax, on the use of property or services within New Jersey.

The use tax is imposed on the following:

— Use of tangible personal property or digital property purchased at retail;

— Use of tangible personal property manufactured, processed, or assembled by the user, if items of the same kind are offered for sale by the user in the regular course of business. In addition, the use of tangible personal property that is manufactured, processed, or assembled by the user is taxable even if the items are not offered for sale in the regular course of business, but are used or incorporated into a structure, building or real property. The mere storage, keeping, retention, or withdrawal from storage of such property, however, without actual use, is not a taxable use; and

— Use of tangible personal property, not acquired for resale, upon which taxable production, processing, fabricating, or imprinting services have been performed; or with respect to which taxable installation, maintenance, or repair services have been performed.

CCH Examples: Use Tax

The following examples illustrate circumstances in which use tax is due:

— items of inventory that are purchased tax free with a resale certificate are given away by the vendor as an advertising promotion; and

— taxable goods or services are purchased out of state for use in New Jersey and no sales tax was collected.

¶1209 Basis of Tax

Law: R.S. 54:32B-2, 54:32B-3, 54:32B-12; Reg. Secs. 18:24-1.4, 18:24-7.4, 18:24-27.2 (CCH NEW JERSEY TAX REPORTS ¶61-110—¶61-190).

The sales tax is imposed on the sales price and the charge for any service whether received in money or other consideration. Credits (other than trade-in allowances), expenses and early-payment discounts are not deductible from the sales price. Sales price includes delivery services, even if the delivery charge is separately stated on the invoice or purchase order.

• *Purchases made with coupons*

Sales tax is due on the discounted price of an item purchased with a vendor coupon, if the vendor receives no reimbursement. Sales tax is due on the full regular price of the item if the vendor is reimbursed. Sales tax is also due on the full regular price of the item when the item is purchased with manufacturer coupons entitling a purchaser to pay a reduced price on the item. For example, nonreimbursable fast food discount coupons, which entitle customers to receive two food or drink products for the price of one, are not subject to sales tax (*Burger King Corp. v. Division of Taxation* (1988 NJ Super Ct) 224 NJSuper 628; CCH NEW JERSEY TAX REPORTS [1979—1989 Transfer Binder], ¶201-382). SSUTA effective October 1, 2005, excludes from the "sales price" definition "discounts, including cash, term or coupons that are not reimbursed by a third party."

Effective January 1, 2009, the law adds language in the definition of "sales price" which sets forth the specific criteria to be met in order for third-party consideration received by the seller to be included within the definition of sales price. N.J.S.A. 54:32B-2(oo)(3).

CCH Tip: Scan Card Discounts

Vendors who receive allowances or reduced prices from their suppliers and who pass these discounts on to their consumers, if the consumers present a scan card issued by the vendor, are only required to collect sales tax on the price charged to the consumers after deducting the discount. Even though the vendor is not required to pass the reduced price on to the consumer and could retain the supplier allowances as additional profit, the allowance will not be treated as a vendor's receipt for the retail sale of an item so long as the vendor passes the discount on to the consumer (*State Tax News*, Division of Taxation, Winter 1999; CCH NEW JERSEY TAX REPORTS, ¶400-673).

• *Federal excise taxes*

Federal excise taxes imposed on manufacturers are included in taxable purchase price. However, when the federal tax is imposed on the purchaser (as in the case of the excise tax on the first retail sale of heavy trucks and trailers), the amount of the U.S. levy, if separately stated, will not be included in the purchase price subject to the New Jersey sales tax.

• *Delivery and Transportation charges*

On and after October 1, 2006, P.L. 2006, c.44, modified the exclusion for delivery charges that are separately stated from the sales price of an item on the invoice, bill, or similar document given to the purchaser. The law provides for tax to be imposed on delivery charges for taxable items and no tax to be imposed on delivery charges for nontaxable items like clothing.

The law defines delivery charges as charges by the seller for preparation and delivery to a location designated by the purchaser of personal property or services including, but not limited to, transportation, shipping, postage, handling, crating, and packing. If a shipment includes both exempt and taxable property, the seller should allocate the delivery charge by using: (1) a percentage based on the total sales price of the taxable property compared to the total sales price of all property in the shipment; or (2) a percentage based on the total weight of the taxable property compared to the total weight of all property in the shipment. Only the portion of the delivery charge that relates to the taxable property or service is subject to tax.

Thus, only delivery charges imposed by the seller of taxable items on the end-user are subject to tax.

Effective January 1, 2009, the law clarifies that if delivering taxable and non-taxable property, the seller is required to tax the percentage of the delivery charge allocated to the taxable property but is not required to tax the percentage allocated to the exempt property. N.J.S.A. 54:32B-2(rr).

• *Trade-in allowances*

Trade-in allowances may be deducted from the sales price if the property traded in is intended for resale by the vendor and is of the same kind as the property purchased. A passenger car and a truck are of "the same kind." The trade-in deduction is not allowed on sales of new manufactured or mobile homes.

• *Finance charges*

Interest, service charges, and finance charges imposed as consideration for the extension of credit and paid by a purchaser are not part of the sales price and are not included in the receipt subject to tax. Interest paid by a lessor on the purchase of tangible personal property intended to be leased to a customer is included in the receipt subject to tax.

• *Canceled sales, returned merchandise, bad debts*

The return form allows a vendor to deduct from gross receipts amounts (excluding tax) refunded or credited for returned goods. The Director is authorized to issue regulations concerning canceled sales, returned goods, and bad debts (for regulation provisions concerning refunds in connection with bad debts, see ¶1410).

• *Import tax surcharge*

The surcharge which an importer has to pay is part of the purchase price and is includable in the tax base, irrespective of whether it is separately stated (*Letter,* Division of Taxation, September 24, 1971).

Lease transactions: See ¶1215.

Alcoholic beverages: See ¶1216.

Vending machines, food and beverages: See ¶1205.

¶1210 Basis of Tax—Use Tax on Property Used Out of State and Later Brought Into New Jersey

Law: R.S. 54:32B-7 (CCH New Jersey Tax Reports ¶ 61-110).

The compensating use tax is imposed on the purchase price of property purchased by a resident outside New Jersey for use outside the state and subsequently brought into the state. However, if it can be shown that the resident used the property outside New Jersey for more than six months, the use tax is imposed on the current market value of the property at the time of its first use in the state, not to exceed the cost of the property.

If tangible personal property is brought into New Jersey for use in the performance of a contract or subcontract for a period of less than six months, the taxpayer has an option under which he may base the tax on the fair rental value of the property for the period of use in New Jersey. However, the option does not apply if the property is to be completely consumed or is to be incorporated into real property located in New Jersey.

Lease transactions: See ¶ 1215.

¶1211 Basis of Tax—Use Tax on Manufacturer's Use of Own Product

Law: R.S. 54:32B-6, 54:32B-7; Reg. Secs. 18:24-7.13, 18:24-7.14 (CCH New Jersey Tax Reports ¶ 60-510).

Manufacturers, assemblers or processors who use their own products in the regular course of their business in New Jersey compute the tax on the price at which they offer items of the same kind for sale or, if items of the same kind are not offered for sale in their regular course of business, on the cost of all materials used in the fabrication, assembly or processing of the product. The mere storage, keeping, retention, or withdrawal from storage of the items by the person who manufactured, assembled or processed the property is not a taxable use. The New Jersey Supreme Court ruled in *Cosmair, Inc.* (NJ SCt 1988) 109 NJ 562, 538 A2d 788; CCH New Jersey Tax Reports [1979—1989 Transfer Binder], ¶ 201-416, that product samples shipped from a New Jersey manufacturer's warehouse for out-of-state delivery, including delivery to a common carrier, and subsequent free distribution to customers, were excluded from use tax.

Special regulations, Reg. Secs. 18:24-7.13, 18:24-7.14, apply to automobiles used by motor vehicle manufacturers and dealers.

¶1212 Basis of Tax—Installment and Credit Sales

Law: R.S. 54:32B-12; Reg. Secs. 18:24-23.1—18:24-23.3 (CCH New Jersey Tax Reports ¶ 61-120, ¶ 61-180, ¶ 61-190).

The full amount of the tax is collected from the customer at the time of the sale, including conditional or credit sales, and must be reported on the return covering the period in which the sale occurs and paid to the Director, regardless of when the installment payments are made by the customer.

By regulation, the Director may provide that tax on receipts from installment sales may be paid on the amount of each installment and upon the date when the installment is due. To date, such regulations have not been issued.

Bad debt deduction: SSUTA defines bad debts by reference to federal law (IRC Sec. 166), except it does not include (1) financing charges or interest, (2) sales or use taxes charged on the purchase price, (3) uncollectable amounts on property that remains in the possession of a seller until the full purchase price is paid, (4) expenses incurred in attempting to collect any debt, or (5) repossessed property. Sellers are permitted to take a bad debt deduction on their sales and use tax return for the period during which the bad debt is written off as uncollectable and is eligible to be deducted for federal income tax purposes. A taxpayer who is not required to file federal income tax returns may deduct a bad debt on a return filed for the period in which the bad debt is written off as uncollectable and would be eligible for a bad debt deduction for federal income tax purposes if the taxpayer was required to file a federal income tax return. Prior law and regulations required a seller to apply for a refund and did not allow an allocation between purchase price and tax, for any payments received on the account (R.S. 54:32B-12.1).

¶1213 Rate of Tax and Bracket Collection Schedule

Law: R.S. 52:27H-80, 54:32B-3, 54:32B-4, 54:32B-6, 54:32B-8.45 (CCH NEW JERSEY TAX REPORTS ¶ 60-110,¶ 60-130).

The retail sales and use tax rate is 7%. The tax is collected according to the following bracket collection schedule:

Amount of Sale	Amount of Tax
$0.01 to $0.10	None
$0.11 to $0.19	0.01
$0.20 to $0.32	0.02
$0.33 to $0.47	0.03
$0.48 to $0.62	0.04
$0.63 to $0.77	0.05
$0.78 to $0.90	0.06
$0.91 to $1.10	0.07

In addition to a tax of 7¢ on each full dollar, a tax is collected on each part of a dollar in excess of a full dollar in accordance with the above formula.

While the bracket schedule does not allow for collecting taxes on sales of less than 11¢, the vendor is required to remit tax on total receipts (however, coin-operated vending machine sales of 25¢ or less receive special treatment, see ¶ 1302).

Public pay phones: For public pay-phone charges paid by coin, the tax is computed to the nearest multiple of 5¢, and is rounded up to the next higher multiple of five if the tax that would otherwise be due is midway between multiples of five.

Urban enterprise zones: A vendor operating a business that is located within an urban enterprise zone may charge sales tax at a reduced rate of 50% of the tax rate on all qualified sales upon obtaining the required certificate of authorization from the state (¶ 1315).

Exemptions: A 50% exemption from the tax on retail sales (other than sales of motor vehicles, alcoholic beverages, or cigarettes) made by vendors (except those primarily engaged in catalog or mail order sales) from a place of business located in a county in which is situated an entrance to an interstate bridge or tunnel connecting New Jersey with a state that does not impose a sales and use tax or imposes a sales and use tax at a 1% rate. Currently, Salem County qualifies for the exemption. For further details, see ¶ 1302.

¶1214 Building and Construction Trades—Related Activities

Law: R.S. 54:32B-2, 54:32B-3, 54:32B-8.22, 54:32B-12; Reg. Secs. 18:24-5.2—18:24-5.12 (CCH NEW JERSEY TAX REPORTS ¶ 60-330).

"Contractor" defined: A contractor is one who engages in a business involving the construction of buildings or structures, or otherwise improving, altering, or repairing real property.

"Fabricator" defined: A fabricator is one who engages in a business involving manufacturing, processing, or assembling property for sale, which, when installed, ordinarily becomes a physical component part of real property.

• *Purchases by contractors*

Materials and supplies: Sales of material and supplies to contractors for use in constructing buildings, structures, or otherwise improving, altering, or repairing real property are sales at retail. Thus, contractors must pay the sales tax at the time of purchase (unless they hold a direct payment permit). The New Jersey Tax Court has held that in the absence of receipt of a direct payment certificate from a contractor, the taxpayer was obligated to collect sales tax on its sales of materials and supplies to contractor *Stephen Little Trucking and Stephen Little v. Director, Division of Taxation*, 19 N.J. Tax 461 (Tax 2001); CCH New Jersey Tax Reports, ¶400-759). However, no tax is due on the purchase of materials, supplies, or services for exclusive use in fulfilling a contract with an exempt organization, for a qualified business in an urban enterprise zone (including certain urban renewal entities which are sole owners of certain operating companies situated within the same zone), or for housing projects financed through the State Housing and Mortgage Finance Agency and other federal, state, or local subsidies. The exemption does not apply to purchases of tools, machines, or machine parts to be used in performance of the project.

Rebate for Off-Track Wagering Facilities Construction Materials: P.L. 2012, c.40, effective August 7, 2012, provides a rebate for tax paid on purchases of certain materials, supplies used for construction of off-track wagering facilities. Legislation provides a grant program to provide a one-time rebate of New Jersey sales and use tax paid for the purchase of certain materials and supplies used for the construction of certain off-track wagering facilities.

Equipment: The purchase, rental, or use of construction equipment by a contractor is taxable even if the purchase, rental, or use is for the fulfillment of a contract with an exempt organization.

Services: A contractor must pay sales tax on the purchase of any of the enumerated services that are subject to tax, unless the service is purchased for use exclusively in fulfilling a contract with an exempt organization. Taxable services include, but are not limited to, fabrication of tangible personal property, installing tangible personal property (unless the installation results in a capital improvement) and maintaining, servicing or repairing real or tangible personal property. (See "Subcontractor" below for rules applied to prime contractor—subcontractor transactions.)

• *Services performed by contractors*

Installing tangible personal property: A contractor must collect tax on the charge for installing tangible personal property unless the installation results in a capital improvement.

The following factors are considered in determining whether an installation of tangible personal property results in a capital improvement: (1) whether the improvement results in an increase in the capital value of the realty; and (2) whether the improvement results in a significant increase in the useful life of the real property.

The installation charge is exempt only if the contractor obtains a Certificate of Capital Improvement, which the contractor accepts in good faith, from the customer.

Landscaping services and installing carpeting and other flooring are not considered capital improvements.

Servicing, maintaining, or repairing real property: A contractor's charge for servicing, repairing, or maintaining real property is taxable, and the contractor collects the tax from the contractor's customer. (The tax should be collected only on the service, since the contractor is responsible for paying tax on the material used in performing the service.) The New Jersey Tax Court has ruled that an out-of-state contractor's labor charges for reconditioning machinery used in a manufacturer's out-of-state plant constituted a use subject to taxation when the reconditioned property was shipped to the manufacturer's New Jersey plant for purposes of inspecting the contractor's work (*Wheaton Industries v. Division of Taxation*, April 1990, 11 NJ Tax 139; CCH New Jersey Tax Reports [1989—1994 Transfer Binder], ¶ 400-075).

The following are not taxable services: (1) services to a residential heating unit which is operated for no more than three independent family units; (2) services rendered by a person not in a regular trade or business offering services to the public; and (3) garbage removal and sewer service, if performed under a contract with a term of at least 30 days.

CCH Tip: Exterminator's Reinspection Services Were Taxable

A fee for reinspection after extermination and further treatment, if necessary, of previously exterminated premises was taxable because the reinspection was part of the initial exterminating service that was subject to tax. Though reinspection services only, with no right to necessary further treatments, are not taxable services, the reinspection with a right to necessary treatments was a taxable warranty that was part of the initial contract even though the reinspection was billed on a yearly basis (*Williams Termite and Pest Control, Inc.*, NJ Tax Court, No. 003650-1997, October 8, 1999; CCH New Jersey Tax Reports ¶ 400-661).

• *Subcontractors*

The following rules apply where a contractor agrees to perform specified operations for another contractor:

—*Materials and supplies:* Purchases of materials and supplies by a subcontractor are subject to the same rules which are applied to purchases by contractors. They are taxable to the subcontractor unless the purchases are for exclusive use in fulfilling a service contract with a prime contractor fulfilling a contract with an exempt organization.

—*Services performed by subcontractors:* A subcontractor does not collect tax on taxable services performed for a prime contractor. The prime contractor collects the tax from the customer. However, the subcontractor retains records to show taxable services were performed for a prime contractor.

• *Fabricators*

Fabricators, as opposed to contractors, purchase their materials as if they were intended for resale. Fabricators who sell their fabricated products to others for installation must collect tax on the sales price of the item. Fabricators who sell and install their own products must collect tax from their customers on the charge for installation, unless the installation results in a capital improvement. If the installation does result in a capital improvement, the fabricator does not collect tax on the installation, but instead must pay use tax on the fabricated product. The use tax is computed on either the price at which items of the same kind are offered for sale by the fabricator, or on the cost of all materials used in fabrication if the fabricator does not make sales of similar items.

• *Out of state contracts*

Materials, supplies, and equipment purchased in New Jersey for out-of-state use are subject to sales and use taxes if the materials, supplies, and equipment are picked up by the contractor in New Jersey. They are not subject to tax if delivered to the out-of-state jobsite by the supplier, common carrier, or unregulated carrier hired by the supplier.

¶1214

Materials, supplies, and equipment purchased outside the state are subject to the New Jersey use tax. The tax is based on the purchase price, except that current market value is the basis for the tax on equipment used outside of New Jersey for more than six months before its use in New Jersey. The use tax is not applicable to property on which a tax was already paid to another state that allows a corresponding exemption to property or services upon which a tax was paid to New Jersey.

¶1215 Lease and Rental Transactions

Law: R.S. 54:32B-2(e)(3), 54:32B-2(f), 54:32B-2(w), 54:32B-2(aa), 54:32B-2(bb), 54:32B-3(a), 54:32B-7, 54:32B-8, 54:32B-12 (CCH NEW JERSEY TAX REPORTS ¶60-460).

• *Leases and Rental Transactions under SSUTA effective October 1, 2005*

Under SSUTA, the provisions of the lease law that have been in effect since 1989 have been repealed for leases entered into as of October 1, 2005. The term "lease or rental" is defined as a transfer of possession or control for consideration, excluding financing transactions and installment sales (R.S. 54:32B-2(aa)). The leasing company is no longer the retail purchaser of property purchased for lease and is no longer the party legally responsible for the tax on the transaction. The 28-day criterion for determining whether a transaction is a lease or a rental is no longer applicable. Rather, sales tax is collected from the lessee, and for leases or rentals with a term of more than six months, the tax continues to be due up-front, in the period in which the lessee takes delivery of the property. The basis for calculating the tax continues to be either the total of the periodic payments required under the agreement, or the original purchase price of the property for leases of more than six months. For leases of six months or less, the basis for calculating the tax is the periodic payment. Specific sourcing rules for leases and rentals are provided in the new law.

Unlike in the old law, in the new law, the words "lease" and "rental" are used interchangeably to mean any transfer of possession or control of tangible personal property for a fixed or indeterminate term for consideration.

A lease or rental does not include any of the following types of transactions:

—transfer of property under a security agreement or deferred payment plan that requires transfer of title upon completion of the required payments;

—transfer of property under an agreement that requires transfer of title upon completion of the required payments and payment of an option price not exceeding $100 or one percent of the total required payments;

—providing tangible personal property along with an operator who is necessary in order for the equipment to function as designed.

Sales tax on a lease or rental for a term of more than six months is paid by the lessee either on the original purchase price of the leased property or on the total of the periodic payments required under the lease agreement. If tax is paid on the original purchase price, then the lessor's subsequent leases or rentals of the same item of property will not be subject to New Jersey sales or use tax. (Whether the tax will be calculated on the purchase price or the total of the periodic payments is negotiable between the lessor and lessee.)

• *Leases entered into prior to October 1, 2005*

For leases entered into prior to October 1, 2005, regardless of whether the property is either removed from or brought into New Jersey after October 1, 2005, the term retail sale includes the purchase of tangible personal property for lease for more than 28 days. If the lessor of tangible personal property purchased for lease elects to pay tax on the sales price determined under the lease payment method, any subsequent lease or rental is a retail sale and a subsequent sale is a retail sale.

Under prior law, for sales and use tax purposes, a lease is a long-term transaction, lasting more than 28 days, while transactions lasting 28 days or less are rentals. If property is rented for a period of 28 days or less, the lessor must collect tax from the lessee on the rental payments made (*Notice to Vendors,* Division of Taxation, July 5, 1989; CCH NEW JERSEY TAX REPORTS [1989—1994 Transfer Binder], ¶ 400-001). Leases that are actually installment sales do not constitute leases for purposes of the sales and use tax, and sales tax must be collected and remitted on the sales price of such property (*State Tax News,* Division of Taxation, January/February 1990; CCH NEW JERSEY TAX REPORTS [1989—1994 Transfer Binder], ¶ 400-034).

The purchase of property for a long-term lease constitutes a retail sale. The lessor is considered the end user and is responsible for payment of the sales tax. However, the subsequent lease of tangible personal property also constitutes a retail sale, and the lessor may therefore present a resale certificate (Form ST-3) when making purchases of property for lease. Tax is due from the lessor at the time of the first lease of the property. The owner of the leased property is considered the lessor for sales and use tax purposes, regardless of whether the lease is assigned to a finance corporation, or whether the name of the finance corporation appears on the lease agreement.

• *Basis of tax prior to October 1, 2005*

At the time of lease, lessors may elect to pay tax on either the purchase price of the property, or on the total of lease payments over the full term of the lease. If the lessor elects to pay tax on the total of lease payments, a subsequent lease of the property constitutes a retail sale subject to tax, and the lessor must again elect whether to pay tax on the purchase price or the total of lease payments. If the lessor has always chosen to pay tax on the total of lease payments, the subsequent sale of the property is also taxable. The total of lease payments does not include any separately stated, nontaxable charges for sales and use tax purposes, such as finance charges. There is no provision for the refund of any portion of the tax paid by the lessor in the event a lease is canceled before the expiration of the term.

The Division of Taxation advises that lessors should not charge tax on lease transactions, but that lessors may be able to pass sales tax costs along to the lessee under the terms of the lease agreement (*Notice to Vendors,* Division of Taxation, July 5, 1989; CCH NEW JERSEY TAX REPORTS [1989—1994 Transfer Binder], ¶ 400-001).

Property may be purchased under an exemption certificate if the property, the use of the property, or the lessee of the property is granted an exemption under the sales and use tax. However, if the property is later leased for a nonexempt use or to a nonexempt person, or converted to a nonexempt use, the property will be subject to tax.

• *Lessor certification in use prior to October 1, 2005*

Lessors are required to issue to the lessee a properly completed "Lessor Certification" (Form ST-40). Issuance of the certificate verifies that the lessor will remit sales tax. Unpaid sales tax may be collected from lessees who do not maintain the properly completed "Lessor Certification" form in their files. The lessor should also issue Form ST-40 when leasing property to an exempt organization, leasing motor vehicles, vessels, or aircraft to out-of-state residents, or leasing property for an exempt use. A copy of the appropriate exemption certificate issued by the lessee must be attached to the form.

• *Sale of leased property prior to October 1, 2005*

If the lessor has always selected the lease payments option, sales tax must be collected and remitted from the purchaser when the leased property is sold. A lessor does not receive a reduction in the tax base for the value of a trade-in of property that had been leased.

¶1215

• *Out-of-state leases prior to October 1, 2005*

If the lessor purchases property outside New Jersey, for lease outside New Jersey, and the lessee brings the property into New Jersey, the lessor must pay use tax. The lessor may elect to pay use tax based on either the original purchase price of the property or the lease payments for the period of use within New Jersey. However, if the property is leased to a nonresident for use outside New Jersey and the lessor accepts a properly completed form ST-10 from the lessee, the lessee, and not the lessor, is responsible for tax if the lessee later brings the property into New Jersey for use.

• *Sale-leaseback transactions*

SSUTA provides a specific exemption for sale-leaseback transactions, which are defined as transactions where the owner of property sells the property to a lessor, who leases it back to the owner within 180 days from when the property was originally placed in service by the owner. A sale-leaseback is treated as a financing transaction, rather than a true lease. Although these transactions were not taxed under prior law, the prior law did not have a specific definition or a 180-day threshold (R.S. 32B-8.57).

Rentals between certain closely related business entities: Effective November 1, 2003, receipts from the rental of tangible personal property, on which sales tax was paid or use tax obligations have been satisfied between related persons not engaged in the regular trade or business of renting that property to other persons, are exempt from the tax imposed under the Sales and Use Tax Act. For the purposes of this section, "related persons" means persons that are 80% or more owned by each other or that are 80% or more owned by the same third parties (Ch. 136 (S704), Laws 2003).

The following chart summarizes the pre-and post-SSUTA rental/lease law:

Summary of Major Changes

	L. 1989, c. 123	L. 2005, c. 126
Terms "lease" or "rental":	Different meaning	Interchangeable
Legal incidence of tax (who is liable to pay the tax):	Lessor paid use tax on leases for terms of over 28 days, while lessee paid sales tax on rentals for terms of 28 days or less.	Lessee pays sales tax, regardless of length of term.
Collection of tax:	Lessor collected tax only on rentals for 28 days or less. Lessor did *not* collect tax on leases over 28 days.	Lessor collects on lease/rental regardless of length of term.
Threshold for determining whether tax is remitted on accelerated basis:	Term of more than 28 days	Term of more than six months.
Refunds if leased property is relocated outside NJ before expiration of lease:	No refund	Allocated refund (certain conditions)

Computers, software, and related services: See ¶ 1203 and ¶ 1204.

¶ 1216 Alcoholic Beverages

Law: R.S. 54:32B-2, 54:32B-3 (CCH New Jersey Tax Reports ¶ 60-260).

Alcoholic beverages are subject to New Jersey sales and use tax.

Alcoholic beverage excise tax: See ¶ 1804.

¶ 1217 Sourcing Rules

SSUTA contains sourcing rules to determine the location of the sale. The definition of "sale" is any transfer of title or possession, for consideration. New Jersey is a destination state, so whether a sale of property is subject to New Jersey sales or use tax is generally based upon where delivery occurs. The new law provides specific sourcing rules which determine the location where the sale, lease or rental is deemed to occur for purposes of applying each state's sales and use tax. In addition to general sourcing rules for sale transactions, there are additional rules for lease and rentals of tangible personal property; of motor vehicles, trucks and certain aircraft; and for sales, lease and rentals of transportation equipment. Generally, sales continue to be sourced based on the location where delivery is taken by the purchaser. There are special sourcing rules for telecommunications (R.S. 54:32B-3.1; 3.2; 3.3; 3.4).

By repealing N.J.S.A. 54:32B-3.2 effective January 1, 2009, the law repeals the MPU sourcing provision which was repealed in the SSUTA. Computer software and related services are sourced according to the Streamlined Sales Tax Governing Board's Rules and Procedures (amended June 18, 2008).

SALES AND USE TAXES

CHAPTER 13
EXEMPTIONS

¶ 1301	In General	
¶ 1302	Exempt Property and Services	
¶ 1303	Exempt Transactions	
¶ 1304	Use Tax Exemptions	
¶ 1305	Manufacturing and Processing Machinery, Apparatus, and Equipment	
¶ 1306	Machinery and Equipment for Utilities	
¶ 1307	Farming Exemption	
¶ 1308	Fuel and Utilities	
¶ 1309	Research and Development Exemption	
¶ 1310	Casual Sales	
¶ 1311	Chemicals and Catalysts Used in Processing	
¶ 1312	Exempt Organizations	
¶ 1313	Exempt Admission Charges	
¶ 1314	Exempt Meals and Occupancies	
¶ 1315	Urban Enterprise Zone Exemptions	
¶ 1316	Ships and Other Vessels; Marine Terminal Services and Equipment	
¶ 1317	Radio and Television Broadcast Production Equipment	
¶ 1318	Facilities Sales Tax Exemption Certificate Program	
¶ 1319	Seven Year Exemption Period from Certain Taxes on Energy for Certain Manufacturers	
¶ 1320	Postconsumer Material Manufacturing Facility Exemption	

¶1301 In General

The discussions below deal with the exemptions from sales and use taxes.

Exemptions include sales for resale (¶1303); food, clothing, and drugs (¶1302); manufacturing and processing machinery and equipment (¶1305); fuel, utilities, and machinery (¶1306, ¶1308); radio and television equipment (¶1317); property for use in farming (¶1307); and casual sales (¶1310).

¶1302 Exempt Property and Services

Law: R.S. 54:4-1.7, 54:32B-2, 54:32B-3, 54:32B-8—54:32B-8.46; Reg. Secs. 18:24-6.1—18:24-6.7, 18:24-17.2 (CCH New Jersey Tax Reports ¶60-240, ¶60-285, ¶60-290, ¶60-300, ¶60-310, ¶60-390, ¶60-400, ¶60-420, ¶60-460, ¶60-510, ¶60-520, ¶60-540, ¶60-550, ¶60-560, ¶60-570, ¶60-600, ¶60-630, ¶60-640, ¶60-665, ¶60-720, ¶60-740, ¶60-750, ¶60-760).

Sales and use tax exemptions apply to receipts from retail sales of the following:

Clothing and footwear: Prior to SSUTA clothing and footwear are exempt except articles made of fur where fur is the component material of chief value of the article. Safety shoes or clothing are exempt, but clothing, footwear, and equipment normally worn for a particular sport are taxable if not suitable for general wear. Also exempt are component materials such as fabric, thread, yarn, buttons, and zippers. Accessories, such as handbags, jewelry, and wallets, are taxable. For illustrative list of articles of clothing and footwear, see Reg. Secs. 18:24-6.1—18:24-6.7.

SSUTA defines "clothing" as all human wearing apparel suitable for general use. Sales of clothing are exempt from tax. Under the prior law, sales of clothing and footwear that were made essentially of fur were subject to tax (R.S. 54:32B-8.4(d)).

Under the new law, fur clothing and footwear are exempt from tax. There is also a new definition of "protective equipment," and a specific exemption for such equipment when necessary for the daily work of the user. Under prior law, protective equipment was generally considered to be exempt clothing when worn as part of a work uniform, so the new definition should not affect the taxability of such products. A new definition of "sports or recreational equipment" supports the position that goods worn for athletic or recreational activity but not suitable for general use are subject to tax (*e.g.,* bowling shoes, cleats, ski boots).

Effective January 1, 2009, the law adds a new definition of "fur clothing" and excludes fur clothing from the clothing exemption. N.J.S.A. 54:32B-8.4. In addition, the law repeals the 6% Fur Clothing Retail Gross Receipts Tax. N.J.S.A. 54:32G-1. Thus, fur clothing is now subject to sales and use tax at a rate of 7%.

Drugs and medicines, medical aids, etc.: Prior to SSUTA prescription drugs and medicines for human use are exempt from tax, as are over-the-counter drugs recommended and generally sold for the relief of pain, ailments, distress or disorder of the human body. Also exempt are diabetic supplies, crutches, artificial limbs, artificial eyes, hearing devices, dentures, corrective eyeglasses, prosthetic aids, orthopedic appliances, tampons and the like, medical oxygen, respiratory equipment, human blood and its derivatives when sold for human use, wheel chairs, transcutaneous electro-neuro stimulators (TENS units), and durable medical equipment, including replacement parts.

SSUTA clarifies and changes the exemption in certain areas.

"Durable medical equipment" remains exempt from tax, and is defined so as to remove the requirement under prior law that the equipment be appropriate for use in the home, and adds the requirement that it not be worn in or on the body.

"Mobility enhancing equipment" remains exempt from tax, and is defined as a separate category of property and refers to property used to provide or increase the ability to move from place to place, (*e.g.,* wheelchairs).

Effective January 1, 2009, the law adds a prescription requirement to the exemption for mobility enhancing equipment. This is intended to clarify that there is no exemption for such equipment when purchased by a medical services provider (*e.g.,* grab bars, wheelchairs, and shower handles are taxable when purchased by a for-profit hospital, doctor's office, etc.). N.J.S.A. 54:32B-8.1.

"Grooming and hygiene products" are defined as soap or cleaning solution, shampoo, toothpaste, mouthwash, anti-perspirant, or suntan lotion or screen, regardless of whether the item meets the definition of over the counter drug. Under prior law, some of these types of products were deemed to be exempt from tax as over the counter drugs if they were "medicated." Under the new law, all grooming and hygiene products will be subject to tax, regardless of medicinal ingredients.

In the health care area, other defined product terms are "prescription," "prosthetic device," "drug," and "over-the-counter drug." All products within these defined categories also remain exempt from tax.

Food and beverages: Prior to SSUTA food, food products, beverages (including noncarbonated soft drinks), dietary foods and health supplements sold for human consumption off the premises are exempt. In addition, the amount of the sales price for which food stamps have been properly tendered in full or partial payment is excluded from the definition of "receipt." Candy, confectionery, and carbonated soft drinks and beverages are taxable. The exemption does not apply to food served by restaurants and caterers, to "take-out food and drink," or to food and beverages sold through vending machines (¶1205), with limited exceptions.

SSUTA defines "candy" as a preparation of sugar, honey, or other natural or artificial sweeteners in combination with chocolate, fruits, nuts or other ingredients or flavorings in the form of bars, drops, or pieces; candy does not include any preparation containing flour or requiring refrigeration. Candy remains subject to sales tax. As a result of the new definition, products such as Twix bars, Milky Ways and most licorice, which have been subject to tax as candy, will now be exempt from tax because they contain flour. The taxability of a candy-like product will depend upon whether it meets the definition of "candy," which will require knowledge of the ingredients.

Under SSUTA, "soft drinks" are defined as non-alcoholic beverages that contain natural or artificial sweeteners, but do not contain milk or milk products; soy, rice or similar milk substitutes; or more than 50% fruit or vegetable juice. Under prior law, a distinction was made between the retail sale of carbonated (taxable) and non-carbonated (exempt) beverages. Beverages such as iced teas and various juice drinks that contain only a small percentage of juice were exempt because they are non-carbonated. As a result of adopting the new definition, this distinction is no longer relevant.

Thus, if non-carbonated beverages meet the above definition, they will be subject to tax as soft drinks. Although bottled water sold at retail remains exempt, flavored water products are now taxable if they contain artificial or natural sweeteners. The taxability of any canned, bottled or boxed beverage depends upon whether it is a soft drink, which will require knowledge of the ingredients. (NOTE: ALL beverages remain subject to tax when sold for on-premises consumption.

Effective January 1, 2009, the law eliminates the language that imposed tax on non-liquid soft drinks (*e.g.,* powdered beverage mixes). N.J.S.A. 54:32B-8.2. This is a technical amendment and does not result in a change in taxability of such products. Since October 1, 2005, powdered beverage mixes have been exempt as food ingredients, pursuant to the SSUTA.

"Prepared food," which includes beverages, is defined as: (1) food sold in a heated state or heated by the vendor; or (2) two or more ingredients combined by the seller and sold as a single item; or (3) food sold with eating utensils provided by the seller. Food that is only cut, repackaged or pasteurized by the seller, as well as eggs, fish, meat, poultry, and foods that contain these raw animal foods, that require cooking by the consumer are not treated as prepared food. The following are NOT treated as "prepared food," unless served by the seller with eating utensils: food sold by a seller that is a manufacturer; food sold in an unheated state by weight or volume as a single item; and bakery items sold as such, including bread, rolls, buns, bagels, donuts, cookies, muffins, etc.

"Food and food ingredients" and "dietary supplements" remain exempt from tax, and both terms are specifically defined in the new law.

Computer software and related services: On July 5, 2011, the Division of Taxation issued a new technical advisory memorandum on software, TB-51R. Computer software means a set of coded instruction designed to cause a computer or automatic data processing equipment to perform a task. N.J.S.A. 54:32B-8.56.

Prewritten computer software is "tangible personal property": The New Jersey Sales and Use Tax Act taxes retail sales of tangible personal property, unless a specific statutory exemption or exclusion applies. "Tangible personal property" includes prewritten computer software including prewritten computer software delivered electronically. Prior to October 1, 2006, software that was transmitted electronically was not treated as taxable tangible personal property, and therefore its sale was not subject to sales or use tax. P.L. 2006, c.44, made the following changes regarding the taxability of software, effective October 1, 2006: 1. expanded the statutory definition of "tangible personal property," explicitly including "prewritten computer software delivered electronically" N.J.S.A. 54:32B-2(g), and 2. limited the exemption for electronically delivered prewritten software, allowing an exemption for sales of electronically delivered prewritten software only when it is to be used directly and exclusively in the conduct of the purchaser's business, trade, or occupation. N.J.S.A. 54:32B-8.56.

Taxability of prewritten software: Prewritten computer software is any computer software, including prewritten upgrades and combinations or portions of two or more prewritten software programs, that is not designed and developed to meet the unique requirements of a specific purchaser and sold for that specific purchaser's exclusive use. N.J.S.A. 54:32B-8.56. The retail sale of prewritten software is taxable. The sale of a license to use prewritten software is treated the same as the sale of outright title to the prewritten software. The use in New Jersey of prewritten computer software purchased at retail without payment of sales or use tax is subject to use tax. N.J.S.A. 54:32B-6.

Custom software: In those exceptional circumstances when software is created, written, and designed for the exclusive use of a specific customer, it is not considered prewritten computer software when sold to the specific customer for whom it was designed. N.J.S.A. 54:32B-8.56. That customer's purchase of this entirely custom-made software is treated as a nontaxable professional service transaction and is not subject to sales tax.

Modified software: The sale of prewritten computer software is taxable regardless of whether the prewritten software is sold in its original form, or combined with other prewritten software programs, or with modifications to meet the purchaser's special needs. However, the seller of modified software has an option to charge a separate fee for the customization service. A separately stated, commercially reasonable charge for the professional service of modifying the software for the customer is not treated as a charge for the sale of prewritten computer software and is therefore exempt from sales tax. N.J.S.A. 54:32B-8.56. If the seller of modified software instead chooses to charge a lump sum, without separately stating the fee for customization services, then the entire charge is subject to sales tax as part of the sale of tangible prewritten software.

Exemption for sales of electronically delivered software used exclusively and directly in conduct of purchaser's business, trade or occupation: There is one exception to the taxability of prewritten software delivered electronically. Sales of prewritten software delivered electronically are exempt if the software is to be used directly and exclusively in the conduct of the purchaser's business, trade, or occupation. N.J.S.A. 54:32B-8.56. This exception does not apply, however, if the software is being delivered by a "load-and-leave" method. If the purchaser of software initially delivered electronically also receives tangible storage media containing the software, then the transaction is not deemed to be a sale of software delivered electronically and is not exempt, even when the software is to be used directly and exclusively in the purchaser's business.

Installation and maintenance of software: Fees for the service of installing software for the customer are subject to sales tax. They are treated as charges for the installation of tangible personal property. N.J.S.A. 54:32B-3(b)(2). The sale of a maintenance contract for prewritten software is generally subject to tax. Software maintenance contracts usually include the provision of updated, supplemental, and corrected software. Contracts covering delivery of such updated, supplemental, and corrected software via tangible storage media are taxable. Contracts for the delivery of such updated, supplemental, and corrected software entirely electronically, with no tangible storage media, are also taxable unless these electronically delivered updates are to

¶1302

be used directly and exclusively in the conduct of the purchaser's business, trade, or occupation. A maintenance contract covering only entirely custom-made updates of custom software, for the exclusive use of the original purchaser, is also nontaxable, regardless of whether delivered electronically or through tangible storage media. If a software maintenance contract covers only the provision of training, consultation, or advice, help and customer support via telephone or online, but no software, then the contract is not taxable.

Sourcing rules: Effective October 1, 2005, the Streamlined Sales and Use Tax Agreement (SSUTA) has been incorporated into the New Jersey Sales and Use Tax Act. P.L. 2005, c.126. The SSUTA sourcing provisions aid a seller by identifying which state's law should be applied to a sale, *e.g.*, the sourcing rules are used to specify which state has the first right to tax tangible personal property or services sourced to that state. Sourcing a sale to a particular state does not mean that the transaction is taxable. The sale may in fact not be taxable under the law of the state to which the sale was sourced.

Sourcing of receipts from sales of prewritten computer software is governed by the following principles:

1. If prewritten computer software is received by the purchaser at a business location of the seller, the retail sale is sourced to that business location. N.J.A.C. 18:24-25.7(a)(1).

2. If prewritten computer software is not received by the purchaser at a business location of the seller, the retail sale is sourced to the location(s) where receipt by the purchaser occurs. Receipt may occur at multiple locations if the seller delivers the software to multiple locations. The transaction is sourced to those locations if the seller receives delivery information from the purchaser by the time of the invoice. N.J.A.C. 18:24-25.7(a)(2).

Other specific exemptions are:

Advertising: Receipts from sales of advertising and promotional materials prepared inside or outside of New Jersey are exempt if they are for distribution by a New Jersey direct-mail advertising or promotional firm to out-of-state recipients. The exemption includes, but is not limited to, receipts from the preparation and maintenance of mailing lists, addressing, separating, folding, inserting, sorting, and packaging advertising or promotional materials and transporting to the point of shipment by the mail service or other carrier. Also exempt is the sale of advertising to be published in a newspaper. Advertising services are not subject to sales tax.

SSUTA defines "direct mail" as printed material delivered or distributed by U.S. Mail or other delivery service to a mass audience or to addresses on a mailing list, including items of tangible property supplied by the purchaser and included in the packaging. Direct mail does not include multiple items of printed material delivered to a single address, *e.g.*, a shipment of flyers in bulk to the purchaser (R.S. 54:32B-2(ss)). SSUTA "advertising and promotional materials" are referred to as "direct mail."

Under prior law, both the printed material and the direct mail processing service were subject to tax when the material was delivered to New Jersey recipients. Both remain subject to tax under the new law. Promotional items sent with printed material remain exempt but are taxed if not sent with printed material. Under prior law, "direct mail" included all promotional material, whether sent with promotional material or not. A new multi-state Certificate of Exemption is available for use by the purchaser of direct mail. The new law also contains specific sourcing rules for direct mail.

Effective January 1, 2009, the law replaces the term "direct mail" with the term "printed advertising material". This does not result in a change of taxability from prior law because the change is consistent with the Division of Taxation's application and use of the term since October 1, 2005. The SSUTA definition of "direct mail" was never intended to define a product, but it was erroneously incorporated into New Jersey law as such. This amendment fixes that error. N.J.S.A. 54:32B-3(b)(5); N.J.S.A. 54:32B-8.39.

The law replaces the term "direct mail processing service" with "mail processing services" for the reason stated above. N.J.S.A. 54:32B-3(b)(5); N.J.S.A. 54:32B-8.39.

Agricultural: Specified property and services used for farming are exempt (¶1307).

Aircraft: Sales of aircraft for use by an air carrier having its principal place of operations in New Jersey and engaging in interstate, foreign, or intrastate air commerce are exempt. The exemption extends to repairs to the aircraft, replacement parts, and machinery or equipment to be installed on the aircraft.

An exemption from New Jersey sales and use tax applies to receipts from repairs made to an aircraft that has a maximum certificated takeoff weight of 6,000 pounds or more noted in the certificate type issued by the Federal Aviation Administration. The exemption for repairs covers machinery or equipment installed on such aircraft and replacement parts for such aircraft.

Bibles: Sales of the Bible or similar sacred scripture are exempt by statute. However, the Division of Taxation, in a notice effective October 1, 1989 (CCH NEW JERSEY TAX REPORTS [1989—1994 Transfer Binder], ¶400-014), advises that it has ceased enforcement of this exemption, and will collect the sales tax on receipts from retail sales of Bibles and other sacred scripture in light of a decision by the United States Supreme Court, holding that such exemptions violate the Establishment Clause of the Fourteenth Amendment to the U.S. Constitution (*Texas Monthly, Inc. v. Bullock,* February 21, 1989; CCH NEW JERSEY TAX REPORTS [1979—1989 Transfer Binder], ¶201-468).

Buses: Sales of buses, including repair and replacement parts and labor, to regulated carriers and to school bus operators for public passenger transportation are exempt.

Chemicals and catalysts used in processing: See ¶1311.

Effluent treatment equipment: Receipts from sales of equipment used exclusively to treat effluent from a primary wastewater treatment facility, which would otherwise have been discharged into New Jersey waters for subsequent reuse in an industrial process or by conveyance equipment used to transport effluent to the treatment facility or to transport the treated effluent to the reuse site, are exempt from New Jersey sales and use tax. To be eligible, the DEP Commissioner must have determined whether the operation of the system in which the equipment is used and reuse of resulting wastewater effluent is or will be helpful to the environment. The tax will be collected by vendor. The tax is refunded to the purchaser by filing for a refund within three years of the date of purchase. The DEP determination of environmental benefit must accompany a refund claim (N.J.S.A. 54:32B-8.36).

Electricity: Receipts from the sale, exchange, delivery, or use of electricity are exempt that are (1) sold for resale, (2) sold by a municipal electric corporation or utility in existence as of December 31, 1995, and used within its municipal boundaries, except if the customer is located within a franchise area (a) served by an electric public utility other than the municipal electric corporation or (b) outside of the franchise area of the municipal electric utility existing as of December 31, 1995, or (3) generated by a facility located on the user's property or contiguous property purchased or leased from the user by the person owning the co-generator, and the electricity is consumed by the on-site end user on the user's property. Ch. 240, Laws 2009, clarifies the meaning of "contiguous property" and removes certain limitations

¶1302

on the exemption from sales and use tax for natural gas and utility service used for cogeneration.

Films, records, etc. for use in communications media: Sales of films, records, tapes, or any type of visual or sound transcriptions to theaters or radio or broadcasting stations or networks, or which are produced for use in such media are exempt. This exemption does not apply if the item is used for advertising purposes.

Receipts from the sale of tangible personal property for use or consumption directly or primarily in the production of film or video for sale are exempt from sales and use tax. The exemption applies to all tangible personal property including motor vehicles, replacement parts without regard to useful life, tools, and supplies but does not apply to property when the use is incidental to film or video production. Receipts from installing, maintaining, servicing, or repairing tangible personal property that is directly used or consumed in the production of film or video for sale are also exempt.

Flags: Sales of the American flag and the flag of the state of New Jersey are exempt.

CCH Caution: U.S. and New Jersey Flags

The exemption does not apply, however, to mere representations of flags or to merchandise with a flag theme. Taxable items include: framed prints, wind socks, stickers, pins, tie tacks and jewelry, tote bags, teddy bears, figurines and red, white and blue ribbons. Public Notice, New Jersey Division of Taxation, June 13, 2003.

Fuel and utilities: See ¶ 1308.

Gold and silver: The sale or storage of gold or silver in the form traded on any licensed contract market or other board of trade or exchange is exempt if the sale fulfills a contract for future delivery or an option to buy or sell. The exemption does not apply if the metal is converted to use by a purchaser.

Installation and maintenance services on property delivered outside of state: See ¶ 1204.

Installation of tangible personal property constituting an addition or capital improvement to real property: See ¶ 1214.

Laundering, etc.: Laundering, dry cleaning, tailoring, weaving, pressing, shoe repairing, and shoe shining are exempt, however, the exemption is only for laundering, etc. of clothing.

Limousines: Receipts from sales of, and repairs to, limousines for licensed limousine operators are exempt. Replacement parts are also exempt.

Machinery and equipment: The exemptions for machinery and equipment used in specific activities are discussed at the following paragraphs: manufacturing, processing, assembling, and refining (¶ 1305); utilities (¶ 1306); farming (¶ 1307); and research and development (¶ 1309).

Maintenance and cleaning services: Garbage removal and sewer services performed on a regular contractual basis for a term of 30 days or more, other than window cleaning and rodent and pest control, are exempt from tax. Also exempt is the maintenance, servicing, or repair of a residential heating unit serving no more than three families living independently and cooking on the premises. Janitorial services, however, are taxable, whether or not performed on a regular contractual basis.

CCH Caution: Parking Lot Sweeping Service

Cleaning parking lots with a vehicle that suctioned dirt and debris into a container located within the vehicle that was then emptied into dumpsters located on the customers' property was not an exempt garbage removal service. However, when the collected debris was removed from the customers' premises after the power sweeping was complete, the services were exempt (*Exterior Power Sweeping,* New Jersey Superior Court, Appellate Division, No. A-3346-97T5, April 30, 1999; CCH NEW JERSEY TAX REPORTS, ¶ 400-631).

Manufactured homes: The sales tax is levied only upon the first sale of a new manufactured or mobile home, based on the manufacturer's invoice price. Consequently, subsequent sales, and sales amounts greater than the ascertainable manufacturer's invoice price, are exempt. In addition, the sale of a used manufactured or mobile home by a person, including a dealer, is exempt from sales and use tax, whether or not the home is installed in a mobile home park.

Meals for elderly or disabled persons: Meals especially prepared and delivered by a government-funded or nonprofit food service project to homebound elderly or disabled persons, or served at a group-sitting to such persons who are otherwise homebound, are exempt.

Motor fuels: Sales of motor fuels subject to the motor fuel tax, sales of fuel to an airline for use in its airplanes, and sales to a railroad for use in its locomotives, are exempt.

Motor vehicles, commercial: Sales, rentals, or leases of commercial motor vehicles, vehicles used in combination with them, and repair and replacement parts for them are exempt. The exemption applies only to vehicles that are registered in New Jersey and (1) have a gross vehicle weight rating in excess of 26,000 pounds (determined by the capacity of the vehicle as specified by the manufacturer), (2) are operated actively and exclusively for the carriage of interstate freight under a certificate or permit issued by the Interstate Commerce Commission, or (3) are registered as farm vehicles or equipment under the Motor Vehicle Statute and have a gross vehicle weight rating in excess of 18,000 pounds.

Municipal parking: Municipal parking, storing, or garaging of a motor vehicle and receipts from charges for use of casino parking spaces or pursuant to an agreement between the Casino Reinvestment Development Authority and a casino operator are exempt.

Newspapers, magazines, and periodicals: Sales of (1) newspapers and (2) magazines and periodicals sold by subscriptions and (3) membership periodicals are exempt from tax whether or not accessed by electronic means. Receipts from sales of advertising to be published in a newspaper are exempt from tax.

Packaging materials and containers: Sales or use of wrapping paper, twine, bags, cartons, tape, rope, labels, nonreturnable containers, reusable milk containers, and all other wrapping supplies are exempt when they are for a use that is incidental to the delivery of tangible personal property. In addition, containers sold for use in a farming enterprise are exempt from tax.

Paper products: Receipts from sales of disposable household paper products, including towels, napkins, diapers, toilet tissues, diapers, cleaning tissues, paper plates, and cups, purchased for household use are exempt from tax.

Printing production machinery and equipment: Sales of production machinery, apparatus, or equipment for use or consumption directly and primarily in the following are exempt from tax: production of newspapers in the production department of a newspaper plant; production of tangible personal property for sale by persons in the business of commercial printing; periodical, book, manifold business form, greeting card or miscellaneous publishing and typesetting, photoengraving, electrotyping and stereotyping; and lithographic plate making. The exemption applies to such items as engraving, enlarging, and development equipment; internal process cameras and news and other similar transmission equipment; composing and pressroom apparatus and equipment; binding apparatus and equipment; type fonts; lead; mats; ink; plates; conveyors; stackers; and sorting, bundling, stuffing, labeling, and wrapping equipment. The exemption extends to supplies for any of the exempt items. The law specifically provides, however, that sales of motor vehicles, typewriters, and other equipment and supplies subject to sales tax are not exempt under these provisions.

Processing and printing services on property delivered outside of state: See ¶1204.

Property purchased for lease: See ¶1215 for SSUTA changes to lease transactions effective October 1, 2005.

Prior to SSUTA receipts from sales of tangible personal property purchased for lease are exempt if the property, the use of the property, or the lessee of the property is granted an exemption under the Sales and Use Tax Act. However, tax is due if the property is later leased for a nonexempt use, leased to a nonexempt person, or converted to a nonexempt use.

Railroad rolling stock, track materials and equipment: Railroads whose rates are regulated by the Interstate Commerce Commission or by the New Jersey Board of Public Utilities may make tax-free purchases of the following: locomotives, railroad cars and other railroad rolling stock, including repair and replacement parts; track materials; and communication, signal and power transmission equipment.

Recycling equipment: Receipts from sales of recycling equipment are exempt from sales and use taxes. For purposes of the exemption, "recycling equipment" means any equipment that is used exclusively to sort and prepare solid waste for recycling or in the recycling of solid waste. The term "recycling equipment" does not include conventional motor vehicles or any equipment used in a process after the first marketable product is produced or, in the case of recycling iron or steel, any equipment used to reduce the waste to molten state and in any process thereafter.

Salem County partial exemption: An exemption from 50% of the tax is provided for retail sales, other than sales of motor vehicles, alcoholic beverages, or cigarettes, made by a vendor from a place of business located in a county in which is situated an entrance to an interstate bridge or tunnel connecting New Jersey with a state that does not impose a sales and use tax, or imposes a tax at a 1% rate. Businesses located in such counties that are engaged primarily in catalogue or mail order sales are not eligible for the exemption. The State Treasurer shall annually designate the county or counties in which this exemption applies. Currently, Salem County qualifies for the 50% exemption, since an interstate bridge connects the county with the State of Delaware, which does not impose a sales and use tax.

Sales by morticians, undertakers, and funeral directors: Tangible personal property sold by morticians, undertakers, and funeral directors is exempt. However, sales to morticians, undertakers, and funeral directors of property for use in conducting funerals are taxable. Limousine services provided in connection with funeral services are not subject to tax.

Ships and other vessels, commercial and government-owned; fuel, supplies, etc.: See ¶1316.

Solar energy devices: Sales of devices or systems designed to provide heating or cooling, or electrical or mechanical power, from solar-generated energy are exempt if they meet standards for qualification. The exemption extends to devices for storing the energy. The exemption does not apply to devices or systems that would be required regardless of the energy source being utilized.

Services not considered telecommunications: Sales of the following telecommunications services are exempt: calls charged at local calling rates made through public pay phones and paid for with coins; one-way radio or television broadcasting transmissions available to the general public without a fee; telecommunications carrier access purchased for resale and cable television subscription charges.

Textbooks: Sales of school textbooks required for use by students in an educational institution approved by the Department of Education or Department of Higher Education are exempt.

Transportation charges: Receipts from the charges for transportation of persons or property are exempt except for delivery charges; transportation services provided by a limousine operator; and the transportation of energy.

See ¶1201 for SSUTA changes effective October 1, 2005.

Trigger locks and firearm vaults: Trigger locks and other devices that make firearms inoperable, as well as firearm vaults that provide secure storage for firearms, are exempt from New Jersey sales and use tax.

Truck rentals to certain freight carriers and truck services by persons not dealing with public: The rental, leasing, licensing, or interchanging of trucks, tractors, trailers, and semitrailers to freight carriers by persons not engaged in renting trucks to the public is exempt from tax. For the exemption to apply, the renting, leasing, licensing, or interchanging must be to, or with persons engaged in, a regular trade or business involving carriage of freight by such vehicles.

Similarly, services with respect to trucks, tractors, trailers, or semitrailers, rendered by persons not engaged directly or indirectly in a regular trade or business offering such services to the public, are exempt.

See also "Motor vehicles, commercial" above.

Urban enterprise zone exemptions: See ¶1315.

Vending machine sales of 25¢ or less: Receipts from coin-operated machines vending tangible personal property at 25¢ or less are exempt, but only if the retailer is primarily engaged in making such sales and maintains satisfactory records. "Primarily engaged in making such sales" means more than one-half of the total receipts from the taxpayer's business are derived from sales through coin-operated vending machines. The exemption does not apply to vending machines sales of food or drink.

Zero emission motor vehicles: Sales of zero emission motor vehicles are exempt from sales and use tax. The exemption is not applicable to partial zero-emission vehicles, including hybrids. The exemption also is not applicable to labor or parts for qualified vehicles.

¶1303 Exempt Transactions

Law: R.S. 54:32B-2, 54:32B-3, 54:32B-8.10, 54:32B-10, 54:32B-12 (CCH New Jersey Tax Reports ¶60-020, ¶60-075, ¶60-420, ¶60-450, ¶60-460, ¶60-570, ¶60-590, ¶60-635, ¶60-650, ¶60-665, ¶60-740).

The following transactions are exempt:

Sales for resale: The resale exemption applies to (1) sales of tangible personal property for resale in the same form as purchased, (2) sales of tangible personal property for resale as converted into or as a component part of a product produced for sale by the purchaser, and (3) sales of tangible personal property for use by the purchaser in the performance of a taxable service (¶1204) where the property so sold becomes a physical component of the property upon which the services are performed, or is later actually transferred to the purchaser of the service in conjunction with the performance of the service (¶1214).

The resale exemption also applies to taxable services (¶1204) purchased for resale. For example, a contractor does not pay the tax on the purchase of taxable services from a subcontractor for resale (¶1214).

¶1303

Property which is purchased exclusively for the purpose of lease or rental is purchased for resale.

A purchaser for resale must furnish to the vendor a resale certificate (Form ST-3). Form ST-3 will cover additional purchases by the same purchaser of the same type of property. However, each subsequent sales slip or purchase invoice based on this certificate must show the purchaser's name, address, and New Jersey certificate of authority number for purposes of verification. Vendors may also accept the Multi-state Tax Commission's Uniform Sales and Use Tax Certificate for resales.

Certificates must be retained by the seller for a period of not less than four years from the date of the last sale covered by the certificate. Certificates must be in the physical possession of the vendor and available for inspection on or before the 60th day following the date of the transaction to which the certificate relates.

Sales exempt under federal law: No tax is imposed on sales which New Jersey is prohibited from taxing under the United States Constitution or federal laws.

Out-of-state sales: There is no specific statutory exemption for sales of tangible personal property delivered outside the state for use outside the state. However, such sales presumably are exempt under the Commerce Clause of the United States Constitution.

Sales of motor vehicles, aircraft, and boats to certain nonresidents: Sales of motor vehicles, aircraft, and boats to a nonresident purchaser are exempt even though the nonresident takes physical possession of the vehicle in New Jersey if the following requirements are met: (1) the nonresident does not have a permanent abode in New Jersey; (2) the nonresident is not engaged in carrying on in New Jersey any employment, trade, business or profession in which the motor vehicle would be used in New Jersey; (3) the nonresident furnishes the vendor adequate evidence of his nonresident status; and (4) the nonresident does not intend to house, moor, base, or otherwise place the aircraft, boat, or other vessel in New Jersey for use on other than a transient basis or for repairs at any time within 12 months from the date of purchase.

Solicitation of sales by catalogs and flyers in interstate commerce only: The U. S. Supreme Court has held that in the absence of any retail outlets, solicitors or property in the state (Illinois), a foreign mail order company could not be required to collect and remit use tax on sales made to residents of the taxing state. The seller's sole activity in the state was solicitation of sales by catalog or flyers followed by delivery of the goods by mail or common carrier as part of a general interstate business (*National Bellas Hess, Inc. v. Department of Revenue* (1967, US SCt) 386 US 753). The *Bellas Hess* decision rested on both Due Process and Commerce Clause considerations. The position taken in *Bellas Hess* that physical presence is required to meet the requirements of the Commerce Clause was specifically reaffirmed by the High Court in *Quill Corp. v. North Dakota* (1992, US SCt) 112 SCt 1904. However, *Quill* overruled the *Bellas Hess* due process objections, holding that physical presence is not required by the Due Process Clause before a state can compel an out-of-state mail-order company to collect its use tax. Therefore, with the *Bellas Hess* due process objection removed, the Court noted that Congress is now free to decide whether, when, and to what extent the states may burden out-of-state mail-order concerns with a duty to collect use taxes.

CCH Tip: Electronic Commerce

The presence of a webpage on a computer server located in New Jersey does not give rise to a sales tax collection responsibility for an out-of-state retailer (*Response to CCH Internet/Electronic Commerce Survey*, Division of Taxation, September 22, 1999; CCH NEW JERSEY TAX REPORTS, ¶ 400-665).

A business organization entering into a contract to provide goods or services or to construct a construction project with certain state and local agencies is required to collect and remit use tax on all sales of tangible personal property delivered into New Jersey. The use tax collection requirement also applies to the contracting entity's affiliates, suppliers and subcontractors.

In a purported technical change, New Jersey expanded its sales and use tax nexus provisions to include agency and affiliate nexus concepts. That is, a seller would be required to collect New Jersey sales tax based on merely having an agent or affiliate that maintains a place of business within the state.

Casual sales: See ¶1310.

Transfers involving corporations and partnerships: Transfers to a corporation for stock when the corporation is being organized, merged, or consolidated, and distributions of property as a liquidating dividend, are exempt. Similarly, contributions of property to a partnership for a partnership interest and distributions of property to the partners by a liquidating partnership, are exempt.

Professional, insurance, or personal service: Professional, insurance, or personal service transactions that involve the transfer of tangible personal property as an inconsequential element for which no separate charges are made are specifically not retail sales. Thus, services of lawyers and accountants are exempt. Barbering and beauty parlor services are also exempt.

¶1304 Use Tax Exemptions

Law: R.S. 54:32B-6, 54:32B-11 (CCH NEW JERSEY TAX REPORTS ¶60-020).

Sales of property or services on which the sales tax has been imposed are exempt from use tax.

Specific compensating use tax exemptions are provided for the use of property or services as follows:

— *Use prior to July 1, 1966:* The use of property that had been used by the purchaser in New Jersey prior to July 1, 1966, is exempt.

— *Purchases made while nonresident:* The use of property purchased by the user while a nonresident of New Jersey is exempt, except that the use is taxable if the property is incorporated into real property in New Jersey in the performance of a contract, or in the case of tangible personal property purchased for lease. Property used in any employment, trade, business, or profession carried on in New Jersey, unless entirely in interstate or foreign commerce, does not qualify for the exemption.

— *Where sale is exempt:* The use of property or services is exempt if the sale of such property or services to a purchaser would be exempt from sales tax.

— *Use of property to make product for sale or for market sampling:* The use of property that is converted into, or becomes a component part of, a product produced for sale or for market sampling by the purchaser is exempt.

— *Paper used in publishing:* The use of paper in the publication of newspapers and periodicals is exempt.

— *Property or services on which a sales or use tax has been paid to another state:* The use of property or services on which a retail sales or use tax was due and paid, without any right to refund or credit, to another state or jurisdiction within another state is not taxable, provided the other state or jurisdiction allows a corresponding exemption when a sales or use tax is paid to New Jersey. The New Jersey use tax, however, does apply to the extent of the difference in rates if the New Jersey tax is higher.

CCH Example: Reciprocity

If a taxpayer makes a purchase in a state that has sales tax reciprocity with New Jersey, a credit is allowed for sales tax paid to that state. For example, if the purchase price is $100 and the sales tax is 4%, the taxpayer pays $4 in sales tax to that state. The New Jersey sales tax at a rate of 7% would be $7; therefore, the taxpayer owes New Jersey use tax of $3.

¶1305 Manufacturing and Processing Machinery, Apparatus, and Equipment

Law: R.S. 54:32B-8.13; Reg. Sec. 18:24-4.4 (CCH New Jersey Tax Reports ¶ 60-510).

Sales of machinery, apparatus, or equipment for use or consumption directly and primarily in the production of tangible personal property by manufacturing, processing, assembling, or refining are exempt. The exemption does not apply if the use of the property is merely incidental to the above activities, nor does the exemption apply to motor vehicles, parts with a useful life of one year or less, natural gas distributed through a pipeline, electricity, utility service, and tools and supplies used in conjunction with the machinery, apparatus, or equipment.

For administrative provisions discussing the exemption, including the meaning of "production" and of "direct and primary use," see Reg. Sec. 18:24-4.4.

See also the heading "Printing production machinery and equipment" at ¶ 1302.

See also "Facilities Sales Tax Exemption Certificate Program" at ¶ 1318.

¶1306 Machinery and Equipment for Utilities

Law: R.S. 54:32B-8.13 (CCH New Jersey Tax Reports ¶ 60-350, ¶ 60-750).

Sales of certain machinery, apparatus or equipment for use by utilities are exempt.

Utilities: Sales of machinery, apparatus, or equipment for use or consumption directly and primarily in the production, generation, transmission, or distribution of gas, electricity, refrigeration, steam, or water for sale or in the operation of sewerage systems are exempt.

Cogeneration facilities: Sales of machinery, apparatus, equipment, building materials, or structures or portions thereof used directly and primarily for cogeneration in a cogeneration facility are exempt from tax. To be exempt, the facility's primary purpose must be the sequential production of electricity and steam or other forms of useful energy used for industrial or commercial heating or cooling. The facility must be designated by the federal Energy Regulatory Commission (or its successor) as a "qualifying facility" pursuant to the Public Utility Regulatory Policies Act of 1978.

Exclusions from exemption: The above exemptions do not apply to sales, otherwise taxable, of machinery, equipment, or apparatus whose use is only incidental to utility activities.

Sales of motor vehicles, parts with a useful life of one year or less, and sales of tools or supplies, although used in connection with the exempt machinery, apparatus, or equipment, are taxable. In determining whether a part has a useful life of one year or less, the purchaser's own treatment of the item for accounting purposes is taken into consideration. The term "year," as used in this rule, means a standard calendar year of 12 months.

¶1307 Farming Exemption

Law: R.S. 54:32B-8.16; Reg. Secs. 18:24-19.1—18:24-19.6 (CCH NEW JERSEY TAX REPORTS ¶60-250).

Sales of tangible personal property and production and conservation services to a farmer for use and consumption directly and primarily in the production, handling, and preservation of farm products for sale are exempt.

The exemption applies to stock, dairy, poultry, fruit, fur-bearing animal, and truck farms, ranches, nurseries, greenhouses and other similar structures used primarily for the raising of agricultural or horticultural commodities, and orchards. Automobiles, energy, and property incorporated into a building or structure, with certain exceptions, are taxable, however. Containers used in farming are exempt.

For detailed explanation of the farming exemption, see Reg. Secs. 18:24-19.1— 18:24-19.6, and *State Tax News,* Division of Taxation, Winter 1995; CCH NEW JERSEY TAX REPORTS, ¶400-421.

¶1308 Fuel and Utilities

Law: R.S. 54:32B-8.7 (CCH NEW JERSEY TAX REPORTS ¶60-750).

Sales of gas, water, steam, fuel, and electricity delivered to consumers through mains, lines, pipe, or in containers or in bulk are exempt.

Sales and use tax applies to receipts from the sale of natural gas and electricity provided to persons in New Jersey. The tax on energy (except for electricity consumed by the generating facility producing it) and utility service (except that used by the facility providing the service) is imposed at the applicable rate on the charge made by the utility service provider. The sales and use tax exemption for gas is modified to specify that it applies to other than natural gas, and the exemption for electricity is deleted. Energy is excluded from the exemption for receipts from charges for transportation of persons or property, and from the exemptions for production and communication equipment, research and development supplies and equipment, manufacturing, and farm supplies and equipment. The enterprise zone exemptions and nonprofit organization exemptions do not apply to purchases of gas and electricity.

A sales and use tax exemption is enacted for retail sales of energy and utility service to certain qualified businesses located within an urban enterprise zone. To qualify for the exemption, the business must employ at least 500 people within the enterprise zone, at least 50% of whom are directly employed in a manufacturing process. Additionally, the energy and utility services must be used or consumed exclusively by that business within the enterprise zone. The exemption also applies to a group of two or more vertically integrated qualified business that are located within a single redevelopment area adopted pursuant to the Local Redevelopment and Housing Law (Ch. 65, Laws 2004).

The exemption allowed for retail sales of energy and utility services is expanded to apply to a qualified business that employs at least 250 people within an enterprise zone. At least 50% of the employees must be directly employed in a manufacturing process. In addition, sales of energy and utility services to a business facility located within a county that has an entrance to an interstate bridge or tunnel connecting New Jersey with a state that does not impose a sales tax or imposes the tax at a rate at least five percentage points lower than the rate in New Jersey are exempt from sales tax. To qualify for the exemption, the business must employ at least 50 people at the qualifying facility and at least 50% of those employees must be directly employed in a manufacturing process. The energy and utility services must also be consumed exclusively at that facility. A qualifying business facility must file an application for the exemption with the chief Executive Officer and Secretary of the Commerce,

Economic Growth and Tourism Commission. The application then will be processed within 20 business days of receipt, and notice of its acceptance or denial will be provided to the applicant. The exemption applies upon notice of approval of the application and expires for any year in which the business fails to meet the requirements. (Ch. 374, Laws 2006).

See ¶ 1319 for seven year exemption period for certain taxes on energy for certain manufacturers.

¶1309 Research and Development Exemption

Law: R.S. 54:32B-8.14 (CCH NEW JERSEY TAX REPORTS ¶ 60-510).

Sales of tangible personal property purchased for use or consumption directly and exclusively in research and development in the experimental or laboratory sense are exempt.

The exemption does not apply to property for use in ordinary testing or inspection of materials or products for quality control, efficiency or consumer surveys, management studies, advertising, promotions or research in connection with literary, historical or similar projects.

Effective January 1, 2009, the law clarifies that the research and development exemption explicitly includes sales of digital property in the exemption. N.J.S.A. 54:32B-8.14.

See also "Facilities Sales Tax Exemption Certificate Program" at ¶ 1318.

¶1310 Casual Sales

Law: R.S. 54:32B-2, 54:32B-8.6 (CCH NEW JERSEY TAX REPORTS ¶ 60-590).

A casual sale of tangible personal property or digital property (that is, an isolated or occasional sale of property that originally had been obtained for use by a person who is not regularly engaged in making retail sales) is exempt from both sales and use tax.

For the sale to qualify as an exempt, casual sale, the owner must conduct such sales on no more than four occasions during the calendar year, and the property must have been acquired for the owner's use (other than resale). However, each sale is not limited to one transaction but may include several transactions occurring over a period of time not to exceed one full week.

The following sales do not qualify as exempt casual sales:

— casual sales of motor vehicles, whether the vehicle is for use on the highways or otherwise;

— casual sales of boats or vessels registered or subject to registration under the New Jersey Boat Act of 1962; and

— sales of tangible personal property purchased for lease that were exempted from sales and use tax.

¶1311 Chemicals and Catalysts Used in Processing

Law: R.S. 54:32B-8.20 (CCH NEW JERSEY TAX REPORTS ¶ 60-510).

Sales of materials, such as chemicals and catalysts, which are used to induce or cause a refining or chemical process, are exempt where such materials are an integral or essential part of the processing operation, but do not become a component part of the finished product.

¶1312 Exempt Organizations

Law: R.S. 54:32B-8.22, 54:32B-9; Reg. Secs. 18:24-8.1—18:24-9.11 (CCH New Jersey Tax Reports ¶60-580).

The sales and compensating use taxes do not apply to any sales or amusement charges by or to certain organizations, or to any use or occupancy by them. The exempt organizations are as follows:

—The state of New Jersey, its agencies, instrumentalities, public corporations (including a public corporation created pursuant to agreement or compact with another state), or political subdivisions where they are the purchasers, users, or consumers. The exemption for sales by these organizations applies only to sales of services or property of a kind not ordinarily sold by private persons.

—The United States, its agencies and instrumentalities, insofar as it is immune from taxation as a purchaser, user, or consumer, or where it sells items not ordinarily sold by private persons. The Division of Taxation has advised that federal credit unions are deemed to be instrumentalities of the United States government and are therefore exempt from the New Jersey sales and use tax (*State Tax News*, Division of Taxation, November 1, 1989; CCH New Jersey Tax Reports [1989—1994 Transfer Binder], ¶400-014a). This exemption applies only to items purchased for use by the credit unions that are for activities reasonably related or incidental to the functions of federal credit unions.

—The United Nations, or any international organization of which the United States is a member, as a purchaser, user, or consumer, or as a seller of items not ordinarily sold by private persons.

—Nonprofit organizations organized and operated exclusively for religious, charitable, scientific, testing for public safety, literary or educational purposes, or for the prevention of cruelty to children or animals. However, sales of motor vehicles by such organizations are taxable unless the purchaser is also an exempt nonprofit organization or an exempt governmental entity. Also, retail sales of tangible personal property by any shop or store operated by an exempt nonprofit organization are taxable unless (1) the purchaser is also an exempt nonprofit organization or an exempt governmental entity, or (2) the organization received the property as a gift or contribution, substantially all of the work in carrying on the business of the shop or store is performed for the organization without compensation, and substantially all of the shop's or store's merchandise has been received as a gift or contribution.

Sales or amusement charges by or to a National Guard or war veterans' organization or post, the Marine Corps League, or an auxiliary unit or society of any of these organizations are exempt.

Occupancy in a hotel operated on the premises of a nonprofit organization in furtherance of the activities of the nonprofit organization is not subject to the tax on hotel occupancy.

Sales made at concession stands found in or on grounds of a state-owned and operated residential veterans facility are exempt.

For regulations detailing organizational and operational requirements for tax-exempt status for nonprofit organizations, see Reg. Secs. 18:24-8.1—18:24-9.11.

Exemption certificates: See ¶1405.

Occupancy or meals: The exempt status of an organization holding a valid exempt organization permit extends to the tax for hotel occupancy and the tax on meals if the vendor is furnished with a copy of the organization's exemption certificate (¶1405) and if all the charges on which the tax was calculated are paid by the organization using organization funds, and there is no reimbursement to the organization for the charges.

Contractors: See ¶1214.

¶1312

¶1313 Exempt Admission Charges

Law: R.S. 54:32B-3, 54:32B-9 (CCH New Jersey Tax Reports ¶ 60-230).

Admission charges of 75¢ or less are exempt (¶ 1207).

Admissions to facilities for participating sports: Charges for admission to, or use of, sporting facilities where the patron participates, such as bowling alleys and swimming pools, are exempt.

Combative sports exhibition: The tax does not apply to admission charges for boxing, sparring, wrestling matches, kick boxing or combative sports exhibitions, events, performances or contests if the charges are taxed under any other New Jersey law (admissions to such contests are generally taxable under Title 5, Chapter 2A, *Boxing, Wrestling and Combative Sports,* at rates varying from 3% to 6% depending upon the total admissions sold). Professional wrestling matches that provide entertainment rather than represent the conducting of a bona fide athletic contest are subject to sales tax because they are no longer subject to the tax governed by the Athletic Control Board.

Admission proceeds to benefit exempt organization: Admission charges are not taxable, except to the extent noted below with respect to admissions to certain athletic games and to dramatic or musical arts performances and motion picture theaters, if all of the proceeds inure exclusively to the benefit of the following:

— The state of New Jersey, its agencies, instrumentalities, public authorities and corporations (including a public corporation created pursuant to agreement or compact with another state);

— A nonprofit exempt organization (as described under "Exempt Organizations" at ¶ 1312);

— Societies or organizations conducted for the sole purpose of maintaining symphony orchestras or operas and receiving substantial support from voluntary contributions;

— National guard or veterans' organizations organized in New Jersey, no part of the net earnings of which inures to the benefit of any private shareholder or individual; or

— Local police or fire departments, or voluntary fire, ambulance, first aid or emergency companies or squads, or police or fire department retirement, pension, or disability funds for members or their heirs.

Exceptions applicable to certain types of admission charges: Special rules limit application of the exemption as follows:

— Admissions to athletic games or exhibitions are taxable unless the proceeds inure exclusively to the benefit of elementary or secondary schools, or, in the case of an athletic game between elementary or secondary schools, the entire gross proceeds inure to the benefit of a nonprofit exempt organization (as described under "Exempt Organizations" ¶ 1312).

— Carnivals, rodeos, and circuses are taxable in any case if there are any paid professional performers or operators.

— Initiation fees, membership fees, or dues charged by certain governmental and charitable health and fitness, athletic, sporting or shopping clubs.

Places to which admission is exempt: Admission charges for admission to the following are nontaxable if no part of the entire earnings inures to the benefit of any stockholders, etc.:

— Admissions to agricultural fairs where the proceeds are for the improvement, maintenance, and operation of such fairs;

— Admissions to historical homes and gardens; and

— Admissions to historic sites, houses, shrines, and museums operated by organizations preserving such historic places.

¶1314 Exempt Meals and Occupancies

Exemptions from the tax on restaurant meals, catered meals, and take-out food are noted at ¶1205. Exempt occupancies of hotel rooms are treated at ¶1206.

¶1315 Urban Enterprise Zone Exemptions

Law: R.S. 52:27H-79, 52:27H-80, 52:27H-80.2, 52:27H-86 (CCH New Jersey Tax Reports ¶60-360).

Retail sales of tangible personal property (except motor vehicles and energy) and sales of services (except telecommunications and utility service) to a qualified business for the exclusive use or consumption of the business within an urban enterprise zone are exempt from sales and use taxes provided that the designation of the enterprise zone by the Urban Enterprise Zone Authority specifically makes this exemption available to a qualified business.

The exemption is taken as a refundable exemption (prior to July 15, 2006, it was an exemption taken at the point of sale whereby businesses located in urban enterprise zones were previously permitted to make tax-free purchases for use in the enterprise zone without paying sales and use tax). Businesses located in enterprise zones, with the exception of certain qualified small businesses with annual gross receipts of less than $1 million, are required to pay tax on their purchases and apply for a refund of the tax paid. Effective for sales made after January 13, 2008, the definition of small business is a qualified entity with annual gross receipts of less than $3 million. The $3 million threshold was increased to $10 million effective February 1, 2009. Contractors may continue to purchase construction materials tax free for UEZ qualified businesses.

P.L. 2011, c.28, signed into law on March 1, 2011, applies to sales or services made or rendered on or after April 1, 2011. The law amends section 20 of P.L. 1983, c.303 (N.J.S.A. 52:27H-79) and allows all qualified urban enterprise zone (UEZ) businesses to be eligible to receive the sales tax exemption at the point of purchase regardless of annual gross receipts. Previously, P.L. 2006, c.34, (amended by P.L. 2007, c.328 and P.L. 2008, c.118) restricted the point-of-purchase exemption from sales and use tax on eligible purchases made by certain small qualified businesses for exclusive use or consumption of such business in the enterprise zone. Larger UEZ businesses had to pay sales tax at the time of purchase and then file for refunds.

In addition, an exemption from 50% of the tax is provided for retail sales made by a certified vendor from a place of business located in an urban enterprise zone and owned or leased and regularly operated by the vendor for the purpose of making retail sales. Therefore, a certified vendor is required to charge sales tax at a rate of 3.5% on all qualified sales.

However, sales of the following items and services by vendors in urban enterprise zones are subject to tax at the full 7% rate:

— alcoholic beverages;

— cigarettes;

— motor vehicles;

— manufacturing machinery, equipment, or apparatus;

— prepared foods;

— meals;

— admissions;

— catalog sales;

— energy

— rooms; and

— taxable services.

To be eligible for either exemption, businesses are required to demonstrate that they will create new employment in the municipality and that they will not create unemployment in other areas of the state, including the municipality in which the urban enterprise zone is located. However, qualified businesses having less than 50 employees are eligible if actively engaged in trade or business within an urban enterprise zone for at least one year prior to zone designation and agreement is made with the municipality in which the zone is located to undertake an investment in the zone in lieu of the employment of new employees. Businesses employing no more than 10 employees must invest at least $5,000; businesses employing more than 10 employees must invest at least $500 per employee.

Vendors must obtain authorization prior to collecting the tax at a reduced rate. An Application for Reduced Sales Tax Collections (Form UZ-1) must be filed in order to receive a certificate of authority to collect tax at the 3.5% rate.

Urban enterprise zones have been designated in several cities. See ¶707 for a list.

A sales and use tax exemption is enacted for retail sales of energy and utility service to certain qualified businesses located within an urban enterprise zone. To qualify for the exemption, the business must employ at least 250 people within the enterprise zone, at least 50% of whom are directly employed in a manufacturing process. Additionally, the energy and utility services must be used or consumed exclusively by that business within the enterprise zone. The exemption also applies to a group of two or more vertically integrated qualified business that are located within a single redevelopment area adopted pursuant to the Local Redevelopment and Housing Law (Ch. 65, Laws 2004).

The sales tax exemption allowed for retail sales of energy and utility services is expanded to apply to a qualified business that employs at least 250 people within an enterprise zone. At least 50% of the employees must be directly employed in a manufacturing process. In addition, sales of energy and utility services to a business facility located within a county that has an entrance to an interstate bridge or tunnel connecting New Jersey with a state that does not impose a sales tax or imposes the tax at a rate at least five percentage points lower than the rate in New Jersey are exempt from sales tax. To qualify for the exemption, the business must employ at least 50 people at the qualifying facility and at least 50% of those employees must be directly employed in a manufacturing process. The energy and utility services must also be consumed exclusively at that facility. A qualifying business facility must file an application for the exemption with the chief Executive Officer and Secretary of the Commerce, Economic Growth and Tourism Commission. The application then will be processed within 20 business days of receipt, and notice of its acceptance or denial will be provided to the applicant. The exemption applies upon notice of approval of the application and expires for any year in which the business fails to meet the requirements. (Ch. 374, Laws 2006).

The New Jersey Urban Enterprise Zone (UEZ) Authority is authorized to make a "UEZ-impacted business district" designation for an economically distressed business district that is negatively impacted by the presence of two or more adjacent enterprise zones in which a reduced sales tax rate is collected. A "qualified business" in a UEZ-impacted district is entitled to an exemption of 50% of the sales tax to the same extent that it is granted to a business in adjacent enterprise zones. Businesses must apply to the Division of Taxation and meet eligibility criteria and annual certification requirements. No tax credits, incentives, programs or benefits of the UEZ Act are available other than sales tax rate reduction.

¶1315

¶1316 Ships and Other Vessels; Marine Terminal Services and Equipment

Law: R.S. 54:32B-8.12 (CCH New Jersey Tax Reports ¶ 60-740).

Sales, repairs, alterations, or conversion of the following vessels are exempt:

— commercial ships (or any component, including cargo containers), barges, and other vessels of 50-ton burden or over, primarily engaged in interstate or foreign commerce;

— vessels, regardless of tonnage, primarily engaged in commercial fishing or shellfishing, including equipment necessary for harvesting fish, shellfish, crustaceans, and other aquatic organisms;

— vessels primarily engaged in commercial party boat sport fishing and subject to annual inspection by the Coast Guard;

— government-owned ships, barges, and other vessels; and

— commuter ferryboats.

Fuel and supplies: Purchases of fuel, provisions, supplies, maintenance and repairs of such vessels are also exempt. The exemption does not apply to articles purchased for the original equipping of a new ship.

Marine terminal services and equipment: Machinery, apparatus, and equipment used at marine terminal facilities to load, unload, and handle cargo carried by commercial ships, barges, and other vessels primarily engaged in interstate or foreign commerce are exempt from the sales and use tax. Also exempt are storage and other services rendered with respect to the loading, unloading, and handling of cargo at a marine terminal facility.

¶1317 Radio and Television Broadcast Production Equipment

Law: R.S. 54:32B-8.13 (CCH New Jersey Tax Reports ¶ 60-640).

Sales of machinery, apparatus, or equipment made to a commercial broadcaster operating under a broadcasting license issued by the Federal Communications Commission or to a provider of cable or satellite television program services are exempt. The machinery, apparatus, or equipment must be used or consumed directly and primarily in the production or transmission of radio or television broadcasts. The exemption does not apply to machinery, apparatus, or equipment used in the construction or operation of towers.

¶1318 Facilities Sales Tax Exemption Certificate Program

Law: R.S. 54:32B-1 *et seq.* (CCH New Jersey Tax Reports ¶ 60-510, 60-750).

A sales tax exemption certificate program is established for approved projects of new business headquarters, manufacturing facilities and research and development facilities in locations that are designated by the New Jersey State Development and Redevelopment Plan as Planning Area 1 or 2 locations. The exemption certificates apply only to property purchased for installation in approved projects, including machinery, equipment, furniture and furnishings, fixtures and building materials. Eligible property does not include motor vehicles, tools, supplies or parts with a useful life of one year or less. A project involving the renovation or expansion of an existing facility that is not in Planning Area 1 or 2 may be eligible to participate at the determination of the secretary if applicable criteria are satisfied.

¶1319 Seven Year Exemption Period from Certain Taxes on Energy for Certain Manufacturers

An exemption is provided from sales tax imposed on energy and utility services and from the transitional energy facility assessment unit rate surcharge. This exemption is to be applied only to a manufacturing facility producing products using recycled materials and satisfying several precise and complex criteria (currently applicable only to one manufacturing facility in the State). The Act provides that the exemption is in effect for seven years, and during that time, the economic effect of allowing the facility's exemption will be reviewed annually. (Ch. 94, Laws 2007).

¶1320 Postconsumer Material Manufacturing Facility Exemption

Receipts from the sale or use of energy and utility service to or by a postconsumer material manufacturing facility for use or consumption directly and primarily in the production of tangible personal property, other than energy, are exempt from New Jersey sales and use tax and the transitional energy facility assessment (TEFA) unit rate surcharge for a period of seven years beginning on January 1, 2010.

Owners of eligible postconsumer material manufacturing facilities will continue to pay the taxes as the price of energy and utility service is collected. The manufacturing facility owner then will have to file for quarterly refunds of the sales and use tax and TEFA surcharge allowable under the exemption within 30 days of the close of the calendar quarter in which the sale or use is made or rendered. If the owner of a postconsumer material manufacturing facility relocates the facility to a location outside New Jersey during the exemption period, the owner of the facility will be required to pay the amount of tax for which an exemption was allowed and refunded.

For purposes of the exemption, a "postconsumer material manufacturing facility" means a facility that:

— receives service under an electric public utility rate schedule that applied only to the owner of the facility on January 1, 2004;

— manufactures products made from "postconsumer material," provided that no less than 75% of the facility's total annual sales dollar volume of such products produced in New Jersey meets the definition of "postconsumer material";

— completes a comprehensive energy audit within the required time period as set out in the law; and

— employs, individually or collectively with affiliated facilities, at least 150 employees in New Jersey as of April 1, 2009.

SALES AND USE TAXES
CHAPTER 14
RETURNS, PAYMENT, ADMINISTRATION

¶1401	Registration
¶1402	Returns
¶1403	Payment of Tax
¶1404	Direct Payment Permits
¶1405	Exemption Certificates
¶1406	Records
¶1407	Bulk Sales
¶1408	Administration
¶1409	Assessment of Tax
¶1410	Refunds
¶1411	Advertising Absorption of Tax
¶1412	Amnesty

¶1401 Registration

Law: R.S. 54:32B-15 (CCH NEW JERSEY TAX REPORTS ¶61-240).

All persons required to collect the tax on sales, services, meals, occupancy and admissions and all persons purchasing tangible personal property for resale or lease must file a certificate of registration with the Director of the Division of Taxation. Registration is required at least 15 days before commencement or opening.

A certificate of authority or duplicate certificate of authority must be displayed at each business location.

There is no registration fee.

SSUT provides for the development of an SSUTA central online registration system which can be used as an alternative to the traditional registration system currently available through the Division of Revenue's website. Central registration constitutes registration with every member state, including those that join after the seller registers. By registering through this system, sellers agree to collect and remit tax on all sales sourced to any member state. Registration under the Agreement does not in and of itself create nexus with New Jersey for any other taxes or fees.

Sellers that register through the central system have the option of choosing between three methods of calculating, reporting and remitting the tax. These methods involve the selection of a Certified Service Provider (CSP), a Certified Automated System (CAS), or using the seller's own proprietary system. Sellers may also report and remit based on traditional means, but there are benefits to utilizing one of the other systems that will not be available for traditional systems. Privacy and confidentiality protections are also addressed.

Optional registration: Persons who are making sales of tangible personal property or services subject to the compensating use tax, and who are not otherwise required to register and collect the tax, can elect to register with the Director. The Director, in his or her discretion, can issue a certificate of authority to collect the tax.

New Use Tax Collection Requirement for Businesses Contracting with State and Local Agencies: A business organization entering into a contract to provide goods or services or to construct a construction project with certain state and local agencies is required to collect and remit use tax on any sales of tangible personal property delivered into New Jersey. The use tax collection requirement also applies to the contracting entity's affiliates, suppliers and subcontractors.

Effective December 31, 2010, the 1986 Reciprocal Agreement between the State of New Jersey and the State of New York providing Cooperative Tax Administration ("Reciprocal Agreement") is ending. Notices, New Jersey Division of Taxation, September 2010.

In a purported technical change, New Jersey expanded its sales and use tax nexus provisions to include agency and affiliate nexus concepts. That is, a seller would be required to collect New Jersey sales tax based on merely having an agent or affiliate that maintains a place of business within the state.

¶1402 Returns

Law: R.S. 54:32B-14, 54:32B-17, 54:32B-24, 54:32B-26, 54:49-3.1; Reg. Secs. 18:24-11.2, 18:24-11.3 (CCH NEW JERSEY TAX REPORTS ¶61-220, ¶89-102).

Sellers that collect more than $30,000 in New Jersey sales and use tax during the preceding calendar year must file a monthly remittance (ST-51) for the first and second months of each calendar quarter (January, February, April, May, July, August, October and November) if the amount of tax due for that month exceeds $500 pursuant to regulation N.J.A.C. 18:24B-1.4. This change was adopted in 2010 in order for New Jersey to remain in compliance with the Streamlined Sales and Use Tax Agreement. If less than $30,000 in New Jersey sales and use taxes has been collected by the seller during the preceding calendar year, a monthly remittance is not required, regardless of the amount of tax due for that particular month. This regulation supersedes N.J.A.C. 18:24-11.2 which requires a monthly remittance if the amount of tax due for the month exceeds $500, regardless of the amount of New Jersey sales and use taxes collected during the preceding month. The monthly remittance continues to be due by the 20th day of the month following the period covered by the return. All sellers registered to collect sales and use tax must file a quarterly return (ST-50) (March, June, September and December) regardless of the amount of sales and use taxes collected and/or accrued in the preceding calendar year.

The postmark date generally determined whether the return was filed on time.

CCH Tip: ST-50/ST-51 Is Paperless

During 2004, the Division of Taxation moved to a totally paperless filing and payment system for New Jersey sales and use tax. Internet filing and telephone filing are available. The phase-out of paper returns is complete and all sales tax filers must file and pay electronically as of 2005. Electronic check, electronic funds transfer and credit card payment is available.

• *Amended returns*

Amended returns, if required, are due within 20 days after notice from the Director.

• *Extensions of time*

The Director may extend the time for filing of returns for a period of not more than three months.

• *Use tax return*

If a purchaser has not paid the tax to the vendor, the purchaser must file a return and pay the tax directly to the Director within 20 days of the purchase.

¶1402

• *Annual business use tax returns*

Businesses and other entities that are not registered venders are required to file an Annual Business Use tax return by May 1 following the year in which the tax liability is incurred. If a nonvender's use tax liability for each of the prior three years was less than $2,000, a return is not required unless a use tax payment is due. Nonvendors that had a minimum $2,000 use tax liability for the three prior years are required to file quarterly returns. If a taxpayer who is filing quarterly has a use tax liability exceeding $500 for the first or second month of the quarter, the taxpayer is subject to monthly filing and payment requirements. Professionals recently subject to self-audit programs that have since filed quarterly returns may now file the ST-18 annual return, unless their use tax liability has been unusually high.

CCH Tip: Non-Reporting Status

A business may file Form C-6205-ST requesting to be placed on a non-reporting basis if it makes no sales of goods or services subject to sales tax, does not lease any goods subject to use tax, and has not had use tax liability averaging over $2,000 during the past three years.

• *Penalties and interest*

Penalty and interest provisions of the State Tax Uniform Procedure Law apply to delinquencies or failure to file returns or pay the tax (¶2010, ¶2011). In addition, certain willful acts and omissions in violation of sales and use tax provisions may result in fine or imprisonment.

¶1403 Payment of Tax

Law: R.S. 54:32B-13, 54:32B-18, 54:48-4.1 (CCH New Jersey Tax Reports ¶61-220).

Payment accompanies the quarterly return or monthly remittance statement (for due dates, see ¶1402).

Taxpayers with an annual tax liability of $10,000 or more are required to pay by electronic funds transfer. Payment by electronic funds transfer is deemed to be made on the date the payment is received by the designated depository.

Motor vehicles and boats: A motor vehicle or a boat or vessel cannot be registered, except in the case of a renewal of registration by the same owner, unless the required proof is given with respect to the sale of the motor vehicle, boat or vessel to the registrant or to the lessor that the sales or use tax has been paid or that no tax is due.

SSUTA, provides no person required to collect SUT shall be held liable for having charged and collected the incorrect amount of SUT by reason of reliance on erroneous data provided by the Director with respect to tax rates, boundaries or taxing jurisdiction assignments or contained in the taxability matrix.

Effective January 1, 2009, the law amends N.J.S.A. 54:32B-14 to provide situations where a purchaser is not liable for tax, interest, or penalty, such as reliance by a certified service provider on erroneous data provided by the Division of Taxation and reliance on erroneous data in the Division's taxability matrix. The relief from liability is limited to the erroneous classification of certain terms in the taxability matrix.

¶1404 Direct Payment Permits

Law: R.S. 54:32B-12 (CCH New Jersey Tax Reports ¶61-250).

Persons who purchase tangible personal property or services under circumstances that make it impossible to determine whether the item or service will be used for a taxable or exempt purpose may apply for a direct payment permit, which waives collection by the vendor and allows the purchaser to pay the tax directly to the Director.

Contractors, subcontractors, and repairmen may pay the tax directly to the Director upon obtaining a direct payment permit, thereby waiving collection of tax by the vendor.

A holder of a valid direct payment permit is also required by regulation to maintain and retain all records for a period of four years after the filing date for the quarterly filing period to which the records pertain.

¶1405 Exemption Certificates

Law: R.S. 54:32B-12 (CCH NEW JERSEY TAX REPORTS ¶ 61-020).

Generally, sales are taxable unless the vendor takes from the purchaser a proper resale certificate or other exemption certificate. The certificate should be signed and indicate the name, address, and certificate of registration number of the purchaser and the basis of exemption.

A seller or lessor who accepts in good faith any exemption certificate, which upon its face discloses a proper basis for exemption, is relieved of any liability for collection or payment of tax upon transactions covered by the certificate.

The New Jersey Division of Taxation has issued a sales and use tax bulletin (TB-66) that addresses the division's policy on good faith, as revised by the Streamlined Sales and Use Tax (SST) Agreement, and its applicability to the acceptance of exemption certificates. Based on revisions to the SST Agreement, good faith as it was commonly understood and applied is no longer applicable at the point of purchase. In other words, sellers are relieved from the tax otherwise due so long as the seller obtains a fully completed exemption certificate or captures the relevant data elements required under the SST Agreement within 90 days of the sale. Good faith is now only a factor during an audit situation. (TB-66)

On and after October 1, 2011, the rules in an audit situation have changed. Specifically, if the seller either has not obtained an exemption certificate or has obtained an incomplete exemption certificate, the seller has at least 120 days after the division's request for substantiation of the claimed exemption to either (1) obtain a fully completed exemption certificate from the purchaser, taken in good faith, which, in an audit situation, means that the seller obtain a certificate claiming an exemption that (a) was statutorily available on the date of the transaction, (b) could be applicable to the item being purchased, and (c) is reasonable for the purchaser's type of business; or (2) obtain other information establishing that the transaction was not subject to the tax. If the seller obtains this information, the seller is relieved of any liability for the tax on the transaction unless it is discovered through the audit process that the seller had knowledge or had reason to know at the time such information was provided that the information relating to the exemption claimed was materially false or the seller otherwise knowingly participated in activity intended to purposefully evade the tax that is properly due on the transaction. The burden is on the division to establish that the seller had knowledge or had reason to know at the time the information was provided that the information was materially false. (TB-66)

Principal exemption certificates are Resale Certificate (ST-3), Exempt Use Certificate (ST-4), Exempt Organization Certificate (ST-5), Farmer's Exemption Certificate (ST-7), Certificate of Capital Improvement (ST-8), Contractor's Exempt Purchase Certificate (ST-13), and Joint Exemption Certificate (Transportation) (ST-14).

CCH Tip: Uniform Resale Certificate

New Jersey now accepts the Multistate Tax Commission's Uniform Sales and Use Tax Certificate—Multijurisdiction. For example, the certificate will be accepted for drop shipments or when the buyer and seller are both registered in New Jersey for sales tax purposes.

The exempt organization certificate need not be used to prove tax-exempt sales to governmental agencies if the vendor retains a copy of the government purchase voucher for each sale made.

Recordkeeping requirements: Sellers are required to maintain copies of exemption certificates they have accepted for exempt sales for four years.

Blanket exemption certificates: Only one exemption certificate is necessary for additional purchases of the same general type, but a record must be kept of each sale covered by a blanket certificate. This certificate should be retained for at least four years from the date of the last purchase covered by the certificate.

Electronic certificates: If the seller and purchaser are electronic trading partners, an electronic certificate is acceptable.

SSUTA: SSUT provides that New Jersey must accept the uniform exemption certificate approved by the Governing Board for all exemptions allowed in the state. New Jersey has specified that as long as the uniform exemption certificate is completed by the purchaser and provided to the seller, the seller is relieved of responsibility for collecting sales tax, even if it is later determined that the purchaser was not eligible for the exemption. The state may also continue to accept its pre-existing exemption certificates.

If a business purchaser of a digital good, computer software delivered electronically, or a service is not the holder of a direct payment permit and knows at the time of purchase that the good, software, or service will be concurrently available for use in more than one location, the purchaser is required to provide to the seller at the time of purchase a multiple points of use (MPU) exemption form disclosing that the good or service will be concurrently available for use in more than one location.

The purchaser must apportion the purchase price of the good or service among the locations, and remit the tax on a direct pay basis. The method a purchaser may use to make the apportionment must be reasonable, uniform, consistent, and supported by the purchaser's business records as those business records exist at the time of consummation of the sale.

Upon receipt of the form, the seller is relieved of all obligation to collect, pay, or remit the tax due. The form will remain in effect for all future transactions between the seller and the purchaser until the form is revoked in writing by the purchaser.

A purchaser is not required to provide the form to a seller if the purchaser is the holder of a direct payment permit. (See ¶ 1404).

¶1406 Records

Law: R.S. 54:32B-16; Reg. Secs. 18:24-2.1—18:24-2.16 (CCH NEW JERSEY TAX REPORTS ¶ 61-260).

Persons required to collect tax must keep records of every purchase, purchase for lease, sale or amusement charge or occupancy in such form as the Director may prescribe. The Director of Taxation has issued regulations with detailed instructions concerning the records to be kept.

Effective January 1, 2009, the law extends the length of time during which sales and use tax records must be maintained from three to four years. N.J.S.A. 54:32B-16. This is a technical revision since records are currently required to be kept for four years, which is the statute of limitations for sales tax.

¶1407 Bulk Sales

Law: R.S. 54:32B-22 (CCH New Jersey Tax Reports ¶60-590).

According to the New Jersey Division of Taxation, the sale, transfer, or assignment in bulk of any part of the whole of a transferee's business assets, other than in the ordinary course of business, is deemed a casual sale and is exempt from tax.

A purchaser, transferee or assignee of some or all of a taxpayer's assets in bulk must give notice to the Director at least 10 days before taking possession of the assets or making payment.

The notice given by registered mail includes the price, terms and conditions of the proposed transfer, and whether or not the taxpayer has indicated that any sales or use taxes are owing and whether the purchaser has knowledge that any taxes are owing. If the notice requirements are not met, or if a claim by the state is not protected, then the purchaser assumes personal liability for any tax.

¶1408 Administration

Law: R.S. 54:32B-2, 54:32B-24 (CCH New Jersey Tax Reports ¶60-030, ¶61-450).

The tax is administered by the Director of the Division of Taxation.

The Director has the authority to treat as vendors the agents of vendors, making the agents jointly responsible with their principals for the collection and payment of tax. For sales tax purposes, salespersons, representatives, peddlers, and canvassers may be treated as the agents of the vendors, distributors, supervisors, or employers under which they operate, from which they obtain the tangible personal property they sell, or for which they solicit business.

¶1409 Assessment of Tax

Law: R.S. 54:32B-19, 54-32B-21, 54:32B-27, 54:49-7, 54:49-18 (CCH New Jersey Tax Reports ¶61-410, ¶61-430, ¶61-520, ¶61-620, ¶89-162).

The tax is self-assessing in that it is based on receipts from sales and collected by the vendor. However, if no return is filed or if the return filed misstates the tax due, the Director may compute the correct amount of tax due according to best available information. Factors which may be used include stock on hand, purchases, rentals, number of employees, etc.

Taxpayers have 90 days after notice of determination within which to apply to the Director for a hearing. Review of the determination following the hearing may be sought by an appeal within 90 days after the giving of notice of such determination, after compliance with statutory conditions for review, including conditions relating to deposit of security for the tax sought to be reviewed.

For appeal procedure, see ¶2005.

• *Limitation period*

Except in cases of a willfully false or fraudulent return with intent to evade the tax, no assessment of additional tax may be made after more than four years from the date on which the return was filed. If no return has been filed, the tax may be assessed at any time. Prior to the expiration of the assessment period, taxpayer may give written consent to extend the limitation period. In such case, the amount of additional tax due may be determined at any time within the extended period. The period may be further extended by subsequent written consents made before the expiration of the extended period.

¶1407

• *Jeopardy assessment*

The Director may make a jeopardy assessment if the collection of the tax is in jeopardy. The collection of any jeopardy assessment may be stayed by the furnishing of security.

• *Seller liability*

P.L. 2011, c.49, also makes changes to seller liability rules. New compliance provisions incorporate SSUTA provisions that relieve certain sellers from liability due to changes in the sales and use tax rate. The Director of the Division of Taxation may not hold a seller liable for failure to collect tax that may be due at a new tax rate if the director provides less than 30 days between the date a change in rate is enacted and the date that change takes effect. However, the relief from liability is limited and further described in the new statute.

¶1410 Refunds

Law: R.S. 54:32B-20, 54:32B-27; Reg. Sec. 18:24-23.2 (CCH New Jersey Tax Reports ¶61-610).

Application for refund or credit of tax erroneously, illegally, or unconstitutionally collected or paid may be filed within four years from the date on which the tax was paid. An application may be made by a customer or a vendor, but in either case the limitation period runs from the time the customer paid the tax to the vendor. A vendor who makes the application must be able to show that the tax has been repaid to the customer.

SSUTA provides that a purchaser may not bring a cause of action against a seller for a refund or credit of overpaid taxes unless the purchaser provided the seller written notice that the purchaser requests the refund or credit containing the information necessary for the seller to determine the validity of the request. A cause of action may not be brought until 60 days after the day on which the seller receives the written notice. Also, in connection with a purchaser's request from a seller of over-collected SUT, a seller shall be presumed to have a reasonable business practice if, in the collection of such SUT, the seller (1) uses either a provider or a system including a proprietary system, that is certified by the State; and (2) has remitted to the State all taxes collected, less any deductions, credits or collection allowances.

If a taxpayer has consented to an extension of the time in which an assessment may be made, the period in which the taxpayer may file an application for a credit or refund does not expire prior to six months after the end of the extended assessment limitation period.

The taxpayer has no right to a revision, refund, or credit of any amount of tax, interest, or penalty which has been determined to be due with respect to which the taxpayer has had a hearing or an opportunity for a hearing or has failed to avail himself or herself of the statutory remedies (¶1409). In cases where an amount of tax, interest, or penalty has been determined by the Director, amounts paid after the determination can be refunded or credited only if the determination is shown to be erroneous, illegal, or unconstitutional or otherwise improper.

• *Bad debts*

Prior to October 1, 2005, the full amount of tax on a conditional or credit sale must be paid with the return covering the period in which the sale is made (¶1212). Regulations provide that if an account receivable in connection with the sale proves to be worthless or uncollectible, the vendor is entitled to a refund of the amount, if any, by which the amount of tax paid by the vendor exceeds the total amount collected from the customer.

SSUTA defines bad debts by reference to federal law and sellers are permitted to take a deduction on their sales and use tax return. Prior law and regulations required a seller to apply for a refund and did not allow an allocation between purchase price and tax, for any payments received on the account (R.S. 54:32B-12.1).

• *Exempt organizations*

An exempt organization that holds a valid exempt organization permit and that has paid the tax on rent for room occupancy in a hotel and on charges for food and drink may apply for a refund of the tax if all the charges on which the tax was calculated were paid by the organization using organizational funds (¶1312).

¶1411 Advertising Absorption of Tax

Law: R.S. 54:32B-14 (CCH NEW JERSEY TAX REPORTS ¶61-210).

Generally, no person required to collect sales or use tax shall advertise or hold out to the public in any manner that the tax is not being collected, that it will be refunded, or that it will not be separately stated or charged. A vendor can apply to the Director for waiver of the requirement for separate statement of the tax if the vendor can show that in the vendor's particular business it would be impractical.

Vendors of goods and services that are subject to the New Jersey Sales and Use Tax may advertise that the vendor will pay the tax for the customer subject to the following conditions: The advertising must indicate that the vendor is paying the tax and may not imply that the sale or charge is exempt from taxation; any sales slip, invoice, receipt or other statement of the price or service charge paid or payable given to the customer must state the tax will be paid by the vendor; and the vendor must pay the tax due on the retail sale or service receipt as trustee for and on account of New Jersey and will have the same liability for the amount of tax as for an amount collected from a customer (Ch. 42 (A.B. 1786), Laws 2003).

¶1412 Amnesty

Law: R.S. 54:32B-17 (CCH NEW JERSEY TAX REPORTS ¶61-450).

Amnesty is no longer available. Under the SSUTA, a seller was granted amnesty under certain conditions. A seller will be granted amnesty for uncollected or unpaid sales or use taxes if the seller was not licensed in the state at any time during the 12-month period prior to New Jersey's participation under the SSUTA agreement, the seller obtains a license within a 12-month period beginning on the date of New Jersey's participation under the SSUTA agreement, and the seller is registered under the SSUTA agreement.

A seller may not receive amnesty for a tax (1) collected by the seller; (2) remitted by the seller; (3) that the seller is required to remit on the seller's purchases; or (4) arising from a transaction that occurred within a time period that is under audit if the seller has received notice of the commencement of an audit and the audit has not been completed, including all administrative and judicial remedies in connection with the audit.

Amnesty granted to a seller applies to the time period during which the seller was not licensed and remains in effect if, for a period of three years, the seller remains registered under the agreement and collects and remits the appropriate taxes. Amnesty will not be allowed where a seller commits fraud or an intentional misrepresentation of a material fact.

PART V
INHERITANCE TAXES
CHAPTER 15
INHERITANCE AND ESTATE TAXES

¶ 1501	Overview
¶ 1502	Inheritance Tax Rates and Exemptions
¶ 1503	Computation of Inheritance Tax
¶ 1504	Taxable Transfers Subject to Inheritance Tax
¶ 1505	Settlement of Domiciliary Disputes
¶ 1506	Property Subject to Inheritance Tax
¶ 1507	Inheritance Tax Deductions
¶ 1508	Computation of Estate Tax
¶ 1509	Returns and Assessment
¶ 1510	Payment and Refund
¶ 1511	Notice and Waivers

¶1501 Overview

New Jersey is one of only a few states with both an estate tax and an inheritance tax. New Jersey has imposed an inheritance tax since 1892. The present New Jersey transfer inheritance tax is imposed by Chapter 33 and following of Title 54, Revised Statutes of New Jersey.

The New Jersey statute imposes a transfer inheritance tax or succession tax at graduated rates upon the fair market value of amounts received by any transferee other than a Class "A" transferee.

Features of the New Jersey transfer inheritance tax include the following:

— An exemption is allowed on transfers to certain charitable and religious institutions, etc.

— For nonresidents, an inheritance tax is imposed only upon the transfer of real property and tangible personal property located in New Jersey. No tax is imposed on intangible property of a nonresident decedent.

— When the taxable property of a nonresident decedent is not specifically bequeathed or devised, the tax is computed on the entire estate and prorated according to the proportion which the taxable property in New Jersey bears to the entire estate.

— Provision is made for reciprocity with other states in the enforcement of domiciliary inheritance taxes.

New Jersey has imposed an estate tax since 1934. The present New Jersey estate tax is imposed by Chapter 38 and following of Title 54, Revised Statutes of New Jersey. The New Jersey estate tax applies only to resident decedents.

Originally, the New Jersey estate tax was enacted to absorb the credit allowable under the federal estate tax law for the amount of death taxes-including the inheritance tax-paid by the decedent. Changes made to the federal estate tax in 2001 gradually phased out the state death tax credit for decedents dying after December 31, 2001. This would have eliminated the New Jersey estate tax.

In response to the change in the federal estate tax law, New Jersey decoupled its estate tax from the federal estate tax. For decedents dying after December 31, 2001, the New Jersey estate tax is based on the maximum allowable state death tax credit as of December 31, 2001—regardless of any subsequent changes to federal estate tax law. The result: taxable estates in excess of $675,000 are subject to New Jersey estate tax.

Historical Background: New Jersey Estate Tax for Decedents Dying 1/1/2002–6/30/2002

The legislation decoupling New Jersey's estate tax from the federal estate tax was enacted on July 1, 2002, but was made effective to decedents dying after January 1, 2002. Although this retroactive tax increase was found by the Tax Court to be constitutional, some estates claimed a refund for New Jersey estate taxes imposed as a result of this retroactive application of the law on the grounds that such imposition would be "manifestly unjust." See *Oberhand v. Director, Division of Taxation*, 193 N.J. 558 (2008), for circumstances determined to be manifestly unjust, and *Rappeport v. Director, Division of Taxation*, 22 N.J. Tax 422 (Tax 2005), for circumstances determined not to be manifestly unjust.

New Jersey transfer inheritance and estate taxes are self-assessing, that is, the taxpayer (executor, administrator or duly authorized estate representative) must compute and pay the tax due.

¶1502 Inheritance Tax Rates and Exemptions

These rates are applicable to estates of decedents dying on or after March 1, 1992.

• *Class exemptions*

Surviving Spouse: Transfers of property to the surviving spouse, domestic partner (for decedents dying on or after July 10, 2004) or civil union partner (for decedents dying on or after February 19, 2007) of a decedent are exempt from the New Jersey transfer inheritance tax.

Class A: Transfers of property to a father, mother, grandparent, child, or children, legally adopted child or children, mutually acknowledged child, stepchild or issue of any child or adopted child of a decedent are exempt from the New Jersey transfer inheritance tax.

Class B: Religious or charitable institutions. [Repealed by Ch. 61, L. 1962, eff. July 1, 1963.]—See "Charitable exemptions" below.

Class C: A brother or sister of a decedent, a wife or widow of a son of a decedent, or a husband or widower of a daughter of a decedent.

Exemption: $25,000 per Class C beneficiary.

Class D: Persons or institutions not otherwise classified.

Exemption: None. However, if the share passing to a Class D beneficiary is less than $500, there is no tax.

• *Rates*

Rates

| | | Class C | | Class D | |
		Tax on Col. 1	Rate on Excess	Tax on Col. 1	Rate on Excess
Value of Share					
(1)	(2)	(3)	(4)	(5)	(6)
$0	$25,000	$0	0%	$0	15%
25,000	700,000	0	11%	3,750	15%
700,000	1,100,000	74,250	11%	105,000	16%
1,100,000	1,400,000	118,250	13%	169,000	16%
1,400,000	1,700,000	157,250	14%	217,000	16%
1,700,000	. . . . .	199,250	16%	265,000	16%

• *Domestic partners*

The Domestic Partnership Act, which establishes domestic partnerships for same sex and opposite sex (age 62 and older) unrelated partners, made significant changes to the transfer inheritance tax, applicable to decedents dying on or after July 10, 2004. The Act exempts all transfers made by will, survivorship, or contract to a surviving domestic partner. This includes a membership certificate or stock in a cooperative housing corporation and the value of any pension, annuity, retirement allowance, or return of contributions. (*Notice*, New Jersey Division of Taxation, August 11, 2004, ¶ 401-008)

• *Civil union partners*

If a decedent's death occurs on or after February 19, 2007, property passing to the decedent's surviving civil union partner is entirely exempt from the tax. In many instances, if all of a decedent's property passes to a surviving spouse/civil union partner, children, stepchildren, parents, grandparents or grandchildren, it will not be necessary to file an inheritance tax return with the New Jersey Division of Taxation. In such cases, as long as the decedent's taxable estate plus adjusted taxable gifts is $675,000 or less, it may be possible to use Form L-8 to secure the release of bank accounts, stocks, bonds and brokerage accounts and if there was any real property in the name of the decedent, Form L-9 (or Form L-9NR for a non-resident survivor) may be filed to release the state's lien on the real property. (*Civil Union Act Implementation*, New Jersey Division of Taxation, February 23, 2007, ¶ 401-258)

The offspring of a biological parent conceived by the artificial insemination of that parent who is a partner in a civil union couple is presumed to be the child of the non-biological partner. *In the Matter of the Parentage of the Child of Kimberly Robinson*, 383 N.J. Super. 165; 890 A.2d 1036 (Ch. Div. 2005) recognized that the non-biological parent of a New York registered domestic partnership recognized in New Jersey is presumed to be the biological parent of a child conceived by the other partner through artificial insemination where the non-biological partner has "show[n] indicia of commitment to be a spouse and to be a parent to the child.". The Civil Union Act also states that "the rights of civil union couples with respect to a child of whom either becomes the parent during the term of the civil union, shall be the same as those of a married couple with respect to a child of whom either spouse or partner in a civil union couple becomes the parent during the marriage." (Sec. 37:1-31(e), R.S., ¶ 94-413c; *Civil Union Act Implementation*, New Jersey Division of Taxation, February 23, 2007, ¶ 401-258)

The Civil Union Act does not affect the treatment of domestic partners for purposes of the transfer inheritance tax unless domestic partners enter into a civil union, thus ending their domestic partner status. (*Civil Union Act Implementation*, New Jersey Division of Taxation, February 23, 2007, ¶ 401-258)

• *Charitable exemptions*

Property passing to or for the use of the State of New Jersey, or to or for the use of a municipal corporation within the state or other political subdivision thereof, for exclusively public purposes is exempt from the New Jersey transfer inheritance tax. Also exempt from the tax is that part of a decedent's estate passing to, or the use of, or in trust for any educational institution, church, hospital, orphan asylum, public library, or Bible and tract society or to, for the use of, or in trust for any institution or organization organized and operated exclusively for religious, charitable, benevolent, scientific, literary, or educational purposes, including any institution instructing the blind in the use of dogs as guides, no part of the net earnings of which inures to the benefit of any private stockholder or other individual or corporation. However, this exemption shall not extend to transfers of property to such educational institutions or organizations of other states, the District of Columbia, territories and foreign countries that do not grant an equal and like exemption of transfers of property for the benefit of such institutions and organizations of New Jersey.

¶1503 Computation of Inheritance Tax

• *Residents*

The inheritance tax is computed upon the fair market value, at the time of death, of the amount in excess of the exemption (if any) that passes to each beneficiary. The exemption, if any, is deducted from the first bracket and the balance is taxable at the rates set out in the table above.

• *Nonresidents*

Where property is specifically devised, the same rates and exemptions apply in the case of nonresidents as in the case of residents. Where property is not specifically devised, the same rates and exemptions apply, but the tax is computed on the entire estate of the nonresident and that proportion taken which represents the proportion of the taxable property in New Jersey to the total estate.

¶1504 Taxable Transfers Subject to Inheritance Tax

• *Residents*

Transfers are taxable when made by:

— will;

— intestate law;

— grant or gift in contemplation of death (unless proof to the contrary is shown, transfers within three years of death are deemed to have been so made); and

— grant or gift intended to take effect at or after death, except bona fide sales or exchanges.

Special types of property interests are treated as follows:

— Dower interest is not taxable:

— The transfer of property through the exercise of a power of appointment is taxable as a transfer from the estate of the donor and not as one from the donee;

— Jointly held property is taxable in full in the estate of the deceased joint tenant except to the extent that it can be shown that the property or a part of it belonged originally to the survivor and never belonged to the decedent, except for the right of a spouse, as surviving joint tenant with his or her deceased spouse, or the right of a domestic partner, as surviving joint tenant with that person's deceased domestic partner, to the immediate ownership or possession and enjoyment of a membership certificate or stock in a cooperative housing corporation, the ownership of which entitles such member or stockholder to occupy the real estate for dwelling purposes as the principal residence of the decedent and spouse or domestic partner;

— Tenancies by the entirety are exempt;

— Insurance proceeds on the life of a decedent payable to a named beneficiary directly or passing to a named beneficiary in trust are exempt from tax (the transfer, relinquishment, surrender or exercise of the right to nominate or change the beneficiary of an insurance contract is exempt);

— War risk insurance is exempt providing the property was not received by the decedent before death;

— Retirement benefits which are a direct result of the decedent's employment under a qualified plan as defined by section 401(a), (b) and (c) or 2039(c) of the Internal Revenue Code, payable to a surviving spouse or domestic partner are exempt;

— Servicemen's annuities payable to beneficiaries other than the decedent's estate or estate representatives are exempt; and

— Federal civil service retirement benefits payable to beneficiaries other than the decedent's estate are specifically exempted.

• *Nonresidents*

The same transfers, where they come within the scope of the statute, are taxable the same as in the case of resident decedents.

¶1505 Settlement of Domiciliary Disputes

The law provides for compromise of state death taxes in cases where there is a dispute over the question of the decedent's domicile.

¶1506 Property Subject to Inheritance Tax

• *Residents*

Real property and tangible personal property within the state and intangible personal property wherever situated are taxable if made the subject of a taxable transfer.

• *Nonresidents*

Real property and tangible personal property within the state are taxable. Intangibles of nonresidents are not taxable in New Jersey.

¶1507 Inheritance Tax Deductions

• *Residents*

The following items are deductible:

— debts of decedent (but only to the excess of the value of the property by which it is secured if the security is without the state);

— reasonable expenses of last illness and funeral;

— ordinary expenses of administration, including executors' and attorneys' fees;

— state and local taxes up to the date of death of decedent; and

— inheritance taxes paid other states.

Mortgages are deductible from the mortgaged property so that in making the return only the value of the equity is shown.

• *Nonresidents*

The same deductions are allowed in the case of nonresident decedents as in the case of resident decedents.

¶1508 Computation of Estate Tax

The New Jersey estate tax is designed to absorb the credit allowable for the payment of state death taxes under the federal estate tax law in effect on December 31, 2001. The New Jersey estate tax is only applicable to resident decedents. The New Jersey estate tax is computed as the maximum federal estate tax credit for state inheritance, estate, succession or legacy taxes allowable under the provisions of the Internal Revenue Code in effect on December 31, 2001. Alternatively, the person responsible for the payment of tax may elect to determine the New Jersey estate tax based on the Simplified Tax System described in ¶1509, below.

For example, a decedent who died on June 30, 2012 with a taxable estate of $5,220,000 would not owe any federal estate tax because his entire estate would be sheltered by the federal estate tax exemption. Under current New Jersey law, a New Jersey estate tax of $420,800 would be due which is the maximum state death tax credit that would have been available to decedent's estate if he had died on December 31, 2001.

The New Jersey estate tax may be reduced by the amount of death taxes actually paid to a U.S. state, territory or the District of Columbia (including New Jersey inheritance tax actually paid). With respect to death taxes paid to jurisdictions other than New Jersey, the reduction is based on the proportion that the out-of-state property bears to the entire taxable estate.

In general, if a federal estate tax return in required to be filed for a decedent's estate, any election made on the New Jersey estate tax return must be consistent with the corresponding election made on the federal estate tax return. For example, it is not possible to make a qualified terminable interest property ("QTIP") election under section 2056(b)(7) of the Internal Revenue Code for purposes of the New Jersey estate tax if a corresponding QTIP election is not made for the same property for federal purposes (assuming a federal estate tax return is required).

Section 3 of the Defense of Marriage Act ("DOMA") defined marriage for all federal law purposes as a legal union only of a man and a woman. Under DOMA, the federal estate tax marital deduction was not available for transfers to a same-sex spouse, civil union partner or domestic partner. The United States Supreme Court struck down this provision on June 26, 2013 in *United States v. Windsor* (Sup. Ct. Doc. No. 12-307, Decided June 26, 2013), recognizing a legally-married same-sex couple as "married" under the Internal Revenue Code. Therefore, the federal estate tax marital deduction now is available for transfers to a legally-married same-sex spouse.

In a decision dated September 27, 2013 the Law Division of the New Jersey Superior Court ruled in *Garden State Equality v. Dow* (Docket No. L-1729-11), that New Jersey must recognize same-sex marriage because partners in civil unions are denied federal benefits in violation of the New Jersey constitution. The *Windsor* case confers "married" status for federal tax purposes only to same-sex couples who are legally married. Civil union partners and domestic partners are not considered "married" for federal tax purposes. Revenue Ruling 2013-17. The federal estate tax does not allow a marital deduction for property passing to a domestic partner or civil union partner.

For New Jersey estate tax purposes, a marital deduction is permitted for transfers to a civil union partner or domestic partner of a decedent dying on or after February 19, 2007. The federal estate tax return of a deceased civil union partner must be prepared and filed as though the decedent were single. To compute the New Jersey estate tax a "dummy" 2001 Form 706 is completed as though the Internal Revenue Code treated a surviving civil union partner and a surviving spouse in the same manner. (Civil Union Act Implementation, New Jersey Division of Taxation, February 23, 2007, ¶401-258.)

¶1509 Returns and Assessment

• *Inheritance tax return*

An inheritance tax return must be filed by the executor or administrator within eight months of the date of death of the decedent. The administration of the statute is charged to the Director of the Division of Taxation in the Department of the Treasury. The estate of a resident decedent files its return on Form IT-R. The estate of a nonresident decedent uses Form IT-NR. Forms may be obtained from the New Jersey Division of Taxation website www.state.nj.us/treasury/taxation/prntinh.shtml.

Often, if all of a decedent's property passes to a surviving spouse, children, stepchildren, parents, grandparents, or grandchildren, it is not necessary to file an inheritance tax return with the Division of Taxation.

• *Future interests*

New Jersey inheritance tax on an executory devise or the transfer of property subject to a contingency or a power of appointment is payable within two months after the transferee comes into enjoyment or possession of the property.

• *Compromise of tax*

The Director of the Division of Taxation has authority to revise, alter, compromise and settle inheritance and estate or transfer taxes where there is reasonable doubt of the state's ability to enforce the tax or there is a reasonable doubt that the tax lien is valid or unimpaired.

CCH Tip: Compromise Tax on Future Interests

Although the inheritance tax may not be due until a future date, it may be advisable to enter into a compromise of the tax with the Division of Taxation that will finally dispose of the tax in exchange for its immediate payment. The compromise proposal can be included on Form IT-R, together with an attached explanation of how the proposed amount was calculated.

• *Final determination*

The District Supervisor of the Transfer Inheritance Tax Branch makes the appraisal but the Director of the Division of Taxation makes the final determination of the tax.

• *Estate tax return*

If the decedent's gross estate plus adjusted taxable gifts (as determined in accordance with federal estate tax law in effect on December 31, 2001) exceeds $675,000, a New Jersey estate tax return must be filed within nine months after the decedent's death. There are two ways of filing the return.

The Form 706 method requires the filing of New Jersey Form IT-Estate together with a 2001 federal Form 706, completed as if the decedent had died on December 31, 2001.

If a federal estate tax return has not been filed (and will not be filed) or is not required to be filed with the IRS, in addition to the Form 706 method a Simplified Tax System method is permitted, provided it produces a tax liability similar to the Form 706 method. Under this alternate method, Form IT-Estate is filed along with New Jersey Form IT-R (inheritance tax return), completed as if the decedent had died on December 31, 2001. The net estate shown on the inheritance tax return is adjusted as follows to determine the value of the estate using the Simplified Tax System: (i) real and tangible property located outside of New Jersey is added, (ii) the proceeds of a life insurance policy owned by the decedent (or transferred within three years of death) paid to any beneficiary other than the decedent's estate, executor or administrator is added, (iii) transfers made within three years of death that are not included in the net estate shown on the inheritance tax return are added, (iv) property passing outright to the surviving U.S.-citizen spouse is deducted, and (v) property passing for charitable purposes is deducted.

If a federal estate tax return is filed for the decedent's estate, a copy must be submitted to the New Jersey Division of Taxation within 30 days of the date of filing of the federal estate tax return. Elections made for purposes of the federal estate tax (e.g., the QTIP election under IRC § 2056(b)(7)) must also be made for purposes of the New Jersey estate tax.

¶1509

• *Appeals*

Any interested person who is dissatisfied with an order, finding, decision, or assessment of the Director may appeal to the Tax Court.

¶1510 Payment and Refund

• *Time for payment*

The tax is due and payable at the date of death of the decedent, and if not paid within eight months (nine months for the estate tax) from such date the executors, administrators, grantees, donees, or trustees shall be required to give bond to the state of New Jersey for payment. The tax is to be paid to the State Treasurer. The same general rules apply in the payment of taxes due from nonresident estates. See "Future interests" section above for an exception to this rule.

• *Receipt for payment*

On payment of the tax a receipt is issued by the Treasurer of the State, and this receipt is the proper voucher in the settlement of estate accounts. No notice of assessment is given until the taxes are paid.

• *Interest and discount*

Interest at the rate of 10% per annum begins eight months after the death of the decedent (nine months for the estate tax) if the tax is not paid within that time. If an extension to pay is granted, interest may be reduced to a 6% rate by the Division of Taxation, but, when the extension expires, the 10% rate applies. In case the decedent dies while a member of the Armed Forces of the United States, interest is not chargeable until the expiration of eight months after receipt of official notification of the death of the decedent by the spouse, parent, or next of kin. There is no discount for advance payment. Money received by executor or administrator for payment of the tax must be paid over to the Treasurer of the State within 30 days.

• *Liability for payment*

The administrators, executors, trustees, grantees, donees or vendees are personally liable for the taxes until they are paid. The statute does not specify that the beneficiary is himself personally liable unless he is a donee, but under the lien and enforcement provisions of the estate and inheritance tax acts the actual liability of the property passing to him can insure the payment and collection of the tax.

• *Reciprocity*

Reciprocity with other states is provided for in the collection of transfer taxes imposed by the state of domicile, where a nonresident estate is being administered in the local probate courts.

• *Refunds*

Refund may be had for taxes paid erroneously if claim is made within three years of the date of payment, or from the date of final determination of the tax by a court of competent jurisdiction. Application should be made to the Director of the Division of Taxation in the Department of the Treasury, who if satisfied that the refund is due, will certify the same and a warrant will be drawn on the State Treasurer for the amount of the refund.

CCH Tip: Protective Claim for Refund

N.J.S.A. 54:38-3 provides that applications for the refund of taxes claimed to have been excessively or erroneously paid must be filed with the Director of the Division of Taxation within three years from the date of payment. In some circumstances, the actual amount of estate tax due may not be determinable within that three year limitations period. To preserve the right to an eventual refund, it is necessary to file a protective claim for refund within the three-year limitations period. The Division of Taxation provides a form on which to make such a protective claim for refund (Form IT-PRC) and states that a protective refund claim will not be deemed to be complete until the form is fully completed. *See Estate of Frank J. Ehringer v. Director, Division of Taxation* (Tax Court of New Jersey, Docket No. 009126-2008), denying a refund of estate tax paid which was filed after the three-year statute of limitations where the protective refund claim was not made.

¶1511 Notice and Waivers

• *Estate tax*

For decedents dying after December 31, 2001, the estate tax is a lien on all property of a decedent until paid, and no property owned by a decedent as of the date of death may be transferred without the written consent of the Director of the Division of Taxation. Consent and waiver procedures are set forth in regulations at N.J.A.C. 18:26-11.1, *et seq.*

• *Decedents dying prior to January 1, 2002*

For deaths occurring before January 1, 2002, the consent of the Director of the Division of Taxation, in the form of a waiver, is required for the transfer to parties other than Class A beneficiaries of New Jersey real estate, stock of New Jersey corporations or banking institutions and deposits with New Jersey banking institutions. If the transfer is to a Class A beneficiary, an Affidavit and Self-Executing Waiver (Form L-8) is required by the transfer agent or bank. The transfer of real estate to a Class A beneficiary requires the filing of a Form L-9, except in the case of real estate held by the decedent and a spouse as tenants by the entirety.

• *Decedents dying after December 31, 2001*

For deaths occurring after December 31, 2001, where the decedent's taxable estate plus adjusted taxable gifts is $675,000 or less, the pre-2002 procedures described above continue to apply. For all other transfers (including those to Class A beneficiaries), a waiver will have to be obtained from the New Jersey Division of Taxation. However, funds held in the name of a decedent in any bank may be transferred to a new account in the same bank in the name of the estate without obtaining a waiver.

• *Transfers not subject to waiver*

Waivers are not required for transfers of salaries, accounts receivable, payments under pension, profit sharing or bonus plans, automobiles, mortgages, and household and personal effects.

• *Release under blanket consent*

The Director of the Division of Taxation, by blanket consent, permits New Jersey banks and other financial institutions to release 50% of all funds on deposit in the name of the decedent, whether in his name individually or jointly. In addition, banks may release funds on deposit for the payment of New Jersey inheritance tax or New Jersey estate tax.

• *Small estates*

Waivers are not required if a resident decedent's gross estate for tax purposes does not exceed $5,000, if the applicant is the spouse of the decedent, or $200, if the applicant is another person. An Affidavit of Surviving Spouse or Affidavit of Next of Kin in Lieu of Administration must be obtained from the Surrogate of the county in which the decedent died a resident before any funds may be released.

- *Waiver prior to final return*

Where circumstances require that a waiver be obtained prior to the filing of the inheritance tax return for a resident decedent, the request for a waiver should be made by the executor, administrator or other proper representative using Form L-4.

- *Nonresidents*

No waivers are required in estates of nonresidents, except for an inheritance tax waiver for real property located in New Jersey. Affidavits of domicile are required to establish that the decedent was legally domiciled in a jurisdiction other than New Jersey.

PART VI
PROPERTY TAXES
CHAPTER 16
REAL PROPERTY TAXES

¶1601	Scope of Chapter
¶1602	Imposition of Tax
¶1603	Property Subject to Tax
¶1604	Property Exempt
¶1605	Homestead Property Tax Reimbursement Program (Senior Freeze)
¶1606	Basis and Rate of Tax
¶1607	Assessment Procedure and Equalization
¶1608	Returns and Payment
¶1609	Administration—Penalties, Refunds, Appeals

¶1601 Scope of Chapter

Property taxes in New Jersey are imposed on real property. Intangible personal property is exempt.

Taxes on real property are levied by the local taxing districts, which assess and collect the taxes under the supervision of the county boards of taxation.

The purpose of this chapter is to give a general picture of the nature and application of the real property tax and the manner of its administration. It is not intended to provide detailed coverage. It covers, generally, the questions of what property is subject to tax, the base and rate of tax, and the requirements for filing returns and making payments.

Ch. 118, Laws 2009, establishes a pilot program in Gloucester County for the transfer of the municipal property tax assessment to the county.

¶1602 Imposition of Tax

(CCH New Jersey Tax Reports ¶20-010).

The local taxing districts assess and collect real property taxes on behalf of the municipality, the county, and school or other districts. Thus, all general property taxes are assessed and collected on one tax bill.

Taxes are levied and collected pursuant to the provisions of the Revised Statutes of New Jersey. Consequently, assessment and collection procedures are generally uniform throughout the state. However, the percentage of true value at which property is assessed varies among the counties (¶1606).

¶1603 Property Subject to Tax

Law: R.S. 40:48E-5, 54:4-1, 54:4-1.16, 54:4-23.2, 54:4-23.8, 54:4-23.12, 54:11-3, 54:29A-7, 54:29A-16, 54:29A-17 (CCH New Jersey Tax Reports ¶20-105—20-335).

All real property is subject to tax unless specifically exempted. For principal exemptions, see ¶1604.

Railroads: Property owned by a railroad and not used for railroad purposes is taxed by the local taxing districts in the same manner as other real property in the district.

Railroad real property used for railroad purposes is classified by the Director, Division of Taxation into the following classes:

— Class I, main stem;

— Class II, real estate used for railroad purposes other than the main stem and facilities used in passenger service; and

— Class III, facilities used in passenger service.

The tax is not imposed on Class I or Class III property (¶1604). Class II property is subject to a state tax (¶1606). The Consolidated Rail Corp. (Conrail) was declared to be exempt from the state-imposed tax on property used for railroad purposes by the Special Court of the Regional Rail Reorganization Act, in *State of New Jersey et al. v. Consolidated Rail Corp. et al.*; CCH NEW JERSEY TAX REPORTS [1979—1989 Transfer Binder], ¶201-459, as a result of the federally provided exemption from state tax (except taxes imposed by a state's political subdivisions) under the Northeast Rail Service Act of 1981.

Farm lands: Special provisions relate to farm land. Under the Farmland Assessment Act the valuation of farm land may, upon application, be limited to its value for agricultural or horticultural use rather than the potential value for residential or industrial development. To qualify, land must be at least 5 acres in size and must be devoted to agricultural or horticultural use in each of two preceding years. The land must also produce a certain amount of gross sales. Applications must be filed with the Tax Assessor by August 1 of pretax year. All structures (except single-use agricultural or horticultural facilities) and farmhouses, including the land upon which situated or used in connection therewith, and other farm structures are valued and taxed by the same standards as other real property. Upon change in use, additional roll-back taxes are imposed.

P.L. 2013, c.43, amends the Farmland Assessment Act for New Jersey property tax purposes, and applicable to tax years commencing with tax year 2015, this legislation requires the State Board of Agriculture and the Department of Agriculture to develop guidelines describing generally accepted agricultural and horticultural practices that may be used by municipal tax assessors, county assessors, county tax administrators, and other appropriate local government officials to assist them in determining whether land may be deemed to be in agricultural use, horticultural use, or actively devoted to agricultural or horticultural use pursuant to the Farmland Assessment Act of 1964. The Division of Taxation will review the guidelines and, upon its approval thereof, adopt them as rules and regulations.

Upon the request of a municipal tax assessor, county assessor, county tax administrator or other appropriate local official, the Division, in consultation with the State Board of Agriculture and the Department of Agriculture will provide advice to assist such individuals in determining whether a particular parcel may qualify for valuation, assessment and taxation based on the agricultural and horticultural activities taking place on the parcel.

The legislation raises from $500 to $1,000 the minimum gross sales of agricultural or horticultural products produced thereon and payments standard for typical agricultural or horticultural lands to qualify for farmland assessment on the first five acres of land. This change does not apply to woodland managed subject to a woodland management plan, which would continue, as under current law, to qualify for farmland assessment with minimum gross sales and payments of $500 or land subject to a forest stewardship plan, which, under current law, has no minimum income qualifying standard for farmland assessment.

The legislation also provides that income imputed to land used for grazing will be income imputed to cropland being used as pasture from time to time, as well as permanent pasture land used for grazing.

¶1603

Landowners who previously met the farmland assessment standards but cannot or do not meet the new standards will not be required to pay the roll-back tax at the time of that disqualification provided they do not abandon the agricultural or horticultural use. However, because at that point the property would no longer be farmland assessed under the new standards, the landowner will then be required to pay the full property taxes on the land.

The legislation allows for the continuation of the farmland assessment under the former minimum income threshold for farms receiving payments from soil conservation programs until the expiration of the existing contract period for the farm.

The legislation also details continuing education and licensing requirements for assessors; establishes State Farmland Evaluation Committee requirements; and explains farmland assessment application requirements.

Ch. 213, Laws 2009, allows any person who owns preserved farmland to construct, install and operate biomass, solar or wind energy generation facilities, structures and equipment on the farm to generate power or heat and to make improvements to buildings or structures on the land for that purpose. These uses now qualify for the preferential treatment provided under the Farmland Assessment Act.

Ch. 256, Laws 2009, establishes forest stewardship and forest certification programs in the Department of Environmental Protection and expands the Farmland Assessment Act of 1964 to provide differential property tax assessment to owners of forest land who implement an approved forest stewardship plan.

Hotels: For any calendar year, hotel owners, subject to the hotel use or occupancy tax, are required to pay either the real property tax or the hotel use or occupancy tax, whichever is greater (¶1903). However, by ordinance the city may require hotel owners to pay both taxes.

Attached personal property: Real property includes personal property affixed to real property or an appurtenance to real property unless

— it can be severed or removed without material injury to either the real property or itself, and the property is not of a type that is ordinarily intended to be permanently affixed to real property, or

— it is machinery, apparatus, or equipment used or held for use in business and is neither a structure nor machinery, apparatus, or equipment whose primary purpose is to enable a structure to support shelter, contain, enclose, or house persons or property (¶1604).

¶1604 Property Exempt

Law: Art. VIII, Sec. 1, Par. 3, N.J. Const.; R.S. 6:1-97, 40:55C-65, 40A:21-1—40A:21-21, 54:4-1, 54:4-1.5, 54:4-1.6, 54:4-1.19, 54:4-3.3—54:4-3.33, 54:4-3.48, 54:4-3.52, 54:4-3.55, 54:4-3.56, 54:4-3.59, 54:4-3.60, 54:4-3.64, 54:4-3.131, 54:4-3.138—54:4-3.149, 54:4-3.153, 54:4-3.154, 54:4-1, 54:4-20, 54:4-8.11, 54:4-8.15, 54:4-8.41, 54:29A-7, 55:14A-20 (CCH NEW JERSEY TAX REPORTS ¶20-505, 20-510).

The following property is exempt from taxation:

• R.S. 54:4-3.3 – state, county, municipal and federally-owned property.

• R.S. 54:4-3.6 – primary provision establishing exemption for various categories of property (religious, charitable, education, moral and mental improvement, hospital).

• R.S. 54:4-3.6a – exemption of property of nonprofit entity used for production of educational television and radio.

• R.S. 54:4-3.9 – exemption of burial grounds and vaults used or intended to be used as burial areas.

- R.S. 54:4-3.10 – exemption of property of fire association, fireman's relief association and volunteer fire company and used exclusively for the purpose of the entity.
- R.S. 54:4-3.11 – exemption of all property used for railroad or canal purposes by a railroad or canal entity.
- R.S. 54:4-3.13 – exemption of property of an association or corporation used to maintain a public fire patrol or salvage corps to protect against fire damage.
- R.S. 54:4-3.15 – exemption of property used by crippled soldiers.
- R.S. 54:4–54:4-3.18 –exemption of turnpike property used by the public without tolls.
- R.S. 54:4-3.24 – exemption of property used by Y.M.C.A., et al.
- R.S. 54:4-3.25 – exemption of property of veterans' associations.
- R.S. 54:4-3.26 – exemption of property of nonprofit fraternal organizations.
- R.S. 54:4-3.27 – exemption of property of volunteer aid and relief organizations.
- R.S. 54:4-3.30 – exemption of dwellings of veterans suffering certain disabilities; surviving spouse's rights.
- R.S. 54:4-3.35 – exemption for residences of district supervisors of religious organizations.
- R.S. 54:4-3.48 – exemption of blast or radiation fallout shelter erected on residential property.
- R.S. 54:4-3.5 – exemption of property used for military purposes.
- R.S. 54:4-3.52 – exemption of historic sites.
- R.S. 54:4-3.54a-c – exemption of certain historical properties.
- R.S. 54:4-3.56 – exemption of equipment for abating or preventing pollution.
- R.S. 54:4-3.59 – exemption of improvement to water supply or sewerage disposal systems.
- R.S. 54:4-3.64 – land for conservation or recreation purposes owned by non-profit organization.
- R.S. 54:4-3.113a – exemption of property used for renewable energy system that is part of or added to a commercial or residential building.
- R.S. 54:4-3.131 – exemption of property used in automatic fire suppression system.
- R.S. 54:4-3.138 – exemption of property of non-profit entity dedicated for a pet cemetery.
- R.S. 54:4-3.154 – exemptions from real property tax provided by municipal ordinance (environmental opportunity zones).
- R.S. 54:4-3.160 – exemptions (health enterprise zone).

Effective July 28, 2009, all projects which are part of the Economic Stimulus Act of 2009 used in furtherance of the educational purposes as defined in that Act are exempt from property taxation. N.J.S.A. 18A:64-85, P.L. 2010, c. 10.

Urban gardens: P.L. 2011, c.35, signed into law on March 1, 2011, and effective immediately, encourages nonprofit corporations and associations to help transform vacant properties located in older urban areas into gardens for growing fresh fruits and vegetables. Existing provisions of law authorize municipalities and counties to lease or sell public property not needed for a public use to nonprofit entities for them to perform specified laudatory public purposes thereon. This law affects lands in cities of the first, second, third, and fourth classes. The cultivation and sale of fresh fruits and vegetables is now among the purposes for which municipalities may lease or sell public land for nominal consideration. Previously, the law allowed for the long-term lease of excess public land, but not the sale thereof, to nonprofits for gardening purposes. Now, the transformation of excess vacant public lands into urban farms is a public purpose and the law affords these lands exemptions from property taxation.

P.L. 2011, c.171, signed on January 5, 2012, and effective immediately, amends various parts of the law to allow all municipalities to sell and lease public property not needed for public purposes to certain nonprofit entities for "urban" farming and gardening purposes. Under the previous law, this practice was restricted to municipalities located in cities of the first, second, third, or fourth class.

Property tax exemption for certain sports and entertainment projects: P.L. 2009, c. 6, enacted on January 27, 2009, and effective immediately, provides that a sports and entertainment project constructed under a redevelopment plan adopted by an eligible city that is owned, used and operated by the eligible city to provide sports and entertainment events, shows, public meetings or events, exhibitions or other expositions shall be deemed to be devoted to an essential public and governmental use and purpose. The property of the sports and entertainment project is exempt from property taxation as well as any special assessments of the State or any local government entity.

Exemption for Renewable Energy Systems Created: Effective October 1, 2008, New Jersey legislation establishes a property tax exemption for a renewable energy system that is part of or added to a commercial or residential building as an accessory use, and that produces renewable energy onsite to provide all or a portion of the electrical, heating, cooling or general energy needs of the building. Ch. 90 (S.B. 241), Laws 2008. "Renewable energy" includes (1) electric energy produced from solar technologies, photovoltaic technologies, wind energy, fuel cells, geothermal technologies, wave or tidal action, methane gas from landfills, a resource recovery facility, a hydropower facility or a biomass facility, and (2) energy produced from solar thermal or geothermal technologies.

To qualify for exemption, property must be certified by a local enforcing agency as a renewable energy system. The owner of real property that is equipped with a certified renewable energy system may have exempted annually from the assessed valuation of the real property a sum equal to the assessed valuation of the real property with the renewable energy system included, minus the assessed valuation of the real property without the renewable energy system included. Application for certification of a system must be made on a form prescribed by the Division of Taxation and provided for the use of claimants by the local enforcing agency. Ch. 90 (S.B. 241), Laws 2008.

Veterans: Honorably discharged veterans and their surviving spouses are entitled to deduct $200 from their tax bill for the 2002 tax year. The deduction will increase to $250 for tax years after 2002. (Certain disabled veterans or their surviving spouses are entitled to a full exemption as noted above.) P.L. 2007, c.317, enacted January 13, 2008, and effective immediately, allows the surviving spouse of a disabled veteran to claim a property tax exemption when the veteran's disability declaration was granted after death.

Senior citizens and disabled persons: Persons 65 years of age or older, or totally and permanently disabled, with income not in excess of $10,000 per year (excluding: social security benefits or—to the extent of the maximum amount of social security payable to, and excludable by, an owner under similar circumstances—Federal Railroad Retirement Act benefits and federal or state pension, disability and retirement benefits that are in lieu of social security benefits; and the capital gain realized from the sale of the taxpayer's principal residence) and meeting certain residency requirements, are entitled to a $250 deduction from the tax on their residence, whether located on land owned by the taxpayer or by someone else. The deduction is also granted to the surviving spouse of a taxpayer who received the deduction under these provisions, provided the survivor was at least 55 when the original taxpayer died and has not remarried. This deduction may be in addition to only the veterans' deduction and the homestead rebate.

Tenant shareholders in cooperatives or mutual housing corporations, otherwise qualifying for the senior citizens' or disabled persons' deduction, are permitted to claim a deduction against property taxes in an amount not to exceed the proportionate share of the tax attributable to the shareholder's unit.

Attached personal property: Real property does not include personal property affixed to real property or an appurtenance to real property. Real property does not include machinery, apparatus, or equipment that is used or held for use in business, which does not have a primary purpose of enabling a structure to support, shelter, contain, enclose, or house persons or property. In a 1997 opinion (*General Motors Corp. v. City of Linden,* NJ Supreme Court, No. A-106, July 21, 1997; CCH New Jersey Tax Reports, ¶ 400-524), the constitutionality of this statute was upheld.

Billboards and radio towers: New Jersey cases have held that billboards and radio towers are exempt from property tax. Wooden billboards qualify as personal property exempt from property tax because they can be removed without material injury to the real property or to the billboard itself, and they are not ordinarily intended to be permanently affixed to the real property (*The R.C. Maxwell Co. v. Galloway Twp.* (1995 App Div) 15 NJ Tax 187, cert den, 142 NJ 457; CCH New Jersey Tax Reports, ¶ 400-470).

Effective January 10, 2002, an exemption was passed for steel advertising signs and structures. The exemption from local taxation for steel outdoor advertising signs is repealed in 2004 and any outdoor advertising sign requiring a permit pursuant to the Roadside Sign Control and Outdoor Advertising Act, along with any supporting structures, are deemed to be real property and are subject to local taxation. The new law applies to assessments made after June 29, 2004 (P.L. 2004, c.42).

Radio broadcast towers are exempt from local property tax as business personal property because they are classified as machinery apparatus or equipment used for business. However, the concrete bases of the towers constitute taxable real property because they are permanently affixed to the land (*Emmis Broadcasting Corp. v. Borough of East Rutherford, et al,* July 23, 1996, NJ Super Ct, App Div; CCH New Jersey Tax Reports, ¶ 400-469).

Manufactured homes: Manufactured homes are taxable only if (1) affixed to the land on a permanent foundation, or (2) affixed on a nonpermanent foundation, but connected to utility systems so they are habitable as a dwelling on a permanent basis. An exemption also is provided if the home is in a mobile home park, but municipalities will set and impose annual municipal service fees.

Abatements for areas in need of rehabilitation: In 1991, the New Jersey Legislature transformed numerous abatement statutes into a uniform series of laws. The relevant statutes now are the Local Redevelopment and Housing Law (N.J.S.A. 40A:12A-1, *et seq.*), the Long Term Tax Exemption Law, (N.J.S.A.40A:20-1, *et seq.*), and the Five Year Exemption and Abatement Law, (N.J.S.A. 40A:21-1, *et seq.*). Properties located in urban enterprise zones generally qualify for these abatements.

Under the Long Term Tax Exemption Law, which is construed in conjunction with the Local Redevelopment and Housing Law, a municipality may grant an exemption for industrial, commercial, residential or other use property for new construction or major rehabilitation. The Local Redevelopment and Housing Law determines what area qualifies for an exemption. Prior to construction of the project, an application and financial agreement are submitted to the municipality and must be approved. The exemption may last a minimum of six years or a maximum of thirty years. The exempted project must be owned, leased or managed by an urban renewal entity qualified under the Long Term Tax Exemption Law. For the term of the exemption, the improvement is exempt and the land remains subject to tax. The urban renewal entity pays a payment in lieu of tax ("PILOT"), based generally upon not less than 2% of project cost or not less than 10% of income for commercial properties. The minimum annual service charge must be at least equal to property taxes paid in the last full year that the property was subject to tax. The PILOT payment must be for a period of at least six years but can last as long as fifteen years. After that, regular taxes may be phased in pursuant to statute.

In addition, a limited property tax exemption is provided for the value of land when housing is to be constructed, acquired, or rehabilitated by an urban renewal entity.

Under the Five Year Exemption and Abatement Law, which is also construed in construction with Local Redevelopment and Housing Law, a municipality may pass an ordinance providing for an exemption and/or abatement for certain property. With regard to one- and two-family dwellings, the ordinance may exempt, for five years, the taxable value of either $5,000, $15,000 or $25,000 of improvements completed on dwellings 20 years or older. In addition, the ordinance may also permit an abatement of some portion of the assessed value as it existed prior to the improvement. With regard to new construction and conversion to one- and two-family dwelling use, an exemption and abatement may also be provided. Regarding multiple dwellings, the ordinance may exempt the value of improvements to multiple dwellings or conversions for five years. In addition, the ordinance may also permit an abatement of some portion of the assessed value as it existed prior to the improvement or conversion. For new construction of multiple dwellings, the ordinance may provide for a payment in lieu of tax to be made to the municipality. With regard to improvements to commercial/industrial property, the ordinance may provide for an exemption up to the value of any improvements. In addition, for new construction, the ordinance may provide for a payment in lieu of tax.

P.L. 2007, c.268, enacted on January 13, 2008, and effectively immediately, permits short-term property tax exemptions to begin immediately following the completion of a project instead of in the next tax year following the tax year when the project was completed.

Under the Environmental Opportunity Zone Act (N.J.S.A. 54:4-3.150, *et seq.*), a municipality may grant ten-year exemptions for qualified real property requiring remediation in environmental opportunity zones. A payment in lieu of tax is measured in terms of a percentage of the taxes otherwise due.

Effective May 6, 2007, the law allows short-term property tax relief for a five-year period for owners of residential property located in a redevelopment area that has been rebuilt or renovated by certain volunteer labor after being destroyed or damaged by fire. The Act enables municipalities to enact an ordinance granting a five-year exemption from property tax on the value of the improvements made in such situations. (Ch. 90, Laws 2007).

Effective May 6, 2007, the law permits municipalities to allow a five-year property tax abatement for certain improvements made on single-family dwellings located in an area declared in need of redevelopment, if half of the occupants of the dwelling qualify for a Federal income tax credit because of permanent and total disability. The tax relief, which will allow the improved property to be assessed based on its value before the renovations or reconstruction, will apply if the improvements were made in order to accommodate the occupants' physical disabilities and the work was done by volunteer labor satisfying certain statutory criteria. (Ch. 91, Laws 2007).

¶1605 Homestead Property Tax Reimbursement Program (Senior Freeze)

Law: R.S. 54:4-6.2—54:4-6.12, 54:4-8.57—54:4-8.74, 54A:9-8.1 (CCH New Jersey Tax Reports ¶ 20-205, 20-245).

Under the terms of the State Budget for FY 2014, only those applicants whose income for 2011 did not exceed $80,000 and whose income for 2012 did not exceed $70,000 (the original limit was $82,880) will be eligible to receive reimbursements for 2012 provided they met all the other program requirements. Residents whose 2012 income was over $70,000 but not over $82,880 will not receive reimbursements for 2012, even if they met all the other program requirements. The Division of Taxation will send notices to these applicants advising them that they are not eligible to receive reimbursements payments for 2012. However, by filing an application by the due date, these residents can establish their eligibility for benefits in future years and ensure that they will be mailed an application for 2013.

Under the terms of the State Budget for FY 2013, only those applicants whose income for 2010 did not exceed $80,000 and whose income for 2011 did not exceed $70,000 (the original limit was $80,000) were eligible to receive reimbursements for 2011 provided they met all the other program requirements. The Division of Taxation sent notices to applicants whose 2011 income was over $70,000 but not over $80,000 advising them that they were not eligible to receive reimbursement payments for 2011.

Residents whose 2011 income was over $70,000 but not over $80,000 did not receive reimbursements for 2011, even if they met all the other program require- ments. However, by filing a 2011 application by the due date, these residents established their eligibility for benefits in future years.

The deadline for filing 2012 reimbursement applications has also been extended to September 16, 2013.

NOTE: Eligibility requirements, including income limits, and benefits available under this program are subject to change by the State Budget.

¶1606 Basis and Rate of Tax

Law: R.S. 54:4-2.25, 54:4-2.26, 54:4-23, 54:29A-7, 54:29A-16 (CCH New Jersey Tax Reports ¶ 20-405, 20-610).

Real property is assessed according to its "full and fair value," which is defined as the price the property would sell for at a fair and bona fide sale by private contract on October 1. However, taxable value is a fixed percentage of true value. The percentage is established for each county by the county board of taxation.

In general, the tax rate is the aggregate of levies in the local taxing district (county, school, municipal, etc.).

Railroads: Property owned by a railroad and not used for railroad purposes is assessed and taxed by the local taxing districts in the same manner and at the same rate as other real property.

The state tax on Class II railroad property (that is, real property used for railroad purposes other than the main stem or facilities used in passenger service) is imposed at the rate of $4.75 for each $100 of the true value of such property.

Dedicated library purposes tax: P.L. 2011, c.38, signed into law on March 21, 2011, and effective immediately, requires municipalities in which a free public library is located or that belong to a joint municipal library to provide for a dedicated library purposes tax on the property tax bill. Specifically, a municipality must pay over to the library or the joint municipal library funds due to the library on a quarterly basis. The law further assures that there will be no net impact on a municipality's non-library purposes adjusted tax levy for the purposes of the cap law. The Director, Division of Local Government Services, Department of Community Affairs is now required to proportionately decrease the adjusted tax levy of affected municipalities to ensure that any statutorily required municipal support of free public libraries is exempt from the calculation of a municipality's adjusted tax levy for the purposes of the 2% levy cap. The Division is required to segregate the municipal library tax on the local property tax bill/abstract of ratables. All system-related changes will be performed by the Office of Information Technology.

CCH Tip: Tax Reduction Aid for Sharing Services

To promote New Jersey property tax relief, the Regional Efficiency Aid Program (REAP) provides state aid for the purpose of reducing property taxes owed on residential property to local governmental units and school districts that regionalize, consolidate, and share services. A formula involving population and other variables will be used to determine the property tax reduction for each residential property. Taxpayers should check with local property tax officials to determine whether their local governments are participating in the program.

¶1607 Assessment Procedure and Equalization

Law: R.S. 54:4-23 (CCH New Jersey Tax Reports ¶20-700).

In general, real property is assessed annually as of October 1 by the local assessors. Assessment appeals generally must be made by the following April 1 (¶1609).

P.L. 2007, c.256, enacted January 13, 2008, and effective immediately, changes the deadline for appeals of certain property tax assessments. When there has been a municipality-wide revaluation or reassessment, a taxpayer or taxing district may appeal to the county board of taxation on or before May 1, or if the assessed value of the property exceeds $1,000,000, may instead file a complaint directly with the State Tax Court.

The local assessors determine the taxable value of the real property by applying to the true value of such real property the percentage level established for the county by the county tax administrator.

Equalization tables are prepared by the Director of the Division of Taxation for use in the distribution of state school aid funds. Ordinarily these tables are adopted by the counties.

P.L. 2013, c.15, enacted January 25, 2013, creates a real property assessment demonstration program to demonstrate a more cost-effective and accurate process of real property assessment administration. The program specifically addresses the systemic costs that result from the losses due to successful tax assessment appeals. The legislation details how many counties may participate in the program, sets out criteria that the counties must meet and specifies the information that counties must provide to the Director of the Division of Local Government services and the Director of the Division of Taxation in order to implement the demonstration program as a demonstration county. Implementation of the demonstration project would take place October 1, 2013.

The New Jersey Supreme Court has held that the reassessment of recently sold property, while leaving undisturbed the appraised valuations of properties in the same class that had not been sold (selective or spot assessments, commonly known as the "welcome stranger" pattern), violated New Jersey's constitutional requirement of uniformity and the federal equal protection clause (*Township of West Milford v. Van Decker*, July 24, 1990, 120 NJ 354, 576 A2d 881; CCH NEW JERSEY TAX REPORTS [1989—1994 Transfer Binder], ¶ 400-070). Effective June 14, 2001, a tax assessor may reassess all or part of a taxing district pursuant to the statutory authority provided in N.J.S.A. 54:4-23.

¶1608 Returns and Payment

Law: R.S. 40A:5-44—40A:5-47, 54:4-34, 54:4-66, 54:4-67, 54:29A-44, 54:29A-46 (CCH NEW JERSEY TAX REPORTS ¶ 89-102, 20-756).

Returns are not required in connection with real property taxes.

Real property taxes are collected in four installments, due February 1, May 1, August 1, and November 1 for municipalities with a January 1 through December 31 fiscal year (the first two installments are based on the prior year's rate and the third and fourth installments are based on the full tax for the current year less the amount charged on the first two installments). Special provisions exist regarding municipalities required to operate on the state fiscal year.

Any municipality with a population of over 35,000 or any municipality that received state funds under the Municipal Revitalization Program in the state fiscal year 1990 or 1991 is required to operate on the state fiscal year, which runs from July 1 to June 30. Municipalities operating on the state fiscal year are authorized to deliver two tax bills a year, each reflecting amounts due for two installments.

Taxes are payable to the local collector of taxes. A taxing district may provide a discount for prepayment of taxes.

Credit card payment of taxes: Counties, municipalities, other local units and courts of New Jersey may permit payment of financial obligations by credit card, debit card, or electronic funds payment. In order to establish a payment system, a governing body of a local unit must pass a resolution that specifies the types of charges, taxes, fees, assessments, fines, or other obligations that may be paid by card or electronically. A service charge may be assessed. Payment of delinquent local unit obligations or for the redemption of local unit liens is prohibited.

Railroads: Property owned by a railroad and not used for railroad purposes is taxed by the local taxing districts in the same manner as other real property.

Every railroad is required to file a schedule of its property as of the preceding January 1 with the Division of Taxation on or before March 1.

The state tax on Class II railroad property (that is, real property used for railroad purposes other than the main stem or facilities used in passenger service) is due December 1.

¶1609 Administration—Penalties, Refunds, Appeals

Law: R.S. 54:3-21, 54:4-66, 54:4-67, 54:4-69, 54:4-78, 54:51A-1 (CCH NEW JERSEY TAX REPORTS ¶ 20-752, 20-770, 20-904, 20-906, 89-202, 89-204, 89-206, 89-208, 89-228).

In general, taxes not paid on the due date are deemed delinquent and remain delinquent until all unpaid taxes (including taxes and other liens subsequently due and unpaid, plus interest) have been fully paid and satisfied. However, a taxing district may provide a 10-day grace period during which no interest is charged. Failure to make a payment on time or a nonpayment may cause the imposition of penalties, such as addition of interest to the tax and sale of real property for delinquent taxes. Penalties in the form of addition of interest vary from district to district. However, governing bodies are authorized to impose interest of up to 8% per year on the first $1,500 of the delinquency, and 18% per year on the amount of delinquency in excess of $1,500, to be calculated from the date the tax was payable until the date that actual payment to the lienholder will be next authorized. Also, governing bodies may impose up to 6% of the amount of delinquent taxes on any taxpayer owing in excess of $10,000 at the end of the calendar year.

• *Appeals*

The main remedy available to taxpayers in connection with property taxes is an appeal from the local assessors to the county board of taxation. An appeal may be dismissed if the first quarter taxes and any prior years taxes and municipal charges have not been paid. If the assessed valuation of the property involved exceeds $1,000,000, the action of the assessors may be appealed directly to the Tax Court, but at least the first quarter taxes and any prior years taxes and municipal charges must have been paid. Further appeals from the county board may be taken to the Tax Court. Any additional taxes then due must be paid. Both the county tax board and Tax Court have jurisdiction to relax the tax payment rules if the "interests of justice" so require. Further appeals from the Tax Court may be taken in the Appellate Division of the Superior Court and in the N.J. Supreme Court.

Both petitions of appeal filed with the county board of taxation and complaints filed directly with the Tax Court must be filed on or before April 1. If a petition of appeal or complaint is filed by a taxpayer or taxing district during the 19 days before April 1, the other party may file a cross-petition of appeal with the county board of taxation or a counterclaim with the clerk of the tax court within 20 days from the date of service of the petition or complaint.

The law provides for refund of overpayments.

Effective May 9, 2013, the governing body of a municipality may adopt a resolution authorizing a municipal employee chosen by the governing body to process, without further action on the part of the governing body, the cancellation of any New Jersey property tax refund, delinquency or the charges and fees imposed by the municipality of less than $10. P.L. 2013, c.54.

PART VII
MISCELLANEOUS TAXES
CHAPTER 17
UNEMPLOYMENT COMPENSATION TAX
(Including Disability Benefits)

¶1701	Scope of Chapter
¶1702	History and Imposition of Tax
¶1703	Coverage
¶1704	Tax Rates
¶1705	Returns and Reports
¶1706	Benefits

¶1701 Scope of Chapter

This chapter discusses briefly the New Jersey Unemployment Compensation Law and the New Jersey Temporary Disability Benefits Law. Its purpose is to give a general idea of the impact of the tax and of the principal provisions. It is not intended to provide a detailed analysis of the law or regulations. It covers, generally, the questions of who is subject to the tax, who is exempt, the base and rate of the tax, and the benefits payable.

¶1702 History and Imposition of Tax

The unemployment compensation law was enacted in 1936. In 1937, it was reenacted and codified as Chapter 21, Title 43, Revised Statutes of New Jersey 1937. It is tied in with the federal unemployment tax as are the similar taxes in other states. The disability benefits law was enacted in 1948 and is codified as Subtitle 9 of Chapter 21, Title 43, Revised Statutes of New Jersey 1937. The two laws are similar in coverage.

The unemployment compensation and disability benefits taxes are levied on both employers and employees.

The unemployment compensation and disability benefits laws are administered by the Division of Unemployment and Temporary Disability Insurance in the Department of Labor and Industry Workforce Development, 1 John Fitch Plaza, P.O. Box 110, Trenton, New Jersey 08625-0058.

¶1703 Coverage

• *Employer*

Employer: Employing unit that has paid remuneration of $1,000 or more in either the current or preceding calendar year. Generally, an employer subject to the FUTA is automatically subject to the New Jersey law.

• *Employment*

Service, including service in interstate commerce, performed for remuneration or under any contract of hire, written or oral, expressed or implied, with certain exceptions which are listed below.

Service performed by individual for remuneration is deemed "employment" unless and until it is shown that such individual is:

(a) free from direction or control;

(b) performing such services outside the usual course of an employer's business, or outside all places of an employer's business; and

(c) customarily engaged in an independently established trade or business.

Service on an American vessel or aircraft is "employment" if the operating office from which it is directed or controlled is within New Jersey.

• *Exemptions*

Generally, services covered by FUTA are automatically covered by New Jersey law.

The following are exemptions:

— Agents of mutual benefit associations compensated solely by way of commissions.

— Certified shorthand reporter providing services to a third party by the reporter who is referred to the third party pursuant to an agreement with another certified reporter or reporting service, on a freelance basis, compensation for which is based on a fee per transcript page, flat attendance fee, or other flat minimum fee, or combination of these.

— Services as a member of a board of directors, board of trustees, board of managers, or committee of a bank, building and loan or savings and loan association, where such services are not the principal employment of such individual.

— Entertainers, musicians, etc., performing services for operators of amusement places, not in excess of 10 weeks in any calendar year for same owner or operator.

— Family employment, *i.e.,* service in employ of son, daughter or spouse and service by child under 18 in employ of parent.

— Fraternal beneficiary societies operating under the lodge system.

— Services for a hospital by a patient of the hospital.

— Insurance agents wholly on a commission basis, exclusive of industrial insurance agents.

— Services for an international organization.

— Interns in the employ of a hospital who have completed a four-year course of training.

— Investment company agents wholly on a commission basis.

— Mutual fund brokers or dealers in the sale of mutual funds or other securities, if they are compensated wholly on commission basis.

— Operators of motor vehicles weighing 18,000 lbs. or more, licensed for commercial use and used for the highway movement of freight, who own their equipment or lease or finance it through other than the entity for whom the services are performed, if they are compensated by receiving a percentage of gross revenue or by a schedule of payment based on distance and weight of the transportation move.

— Outside travel agents using facilities provided by a travel agent if the outside agent acts as an independent contractor, is paid on a commission basis, sets his or her own work schedule, and receives no benefits, sick leave, vacation, or other leave from the travel agent owning the facilities.

— Real estate salespersons or brokers wholly on a commission basis.

— Service covered by the federal unemployment compensation system.

¶1703

— Service performed in the sale or distribution of merchandise by home-to-home salespersons or in-the-home demonstrators whose remuneration consists wholly of commissions or commissions and bonuses.

— Service by a student for a school, college or university in which the student is enrolled and is in regular attendance or by the spouse of such student if the spouse's employment is under a program of aid to student.

— Service by student for nonprofit or public program. Not applicable if program is established by employer or group of employers.

— Student nurses in employ of hospital or training school while attending training school.

— Union services—service as members of local union committee reimbursed for time lost from work or as part-time officer of local union if remuneration is less than $1,000 a year.

— Services for a veterans' organization or an auxiliary thereof.

• *Agricultural and domestic employers*

Agricultural labor is covered if performed for an employer who employed 10 or more individuals in such service in each of 20 different weeks in the current or preceding calendar year or paid cash remuneration of $20,000 or more for such service in any quarter of the current or preceding calendar year. When agricultural labor is supplied by a crew leader, the employing unit for which the services are performed is the employer of the crew members unless the crew leader is registered under the Migrant and Seasonal Agricultural Worker Protection Act, or substantially all of the crew members operate or maintain mechanized equipment that is provided by the crew leader. In either of these instances, the crew leader is the employer.

Domestic service in a private home is covered if performed for an employer that paid cash remuneration of $1,000 or more in any quarter of the current or preceding calendar year for such service.

• *Government and nonprofit employers*

Tax-exempt nonprofit organizations are mandatorily covered. Also covered are state governmental entities, including political subdivisions. The following services performed for nonprofit organizations or the state are not covered:

— Church or organization operated for religious purposes and which is controlled by a church.

— Religious duties of a minister or a member of a religious order.

— Inmates of custodial or penal institutions.

— Elected officials.

— Members of a legislative body or the judiciary.

— Members of the State National Guard or Air National Guard.

— Employees serving on a temporary basis in the case of a fire, storm, snow, earthquake, flood or similar emergency.

— Individuals in major nontenured policy-making or advisory positions.

— Patients employed in a rehabilitation facility or sheltered workshop.

— Individuals receiving unemployment work-relief or work-training under a program financed by a federal agency or an agency of a state or political subdivision.

— Nonprofit organizations may pay contributions or elect the reimbursement financing method of paying for benefits. State governmental entities must make payments in lieu of contributions, unless an election is made to pay contributions. Under the reimbursement method, payments equal to the full

¶1703

amount of regular plus one-half (full for governmental entities) the amount of extended benefits paid are required. Workers of employers who elect or are required to make reimbursement payments do not pay contributions unless the employer is covered by the state plan under the Temporary Disability Benefits Law. Any nonprofit organization that elects reimbursement financing must execute and file a surety bond or deposit money.

• *Wages*

All remuneration paid for personal services, including commissions and bonuses and cash value of all remuneration paid in any medium other than cash, but including only an amount determined annually as 28 times the statewide average weekly remuneration paid to workers, raised to the next higher multiple of $100. If the amount so determined for any year is less than the amount determined for the previous year, the greater amount will be used. The 2013 wage base is $30,900 and the 2014 wage base is $31,500. Remuneration paid within and without the state, and remuneration paid by predecessors, is included in the taxable wage base. Ordinarily, "wages" includes vacation pay but not dismissal payments which employer is not required to make. Gratuities regularly received from other than an individual's employer are "wages" if reported in writing to the employer. If not so reported, the individual's wages are determined in accordance with minimum wage rates or the amount of remuneration actually received from the employer, whichever is higher. Also service charges, distributed in lieu of customary gratuities or tips, are specifically included as wages.

Disability Benefits

• *Coverage*

"Covered employer" means an employer subject to the Unemployment Compensation Law, and specifically includes the State of New Jersey, including Rutgers, the State University, the University of Medicine and Dentistry of New Jersey and the New Jersey Institute of Technology. "Covered individual" means any person who is in employment as defined in the Unemployment Compensation Law for which he or she is entitled to remuneration from a covered employer, or who has been out of such employment for less than two weeks. However, a covered individual who is employed by the State of New Jersey, including Rutgers, the State University, the University of Medicine and Dentistry of New Jersey, and the New Jersey Institute of Technology, or by any governmental entity that elects to become a covered employer, will not be eligible for disability benefits until he or she has exhausted all sick leave accumulated under the classified service of the State, under terms and conditions similar to classified employees, under terms and conditions pursuant to laws of New Jersey, or as the result of a negotiated contract with any governmental entity that elected to become covered.

• *Wages*

"Wages" means compensation payable by covered employers to covered individuals for personal services, including commissions, bonuses, and the cash value of compensation payable in any medium other than cash. For the limitation on the amount of taxable wages during a calendar year, see the discussion of tax rates, below.

A person who depends for healing upon prayer or spiritual means is exempt from provisions of the Act upon filing the required statement.

¶1703

¶1704 Tax Rates

Unemployment Compensation

- *Standard rate*

Employer—5.4%. Note that certain factors may increase or decrease this rate— see below. New employer rates depend upon the fund reserve ratio in effect for a rate year and can be either 2.8%, 3.1%, or 3.4%.

- *Worker's contributions*

Each worker is required to contribute to the unemployment compensation fund 0.3825% of wages paid. Contributions for workers of "governmental reimbursable employers" will be at the rate of 0.0825%. That is of wages paid with respect to employment with the State of New Jersey or any other governmental entity or instrumentality electing or required to make payments in lieu of contributions.

Effective January 1, 2012 to December 31, 2012, all workers will pay a rate of 0.08% to cover Family Leave Insurance; the rate increases to 0.1% for January 1, 2013 to December 31, 2013 (DLWD Communication).

Note that workers also contribute 0.0425% to the Workforce Development/ Supplemental Workforce Funds.

No contributions are made by workers who are exempt from coverage.

Employers must withhold employees' tax from their wages. Failure to do so renders the employer liable for the tax.

- *Experience rates*

An employer's contribution rate for any experience rating year beginning July 1 may be varied from the standard rate if it qualifies for an experience rating by having at least three calendar years throughout which any individual in its employ could have received benefits. Once this qualification is met, the employer's history of contributions, benefit charges and annual payrolls is used to calculate a "reserve ratio" classification, which along with the trust fund reserve ratio in effect for the rate year determines the applicable contribution rate.

An employer's reserve ratio is determined by finding the difference between its total benefits charged and total contributions paid for all years prior to the beginning of the calendar year and calculating the difference as a percentage of annual average payroll for the last three or five years, whichever is higher. If the total contributions paid exceed total benefits charged, the result is a positive reserve ratio. Should benefit charges exceed contributions paid, the result is a negative reserve ratio. The Experience Rating Tax Table within the law has a breakdown of the entire range of possible positive and negative ratios. Contribution rates are computed by matching the employer's reserve ratio classification with one of five schedules in effect based on the unemployment trust fund reserve ratio (see below).

If no contributions were paid on wages in any calendar year used in determining the average annual payroll of an eligible employer, its rate is specially assigned as follows:

(1) if the employer has a positive reserve balance, its rate will be the higher of the highest rate in effect for positive-balance employers for that period or 5.4%; and

(2) if the employer has a negative reserve balance, its rate will be the highest in effect for deficit-balance employers for that period.

An Unemployment Trust Fund Reserve Ratio will be determined by dividing the balance in the fund as of the prior March 31 by total taxable wages reported by all employers during the last calendar year. Depending on this reserve ratio, each employer, including new employers, will pay rates under one of five schedules in the law.

— Schedule A, ranging from 0.3% to 2.4% for positive-balance employers and from 3.4% to 5.4% for negative-balance employers, with new employers paying 2.8%, is in effect when the reserve ratio is 1.4% or more.

— Schedule B, ranging from 0.4% to 3.0% for positive-balance employers and from 4.3% to 5.4% for negative-balance employers, with new employers paying 2.8%, is in effect when the reserve ratio is 1.0% to 1.39%.

— Schedule C, ranging from 0.5% to 3.6% for positive-balance employers and from 5.1% to 5.8% for negative-balance employers, with new employers paying 2.8%, is in effect when the reserve ratio is 0.75% to 0.99%.

— Schedule D, ranging from 0.6% to 4.0% for positive-balance employers and from 5.6% to 6.4% for negative-balance employers, with new employers paying 3.1%, is in effect when the reserve ratio is 0.50% to 0.74%.

— Schedule E, ranging from 1.2% to 4.3% for positive-balance employers and from 6.1% to 7.0% for negative-balance employers, with new employers paying 3.4%, is in effect when the reserve ratio is 0.49% or under.

Each employer's rate under these schedules will, however, be reduced by 0.1% if the fund ratio is equal to or greater than 3.5% except for those negative-balance employers with a deficit reserve ratio of negative 35% or under. Each employer subject to this reduction must, in turn, contribute 0.1% to the Workforce Development Partnership Fund.

In addition, each employer's rate is further reduced by 0.0175% and a like amount must be contributed to the Supplemental Workforce Fund for Basis Skills. However, during any year in which the fund reserve ratio is at least 3.5%, there is no decrease in the rate of a negative-balance employer with a deficit reserve ratio of negative 35% or under. The rate of an employer with a deficit reserve ratio of negative 35% or under may not be reduced to less than 5.4% and no other employer's rate may be reduced to less than zero.

Rates are increased by a 10% factor if the unemployment trust fund reserve ratio as of the prior March 31 is less than 0.5%.

A $1 annual surcharge is assessed for each employee of employers covered under the Unemployment Compensation Law, to be deposited in the Catastrophic Illness in Children Relief Fund. The surcharge is collected by the Controller for the Unemployment Compensation Fund.

An employer transferring into New Jersey from another state an operation that establishes at least 50 full-time jobs within 180 days of the transfer may be entitled to a reduced rate of contributions ranging from 1.0% to 1.3%, depending on the fund reserve ratio for the year. Such an employer must have acquired in the other state an employer reserve ratio of at least 11% and must demonstrate that this experience in the other state may be considered indicative of future experience in New Jersey.

For the period of July 1, 2013, through June 30, 2014, rates are determined under Column E. Rates under that column range from 1.2% to 4.3% for positive-balance employers and from 6.10% to 7.0% for negative balance employers, with new employers paying 3.4%. (Note that these are basic rates and do not reflect any subsidiary taxes or reductions.)

• *Voluntary payments*

May be made during 30-day period (may be extended for 60 days for good cause) following date of mailing of notice of employer's rate, but not more than 120 days after start of contribution year. If the employer obtains an extension, and then fails to make the payment, it will incur a penalty of 5% or $5, whichever is greater, not to exceed $50. Basic rates assigned where the employer does not have 3 years of experience, rates assigned where the employer has had at least 1 out of the past 3 calendar years during which no contributions were paid, and rates assigned to employers who are delinquent in payment of contributions for prior years, are not affected by voluntary contributions.

• *Disability tax rates*

There are additional employment taxes levied against both employers and employees in order to fund benefits paid under the New Jersey Temporary Disability Insurance Law. Each worker contributes 0.5% of wages paid to the state disability benefit fund with respect to the worker's employment with a government employer electing or required to pay contributions or a nongovernmental employer, including certain nonprofit organizations, unless the employer is covered by an approved private disability plan or is exempt. Effective January 1, 2012 to December 31, 2012, the rate is reduced to 0.2%. For January 1, 2013 to December 31, 2013 the rate increases to .36%. New employers pay at a standard "preliminary" rate of 0.5% that may increase to as much as 0.7% if the fund balance is low. Preliminary rates based on experience are available after three calendar years of employment. Where contributions minus benefit charges exceed a $500 basis, preliminary rates range from 0.1% to 0.2% provided that the ratio of the excess equals or exceeds 1% of the employer's average annual payroll. Where charges exceed contributions by $500, preliminary rates range between .35% to .75%. Where contributions credited exceed benefits charged by no more than $500 plus one percent of average annual payroll, or benefits charged exceed the contributions credited by no more than $500, the preliminary rate is .25%.

The preliminary rates in turn are subject to adjustment depending upon the balance in the state disability benefit fund. Final rates range from between 0.1% to 1.10%. For further details, see the discussion of disability benefits, below.

Disability Benefits

• *Tax rates*

Employers must pay contributions to the disability benefits fund at rates that range from 0.1% to 1.10%, unless they establish a private disability plan that meets with the approval of the Commission. The determining factors in obtaining a given employer's rate are:

(1) the length of time it has been an employer;

(2) its "account balance," *i.e.,* the contributions the employer has paid as measured against the amount of benefits that have been charged to it; and

(3) the amount of money in the disability fund.

Preliminary rates are assigned all employers based on the length of their employment history and their account balance. There rates are in turn subject to possible adjustment depending on the disability fund balance before final rates are assigned.

Ordinarily, the employer whose employment experience is limited—specifically, the employer who has not paid contributions with respect to employment in each of the three calendar years preceding the fiscal year beginning July 1—is assigned a preliminary contribution rate of 0.50%. However, if the fund balance is low, the rate for such employers can be adjusted up to 0.7%.

Employers that have met the three-year experience requirement are divided generally into two categories: those whose accounts show that the total contributions they have paid exceed the total amount of benefits charged plus 1% of average annual payroll by more than $500, and those whose accounts show a nearly reverse situation, *i.e.,* benefits charged exceed contributions credited by more than $500. Depending on their accounts' percentage of excess (contributions over benefits charged plus 1% of annual payroll in the first group, benefits charged over contributions in the second) the preliminary rate for employers in the first group will be 0.1%, 0.15% or 0.2%; the preliminary rate for employers in the second group will be 0.35%, 0.45%, 0.55%, 0.65%, or 0.75%. The employer whose contributions exceed benefits charged by no more than $500 plus 1% of the employer's average annual payroll, and the employer whose benefit charges exceed contributions credited by no more than $500, are assigned a preliminary rate of 0.25%. Preliminary rates may not vary from year to year beyond certain limits: an increase in the preliminary rate may not exceed 0.2% of wages, and a decrease may not exceed 0.1% of wages, from the preliminary rate determined for the preceding year.

Depending on the state of the fund, the preliminary rates described above may be increased or decreased. Certain limitations apply to increases. Prior to July 1 of each calendar year a determination is made whether the amount of the state disability benefits fund as of December 31 of the preceding year (including contributions for the year paid in January) is more than the amount withdrawn from the federal unemployment compensation trust fund plus the amount in the separate unemployment disability benefits account. If so, the total wages on which contributions were paid through the preceding calendar year is divided into the excess. The resulting percentage serves as the basis for any rate adjustments.

If the resulting percentage is 1.25% or higher, 1.25 is subtracted from the percentage and the difference, adjusted to the nearest 0.05%, is used to decrease preliminary rates. No rate may be reduced below 0.10%, however, and no reduction is made in the case of an employer that is ineligible for a calculated preliminary rate (assigned a rate of 0.50%) or an employer with benefit charges that exceed contributions by more than $500.

If the resulting percentage is less than 1.25% but not less than 0.75%, there is no adjustment and preliminary rates become final rates.

If the resulting percentage is less than 0.75% but more than 0.25%, the percentage is subtracted from 0.75% and the difference, adjusted to the nearest 0.05%, is used to increase preliminary rates. Limitations require that preliminary rates of 0.20% or less cannot be increased beyond 0.25%, that preliminary rates of 0.25% cannot be increased beyond 0.50%, and that preliminary rates of 0.35% and higher cannot be increased beyond 0.75%.

If the resulting percentage is equal to or less than 0.25%, final rates will be:

— 0.40% if the preliminary rate is 0.20% or less;

— 0.70% if the preliminary rate is 0.25% or 0.50%; and

— 1.1% if the preliminary rate is 0.35%, 0.45%, 0.55%, 0.65% or 0.75%.

Note that the State of New Jersey pays an annually established rate that will balance the State's account, but not less than 0.1% each fiscal year.

Employers are also assessed for administrative costs, and provision is also made for a special assessment when there is a deficit in the Disability Account. In addition, there is a state plan employer experience rating assessment rate.

Employers who establish their own disability benefit plan are not required to contribute to the State fund but they may be liable for assessments to cover amounts expended by the Division in connection with the supervision of private plans. Such assessment against an employer may not exceed $1/20$ of 1% of its taxable payroll.

Each worker pays 0.5% to the state disability benefits fund; 0.2% effective January 1, 2012 to December 31, 2012 only.

Any employee who paid contributions for disability benefits purposes in an amount exceeding the required percent of taxable wages by reason of working for more than one employer may obtain refund of such excess. Also, any employee who

¶1704

is a taxpayer and entitled to a refund may, in lieu of such refund, claim a credit in the full amount of the refund against the tax otherwise due on his or her New Jersey gross income for that tax year. A similar credit is granted for excess employee unemployment compensation taxes.

Effective January 1, 2012, all workers will pay a rate of 0.08% to cover Family Leave Insurance (FLI). This provides up to six weeks of FLI benefits for the care of a family member suffering from a serious health condition, a newly born child or a newly adopted child. See "Tax Rates" under the "Unemployment Insurance" section of this chart, above, for other taxes required of workers.

Employers must withhold employees' tax from their wages. Failure to do so renders the employer liable for such tax.

Only an amount determined annually as 28 × the statewide average weekly remuneration paid to workers, raised to the next higher multiple of $100, is taxable. If the amount so determined for any year is less than the amount determined for the previous year, the greater amount will be used. This limitation applies to both employer and employee contributions. The taxable wage base for 2012 is $30,300 and the taxable wage base is $30,900 for 2013.

¶1705 Returns and Reports

Unemployment Compensation

• *Tax forms*

Tax: All employers must file and pay the Employer's Quarterly Report, NJ927, and through electronic transmission. Form NJ-927, Employer's Quarterly Report, is due quarterly on or before the 30th day after the close of the quarter. The Employer's Quarterly Report includes forms NJ927, NJ927W and NJ927H. Electronic means includes, but not limited to, secure file transfer protocol (SFTP) or DOR's online web application. There is no extension should the due date fall on a weekend or holiday.

• *Wages*

Form WR-30, Employer Report of Wages Paid, must be filed quarterly on the same due date for the contribution report. All employers and all third-party payroll processors who report in excess of 4 employees for any calendar quarter must file via electronic means. The filing of form WR-30 via electronic means either by secure file transfer protocol or online.

Disability Benefits

Contribution reporting under the Disability Benefits Law is included in Form UC-27B (see the preceding unemployment insurance chart). Within seven days after mailing of request, employer should notify Division of any information as to claimant's eligibility. Within two working days after receipt of Form DS-8, employer should notify Division of any information as to claimant's eligibility or duration of payments to be made. If, after receipt of Form DS-8, employer acquires information that may render claimant ineligible or reduce rate or amount of benefits, the employer should forward same to Division immediately.

¶1706 Benefits

Unemployment Compensation

• *Base year*

First four of the last five completed calendar quarters immediately preceding an individual's benefit year. Alternate base period available to individual who, immediately preceding the benefit year, was subject to a disability compensable under the temporary disability law or a workers' compensation law.

• *Benefit year*

364 days beginning with day on which valid claim is filed.

• *Weekly benefit amount*

60% of the claimant's average weekly wage. Maximum is determined under an "escalator" provision and set at 56 $^2/_3$ % of the statewide average weekly wage. The maximum is $611 for 2012 and $624 for 2013, including any dependents' benefits that may be payable. Dependency allowances are payable equal to 7% of the individual's weekly benefit amount for the first dependent, and 4% each for the next two dependents, up to a total of three dependents. Partial unemployment benefits: weekly benefit is reduced by any earnings that exceed 20% of weekly benefit (fractions of a dollar disregarded) or $5, whichever is larger.

Note that, claimants may now elect to have income taxes voluntarily withheld from their unemployment insurance benefit payments.

• *Maximum total benefits*

Three-fourths of the claimant's base weeks from all employers in the base year multiplied by the weekly benefit rate rounded to the next-lower dollar, and limited to not more than 26 × the weekly benefit rate.

• *Benefit eligibility requirements*

An individual is eligible if he:

(a) has established at least 20 base weeks within the base year; or has earning not less than 1,000 times the minimum wage in effect on October 1 of the calendar year preceding the calendar year in which the benefit year commences, adjusted to the next higher multiple of $100. An alternative base week qualification amount that is equal to 20 × the state minimum hourly wage (total—$145 in 2012 and 2013) and an alternate earnings eligibility test that is equal to 1,000 × the state minimum hourly wage (total—$7,300 in 2012 and 2013) are established for individuals who do not meet the regular requirements;

(b) has earned at least 6 × the previous weekly benefit amount and has at least 4 weeks of employment since the beginning of the immediately preceding benefit year, in order to qualify for a second benefit year;

(c) is able and available for work and actively seeking work;

(d) serves a waiting period of one week; and

(e) participates in reemployment services if required.

The waiting period week becomes compensable, however, when benefits become payable for the third consecutive week next following the waiting period. Individual on vacation without pay is not deemed unavailable or ineligible if vacation resulted from collective bargaining agreement or other action beyond his control. In regard to "unemployment disability benefits," see below.

To qualify for benefits, an agricultural worker must establish 20 base weeks, earn 12 × the statewide average weekly wage, or perform at least 770 hours of service in agricultural labor.

An officer of a corporation or a person who has more than a 5% equitable or debt interest in the corporation, whose claim for benefits is based on wages from the corporation, will not be deemed unemployed in any week during his term of office or ownership of the corporation.

Benefit eligibility of persons attending approved training programs or attending before a court in response to a summons for jury duty is preserved by a special provision of law.

¶1706

Benefits are not payable based on services in a research, instructional or principal administrative capacity for an educational institution during vacations or sabbatical leaves.

Benefits are not payable based on nonprofessional services in an educational institution during vacations. Retroactive payments of benefits are possible under certain circumstances.

Benefits are not payable to a professional athlete during periods between sport seasons if there is reasonable assurance that he or she will perform services in both seasons.

An alien is disqualified unless he or she has been lawfully admitted for permanent residence or is otherwise permanently residing in the United States under color of law.

An individual will not be considered unavailable or ineligible solely due to attendance at the funeral of an immediate family member, provided the duration of the attendance does not extend beyond two days.

• *Disqualification periods*

Voluntary leaving without good cause attributable to the work—until the individual has been employed for 4 weeks and has earned at least 6 × his or her weekly benefit.

Discharge for gross misconduct connected with the work—until the individual has been employed for 4 weeks and has earned at least 6 × the weekly benefit. No benefit rights may accrue based on wages from the employer who discharged the individual for services rendered prior to the day of discharge.

Discharge or suspension for misconduct connected with work—six weeks. Disqualification does not apply if the employer rescinds the discharge, but if the claimant is restored to employment with back pay, he or she must return any benefits received for weeks covered by the back pay.

Refusal of suitable work without good cause—four weeks.

Labor dispute—duration of dispute.

An individual's weekly benefit amount is reduced by the amount of any governmental or other pension, retirement or retired pay, annuity, or other similar periodic payment based on previous work, but not below zero. If provisions of the FUTA permit, the Commissioner may prescribe by regulations either or both of the following:

(1) that such reduction will apply only in the case of a pension, retirement or retired pay, annuity or other similar periodic payment under a plan maintained or contributed to by a base period or chargeable employer; and/or

(2) that the amount of such reduction will be determined by taking into account contributions made by the claimant for the pension or retirement payment.

The amount of benefits payable to an individual who is involuntarily and permanently separated from work prior to the date at which the individual could retire with full pension rights is not reduced because he or she receives a lump-sum payment in lieu of periodic pension, retirement, or annuity payments, except that benefits may be reduced during the week in which he receives the lump sum.

Receipt of remuneration in lieu of notice—weeks in which received.

Receipt of disability benefits under the Temporary Disability Benefits Law—period of receipt.

Receipt of unemployment benefits under another law—weeks in which received.

¶1706

False or fraudulent representation to obtain benefits—disqualified for one year.

Student in full attendance at, or on vacation from an educational institution—disqualified unless attending a training program to enhance employment opportunities or unless the student earned sufficient base-year wages while attending school to establish a claim.

Disability Benefits

Disability benefits are payable with respect to unemployment of any covered individual who has suffered any accident or sickness not arising out of and in the course of his or her employment or, if so arising, not compensable under the workers' compensation law, and resulting in the worker's total disability to perform any work for remuneration.

No benefits are payable:

— to any individual for any period during which he or she is not under the care of a legally licensed physician, dentist, podiatrist, practicing psychologist, chiropractor or optometrist;

— for any period of disability due to willfully or intentionally self-inflicted injury; for any period during which claimant performs work for remuneration;

— in a weekly amount which together with any remuneration the individual continues to receive from his or her employer would exceed the regular weekly wages immediately prior to disability;

— for any period during which a covered individual would be disqualified because of a labor dispute unless the disability commenced prior to such disqualification.

The weekly benefit amount is computed as $66^2/3$ % of the individual's average weekly wage, subject to a maximum of 53% of the statewide average weekly wage. The maximum weekly benefit amount is $559 in 2011, $572 for 2012; and $584 for 2013. The base week amount is $145 in 2012 and 2013.

Unemployment disability benefits are payable to individuals who become disabled while unemployed and, except for their inability to work because of disability, would be entitled to unemployment compensation benefits.

To be eligible for benefits, individuals must have established 20 base weeks in the 52-week period preceding commencement of the disability, or earn $7,300 in 2012 and 2013, in such 52-week period, and they must have served a waiting period of seven days. The waiting period week is compensable if benefits are payable for three consecutive weeks. The maximum total amount of benefits payable is 26 times the claimant's weekly benefit amount.

The maximum amount is computed to the next lower multiple of $1 if not already a multiple thereof.

If individual qualifies during a benefit year for both disability benefits and unemployment compensation benefits under the New Jersey laws, maximum amount payable shall be $1^1/2$ times maximum amount payable under one law.

¶1706

MISCELLANEOUS TAXES
CHAPTER 18
OTHER STATE TAXES

¶1801   Scope of Chapter
¶1802   Insurance Taxes
¶1803   Motor Vehicle Registration
¶1804   Alcoholic Beverage Taxes
¶1805   Cigarette and Tobacco Products Tax
¶1806   Realty Transfer Tax
¶1807   Utilities Taxes
¶1808   Motor Fuels Tax
¶1809   Motor Fuels Use Tax
¶1810   Motor Passenger Carrier Taxes
¶1811   Spill Compensation and Control Tax
¶1812   Casino Taxes and Fees
¶1813   Annual Tax Imposed on Internet Gaming Gross Revenues
¶1814   Major Hazardous Waste Facilities Tax
¶1815   Sanitary Landfill Facility Taxes
¶1816   Litter Control Fee
¶1817   Petroleum Products Gross Receipts Tax
¶1818   Waterfront Commission Payroll Tax (Joint New York-New Jersey Compact)
¶1819   Domestic Security Fee
¶1820   Tax on Certain Cosmetic Medical Procedures
¶1821   Fees on Outdoor Advertising Space
¶1822   Interim Assessment on HMOs
¶1823   Assessment on Licensed Ambulatory Care Facilities
¶1824   Tire Fee
¶1825   Mobile Telecommunications Fee
¶1826   Air Toxics Surcharge
¶1827   Fur Clothing Retail Gross Receipts Tax and Use Tax
¶1828   Luxury Vehicle/Gas Guzzler Tax
¶1829   Non-Residential Development Fee

¶1801 Scope of Chapter

This chapter outlines briefly the New Jersey State taxes that have not already been covered in the Guidebook. The purpose is merely to indicate in general terms who is subject to the tax, who is exempt, the basis and rate of tax, report and payment requirements, and who administers the tax.

¶1802 Insurance Taxes

Law: R.S. 17:22-6.59, 17:22-6.64, 17:22-6.75, 17:30A-1—17:30A-15, 17:32-15, 17:35-8, 17:35-19, 17B:32A-1—17B:32A-19, 27:26A-15, 54:16-1—54:18A-11, 54:48-4.1, 54:49-1—54:50-23 (CCH New Jersey Tax Reports ¶¶88-020, 88-030).

Taxable: Domestic and foreign insurance companies, including health service corporations, pay a tax on taxable premiums.

Marine service corporations do not pay a tax on premiums, but are subject to a tax on underwriting profits.

Foreign fire companies are subject to a firemen's relief association tax, as well as the general premium tax, but the payments on the relief association tax are credited to the premium tax.

Foreign insurance companies are also subject to retaliatory taxes.

Exempt: Fraternal beneficiary and death benefit societies are exempt.

Basis of tax: Life insurance companies are taxed on their taxable premiums, which include all gross contract premiums collected by the company and all of its affiliates, except premiums for reinsurance and premiums for annuity considerations, less certain specified deductions. Non-life companies generally are taxed on gross premiums and assessments, except reinsurance premiums less certain deductions. For both life and non-life companies the maximum taxable premiums cannot exceed 12.5% of the company's total premiums collected.

The tax on marine companies is based on the ratio of annual underwriting profits from premiums written in the state to premiums written within the U.S.

The tax on foreign fire companies is based on taxable premiums.

For periods beginning January 1, 2005, the insurance premiums tax is imposed on all premiums of health services corporations and on any life, accident or health insurance corporation which a health services corporation owns stock in, controls or otherwise becomes affiliated with. The maximum tax rule capping taxable premiums at 12.5% of total premiums for any company whose taxable premiums in New Jersey exceed 12.5% of its total taxable premiums excludes all health service corporations from the benefit of the cap.

CCH Tip: Reconciliation of Premiums Cap with Retaliatory Tax

The premium tax cap of 12.5% that applies to domestic and foreign insurers is intended to encourage insurance companies to conduct more business in New Jersey, while the retaliatory tax is designed to protect New Jersey insurers from another states' imposition of taxes or other costs of doing business that are higher than that of New Jersey. The interpretation of both tax statutes, as they applied to an Ohio insurer, had to be reconciled in order to preserve the intention of each. Separately applied, the benefits of the premium tax cap would be lost and the retaliatory tax would fail to promote the *even-handed treatment* of New Jersey insurers by other states. Therefore, the premium tax cap, as it is applied to foreign insurers, should not be included in calculating the retaliatory tax. (*American Fire & Casualty Company v. New Jersey Division of Taxation,* 189 N.J. 65 (2006), CCH NEW JERSEY TAX REPORTS, ¶ 401-222.

Rate of tax: On life and non-life companies generally the premiums tax is imposed at the rate of 2%. An additional premiums tax is imposed at the rate of 0.1%. The tax on group accident and health insurance and legal insurance premiums is 1%, plus an additional premiums tax of 0.05%. For the year 2009, the regular premiums tax rate on group accident and health insurance and legal insurance premiums is increased to 1.35%. For 2009, dental service companies are also subject to the 1.35% and 0.05% premiums taxes.

     — Marine companies—5% of the average annual underwriting profit, plus an additional tax of 0.25%.

     — Surplus lines coverage—5% beginning 2009; 3% for prior years.

     — Unauthorized insurance—3%.

Credits: Effective January 13, 2008, a business that makes $75,000,000 of qualified capital investment in a business facility in an urban transit hub and employs at least 250 full-time employees at that facility may qualify for tax credits equal to 100% of the qualified capital investment that may be applied against the insurance gross premiums tax (see ¶708A).

Effective for tax returns due on or before March 1, 2014, domestic insurance companies (other than marine insurance companies) can reduce their premiums tax liabilities by 5% of any retaliatory tax liability incurred for that same filing period under the laws of any other state in which the insurance company transacts business. After March 1, 2014, the available percentage reduction will increase 1% per year until reaching 15% of any retaliatory tax liability for the filing due on or before March 1, 2024.

Before 2008, when the credit expired, employers were allowed a credit for voluntarily providing commuter transportation benefits based upon a direct expenditure made after the taxpayer had registered with and been certified by the Department of Transportation. Employers could claim a tax credit in an amount equal to 10% of the cost of commuter transportation benefits provided, up to a maximum amount per participating employee (see ¶713 for current maximum amount). The total amount of the credit allowed for an accounting or privilege period could not exceed 50% of the tax liability that otherwise would have been due after first applying the credits allowed under any other law, and could not reduce the amount of tax liability to less than the statutory minimum.

Returns: Generally, insurance companies must file an annual return by March 1 with the Commissioner of Insurance. Life insurance companies file an annual report with the Commissioner of Insurance by March 15. Marine companies must file their return by April 1 with the Commissioner of Banking and Insurance. The reports of all companies are filed with the Director of the Division of Taxation; however, a "duplicate original" of the return must be filed with the Commissioner of Insurance. Surplus lines agents must file quarterly reports with the Commissioner of Insurance. Foreign fire companies file their returns with the treasurers of the local firemen's relief associations.

The examination of returns and the assessment of additional taxes, penalties and interest will be as provided in the State Tax Uniform Procedure Law (¶2001).

Payment: Premium taxes on domestic and foreign insurance companies generally are payable to the Director of the Division of Taxation, with any balance of tax due for the preceding year payable on March 1, along with an installment payment for the current year equal to 50% of the total tax for the preceding year. Domestic and foreign companies pay the second installment, equal to 50% of the preceding year's tax, on June 1.

The premium tax on foreign fire companies is due March 1, but credit is given for the amount paid on March 1 to the firemen's relief associations. Marine companies must pay their tax within 15 days of billing.

Taxpayers with an annual tax liability of $10,000 or more are required to pay by electronic funds transfer.

Special assessments: Surplus lines insurers are assessed a one-time payment of $25,000 and an additional assessment of not more than 4% of net direct written premiums, to be paid quarterly.

An assessment is authorized against insurers for purposes of funding the New Jersey Life and Health Insurance Guaranty Association, established to pay benefits and protect insureds from hardship due to impairment or insolvency of member insurers. Member insurers are assessed separately, at such time and for such amounts as the board of directors finds necessary. Assessments are due 30 days or more following written notice. An offset of 10% of the amount of assessments for each of the five calendar years following the second year after the year in which those

¶1802

assessments were paid is allowed against New Jersey insurance premiums taxes (up to 20% of the insurer's premiums tax liability in any one year).

Insurers doing business in New Jersey are subject to a Property-Liability Insurance Guaranty Fund assessment not to exceed 2% of the insurer's net direct written premiums for the preceding calendar year.

Administration: The taxes are administered by the Commissioner of Insurance and by the Director of the Division of Taxation, subject to the provisions of the State Tax Uniform Procedure Law (Chapter 20).

¶1803 Motor Vehicle Registration

Law: R.S. 17:33B-63, 39:3-1—39:3-42 (CCH New Jersey Tax Reports ¶ 50-110, 50-120).

Persons subject to tax: Registration fees are imposed on the operation and ownership of commercial and noncommercial motor vehicles, including automobiles, omnibuses, trucks, tractors, trailers, semitrailers, motorcycles, and motorized bicycles.

Exemptions: Among the vehicles exempted from registration fees are motor vehicles of nonresidents under reciprocal provisions, governmental vehicles, certain vehicles of blind or disabled veterans, ambulances owned by nonprofit organizations, and self-propelling vehicles not used for the conveyance of persons or property (such as steam road rollers).

Basis and rate: The registration fees are based on the weight and model year of the vehicle to be registered, except in the case of commuter vans and motorcycles. Registration fees for commercial motor vehicles (trucks, road tractors, and truck tractors) and non-commercial trucks are based on gross weight of vehicle and load. Additional fees are imposed on different classes of vehicles.

Returns and payments: No returns are required to be filed. Fees are payable at the time the annual registration application is submitted.

Administration: The motor vehicle registration provisions are administered by the Motor Vehicle Commission, CN 016, Trenton, New Jersey 08625.

¶1804 Alcoholic Beverage Taxes

Law: R.S. 54:43-1, 54:45-1, 54:48-4.1 (CCH New Jersey Tax Reports ¶ 35-110—35-150).

Persons subject to tax: Excise taxes are imposed on the sale of alcoholic beverages in New Jersey or upon any delivery of alcoholic beverages made within or into New Jersey. License fees are collected from persons connected with the trade.

Basis and rate: Taxes are paid on a gallonage basis at the following rates:

Type of Liquor Taxed	Rate per gallon
Beer, Cider (3.2% to 7% alcohol)	$0.12
Liquors	4.40
Wines, Sparkling Wines, Vermouth, and Cider (more than 7% alcohol)	0.70

P.L. 2009, c. 71 increases the alcoholic beverage tax rate imposed on certain alcoholic beverages by 25% effective August 1, 2009. The tax rate imposed on liquor is increased to $5.50 per gallon; the rate on wine, vermouth and sparkling wine is increased to $0.875 per gallon; and the rate on hard cider is increased to $0.15 per gallon. The law also dedicates certain additional revenues generated by the tax to the Health Care Subsidy Fund.

Alcoholic beverages are also subject to the 7% sales and use tax (¶ 1816).

Returns and payments: Reports covering the preceding two months must be filed on or before the 15th day of the month following each two-month period. Payment accompanies the report.

Taxpayers with an annual tax liability of $10,000 or more are required to pay by electronic funds transfer.

Administration: The alcoholic beverage taxes are administered by the Director of the Division of Taxation and by the Director of the Division of Alcoholic Beverage Control.

¶1805 Cigarette and Tobacco Products Tax

Law: R.S. 54:40A-1—54:40A-44, 54:40B-1—54:40B-14, 54:48-4.1 (CCH New Jersey Tax Reports ¶ 55-110—55-150, 55-165—55-180).

Cigarettes

Persons subject to tax: A tax is imposed on the sale, use, or possession for sale or use within New Jersey of all cigarettes. The tax is paid by the purchase of stamps or decals, which are affixed on each package of cigarettes by the distributors.

License fees are payable by distributors, wholesale dealers, manufacturers, manufacturer's representatives, retail dealers, retail dealers operating vending machines, and consumers.

Sales to the state of New Jersey, its agencies and its political subdivisions are expressly taxable.

Exemptions: No tax is imposed on cigarettes or the sale of cigarettes that New Jersey is prohibited from taxing under the United States Constitution or Federal law (for example, sales to the United States or its agencies and sales in interstate commerce are exempt). Also exempt are purchases by authorized agents of the United States Veterans Administration from donations for free distribution to and consumption by veterans in state hospitals.

Basis and rate: Effective July 15, 2006, the tax rate is $2.575 per pack of 20 cigarettes, increasing the tax on a pack by $0.175 (Ch. 37, Laws 2006). Effective October 1, 2004, cigarettes cannot be sold in packs of fewer than 20 (Ch. 96, Laws 2004).

P.L. 2009, c. 70, raised the cigarette tax rate effective July 1, 2009. The rate increased $0.125 per pack of 20 cigarettes from $2.575 to $2.70. The law also dedicates additional revenue to the Health Care Subsidy Fund.

In addition, cigarettes are subject to the 7% New Jersey sales tax.

Public Law 2005, c.85, enacted on May 4, 2005, and effective November 1, 2005, requires that retail sales of cigarettes may be made only when the purchaser is in the physical presence of the seller, unless the seller has fully complied with certain requirements, including collecting or verifying payment of applicable State cigarette and sales and use taxes and verifying certain information about the purchaser.

Returns and payment: The tax is paid by the affixing of stamps or meter impressions by the distributors. Monthly reports are due by the 20th of each month for the preceding calendar month. Authorized proof of payment must be made by affixing heat applied decals, either by hand or by machine.

Administration: The tax is administered by the Director of the Division of Taxation.

Tobacco Products

Persons subject to tax: A wholesale sales tax is imposed on the receipts from sales of tobacco products (other than cigarettes) by distributors or wholesalers to retail dealers or consumers. Examples of taxable tobacco products are cigars, little cigars, cigarillos, chewing tobacco, pipe tobacco, smoking tobacco and their substitutes, and snuff. Cigarettes are exempt from the tobacco products tax.

Distributors and wholesalers are required to collect the tax from the retailer or consumer when they collect the receipts for the products. The distributors and wholesalers must give the retailer or consumer an invoice, receipt, or other statement on which the tax is separately stated.

Distributors and wholesalers beginning business or opening new places of business must file applications for registration within three days of beginning business.

Records of all sales of tobacco products must be kept by distributors and wholesalers, including a true copy of each invoice, receipt, statement or memorandum for all sales of tobacco products. The records must be available for inspection by the Division of Taxation for three years from the date of transaction.

Basis and rate: The wholesale sales tax on tobacco products is imposed at the rate of 30% of the receipts from tobacco product sales by distributors or wholesalers to retail dealers or consumers. If the distributor or wholesaler has not collected the 30% tax from either the retailer or consumer, the retailer or consumer is subject to a compensating use tax at 30% of the price paid or charged for the tobacco product. Effective August 1, 2006, moist snuff (*e.g.* chewing tobacco) is taxed at $.75 per ounce. Previously, most snuff was taxed with other tobacco products. (Ch. 37, Laws 2006).

Returns and payment: Distributors and wholesalers must file returns for the preceding month and pay the taxes imposed to the Director on or before the 20th of each month. The tax must be paid whether or not the tax has actually been collected from the customer by the time the return is due.

If a retail dealer or consumer is responsible for payment of the tax, as a result of the failure of the distributor or wholesaler to collect the tax, the retailer or consumer will be responsible for remitting a compensating use tax directly to the Division of Taxation, within 20 days of the date on which the tax was required to be paid.

If a return is not filed or, in the opinion of the Director of the Division of Taxation, is incorrect or insufficient, the Director may determine the amount of tax due from the information available. In addition, any person failing to file a return or to pay over any tax due to the Director is subject to penalties and interest.

Taxpayers with an annual tax liability of $10,000 or more are required to pay by electronic funds transfer.

Administration: The tax is administered by the Director of the Division of Taxation.

¶1806 Realty Transfer Tax

Law: R.S. 46:15-5—46:15-11, 46:16-7 (CCH New Jersey Tax Reports ¶34-201—34-213).

Persons and conveyances subject to tax: The realty transfer tax is imposed on the grantor of each deed, instrument or writing conveying real property for a consideration of $100 or more. An instrument creating a leasehold interest for 99 years or more, a proprietary lease of a cooperative unit and any assignment of such lease are also taxable.

The New Jersey Supreme Court determined that the application of recording and realty transfer tax provisions to the transfer of ownership in cooperative housing units only if created after May 7, 1988, was constitutional. The differential tax treatment accorded cooperatives created before and after May 7, 1988, did not violate equal protection requirements and was justified by concerns for administrative convenience and expense (*Drew Associates v. Travisano,* January 31, 1991, 122 NJ 249, 584 A2d 807; CCH New Jersey Tax Reports, ¶400-097).

¶1806

Exemptions: The tax does not apply to any deed

— for a consideration of less than $100,

— by or to the United States, the state of New Jersey, or any instrumentality, agency, or subdivision thereof,

— solely providing for or releasing security for a debt or obligation,

— confirming or correcting a deed previously recorded,

— on a sale for delinquent taxes or assessments,

— on partition,

— by a receiver, trustee in bankruptcy or liquidation, or assignee for the benefit of creditors,

— eligible to be recorded as an "ancient deed" (R.S. 46:16-7),

— acknowledged or proved on or before July 3, 1968,

— between husband and wife, or parent and child,

— conveying a cemetery lot or plot,

— in specific performance of a final judgment,

— releasing a right of reversion,

— previously recorded in another county with full realty transfer taxes paid,

— by an executor or administrator to a devisee or heir to effect distribution of a decedent's estate in accordance with the decedent's will or the intestate laws of New Jersey, and

— recorded within 90 days following the entry of a divorce decree, which dissolves the marriage between the grantor and grantee.

Basis and rate: Effective July 14, 2003, new rates apply. The tax is imposed at the rate of $2.00 per $500 of consideration not in excess of $150,000. An additional tax of $3.35 per $500 of consideration in excess of $150,000 but not in excess of $200,000 is also imposed. An additional tax of $3.90 is imposed for every $500 of consideration in excess of $200,000 (P.L. 2003, c.113). The new law does not increase the Realty Transfer Fee rates on transfers by senior citizens, blind or disabled persons or on the transfer of property that is low and moderate income housing.

Before July 14, 2003, the tax was imposed at the rate of $1.75 per $500 of consideration. An additional tax of 75¢ per $500 of consideration in excess of $150,000 was also imposed. Thus, for the amount of the deed over $150,000, the tax was $2.50 per $500 of consideration.

Increased Realty Transfer Fees: Transfers of real property for consideration in excess of $350,000 are subject to a new "general purpose" realty transfer fee of $0.90 for each $500 of consideration up to $550,000, $1.40 for each $500 of consideration between $550,000 and $850,000, $1.90 for each $500 of consideration between $850,000 and $1,000,000 and $2.15 for each $500 of consideration in excess of $1,000,000. The new law also imposes a separate fee on the purchaser of residential real property for consideration in excess of $1,000,000 equal to 1% of the entire consideration. Both fees are in addition to the current realty transfer fees and are applicable to transfers of real property occurring on or after August 1, 2004 (P.L. 2004, c.66).

Consideration, the basis of tax, includes the remaining amount of any prior existing mortgage, lien or other encumbrance (except liens for property taxes, sewerage or water charges, and like encumbrances of a current and continuing nature that are usually adjusted between buyer and seller). In the case of a leasehold interest, the consideration is the property's "assessed value" on the date of the transaction adjusted to reflect "true value" in accordance with the county percentage level for the current year. In the case of property sold under execution or pursuant to any writ, judgment or order, the basis is the amount bid for the property plus the remaining amount of superior mortgages, liens or encumbrances constituting "consideration."

Partial exemption: The following transfers are exempt from a portion of the tax:

— Sales of one- and two-family, owner-occupied residences owned by senior citizens, blind persons, and disabled persons who are sellers in the transactions are exempt from $1.25 of the tax for each $500, or fraction thereof, of consideration (such sales are also exempt from the supplemental fees that became effective July 14, 2003). The partial exemption does not apply to property owned jointly (other than by a husband and wife) if even one owner is not a senior citizen, blind, or disabled.

— Sales of low- and moderate-income housing are exempt from $1.25 of the tax for each $500, or fraction thereof, of consideration (such sales are also exempt from the supplemental fees that became effective July 14, 2003). This housing includes residential premises or parts thereof, affordable according to the federal Department of Housing and Urban Development or other recognized standards for home ownership and rental costs. The housing must be occupied or reserved for occupancy by households with a gross income of not more than 80% of the median gross household income for households of the same size within the housing region, but including only premises subject to resale controls pursuant to contractual guarantees.

— Transfers of title to real property upon which there is new construction are exempt from $1 for each $500, or fraction thereof, of consideration not in excess of $150,000. However, under Ch. 113, Laws 2003, an additional supplemental fee is imposed on such transfers at the rate of $1 for each $500, or fraction thereof, of consideration not in excess of $150,000.

Collection of tax: The tax is paid to the county recording officer at the time the deed is presented for recording.

1% Realty Transfer Tax on Commercial Property: For transfers of real property occurring on or after August 1, 2006, New Jersey imposes an additional 1% realty transfer fee on purchasers of commercial property for over $1 million of consideration. The 1% tax is imposed on the purchaser and applies to the entire consideration, not just the amount of consideration over $1 million. The additional 1% tax previously applied only to residential purchasers. Taxpayers can obtain a refund of the additional 1% tax for any transfer of commercial real property pursuant to a contract that was fully executed before July 1, 2006, provided that the deed is recorded on or before November 15, 2006.

Additionally, New Jersey imposes a 1% entity level tax for transfers of controlling interests (more than 50%) in entities that own a controlling interest (more than 50%) in commercial real estate with a value in excess of $1 million. That 1% entity-level tax also applies to transfers occurring on or after August 1, 2006. In determining whether there has been a transfer of a controlling interest, transactions which occur within six months of each other are presumed to constitute a single sale or transfer. However, there is an exemption from tax for transfers of controlling interests in entities that are incidental to a corporate merger or acquisition if the equalized assessed value of the real property transferred is less than 20% of the total value of all assets transferred in the merger or acquisition. Additionally, there is an exemption to the 1% entity level tax for transfers of controlling interests in entities completed prior to November 15, 2006, pursuant to a contract or other binding agreement that was fully executed before July 1, 2006. (Ch. 33, Laws 2006).

¶1807 Utilities Taxes

Law: R.S. 27:26A-15, 48:2-59—48:2-60, 54:29A-13—54:29A-14, 54:29A-44, 54:29A-46, 54:30A-16—54:30A-30, 54:30A-49—54:30A-68, 54:48-4.1, Ch. 162, Laws 1997 (CCH NEW JERSEY TAX REPORTS ¶80-101—80-200).

In addition to the utility taxes detailed below, an administrative expense assessment is levied against each public utility, at a rate not to exceed $1/4$ of 1% of its gross intrastate operating revenue for the preceding calendar year. The minimum assessment is $500.

I. Railroads

Taxable: All railroads other than street railways or traction companies operating in New Jersey are subject to a franchise tax.

Basis and rate: The tax is imposed at the rate of 10% of net railway operating income of the preceding year allocated to New Jersey. Net railway operating income of each system (and of each railroad not part of a system) is allocated to New Jersey in the proportion that the number of miles of all track over which the railroad or system operate in New Jersey bears to the total number of miles of all track over which it operates. The minimum tax is $100 where total allocated railway operating revenues do not exceed $1 million, and $4,000 as to all other taxpayers.

Returns and payment: Returns of schedules of operating revenues are due on or before April 1 and are filed with the Division of Taxation. The franchise tax is assessed by the Director and is payable on or before June 15.

Taxpayers with an annual tax liability of $10,000 or more are required to pay by electronic funds transfer.

II. Sewerage and Water Corporations Using Public Streets or Places

Taxable: Sewerage and water corporations using public streets, highways, roads, or other public places in New Jersey are subject to gross receipts tax under R.S. 54:30A-49—54:30A-68. Persons or business entities owning or operating cogeneration facilities are not subject to tax.

Basis and rate: The tax is imposed at the rate of 5% of such proportion of the gross receipts of the taxpayer for the preceding calendar year as the length of the lines or mains in New Jersey located along, in, or over any public street, highway, road, or other public place, exclusive of service connections, bears to the whole length of its lines or mains, exclusive of service connections. A 0.625% surtax is also imposed on the same receipts.

When the gross receipts of any taxpayer for any calendar year do not exceed $50,000, the tax is computed at the rate of 2%. In such case the surtax rate is 0.25% imposed on the same receipts.

An additional tax is imposed at the rate of $7\frac{1}{2}\%$ on the gross receipts of the taxpayer for the preceding calendar year from its business over, on, in, through, or from its lines or mains in the State of New Jersey. A 0.9375% surtax is also imposed on such receipts.

Returns and payment: Returns showing gross receipts for the preceding calendar year are filed on or before February 1 with the Director of the Division of Taxation, who assesses the taxes. The taxes (after certain deductions) are paid to the Director in three installments: 35% within 15 days of certification by the Director, another 35% by August 15, and the remaining 30% by November 15. By June 1, taxpayers must make a prepayment equal to 55% of any increase in taxes due during the preceding calendar year over the amount due in the second preceding year. The surtaxes (after credit for prepayment) are payable to the state on or before May 1, together with a prepayment of tax for the ensuing year equal to 50% of the tax liability for the preceding calendar year.

¶1807

III. Gas and Electric, Heat and Power Corporations Using Public Streets or Places

Gas, electric, gas and electric, and municipal electric corporations public utilities are subject to the corporate business (income) tax (¶703), sales and use tax (¶1308), and, through 2013, a transitional tax.

Prior to 1998, gas and electric light, heat and power corporations using or occupying the public streets, highways, roads or other public places in New Jersey were subject to an annual franchise tax under either R.S. 54:30A-17 *et seq.* or 54:30A-49 *et seq.*

IV. Telephone, Telegraph, and Cable Companies and Other Utilities

Telecommunications companies are subject to the corporate business (income) tax (¶703), sales and use tax (¶1804), and, for five years, a transitional tax.

Prior to 1998, telephone, telegraph, and cable companies and other utilities using public streets or other public places, but not included in categories II or III above, were subject to tax under either R.S. 54:30A-17 *et seq.* or 54:30A-49 *et seq.*

¶1808 Motor Fuels Tax

Law: R.S. 48:4-3, 54:39-1—54:39-75, 54:48-4.1 (CCH New Jersey Tax Reports ¶40-110—40-170).

Persons subject to tax: An excise tax is imposed on motor fuels sold or used in the state. The tax is paid by distributors, importers, and jobbers.

Exemptions: Fuels sold for official use to the federal government, New Jersey or its political subdivisions, or any departments or agencies of such governments, are exempt. Sales for export and from one licensed distributor to another are also exempt.

The following uses of fuel are exempt (that is, if the tax has been paid, claims for reimbursement may be filed): jitneys operating in municipalities and subject to motor passenger carrier taxes (¶1810); buses providing regular route service under R.S. 48:4-3 or under a contract with the New Jersey Transit Corporation or under a contract with a county for special or rural transportation bus service; buses providing commuter bus service that receive or discharge passengers in New Jersey; agricultural tractors not operated on a public highway; farm machinery; aircraft; ambulances; rural free delivery carriers; vehicles run only on rails or tracks (or in substitution); highway motor vehicles operated exclusively on private property; cleaning vehicles; fire engines and fire-fighting apparatus; stationary machinery and vehicles or implements not designed to transport persons or property on public highways; heating and lighting devices; fuels previously taxed and later exported; emergency vehicles used exclusively by volunteer first-aid or rescue squads; and motorboats or motor vessels (1) used exclusively for oyster and clam farming or for commercial fishing or for Sea Scout training, or (2) while being used for hire for fishing parties, sightseeing or excursion parties.

Basis and rate: The general motor fuels tax is imposed at the rate of 10.5¢ per gallon, but several special rates apply.

The tax on special fuels (diesel) is 13.5¢ per gallon.

Gasohol is taxed at the general motor fuels tax rate.

Liquefied petroleum gas and liquefied or compressed natural gas sold or used to propel motor vehicles on public highways is taxed at $5^{1}/4$¢ per gallon.

Aviation fuel is taxed at 12.5¢ per gallon. Gasoline jobbers and distributors are subject to an additional tax of 2¢ per gallon on fuel, including turbine fuel, distributed to general aviation airports.

Reports and payment: Distributors, importers, storage facility operators, and jobbers file reports on or before the 20th day of each month, covering the preceding calendar month. The tax on fuel distributed to general aviation airports must be paid by the 20th day of each month. Other dates apply for special licensees.

Payment of tax accompanies the report.

Taxpayers with an annual tax liability of $10,000 or more are required to pay by electronic funds transfer.

Administration: The tax on motor fuels is administered by the Division of Taxation.

The examination of returns and the assessment of additional taxes, penalties, and interest will be as provided by the State Tax Uniform Procedure Law.

P.L. 2007, c.221, enacted January 3, 2008, and effective on that date, increases the monetary penalties for violations of the law governing retail sales of motor fuels.

Money paid in error may be refunded. No refund may be made if more than four years has elapsed from the time the erroneous payment was made.

Motor Fuel Tax Act: P.L. 2010, c. 22, was signed into law on June 30, 2010.

The Act modernizes the system for assessing the taxes on highway motor vehicles. Those taxes are principally dedicated by the New Jersey Constitution to the costs of the State transportation system.

The law changes the point of taxation of diesel fuel from the retail level to the level at which it is removed from the bulk fuel storage and distribution system of refineries, pipelines, ships and barges at a terminal. It also changes the point of taxation of gasoline from the distributor level to the terminal level.

The Act includes requirements for transporting and labeling dyed fuel, and penalties for mishandling dyed (tax exempt) fuel and for using dyed fuel in highway vehicles. The law also authorizes the co-collection of petroleum products gross receipts tax with the motor fuel taxes when feasible.

Also, on October 6, 2010, by P.L. 2010, c. 79, the previously enacted Motor Fuel Tax Act, as explained above, was amended to make a number of technical changes that will allow more effective implementation of the new taxation system and postpone the operative date of the new law from October 1, 2010, to January 1, 2011, to allow time for necessary re-licensing and other administrative issues. Among other technical corrections, the amendments assure that heating oil dealers are not required to be licensed as motor fuel tax dealers; clarify that fuel transporters are not among those required to pre-collect the motor fuel tax; and correct an error in the original Act that exempted aviation grade kerosene as a taxable fuel.

P.L. 2011, c.152, signed into law on January 5, 2012, and effective the 120th day following its enactment, or May 4, 2012, provides that price signs posted by a retail motor fuel dealer on the dealer's premises and visible from any adjacent roadway shall include the price per gallon, or the price per gallon and per liter, for both cash and credit card purchases of motor fuel in accordance with regulations prescribed by the Director of the Division of Taxation.

P.L. 2011, c.164, signed into law on January 5, 2012, and effective immediately, amends subsection e. of section 201 of P.L. 1938, c.163 (N.J.S.A. 56:6-2) to stipulate that a consumer who earns credits through purchases on a credit card, debit card, or rewards card may utilize those credits to receive a rebate, allowance, concession, or benefit when that person purchases motor fuels.

The use of credits earned through purchases on a credit card, debit card, or rewards card would not change the retail price of motor fuel displayed pursuant to section 3 of P.L. 1952, c.258 (N.J.S.A. 56:6-2.3); and the retail dealer would not bear the cost of the rebate, allowance, concession, or benefit received by the motor fuel purchaser, except for a processing fee assessed in the ordinary course of business.

¶1809 Motor Fuels Use Tax

Law: R.S. 54:39A-1—54:39A-24, 54:48-4.1 (CCH NEW JERSEY TAX REPORTS ¶40-210—40-270).

Persons subject to tax: The motor fuels use tax is imposed on users of fuel in New Jersey operations of buses seating more than 10 passengers, road tractors, truck tractors, and trucks with a gross or registered weight of more than 18,000 pounds alone or in combination with a motor vehicle. The tax applies to the fuel used in New Jersey that is in excess of the amount on which the motor fuels tax (¶1808) has been paid.

A rental company is also a taxable user in the case of a rental vehicle.

A user must obtain an identification card, and an identification marker must be affixed to each vehicle. Cards and markers are valid from April 1 through the following March 31. Temporary permits may be issued for a period up to 25 days pending application for, and the issuance of, cards and markers.

A user whose vehicles make no more than six trips in New Jersey during a 12-month period may apply for a single-trip permit, good for 96 hours, in lieu of all other requirements of the use tax law.

The fee for each original identification marker or any replacement marker is $5. The fee for temporary markers is $5, and for single trip markers, $2.50.

Exemptions: The following vehicles are exempt: vehicles of public utilities, or operating under contract with New Jersey Transit, or under contract with a county for special or rural transportation bus service subject to the Transit's jurisdiction; those providing commuter bus service that receive or discharge passengers in New Jersey; school buses and buses on authorized routes in a municipality; government vehicles; vehicles with dealer, manufacturer, converter or transporter plates; special mobile equipment; vehicles in nonprofit operations of religious or charitable organizations; and farm vehicles not for hire and vehicles for transporting farm labor.

Basis and rate: The use tax is imposed at the motor vehicle fuel tax rate (¶1808) on the amount of motor fuel used in New Jersey. The amount is computed by multiplying the total amount of motor fuels used by a fraction, the numerator of which is miles traveled in New Jersey, and the denominator of which is total miles traveled everywhere. Credit is allowed to the extent of any New Jersey motor fuel tax which has been paid.

Reports and payment: Reports for each calendar quarter are due on the last day of April, July, October, and January. Payment accompanies the reports.

Taxpayers with an annual tax liability of $10,000 or more are required to pay by electronic funds transfer.

Annual reports may be permitted in the case of users who make all their fuel purchases in New Jersey.

Administration: The motor carrier road tax is administered by the Motor Vehicle Commission, CN 016, Trenton, New Jersey 08625-0016.

The examination of returns and the assessment of additional taxes, penalties, and interest will be as provided by the State Tax Uniform Procedure Law.

A claim for refund must be filed within four years after payment of tax. No claim for refund is permitted after proceedings on appeal have been commenced. If the Director, upon examination of the refund claim, determines that there has been an overpayment of tax, the amount of the overpayment will be refunded.

¶1809

¶1810 Motor Passenger Carrier Taxes

Law: R.S. 48:4-1—48:4-35, 48:16-23—48:16-28 (CCH NEW JERSEY TAX REPORTS ¶50-210, 50-220).

Interstate buses: Interstate buses are required by statute to pay a state mileage tax of 0.5¢ for each mile or fraction thereof operated over New Jersey highways. Interstate buses are defined as buses operated over any New Jersey highway for the purpose of carrying passengers from a point outside New Jersey to another point outside the state, from a point outside the state to a point within New Jersey, or from a point within the state to a point outside New Jersey. The law provides exemptions from the interstate bus tax for regular route commuter bus service from or to a point in New Jersey, and for buses operated under contract with the New Jersey Transit Corporation or under contract with a county for bus service subject to New Jersey Transit's jurisdiction.

However, the New Jersey Supreme Court has held that the autobus excise tax violates the Commerce Clause of the United States Constitution because it discriminates against interstate commerce (*Continental Trailways, Inc.*, May 27, 1986, 102 NJ 526, 509 A2d 769; CCH NEW JERSEY TAX REPORTS, ¶201-316). Petitions for certiorari were dismissed by the U.S. Supreme Court (Docket Nos. 86-843 and 86-879, April 6, 1987). As a result, the Division of Motor Vehicles is no longer collecting the tax.

Jitney operators: Jitney operators are required to pay a local tax on gross receipts derived from operation within a city. Autobuses with a carrying capacity of less than 14 passengers operated wholly within a single municipality, or autobuses with a carrying capacity of less than 21 passengers operated wholly within the limits of less than five contiguous municipalities, constitute jitneys. Jitney operators must pay to each city 5% of the same proportion of gross receipts as the length of the route in the city bears to the length of the entire route. Fourth-class cities (resort cities bordering on the Atlantic Ocean) may impose special license fees in lieu of monthly franchise taxes.

Jitney owners or operators are required to file reports on or before the 10th day of each month covering the preceding calendar month with the city treasurer of each city in which the jitney is operated. Payment of tax must accompany the return.

¶1811 Spill Compensation and Control Tax

Law: 54:10-23.11b, 54:10-23.11h; Reg. Sec. 18:37-1.1 *et seq.* (CCH NEW JERSEY TAX REPORTS ¶ 34-010—34-040).

The Spill Compensation and Control Tax is imposed on owners and operators of refineries, storage or transfer terminal, pipelines, deep water ports or drilling platforms used to refine, store, produce, handle, transfer, process or transport hazardous substances, including petroleum products, to insure compensation for cleanup costs and damages associated with any hazardous substance discharge. The tax is applicable if the facility has total combined above ground or buried storage capacity of 20,000 gallons or more for hazardous substances other than petroleum or petroleum products and 200,000 gallons or more for hazardous substances of all kinds, excluding underground storage tanks used solely to store heating oil for on-site consumption.

The rate through December 31, 2003, was $1.50 per barrel for petroleum products and precious metals, and the greater of $1.50 per barrel or 1% of fair market value plus $0.25 per barrel for nonpetroleum hazardous substances.

Increased Taxes on Hazardous Substances: The tax imposed on transfers of hazardous substances is increased from $0.015 to $0.023 per barrel for petroleum or petroleum products, precious metals, elemental phosphorus, or in certain circumstances, antimony or antimony trioxide. All other hazardous substances will be taxed at 1.53%

of the product's fair market value. That tax replaces the current tax that is imposed at the greater of: 1) $0.0150 per barrel; or 2) 1.0% of the product's fair market value plus $.0025 per barrel. Both changes are retroactive to January 1, 2004 and taxpayers are required to file amended tax returns and pay any additional taxes owed by September 2004.

¶1812 Casino Taxes and Fees

Law: R.S. 5:12-139—5:12-152 (CCH New Jersey Tax Reports ¶34-110—34-140).

Taxable: Operators of gambling casinos must obtain licenses. The initial fee (based on investigatory expenses) is at least $200,000. The fee for annual renewal (based on regulatory expenses) is at least $100,000. Licensees are subject to the casino control tax. An additional annual license fee of $500 is imposed on each slot machine.

Basis and rate: The casino control tax is imposed at a rate of 8% of gross revenues. "Gross revenue" is defined as the total sum received from gaming operations, whether collected or not, minus the amount paid out as winnings (excluding the cash equivalent value of any merchandise or thing of value included in a jackpot or payout from the total of all sums paid as winnings to patrons, effective August 14, 2002), reduced by the lesser of 4% of the remainder or a reasonable amount for uncollectible patron checks.

An additional investment alternative tax is imposed at the rate of 2.5% of gross revenues, beginning after the second month of operation at the facility. However, an investment tax credit is available equal to twice the amount of the investment in certain bonds or other authorized investments.

Additional taxes, enacted in 2003, are discussed below.

Returns and payment: Casino control tax returns and payment are due by March 15 on the basis of gross revenue received in the previous calendar year. The additional fees for slot machines are due July 1.

The investment alternative tax is due April 30 for revenues from the previous calendar year. Partial payments of 1.25% of estimated gross revenues are due on the 15th day of the first, fourth, seventh, and 10th month of each year. The partial payments are calculated on the estimated gross revenues for the three months preceding the due dates.

Taxpayers with an annual tax liability of $10,000 or more are required to pay by electronic funds transfer. The threshold amount decreased from $50,000.

Administration: Licenses are issued and the taxes are administered by the Casino Control Commission. Prior to May 1, 2011, the gross revenue tax, the casino hotel room fee and the multi-progressive slot machine revenue tax were also administered by the Commission. P.L. 2011, c.19, signed into law on February 1, 2011, and effective immediately, provides for an orderly transition of responsibilities and functions from the Casino Control Commission to the Division of Gaming Enforcement by May 1, 2011. The Division of Taxation now administers and collects several taxes that were previously administered and collected by the New Jersey Casino Control Commission. These taxes include the gross revenue tax, the casino hotel room fee, and the multi-casino progressive slot machine revenue tax. Taxpayers that were required to file and remit tax returns under the prior version of the Casino Control Act must now file tax returns and make payment to the Division of Taxation. This requirement is applicable to returns for the above-listed taxes that are due after April 30, 2011.

Additional taxes: P.L. 2003, c.116, effective July 1, 2003, imposes a state tax of 4.25% on casino licensees on the value of rooms, food, beverages and entertainment that they give away free or at a reduced price as a "complimentary." For those "complimentaries" provided at a reduced price, the 4.25% tax is calculated on the value of the room, food, beverage or entertainment, reduced by any consideration paid by the customer. This tax, payable by the casino licensee, is in addition to any tax due under the Sales and Use Tax Act on receipts from the sale of food, beverages, room occupancies and entertainment.

Ch. 128, Laws 2004, enacted August 30, 2004, and effective on that date, provides for the gradual phase-out of the tax on casino "complimentaries" until the tax expires on June 30, 2009. It also transfers from the Division of Taxation to the Casino Control Commission the responsibility for administering the casino complimentaries tax, the casino adjusted net income tax, the multi-casino slot machine tax, the casino parking fee and the $3 casino hotel occupancy fee.

In addition, Ch. 116, Laws 2003, increases the Atlantic City casino hotel parking fee from $2.00 to $3.00, imposes a $3.00 per day fee on each hotel room occupied by a guest in a casino hotel, an 8% gross revenue tax on companies that administer and service multi-casino progressive slot machine systems, and (for state fiscal years 2004 through 2006) a 7.5% tax on the calendar year 2002 adjusted net income of casino licensees.

¶1813 Annual Tax Imposed on Internet Gaming Gross Revenues

Ch. 27, Laws 2012, imposes an annual tax on Internet gaming gross revenues in the amount of 15% of such gross revenues, which must be paid into the Casino Revenue Fund. The 8% tax on casino gross revenues will not apply to Internet gaming gross revenues. However, the investment alternative tax will apply to Internet gaming gross revenues, except that the investment alternative tax on these revenues will be 5% and the investment alternative will be 2.5%, with the proceeds thereof used as provided by law.

The legislation is effective February 26, 2013, but will remain inoperative until the date selected by the Division of Gaming Enforcement pursuant to pending legislation.

¶1814 Major Hazardous Waste Facilities Tax

Law: R.S. 13:1E-49—13:1E-91 (CCH New Jersey Tax Reports ¶34-410).

Taxable: A tax is imposed on the owner or operator of any "major hazardous waste disposal facility," defined as a commercial facility with the capacity to treat, store, or dispose of more than 250,000 gallons of hazardous waste, or the equivalent. The provisions do not apply to a facility that would be included solely because of the recycling or refining of hazardous wastes that are, or contain gold, silver, osmium, platinum, palladium, iridium, rhodium, ruthenium, or copper.

Basis and rate: The tax generally is at the rate of 5% of the previous year's gross receipts. The Hazardous Waste Facilities Siting Commission may increase the tax after consideration of a petition by the municipality where the facility is located, or may reduce the tax upon petition by the owner or operator, or on its own motion.

Returns and payment: The owner or operator of the facility must file a statement of the previous year's gross receipts with the chief fiscal officer of the municipality where the facility is located, and pay the tax, by January 25 annually.

If the facility is exempt from real property tax because it is located on a site owned by a public agency, the owner or operator must pay the municipal chief fiscal officer a sum equivalent to the property tax which would otherwise be due. Payment must be made by December 31 annually.

Administration: Provisions regulating the facilities are administered by the Hazardous Waste Facilities Siting Commission and the Department of Environmental Protection.

¶1815 Sanitary Landfill Facility Taxes

Law: R.S. 13:1E-28, 13:1E-28.1, 13:1E-28.2, 13:1E-137—13:1E-176, 54:48-4.1 (CCH NEW JERSEY TAX REPORTS ¶ 34-520, 34-590).

Landfill closure tax: The owner or operator of a sanitary landfill facility is required to pay a tax equal to 50¢ per ton or 15¢ per cubic yard (or equivalent) of solid waste accepted for disposal and 0.2¢ per gallon of liquid waste accepted for disposal.

Solid waste services tax: For 2006, a tax of $1.55 per ton or 46.5¢ per cubic yard of solids is imposed on the owner or operator of a sanitary landfill facility for waste accepted for disposal. Effective January 1, 2007, the tax is $1.60 per ton or 48¢ per cubic yard. The tax rate for solid waste in liquid form, reportable in gallons, remains at 0.2¢ per gallon.

P.L. 2007, c.311, enacted on January 13, 2008, imposes a $3 per-ton recycling tax, effective immediately, on solid waste accepted for disposal or transfer at a solid waste facility as well as on solid waste collected by a solid waste collector that transports solid waste for transshipment or direct transportation to an out-of-state disposal site. In addition, the Act provided for expiration of the solid waste services tax on February 1, 2008. Recycling tax revenues are deposited in the State Recycling Fund, administered by the Department of Environmental Protection, and used for the purposes enumerated in the Act.

P.L. 2008, c.6, enacted March 26, 2008, deferred the effective date of the recycling tax, which was enacted by P.L. 2007, c.311. The effective date is now April 1, 2008. Entities subject to the recycling tax are required to register with the Division of Taxation by April 1, 2008, and the first quarterly recycling tax returns and tax payments are due July 20, 2008. The provisions delaying the effective date of the tax are retroactive to January 13, 2008. The Act also adds type 27-A asbestos-containing waste to the list of types of waste included within the definition of solid waste. In addition, the Act treats recycling tax revenue as an exclusion to be added to calculations of the adjusted local property tax levy.

Host community benefits tax: The owner or operator of a sanitary landfill facility is required to pay an "economic benefit" tax to the municipality within which the facility is located of not less than $1 per ton of solids on all solid waste accepted for disposal at the facility during the previous calendar year. In addition, the owner or operator of a solid waste transfer station is required, on at least a quarterly basis, to pay the municipality within which it is located, as part of a district solid waste management plan, an "economic benefit" tax of at least 50¢ per ton of all solid waste accepted for transfer at the transfer station.

Municipalities with a population of 1,500 or more persons per square mile, that share a common boundary along a sanitary landfill located within another municipality, are entitled to an economic benefit in consideration for the proximity of the landfill, provided the landfill is county operated and received more than 600,000 tons of solid waste in 1988. In such instances, the owner or operator of the landfill must pay the municipality between $0.50 and $1.50 per ton for all solid waste accepted for disposal at the sanitary landfill during the previous calendar year. The economic benefit may be in the form of an exemption from all fees and charges for the disposal of solid waste generated within its boundaries and/or the receipt of a lump sum cash payment.

Exemptions: Waste collected pursuant to a contract signed after January 1, 1982, to dispose of waste generated exclusively by any agency of the federal government is exempt from tax. Waste products resulting from the operation of a resource recovery facility are exempt from the solid waste services tax. However, solid wastes which bypass the incineration process at the taxpayer's resource recovery facility are not exempt from landfill disposal taxes as waste products resulting from the operation of a resource recovery facility (*Pollution Control Financing Authority of Warren County, New Jersey v. New Jersey Department of Environmental Protection,* March 28, 1991, 123 NJ 356, 587 A2d 626; CCH NEW JERSEY TAX REPORTS, ¶ 400-116).

Payments and returns: Returns and payments of tax are due by the 20th day of the month following acceptance of waste on which the tax is levied.

Taxpayers with an annual tax liability of $10,000 or more are required to pay by electronic funds transfer.

¶1816 Litter Control Fee

Law: R.S. 13:1E-99.1 (CCH NEW JERSEY TAX REPORTS ¶ 34-610).

Manufacturers, wholesalers, and distributors of "litter-generating products" must pay a tax of 0.03% of taxable sales of the products within New Jersey. Retailers of the products pay a tax of 0.0225% of taxable sales of the products within the state except that retailers with less than a certain amount of annual retail sales of the products are exempt from the tax (see discussion below).

Paper products subject to tax do not include newspapers or magazines (see also the exemption for roll stock noted below). All other paper products are subject to tax, including other printed material such as advertising flyers, brochures, or pamphlets.

The Clean Communities and Recycling Grant Act was recently signed into law in New Jersey as P.L. 2002, c.128. This Act imposes a litter control fee on manufacturers, wholesalers, distributors and retailers on their sales of litter-generating products within or into New Jersey. The litter control fee is essentially identical to the litter control tax which was imposed in New Jersey from 1986 through 2000 under N.J.S.A. 13:1E-99.1. The litter control tax terminated on December 31, 2000. There was no tax or fee on the gross receipts from sales of litter-generating products for the 2001 calendar year. The litter control fee is similar to the expired litter control tax and is imposed annually on the previous calendar year's gross receipts from sales of litter generating products. It is due and payable on March 15th of each year. The fee rates and litter-generating product categories remain the same. Revenues from the litter control fee furnish support to the Clean Communities Program for litter pickup and removal, and provide recycling grants to New Jersey counties and municipalities. Unlike the prior litter control tax, the new litter control fee exempts:

— All retailers with less than $500,000 in annual retail sales of litter-generating products (the prior tax had a $250,000 retail sales exclusion);

— Restaurants if more than 50% of their food and beverage sales are for on-premises consumption (but continues to include restaurants with 50% or more of sales of food and beverages for off-premises consumption); and

— Paper product sales of roll stock produced by paper product manufacturers and wood pulp.

The new litter control fee applies retroactively to the year beginning January 1, 2002. Thus, the 2002 return will include the gross receipts from all sales of litter-generating products back to that date. The return and fee payment were due on or before March 15, 2003. Litter control fee returns and instructions were sent to all businesses that were eligible for the litter control tax.

¶1817 Petroleum Products Gross Receipts Tax

Law: R.S. 54:15B-1—54:15B-12, 54:48-4.1 (CCH NEW JERSEY TAX REPORTS ¶ 34-301—34-308).

Companies engaged in the refining and/or distribution of petroleum products are subject to tax on the gross receipts derived from the first sale of petroleum products within New Jersey. First sales of petroleum products for export or first sales of petroleum products to the United States government for use in a federal government function or operation are not subject to the tax. Companies that import or cause petroleum products to be imported into New Jersey for their own use or consumption, and are not otherwise subject to the tax, must pay tax if the consideration given or contracted to be given for deliveries of petroleum products during a quarterly period exceeds $5,000.

The term "petroleum products" means refined products made from crude petroleum and its fractionation products, through straight distillation of crude oil or through redistillation of unfinished derivatives. The term does not include numbers 2, 4, and 6 heating oil, kerosene, and propane gas used exclusively for residential purposes.

The term "first sale of petroleum products" means the initial sale of a petroleum product delivered to a location within New Jersey. Book or exchange transfers of petroleum products are excluded, provided the products are intended to be sold in the ordinary course of business.

Commencing January 1, 2001, there is a three-year phase-out of the petroleum products gross receipts tax for fuel used to generate certain electricity of a utility, cogeneration facility or wholesale generation facility that is sold for resale or to certain end users. Companies subject to the tax must, within 20 days following the first taxable transaction, register with the Director of the Division of Taxation.

Exemptions: Receipts from the sales of petroleum products used by marine vessels engaged in interstate or foreign commerce and sales of aviation fuels used by common carriers in interstate or foreign commerce, other than the "burnout" portion, are excluded from tax. An exclusion is also provided for sales of asphalt, sales of polymer grade propylene used in the manufacture of polypropylene, sales of petroleum products to governmental entities, and sales of petroleum products to certain qualified nonprofit organizations made pursuant to a written contract extending for one year or longer.

Basis and rate: Most petroleum products, such as lubricating oils, are subject to a tax equal to 2.75% of the gross receipts derived from the first sale within the state. Liquid fuels are taxed at a per-gallon rate determined by the average retail price of unleaded regular gasoline. The minimum per-gallon rate on liquid fuels is set at 4¢ per gallon.

Credits: A company will be allowed a credit against the tax if a purchaser of petroleum products first sold within New Jersey sells those products for exportation and use outside New Jersey, provided that (1) the purchaser issues a certificate evidencing a sale outside New Jersey, and (2) the company liable for the tax has paid to the purchaser an amount equal to the tax imposed on gross receipts derived from the first sale to the purchaser within New Jersey. A credit is also provided for companies that import or cause to be imported petroleum products for use or consumption within New Jersey and subsequently export the petroleum products for sale or use outside the state.

Returns and payments: Petroleum product tax returns and payment are due the 25th day of each month for gross receipts derived from the preceding month, and a sworn reconciliation return is due the 25th day of April, July, October, and January. If a return is not filed, or if in the opinion of the Director of the Division of Taxation the return is determined to be incorrect or insufficient, the Director may determine the amount of tax due from the information available. In addition, if gross receipts from a transaction are not indicative or representative of the market price because of an affiliation of interests between the subject company and the purchaser, the Director may utilize external indices to establish the taxable gross receipts. Notice of the Director's determination must be given to the company liable for the tax, and will

¶1817

become final and irrevocable unless the company requests a hearing within 30 days after receipt of the notice.

Licensed distributors, "commercial consumers" (which include companies that purchase, consume, blend, or distribute substantial quantities of petroleum products in New Jersey), and companies making certain sales to nonprofit entities or to qualified governmental entities may elect, subject to approval by the Director, to be recognized as a licensed company and pay taxes directly to the Division of Taxation.

Taxpayers with an annual tax liability of $10,000 or more are required to pay by electronic funds transfer.

In Technical Bulletin TB-65, New Jersey Division of Taxation, April 21, 2011, the New Jersey Division of Taxation has issued guidance regarding products that are subject to the petroleum products gross receipts tax. The tax applies to gross receipts from the first sale or use of petroleum products in New Jersey.These sales are subject to a tax rate of 2.75% except for fuel oil, aviation fuel and motor fuels, which are taxed at a fixed rate of $0.04 a gallon. The guidance defines petroleum products, discusses product exemptions, and lists petroleum products subject to tax.

¶1818 Waterfront Commission Payroll Tax (Joint New York-New Jersey Compact)

Law: R.S. 32:23-58, 32:23-74 (CCH New Jersey Tax Reports ¶ 33-085).

A joint compact between New York and New Jersey created the Waterfront Commission of New York Harbor and provided for the imposition of a payroll tax on each employer of longshoremen, pier superintendents, hiring agents, and port watchmen within the Port of New York District. The proceeds of the tax are used to defray the expenses of the Waterfront Commission.

The rate has decreased from 2% to 1.98%, effective July 1, 2007 through June 30, 2008.

Returns and payments are due on or before the 15th day of January, April, July, and October covering the preceding calendar quarter.

The assessment is administered by the Waterfront Commission of New York Harbor, 42 Broadway, New York, New York 10004.

¶1819 Domestic Security Fee

Law: Reg. Sec. 18:40-1.1—18:40-1.12; Ch. 34 (A.B. 2506), Laws 2002 (CCH New Jersey Tax Reports ¶ 60-570).

The Domestic Security Fee legislation provides for the imposition of a $5 per day fee on motor vehicle rental companies. The fee is applicable to motor vehicles rented without a driver under rental agreements for a period up to and including 28 days. The rental fee is due from the rental company whether the renter or any third party pays for the rental or reimburses the rental company for the fee. For purposes of this legislation, "lease agreement" means any agreement for a stated term of more than 28 days (usually six months or longer) that requires the party leasing from a rental company to pay for state motor vehicle registration, maintain the vehicle for ordinary wear and tear at his own expense, and purchase liability and casualty insurance for the vehicle. If a company is simply leasing motor vehicles and the lease agreements entered into contain a stated term of more than 28 days, the company would not be responsible for the domestic security fee.

¶1820 Tax on Certain Cosmetic Medical Procedures

Law: R.S. 54:32E-1 (CCH NEW JERSEY TAX REPORTS ¶60-520).

A 6% tax is imposed on the gross receipts from certain cosmetic medical procedures. Cosmetic medical procedures are any medical procedure performed on an individual which is directed at improving the subject's appearance and which does not meaningfully promote the proper function of the body or prevent or treat illness or disease. Those procedures specifically include cosmetic surgery, hair transplants, cosmetic injections, cosmetic soft tissue fillers, dermabrasion and chemical peel, laser hair removal, laser skin resurfacing, laser treatment of leg veins, sclerotherapy and cosmetic dentistry. A cosmetic medical procedure does not include any surgery or dentistry performed on abnormal structures caused by or related to congenital defects, developmental abnormalities, trauma, infection, tumors or disease, including procedures to improve or give a more normal appearance. The tax is imposed on the subject of the procedure and must be collected by the person billing for the procedure.

The tax also applies to amounts charged for goods or facility occupancies, such as hospitalization or clinic stays, required for or directly associated with a cosmetic medical procedure.

P.L. 2011, c.189, signed into law on January 17, 2012, and effective immediately, phases out the cosmetic medical procedure gross receipts tax, which is paid pursuant to P.L. 2004, c.53 (N.J.S.A. 54:32E-1 et seq.). The current 6% rate will be reduced to 4% on taxable services performed on or after July 1, 2012, but before July 1, 2013. It is further reduced to 2% on taxable services performed on or after July 1, 2013, but before July 1, 2014, and eliminated entirely on taxable services performed on or after July 1, 2014.

¶1821 Fees on Outdoor Advertising Space

Law: R.S. 54:4-11.1 (CCH NEW JERSEY TAX REPORTS ¶60-240).

An outdoor advertising space fee was previously imposed (no fee was imposed effective July 1, 2007). Applicable to receipts from July 1, 2003, through June 30, 2006, a 6% tax was imposed on gross amounts collected by a retail seller for billboard advertising space. For the period from July 1, 2006 through June 30, 2007, the fee was reduced to 4%. Effective July 1, 2007, there was no rate or fee.

¶1822 Interim Assessment on HMOs

Law: R.S. 26:2J-47 (CCH NEW JERSEY TAX REPORTS ¶88-110).

Commencing in fiscal year 2005, the Commissioner of Banking and Insurance issued a special interim assessment in the amount of 1% on the net written premiums received by each HMO granted a certificate of authority to operate in New Jersey. The new law also requires a study to examine and compare how HMOs, service corporations, insurers and other health care delivery systems and providers are taxed, how they contribute to charity care for the uninsured and whether adjustments need to be made to the current tax structure to respond to the evolution of the industry.

HMO Premiums Tax Increase: New Jersey has increased the annual assessment on net written premiums received by health maintenance organizations (HMOs), from one percent to two percent. That increase is effective for assessments made for the 2007 and subsequent fiscal years. (Ch. 43, Laws 2006).

¶1820

¶1823 Assessment on Licensed Ambulatory Care Facilities

Law: R.S. 26:2H-18.57 (CCH New Jersey Tax Reports ¶34-627).

In Fiscal Year (FY) 2005, an ambulatory care facility with at least $300,000 in gross receipts will pay an assessment equal to 3.5% of its gross receipts or $200,000, whichever amount is less. The assessment will be payable to the New Jersey Department of Health and Senior Services (Department) in four installments, with payments due October 1, 2004, January 1, 2005, March 15, 2005 and June 15, 2005. The Commissioner of Health and Senior Services is directed to provide notice no later than August 15, 2004 to all facilities that are subject to the assessment that proof of gross receipts for the facility's tax year ending in calendar year 2003 must be provided by the facility to the commissioner no later than September 15, 2004. If a facility fails to provide proof of gross receipts by that date, the facility will be assessed the maximum rate of $200,000 for FY 2005.

For FY 2006, the commissioner will use the calendar year 2004 data on patient visits, charges and gross revenues, submitted by the facility to calculate a uniform gross receipts assessment rate to be applied to each facility that is subject to the assessment with gross receipts over $300,000. The FY 2006 rate shall be calculated so as to raise the same amount in the aggregate as was assessed in FY 2005, but no facility will pay more than $200,000. A facility will pay its assessment in four payments to the Department, as specified by the commissioner.

Beginning in FY 2007 and each year thereafter, the uniform gross receipts assessment rate calculated for FY 2006 shall be applied to each facility subject to the assessment with gross receipts over $300,000, but no facility will pay more than $200,000. A facility shall pay its assessment in four payments to the Department, as specified by the commissioner.

¶1824 Tire Fee

Law: R.S. 54:32F-1 (CCH New Jersey Tax Reports ¶60-570).

A fee of $1.50 is imposed on the sale of new motor vehicle tires, including tires sold as a component part of a new motor vehicle either sold or leased in New Jersey. The fee must be collected from the purchaser by the vendor, and generally must be stated separately on any bill, invoice, receipt, or similar document. However, the fee will not be considered part of the receipt for purposes of determining sales tax.

¶1825 Mobile Telecommunications Fee

Law: R.S. 52:17C-18, 52:17C-20 (CCH New Jersey Tax Reports ¶34-616).

Applicable to billing periods ending on or after July 1, 2004, for most services, and to billing periods ending on or after August 1, 2004, for certain services, a $.90 fee is imposed on periodic billing to mobile telecommunications and telephone exchange customers. The fee shall be used to fund the "911" system and certain other emergency response systems. All businesses required to collect the "911" system response fee must register to do so and file quarterly returns (Form ERF-100) for each quarter even if no fees were due for that quarter. Filing and payment must be done electronically.

¶1826 Air Toxics Surcharge

Law: R.S. 13:1D-60 (CCH New Jersey Tax Reports ¶34-621).

An annual surcharge, ranging from $.10 to $10.00 per pound of toxic substance, is imposed depending on the category of toxin on toxic air emissions at certain kinds of facilities. A portion of the revenue from this fee will be used to improve security at nuclear power plants in the State.

Public Law 2005, c.141, enacted July 7, 2005, effective immediately, repeals the air toxics surcharge imposed under P.L. 2004, c.51, and applies retroactively to calendar year 2004 and calendar year thereafter.

¶1827 Fur Clothing Retail Gross Receipts Tax and Use Tax

Law: R.S. 54:32G-1 (CCH New Jersey Tax Reports ¶ 60-290).

Gross Receipts Tax and Use Tax: New Jersey enacted a 6% gross receipts tax and compensating use tax on retail sales of fur clothing effective July 15, 2006. Sales of fur clothing were excluded from sales and use tax as of October 1, 2005 as a result of New Jersey's enactment of legislation adopting the Streamlined Sales Tax Agreement's definition of clothing. The fur tax is not part of the sales and use tax but is a separate gross receipts tax. (Ch. 41, Laws 2006).

P.L. 2008, c. 123, repealed the Fur Clothing Retail Gross Receipts Tax and Use Tax effective January 1, 2009. The final return for the quarter ending December 31, 2008, was due January 20, 2009. Beginning January 1, 2009, sales of fur clothing are subject to sales tax at the rate of 7%.

¶1828 Luxury Vehicle/Gas Guzzler Tax

New Jersey enacted a .4% "one-time supplemental titling fee" on new luxury vehicles priced over $45,000 and on vehicles with an average fuel efficiency (average of highway and city ratings) below 19 miles per gallon. The .4% tax applies to vehicles for which certificates of ownership are issued on or after July 15, 2006. (Ch. 39, Laws 2006).

¶1829 Non-Residential Development Fee

On July 17, 2008, New Jersey enacted the Statewide Non-Residential Development Fee Act, sections 32-38 of P.L. 2008 c. 46. This Act imposes a 2.5% fee on new construction of and additions to non-residential development in the State of New Jersey. Monies collected pursuant to this fee will support the development of affordable housing throughout the State, including funding the Urban Housing Assistance Fund which was created as part of the same piece of legislation. The Act was passed as part of sweeping reforms to the New Jersey Fair Housing Act.

Effective July 27, 2009, legislation exempts certain property from the 2.5% development fee imposed by the Statewide Non-Residential Development Fee Act.The measure modifies the Act to exempt property that received site plan approval from a municipality or from the New Jersey Meadowlands Commission before July 1, 2010, from the fee imposed by the Act, provided that a permit for the construction of the building is issued by the local enforcing agency prior to July 1, 2013. The legislation halts application of the fee to projects that have been referred to a planning board by the state or by another public agency prior to July 1, 2010, pending the same permit restrictions. A.B. 4048, Laws 2009.

PART VIII

LOCAL TAXES

CHAPTER 19
LOCAL TAXES

¶ 1901	Scope of Chapter
¶ 1902	Tax on Tangible Personal Property of Local Exchange Telephone, Telegraph, and Messenger System Companies
¶ 1903	Hotel Use or Occupancy Tax
¶ 1904	Atlantic City Luxury Tax
¶ 1905	Trenton Business License Tax
¶ 1906	Newark Taxes
¶ 1907	Jersey City Parking Tax
¶ 1908	Elizabeth Parking Tax
¶ 1909	Cape May County Tourism Tax
¶ 1910	Atlantic City Parking Fee at Casino Hotels
¶ 1911	Municipal Surcharge on Charges for Admission to Major Places of Amusement
¶ 1912	Admission Surcharges
¶ 1913	Motor Vehicle Rental Tax

¶1901 Scope of Chapter

This chapter deals briefly with the tax on business tangible personal property of telephone, telegraph, and messenger system companies and the hotel use or occupancy tax. Specific treatment is also given to the Atlantic City sales tax, the Trenton business license tax, the Jersey City and Elizabeth parking tax, and the Newark parking and payroll tax. The summaries indicate who is subject to the tax, exemptions, the basis and rate of tax, report and payment requirements, and by whom the tax is administered.

The local taxation of real property is covered in Chapter 26.

¶1902 Tax on Tangible Personal Property of Local Exchange Telephone, Telegraph, and Messenger System Companies

Law: R.S. 54:4-1, 54:4-2.48, 54:11A-6.1 (CCH NEW JERSEY TAX REPORTS ¶ 20-295, 89-102).

Taxable: Business tangible personal property of local exchange telephone, telegraph, and messenger system companies is subject to local personal property taxation.

Exempt: Inventories are expressly excluded.

Basis and rate: Business tangible personal property used by local exchange telephone, telegraph, and messenger system companies is taxed at a percentage of true value. This percentage generally will be the average ratio of assessed to true value of real property in the taxing district as established by the Director of the Division of Taxation for the purpose of distributing school aid funds. The assessment date is October 1.

The property is locally taxed at the general real property tax rate of the taxing district in which the property is found.

Returns and payment: Returns must be filed with the Director before September 1. Payment is made to the local collectors at the same time.

Administration: The tax is administered by the local tax assessors and collectors.

¶1903 Hotel Use or Occupancy Tax

Law: R.S. 40:48E-1—40:48E-6 (CCH New Jersey Tax Reports ¶ 60-480).

New Jersey imposes a state hotel and motel occupancy tax at the rate of 5% of the rent paid. The 5% tax is in addition to the state's 7% sales tax. Special rate provisions apply for those municipalities that already impose local taxes or fees on hotel/motel occupancies:

— In Atlantic City, 4% sales tax, 9% luxury tax, and 1% state occupancy fee;

— In Newark and Jersey City, 7% sales tax, 6% local hotel tax, and 1% state occupancy fee;

— In The Wildwoods, 7% sales tax, 2% tourism sales tax, 1.85% tourism assessment, and 3.15% state occupancy tax.

First-class cities or second-class cities in which there is an international airport terminal are authorized to impose, by ordinance, a tax on charges for the use or occupation of hotel rooms, not to exceed 6%. Currently, only the City of Newark imposes the tax. The tax is in addition to the sales and use tax imposed on hotel room occupancies.

P.L. 2010, c.55, signed into law on August 18, 2010, and effective immediately, revises the hotel/motel occupancy tax permitted to be imposed by municipalities under P.L. 2003, c.114. The Act amends section 7 of P.L. 2003, c.114 (N.J.S.A. 40:48F-5) to require the State Treasurer to include with the periodic distribution of tax revenue to each subject municipality a list of all of the hotels and motels therein that submitted municipal occupancy tax revenue to the State for the reporting period. The new law also requires every municipality that has adopted an ordinance imposing the occupancy tax to annually provide to the State Treasurer on or before January 1 of each year a list of the names and addresses of all of the hotels and motels located in the municipality, and also the name and address of any hotel or motel that commences operation after January 1 of any year. This additional reporting requirement will aid in more effective tax administration. Finally, the Act makes unpaid occupancy taxes a municipal lien on the real property comprising the delinquent hotel or motel. This requires the State Treasurer to provide to a subject municipality written notification of nonpayment of local hotel/ motel taxes. The municipality would then be authorized to act as the collection agent for the outstanding balance of taxes due and owing to it in place of the State Treasurer.

Returns and payment: For any calendar year, hotel owners are required to pay the greater of the real property tax (ad valorem taxes, payment in lieu of taxes, or payment of annual service charges) or the hotel use or occupancy tax. A city imposing a hotel use or occupance tax by ordinance may require a hotel located within the municipality to pay both the real property tax and the hotel use or occupance tax. (Ch. 97, Laws 2006).

If the quarterly installment of the real property tax is less than that of the hotel use or occupancy tax, the hotel owner must pay only the hotel use or occupancy tax. If the quarterly installment of the real property tax is greater than the quarterly installment of the hotel use or occupancy tax, the hotel owner must pay the hotel use or occupancy tax, plus a supplemental payment equal to excess of property tax over the hotel use or occupancy tax.

Refunds: If the total of hotel use and occupancy payments other than supplemental payments exceeds the total real property tax for the year, the owner is refunded the total amount of supplemental payments made throughout the year. If the total payments made other than supplemental payments does not exceed the total property tax for the year, but total payments made including supplemental payments does exceed the total property tax for the year, the owner is refunded the difference between the total property tax and the sum of the hotel or occupancy tax paid plus the supplemental payments made. Refunds are paid to the hotel owner without interest by July 1 of the succeeding year or 15 days after the adoption of the budget by the municipal council, whichever is later.

Administration: The tax is collected on behalf of the city by persons collecting the use or occupancy charge from the hotel customer and remitted to the chief fiscal officer of the city.

¶1904 Atlantic City Luxury Tax

Law: R.S. 40:48-8.15—40:48-8.44, 54:32B-8.19; Reg. Secs. 18:25-1.5, 18:25-2.4 (CCH NEW JERSEY TAX REPORTS ¶60-230, ¶61-720).

Taxable: Atlantic City imposes a tax on specified retail sales or sales at retail occurring within the city limits.

"Retail sale" or "sale at retail" is defined to include:

— Any sale in the ordinary course of business for consumption of whiskey, beer, or other alcoholic beverages by the drink in restaurants, cafes, bars, hotels, and similar establishments;

— Any cover, minimum, entertainment, or other similar charge made to any patron of any restaurant, cafe, bar, hotel, or other similar establishment;

— The hiring (with or without service) of any room in any hotel, inn, rooming, or boarding house;

— The hiring of any rolling chair, beach chair, or cabana; and

— Admissions to any theater, moving picture, show, pier, exhibition or place of amusement, except admissions to boxing, wrestling, kick boxing, or combative sports events, matches, or exhibitions subject to the gross receipts tax.

Room and apartment rentals are also taxed, with certain exemptions noted below.

Exempt: Sales not included with the above definition of "retail sale" and "sale at retail" are exempt. Also exempt are casual or isolated sales, sales to or by the State of New Jersey or its political subdivisions, sales exempt under federal law, and sales by a church or bona fide nonprofit charitable association.

The following rental payments are also exempt: (1) rentals by permanent residents; (2) rentals paid directly by an agency of New Jersey state, county, or municipal government, or by a federal agency; (3) rentals received by a church or nonprofit charitable organization; (4) isolated rentals by a person not engaged in a course of repeated and successive transactions of like character; (5) the portion of a room rental attributed to food service; and (6) the rental of apartments for a period of eight weeks or more.

Rate of tax: Atlantic City is authorized to impose the tax at a rate of 3% or less on sales of alcoholic beverages, and at a rate of 9% or less on other taxable sales. Currently, the city imposes the tax at the authorized limits. Sales that are subject to both the Atlantic City luxury tax and the New Jersey sales and use tax are taxed at a combined rate, limited to a maximum of 13% (luxury tax at 9% and sales tax at 4%). Sales subject only to New Jersey sales and use tax are taxable at a rate of 7%. Sales of alcoholic beverages by the drink in Atlantic City are taxable at the combined rate of

10% (luxury tax at 3% and sales tax at 7%). Sales of package goods are subject only to New Jersey sales and use tax at the rate of 7%.

Reports and payment: Reports are required to be filed by vendors with the Division of Taxation on or before the 20th day of each month covering receipts for the preceding calendar month.

Taxes are paid by the purchaser to the vendor who remits the tax to the Director. Payment accompanies the return.

Administration: The tax is administered by the Director of the Division of Taxation.

¶1905 Trenton Business License Tax

Code of the City of Trenton, New Jersey, Ch. 146: Licensing (CCH New Jersey Tax Reports ¶33-100).

Taxable: Persons engaging in, or carrying on, the business of selling any goods, wares, merchandise, commodities, chattels, or any tangible personal property at retail or wholesale, or both, are subject to the Trenton general business license tax.

A separate tax is applicable to persons engaged in certain businesses, trades, or occupations that are subject to the Trenton specific business license tax. Such persons are not also subject to the Trenton general business license tax.

Exemptions: Persons licensed or regulated by the City of Trenton under other ordinances, and alcoholic beverage licensees are exempt. Also exempt are certain enumerated utilities except for sales of electric and gas appliances to be used for the consumption of gas or electricity and held for resale and not for production, transmission, or distribution of gas or electric energy.

Basis and rate: License tax is graduated according to total gross annual sales as follows (Code of the City of Trenton, New Jersey, Ch. 146: Licensing, Sec. 146.8: License Fees):

Total Gross Sales		License Fees
Less than $5,000		$11.00
$5,000 and less than	20,000	22.00
20,000 and less than	50,000	44.00
50,000 and less than	100,000	71.50
100,000 and less than	150,000	99.00
150,000 and less than	200,000	137.50
200,000 and less than	250,000	176.00
250,000 and less than	300,000	209.00
300,000 and less than	350,000	247.50
350,000 and less than	400,000	275.00
400,000 and less than	450,000	313.50
450,000 and less than	500,000	357.50
500,000 and less than	550,000	412.50
550,000 and less than	600,000	440.00
600,000 and less than	650,000	467.50
650,000 and less than	700,000	495.00
700,000 and less than	750,000	522.50
750,000 and less than	800,000	550.00
800,000 and less than	850,000	605.00
850,000 and less than	900,000	660.00
900,000 and less than	950,000	687.50
950,000 and less than	1,000,000	715.00
1,000,000 and above		828.00

Late payments made for the period January 1 through January 31 are subject to a 7% penalty. Thereafter, an additional 1.5% will be imposed for each delinquent calendar month.

A credit of $350 is deducted from the above fees by all licensees who are required to pay an annual fee of $350 or more for a state license and who are also required to pay a state tax imposed upon the sale of commodities by the licensee.

"Total gross annual sales" means all sales, regardless of the place where the sale was solicited, or place where the contract of sale was consummated, or the place of delivery, without deductions for any purpose. In determining the license fee for any particular year, the sales to be used are the sales for the year next preceding the current license year. Adjustments are made where business was not conducted for the whole of the previous year, and estimates in the case of new businesses.

License, reports, and payment: License applications must be filed with the City Clerk prior to January 31 or before commencing business. A separate license is required for each place of business.

No reports are required other than the annual license applications.

Payment of the license fees is made to the City Clerk.

Administration: The tax is administered by the City Clerk.

¶1906 Newark Taxes

Law: R.S. 40:48C-1, 40:48C-6—40:48C-8, 40:48C-14—40:48C-19 (CCH New Jersey Tax Reports ¶ 33-090).

The City of Newark imposes a parking tax and a payroll tax.

• *Employer payroll tax*

Taxable: Employers having a payroll in excess of $2,500 in any calendar quarter are subject to tax.

Exempt: Federal, state, or local government or interstate agencies (including their agencies or instrumentalities), certain foreign insurance companies, and authorized nonprofit religious, charitable, or educational institutions are exempt.

Basis and rate: The tax is imposed at the rate of 1% on remuneration paid to employees for services performed within Newark, or for services performed both within and without the city if they are performed in New Jersey and supervised from Newark. Domestic service in a private residence is excluded.

Reports, payment, administration: Quarterly reports and payment are required. Reports are sent to, and checks made payable to, City of Newark—Payroll Tax. The tax is administered by the Newark Director of Finance.

P.L. 2007, c.294, enacted January 13, 2008, and effective immediately, amends the Local Tax Authorization Act to permit municipalities that impose payroll taxes by ordinance to enact ordinances allowing the assessment of interest charges on delinquent payroll taxes owed to the municipality.

• *Parking tax*

Tax and rate: A tax at the rate of 15% is imposed on fees for parking, garaging, or storing of motor vehicles, other than parking in a garage which is part of a private one- or two-family dwelling.

P.L. 2007, c.296, enacted January 13, 2008, and effective immediately, authorizes municipalities to enact ordinances imposing a 7% "special event" parking tax surcharge on charges for parking, garaging or storing motor vehicles for special events held in the municipality on weekday evenings, weekends and holidays. Newark has enacted such an ordinance effective in 2008.

See also "Hotel Use and Occupancy Tax" at ¶ 1903.

See also "Municipal Surcharge on Charges for Admission to Major Places of Amusement" at ¶1911.

¶1907 Jersey City Parking Tax

Law: R.S. 40:48C-1, 40:48C-6—40:48C-8, 40:48C-14—40:48C-19 (CCH NEW JERSEY TAX REPORTS ¶60-740).

Jersey City imposes a parking tax.

Tax and rate: Jersey City imposes a tax at the rate of 15% on fees for parking, garaging, or storing of motor vehicles (other than fees from parking in garages leased to tenants and part of multiple dwellings with six or fewer families). Authority to impose the tax is in effect through December 31, 2004.

Exempt: No tax is imposed with respect to any parking, garaging, or motor vehicle storage fees charged by religious, charitable, or educational institutions or by nonprofit organizations.

Reports, payment, administration: Quarterly reports and payment are made to the Business Administrator of Jersey City, who administers the tax.

¶1908 Elizabeth Parking Tax

Law: R.S. 40:48C-1.2, 40:48C-6—40:48C-8 (CCH NEW JERSEY TAX REPORTS ¶60-740).

Tax and rate: The City of Elizabeth imposes a tax at the rate of 15% on fees for parking, garaging, or storing motor vehicles at Newark International Airport.

Exempt: No tax is imposed on fees for parking in a garage that is part of premises occupied solely as a private one- or two-family dwelling.

Reports and payment: Reports must be filed with the Director of Finance of the City of Elizabeth. Payment of tax must be made within 30 days of the end of the month during which taxable fees are collected.

¶1909 Cape May County Tourism Tax

Law: R.S. 40:54D (CCH NEW JERSEY TAX REPORTS ¶60-230, ¶61-720).

A tourism improvement and development tax may be imposed by any two or more contiguous municipalities in Cape May County. Currently, Wildwood, Wildwood Crest, and North Wildwood have adopted ordinances authorizing the tourism tax at the rate of 2%. The tax is in addition to the 7% state sales tax, and is imposed on predominantly tourism related sales, which include the following items:

— hotel room occupancy rental;

— sale of food and drink by restaurants, taverns, or other establishments for consumption on or off premises, including mobile vendors and other sellers of prepared food, or by caterers (but not from coin-operated vending machines); and

— admissions charges to any place of amusement, including charges for admission to amusement rides, sporting events and exhibitions, dramatic or musical arts performances, motion picture theaters, and cover charges in nightclubs and cabarets.

In addition, a 1.85% tourism assessment on hotel room rentals became effective April 1, 2003.

¶1910 Atlantic City Parking Fee at Casino Hotels

Receipts from the minimum $3 per day Atlantic City parking fee imposed on the use of casino parking spaces are exempt from New Jersey sales and use tax. There also is an exclusion for parking charges or fees imposed pursuant to an agreement between the Casino Reinvestment Development Authority and a casino operator which was in effect as of June 28, 2007. Any amount collected over and above these fees remains subject to sales tax.

¶1911 Municipal Surcharge on Charges for Admission to Major Places of Amusement

P.L. 2007, c.302, enacted on January 13, 2008, and effective immediately, authorizes municipalities to adopt ordinances imposing a 5% surcharge on admission charges to certain major places of amusement that are also subject to New Jersey sales tax pursuant to N.J.S.A. 54:32B-3(e)(1). The surcharge is to be collected by the same people who collect the admission charges from customers, who must then remit the surcharges collected and submit monthly tax returns reporting the surcharge to the Division of Taxation. Revenue from this surcharge collected in each municipality is distributed to each municipality by the State Treasurer.

Ch. 84, Laws 2013, effective July 17, 2013, allows a municipality to set the surcharge at an amount up to 5% of the admission charge to a major place of amusement.

¶1912 Admission Surcharges

Cities of the second class, excluding municipalities subject to the Municipal Rehabilitation and Economic Recovery Act, where a major place of amusement is located, are allowed to impose a surcharge of up to $2 on each admission charge that is subject to sales tax and a $2 surcharge on parking for that place of amusement. Any such surcharge imposed must be separately stated on any bill, receipt, invoice or similar document provided to the patron but is not considered part of the sale price for purposes of determining sales and use tax. These revenues are required to be appropriated for redevelopment purposes.

A surcharge imposed pursuant to a municipal ordinance must be collected on behalf of the municipality by the person collecting the admission charge or parking fee from the customer.

¶1913 Motor Vehicle Rental Tax

A municipality with a population over 100,000, and within which is located a commercial airport that provides a minimum of 10 regularly scheduled commercial airplane flights per day, is authorized to impose up to a 5% tax on the rental fee of motor vehicles, excluding taxes and surcharges. The revenue will fund eligible purposes, mainly consisting of redevelopment plan activities.

PART IX
ADMINISTRATION AND PROCEDURE
CHAPTER 20
STATE TAX UNIFORM PROCEDURE LAW

¶ 2001	In General—Administrative Bodies
¶ 2002	Assessments by the Director of the Division of Taxation
¶ 2003	15-Day Period for Payment of Special Assessment
¶ 2004	Protest—Request for Hearing
¶ 2005	Appeals
¶ 2006	Refunds
¶ 2007	Personal Liability of Taxpayer—Tax Liens—Warrant
¶ 2008	Tax Payment or Provision for Payment as Condition to Dissolution, Withdrawal, Merger, or Consolidation
¶ 2009	Examination of Property, Books, and Records
¶ 2010	Penalties and Interest
¶ 2011	Criminal Penalties
¶ 2012	Security
¶ 2013	Certificate of Debt
¶ 2014	Closing Agreements and Compromises
¶ 2015	Limitations on Assessment
¶ 2016	Taxpayer Remedies—Action for Damages Against the State
¶ 2017	Contractor Registration Changes
¶ 2018	License Suspension of Tax-Noncompliant Businesses
¶ 2019	Liability of Fiduciary Agents for Certain Taxes
¶ 2020	Multiple Taxes: Enhancement of Tax Compliance Measures Enacted
¶ 2021	Use of Fraud Prevention Contractors

¶2001 In General—Administrative Bodies

Law: R.S. 54:48-1—54:52-19 (CCH NEW JERSEY TAX REPORTS ¶ 20-032, 20-036, 89-060, 89-082).

The State Tax Uniform Procedure Law, Chapters 48 through 52 of Title 54 of the New Jersey Revised Statutes, supplements the assessment and collection provisions of the various taxes administered by the Director of the Division of Taxation. The uniform provisions apply to each tax unless the contrary is indicated in the law imposing the particular tax.

Although the object of the State Tax Uniform Procedure Law is administrative uniformity in the procedure to be followed by taxpayers in relation to any state taxes and in the remedies that may be resorted to by the state to collect the taxes, differences in procedure or remedies provided in the law imposing a particular tax are always given effect.

• *Administrative bodies*

The following is a description of tax administrative bodies in New Jersey. The administrative bodies maintain offices in the state capital, Trenton.

Division of Taxation, Department of Treasury

The Department of the Treasury, Division of Taxation, is the chief tax administration agency in New Jersey. It is located at 50 Barrack Street, CN 269, Trenton, New Jersey 08695, (609) 292-6400. It administers and collects the following taxes:

Alcoholic beverage tax (with Department of Law and Public Safety)
Atlantic City casino parking fee
Atlantic City luxury sales tax
Cape May County tourism sales tax
Casino gambling tax
Cigarette tax
Corporation business (franchise) tax on net worth and income
Corporation income tax
Estate tax
Excise tax on certain utilities
Fuel taxes (with Department of Law and Public Safety)
Inheritance tax
Insurance tax (Commissioner of Insurance)
Litter control tax
Personal income tax
Petroleum products gross receipts tax
Public utilities franchise tax
Railroad franchise tax
Railroad property tax
Realty transfer fee
Sanitary landfill taxes
Sales and use tax
Savings institutions income tax
Spill compensation and control tax
Tobacco products tax

The Division of Taxation maintains a website at

http://www.state.nj.us/treasury/taxation

State Treasurer

The State Treasurer administers and collects the corporate annual fee and the corporate organization and qualification fees.

Department of Law and Public Safety

The Motor Vehicle Commission administers and collects the motor vehicle registration fees and motor fuels use tax.

The Alcoholic Beverage Control Division (with the Department of Treasury) administers and collects the alcoholic beverage tax.

Department of Insurance

The Commissioner along with the Department of Treasury, administers and collects the tax on insurance companies.

Department of Labor

The Commissioner administers and collects the unemployment and disability benefit tax.

Department of Environmental Protection

Remediation funding source surcharge.

Local Taxing Officers

The Local Taxing Officers administer and collect the general property tax and hazardous waste facilities tax.

¶2002 Assessments by the Director of the Division of Taxation

Law: R.S. 54:49-5—54:49-7 (CCH New Jersey Tax Reports ¶20-758, 20-766, 89-162, 89-164, 89-168).

The State Tax Uniform Procedure Law gives the Director of the Division of Taxation the power to make assessments.

Deficiency assessment where a return was filed: The Director may determine that there is a deficiency with respect to the payment of tax upon examination of the taxpayer's return and/or an audit or investigation. The director assesses the additional taxes, penalties, and interest (imposed as in the case of delinquent payment— see ¶2010), gives notice of the assessment to the taxpayer, and makes a demand upon the taxpayer for payment.

Arbitrary assessment—If no report was filed: If the taxpayer fails to file a report as required, the director may estimate the tax liability from any available information and may assess taxes, fees, penalties, and interest due from the taxpayer. The Director must give notice to the taxpayer and make demand upon the taxpayer for payment.

Jeopardy assessments: The Director is authorized to make an arbitrary assessment, even if no return is due, in the case of taxpayers who intend to: depart quickly from New Jersey; remove from New Jersey their property or any property subject to New Jersey state tax; conceal themselves, their property or other property; discontinue business; or do any other act tending to prejudice or render ineffectual proceedings to assess or collect tax. Under such arbitrary assessment, the Director may proceed to collect the tax or compel security for the tax and thereafter give notice of the finding to the taxpayer, together with a demand for an immediate report and immediate payment of the tax.

¶2003 15-Day Period for Payment of Special Assessment

Law: R.S. 54:49-8, 54:49-9 (CCH New Jersey Tax Reports ¶20-766, 89-168).

The State Tax Uniform Procedure Law requires the taxpayer to pay all taxes, penalties, and interest within 15 days after a demand by the director following an arbitrary or jeopardy assessment (¶2002) and provides that if the sum demanded is not paid within 15 days, an additional penalty in the amount of 5% of the tax is imposed.

¶2004 Protest—Request for Hearing

Law: R.S. 54:49-18 (CCH New Jersey Tax Reports ¶20-904, 20-906, 89-228).

A taxpayer has 90 days after the giving of notice of an assessment or finding in which to file a written protest, setting forth the reason for the protest and requesting a hearing. Filing of the protest does generally stay collection of the tax until 90 days after the director's final determination, provided the taxpayer furnishes security where required. Security is generally not required where the amount in controversy is less than $10,000. Security is required, however, where an arbitrary assessment is made upon a taxpayer's failure to file a report or upon a determination that a taxpayer intends to abscond, conceal, or remove property from the state, or discontinue business. Contested assessments of $10,000 or more do not require security, unless the director determines that there is a substantial risk of the taxpayer's failure or inability to pay a liability, based on the taxpayer's compliance history and financial condition.

CCH Caution: Timely Filing

Ninety-day time limit for filing a gross income tax appeal from a final determination when that determination is sent to the taxpayer by certified mail begins to run on the date the taxpayer signed the certified mail return receipt for his determination letter, rather than on date that the determination letter was mailed (*Liapakis v. Director, Division of Taxation,* 363 N.J. Super. 96 (App. Div. 2003)).

The time for appeal commences from the date of the Director's final determination.

¶2005 Appeals

Law: R.S. 54:51A-13—54:51A-23 (CCH New Jersey Tax Reports ¶20-906, 89-236).

An appeal from an action, proceeding, ruling, decision, order, or judgment of the Director of the Division of Taxation is made to the New Jersey Tax Court. A taxpayer has 90 days in which to file an appeal to the Tax Court. The time to appeal to the Tax Court begins from the date of the Director's final determination.

Appeal to the Tax Court is the exclusive remedy of a taxpayer in controversies over decisions of the Division of Taxation or any other state taxing authority.

Except as specifically provided otherwise (as is the case for arbitrary assessments where the taxpayer withholds a report or arbitrary assessments where the taxpayer intends absconding), a complaint filed in the Tax Court will stay the collection of the tax at issue and the enforcement by entry of a judgment. A stay of collection of tax or enforcement by entry of a judgment will expire and be of no effect upon the entry of a judgment by the Tax Court determining that all or any part of the tax assessed is due and owing.

A prevailing taxpayer in a court proceeding in connection with the determination, collection, or refund of any tax, penalty, or interest may be awarded a judgment or settlement for reasonable litigation costs, not to exceed $15,000, incurred in the proceedings, based upon (1) the reasonable expenses of expert witnesses, (2) the reasonable costs of studies, reports or tests, and (3) the reasonable fees of attorneys, not to exceed $75 per hour unless the court specially determines the existence of a special factor. The award may be made only for the costs allocable to the state, and not to any other party. No award may be made with respect to any portion of the proceedings during which the prevailing taxpayer has unreasonably protracted the proceedings. The term "prevailing taxpayer" refers to a taxpayer who, in the decision of the court, establishes that the position of the state was without reasonable basis in fact or law.

Whenever it appears to the court that proceedings have been instituted or maintained by the taxpayer primarily for delay, that the taxpayer's position in the proceedings is without grounds, or that the taxpayer unreasonably failed to pursue administrative remedies, the state may be awarded a judgment or settlement for its reasonable litigation costs, not to exceed $15,000, incurred in the proceedings.

CCH Caution: Contested Issues

Effective January 1, 2002, the statute of limitations is tolled with regard to any "contested issue" disputed by a taxpayer in the New Jersey Tax Court for later years that are not part of the litigation (Ch. 6, Laws 2002).

¶2006 Refunds

Law: R.S. 54:49-14—54:49-16; Reg. Sec. 18:2-5.9 (CCH New Jersey Tax Reports ¶ 20-752, 20-815, 89-204, 89-224).

Claims for refund are filed under oath with the Director of the Division of Taxation. If a taxpayer files a protest or appeal, a refund claim must be filed after the final determination in the taxpayer's favor and is not required or permitted prior to the final determination. Taxpayers that fail to file a protest of an assessment within 90 days have waived their right to file a refund claim regarding the items assessed.

Limitation period: Claims may be filed within four years after the payment of any original or additional tax, unless a shorter limit is fixed by the law imposing the tax. A three-year limitation is specified for personal income tax.

The signing of an agreement by the taxpayer and the Director extending the period for assessment specifically extends the period for filing a claim for refund. Each taxpayer is required to file a separate refund claim. A refund claim on behalf of a class is not permitted. Where a tax is declared to be discriminatory in a final judicial decision from which all appeals have been exhausted, the director may refund or credit only the discriminatory portion of the tax. For sales and use tax purposes, a taxpayer is allowed an additional six months beyond the expiration of the extension agreement to file a refund claim for taxes paid on receipts for transactions occurring during periods covered by the agreement, regardless of whether a deficiency assessment was made.

Requirements for appeal: A taxpayer may not be precluded from claiming a refund of an assessment of additional tax solely on the ground that the taxpayer did not protest or appeal from the assessment. A taxpayer may file a claim for a refund if (1) the taxpayer neither protested nor appealed from the assessment, (2) the taxpayer paid the assessment in full within one year after the expiration of the period allowed for filing a protest of the assessment, (3) the taxpayer files the claim for refund within 450 days of the expiration of the period allowed for filing such a protest, and (4) the amount of the refund claimed does not exceed the amount of the assessment paid.

If, upon examination of a refund claim, it is determined that there has been an overpayment of tax, the amount of the overpayment and the interest on the overpayment, if any, will be credited against any liability of the taxpayer under any state tax law. If the taxpayer has no liability, the taxpayer will be entitled to a refund of the tax so overpaid and the interest on the overpayment, if any.

Interest: Overpayments of tax accrue interest at the prime rate as determined by the Director. Interest accrues from the later of the date on which the taxpayer files a claim for refund or requests adjustment, the date on which the tax is paid or the due date of the report or return. No interest may be paid on an overpayment of less than $1, nor upon overpayments refunded within six months after the later of the last date prescribed (or permitted by extension of time) for filing the return or the actual date on which the return is filed. In the case of erroneous tax payments, interest will be paid on refunds not paid within six months after the claim for refund was filed.

The taxpayer must be notified if the claim for refund is rejected in whole or in part.

¶2007 Personal Liability of Taxpayer—Tax Liens—Warrant

Law: R.S. 54:49-1, 54:49-13, 54:49-13a (CCH New Jersey Tax Reports ¶20-760, 89-174).

Any state tax, fee, interest, or penalty becomes a personal debt of the taxpayer to the state, recoverable in the New Jersey courts, on its due date. The debt, whether sued on or not, is a lien on all the property of the debtor, except as against an innocent purchaser for value in the usual course of business and without notice, and except as may be provided to the contrary in any other law, and has preference in the distribution of assets, whether in bankruptcy, insolvency, or otherwise.

The Director of the Division of Taxation may release any property from the lien of any certificate, judgment, or levy procured by him or her upon either the payment of adequate consideration or the deposit of adequate security.

The director is also authorized to issue a warrant, to the sheriff of any county or to an officer or employee of the Division of Taxation, for a levy upon and sale of the property of any person liable for a state tax.

¶2008 Tax Payment or Provision for Payment as Condition to Dissolution, Withdrawal, Merger, or Consolidation

Law: R.S. 54:50-12—54:50-18 (CCH New Jersey Tax Reports ¶20-758, 20-760, 89-176).

Until all state taxes (including fees, penalties, and interest) are paid, or provision for payment has been made as noted below, no domestic corporation or foreign corporation subject to New Jersey tax may merge or consolidate into a foreign corporation not authorized to do business in New Jersey, no domestic corporation may dissolve, and no domestic or foreign corporation may distribute its assets in dissolution or liquidation to any shareholder. The provisions do not apply to a merger or consolidation into a domestic or authorized foreign corporation.

The Secretary of State is not permitted to accept a certificate of dissolution, merger or consolidation, or issue a certificate of withdrawal to a foreign corporation, unless the company files a tax clearance certificate issued by the Director of the Division of Taxation not more than 45 days prior to the effective date of the corporate action.

Generally, the Director will issue a tax clearance certificate only if all taxes due have been paid, including taxes shown on an estimated return for the period between the due date of the last regular return and the effective date of the action. However, the tax clearance may be obtained without prior payment of the estimated taxes if

— another domestic or authorized foreign corporation certifies that it will make timely payment of all taxes due by the company applying for clearance, and that the certifying company has a net worth of at least 10 times the amount of taxes paid by the applicant for the last complete tax year, or

— in the case of dissolution, or distribution of assets in dissolution or liquidation, timely payment is guaranteed by the shareholders of domestic or authorized foreign corporations which own a majority of the applicant's stock, or by a domestic or authorized foreign corporation acquiring the applicant's assets in exchange for the guarantor's stock. An opinion by a New Jersey attorney that all requirements have been met must be included.

The Director may also require evidence that an unauthorized corporation which is a party to the transaction has paid any taxes owed to the state.

Effective July 1, 2007, the law establishes a tax clearance certificate requirement for awards or certain monetary and financial incentives offered to businesses by State departments, agencies, instrumentalities and independent authorities. The Act prescribes that as a precondition for obtaining an award of business assistance or incentives, such as grants, loans and other financial assistance (but not including tax credits or tax exemptions), the applicant must obtain a tax clearance certificate from the Division of Taxation showing that it has filed its required tax returns and paid any taxes, fees or penalties and interest due. (Ch. 101, Laws 2007).

¶2009 Examination of Property, Books, and Records

Law: R.S. 54:50-2 (CCH NEW JERSEY TAX REPORTS ¶ 20-768, 89-142).

The Director of the Division of Taxation has the power to make an examination of the taxpayer's place of business, tangible personal property, books, records, papers, vouchers, accounts and documents.

¶2010 Penalties and Interest

Law: R.S. 54:48-2, 54:49-3, 54:49-4, 54:49-6, 54:49-9, 54:49-9.1, 54:49-11 (CCH NEW JERSEY TAX REPORTS ¶ 17-250, 20-752, 61-530, 89-204).

The penalty and interest provisions of the State Tax Uniform Procedure Law apply to all state taxes except the inheritance tax and the public utility franchise and gross receipts taxes.

• *Penalty for failure to file return on time*

A taxpayer who fails to file a return within the prescribed time is liable for a late filing penalty of $100 for each month or fraction thereof that the return is delinquent, plus a penalty of 5% per month or fraction thereof of the underpayment, not to exceed 25% of the underpayment, except that if no return has been filed within 30 days of the date on which the first notice of delinquency in filing the return was sent to the taxpayer, the penalty will accrue at 5% per month or fraction thereof of the total tax liability, not to exceed 25% of the tax liability.

• *Penalty for amnesty eligible liability*

From April 15, 2002, until June 10, 2002, New Jersey had a Tax Amnesty Program for state liabilities for tax returns due on and after January 1, 1996, but prior to January 1, 2002. After June 10, 2002, an unabatable 5% penalty will be imposed, and an additional collection fee may also be imposed, for any liability that was eligible for the amnesty. This is in addition to all other penalties, interest and other costs (Ch. 6, Laws 2002).

In 2009, a tax amnesty program was held for state tax liabilities for returns due on or after January 1, 2002, and before February 1, 2009. The additional 5% penalty will be imposed for any amnesty eligible liability.

• *Penalty for underpayment of tax required to be shown on return*

Unless any part of an underpayment of tax required to be shown on a return or report is proven to be due to reasonable cause, an amount of 5% of the underpayment will be added to the tax.

• *Interest for failure to pay tax on or before due date*

The interest rate on deficiencies and delinquent taxes is charged at 3% plus the prime rate, assessed for each month or fraction thereof, compounded annually at the end of each calendar year, for failure to pay tax.

The interest rate on underpayments of tax is 9% from April 1, 2008, to December 31, 2008. The rate for the first three months of 2008 (January 1 to March 31, 2008) was 10.5%.

When an extension of time for filing has been granted, interest accrues from the date that the tax was originally due to the date of actual payment. Any amount of tax unpaid after the time period prescribed by law or pursuant to an extension of time, is considered an underpayment.

R.S. 54:48-2 defines "prime rate" as the rate quoted as of December 1 of the calendar year immediately preceding the calendar year in which payment was due. If the Director determines that the prime rate quoted by commercial banks to large businesses varies by more than one percentage point from the rate otherwise determined, the Director will redetermine the prime rate to be that quoted prime rate for subsequent calendar quarters of the calendar year in which payments become due.

• *Failure to pay taxes, penalties, or interest*

An additional penalty (in addition to any other penalty or interest) of 5% of the tax is imposed if an arbitrary or jeopardy assessment is not paid within 15 days of demand.

If any part of an assessment is due to civil fraud, a penalty will be added in the amount of 50% of the assessment.

• *Power to remit penalties and interest*

If the failure to pay tax when due is explained to the satisfaction of the Director of the Division of Taxation, the Director may remit or waive the payment of any penalty, in whole or in part. The Director may also remit or waive the payment of any interest charge in excess of the rate of three percentage points above the prime rate, including any such penalty or interest with respect to deficiency assessments.

The Director must waive the payment of any part of a penalty or any part of interest attributable to the taxpayer's reasonable reliance on erroneous advice furnished to the taxpayer in writing by an employee of the Division of Taxation acting in the employee's official capacity, provided that the penalty or interest did not result from the taxpayer's failure to provide adequate or accurate information.

- *Voluntary disclosure*

A taxpayer who contacts the Division of Taxation in order to file delinquent returns and makes full payment of liabilities plus interest will not be subject to civil or criminal penalties, provided the Division did not notify the taxpayer of the delinquency prior to the voluntary disclosure (*State Tax News*, Division of Taxation, Spring 1993; CCH NEW JERSEY TAX REPORTS, ¶ 400-257).

¶2011 Criminal Penalties

Law: R.S. 54:52-8, 54:52-10 (CCH NEW JERSEY TAX REPORTS ¶ 20-770, 89-208).

It is a crime of the third degree to fail to file a report with intent to defraud the state or evade the tax, penalty, or interest that is due or to prepare or assist in preparing a false or fraudulent return or statement.

¶2012 Security

Law: R.S. 54:49-2 (CCH NEW JERSEY TAX REPORTS ¶ 89-178).

The Director of the Division of Taxation may require a bond or other security if he or she finds that the collection of tax, interest, or penalties may be prejudiced.

¶2013 Certificate of Debt

Law: R.S. 54:49-12 (CCH NEW JERSEY TAX REPORTS ¶ 89-178).

As an additional remedy for the collection of tax, the Director of the Division of Taxation may issue a certificate of debt to the Clerk of the Superior Court. The clerk dockets the certificate as if it were a judgment, and the Director may proceed on the certificate as if it were a judgment.

¶2014 Closing Agreements and Compromises

Law: R.S. 54:53-1—54:53-15 (CCH NEW JERSEY TAX REPORTS ¶ 20-762, 89-186).

The Director of the Division of Taxation is authorized to enter into a written agreement concerning liability for any state tax. A case may not be reopened as to matters covered by a closing agreement except on a showing of fraud, malfeasance, or misrepresentation of fact. The Director may also compromise criminal and civil penalties arising under the tax laws, but only when there is doubt as to liability or collectability.

The Director may compromise the time for payment of a liability arising under the state tax laws, but only on the grounds that the equities of the taxpayer's liability indicate that a compromise would be in the state's interest and that without such a compromise the taxpayer would experience extreme financial hardship. A delayed payment or installment payment compromise agreement must include interest on the unpaid balance of the liability at the rate of three percentage points above the prime rate. No compromised matters may be reopened unless there has been falsification or concealment of assets by the taxpayer, mutual mistake as to a material fact that would cause a contract to be set aside, or a significant change in the financial condition of a taxpayer with whom the Director has entered into an agreement regarding the time for payment of a tax liability. In the latter instance, the Director may require the taxpayer to provide periodic statements of financial condition. Action may be taken by the Director against taxpayers with whom the Director has entered into an agreement regarding the time for payment of a tax liability, provided the Director gives notice 30 days before the date of any action and the notice includes a statement of the reasons the Director has for believing a significant change in the financial condition of the taxpayer has occurred. An offer in compromise will not be accepted unless the taxpayer waives the time limit on assessment or collection of the liability.

¶2015 Limitations on Assessment

Law: R.S. 54:49-6 (CCH New Jersey Tax Reports ¶ 20-768, 89-144).

Assessments of additional tax may not be made more than four years from the date of filing of a return. However, tax may be assessed at any time in the case of a false or fraudulent return with intent to evade the tax, or failure to file a return. If a shorter time for the assessment of additional tax is fixed by the law imposing the tax, the shorter time governs. Taxpayers may consent in writing to an extension of time for assessment of tax, in which case the amount of such additional tax due may be determined at any time within the extended period. The period may be further extended by subsequent consents in writing made before the expiration of the extended period.

¶2016 Taxpayer Remedies—Action for Damages Against the State

Law: R.S. 54:51A-23 (CCH New Jersey Tax Reports ¶ 20-906, 89-236).

If an employee of the Division of Taxation knowingly disregards any tax law, administrative provision, or regulation in the collection of any tax, or knowingly, recklessly, or negligently fails to release a lien against or bond on a taxpayer's property, then the taxpayer may, within two years from the date that the taxpayer could reasonably discover the actions of the employee or Director, bring an action for damages against the state in the Tax Court. The damages must be limited to the actual direct economic damages suffered by the taxpayer as a proximate result of the actions of the employee, plus costs, reduced by the amount of such damages and costs as could reasonably have been mitigated by the taxpayer. Such civil action will be the exclusive remedy for recovering damages resulting from such actions.

¶2017 Contractor Registration Changes

Law: R.S. 52:32-44 (CCH New Jersey Tax Reports ¶ 60-420).

Ch. 57, Laws 2004, enacted June 29, 2004, and effective immediately, but remaining inoperative until September 1, 2004, extends to local government agencies the requirement that public entities may enter into public contracts with providers of goods and services only if they have presented documentation showing that they are registered with this State for tax purposes. The Act also provides that these providers of goods and services and their affiliates must remit sales or use tax on tangible personal property delivered to a retail buyer in this State.

¶2018 License Suspension of Tax-Noncompliant Businesses

Law: R.S. 54:50-9, 54:50-24, 54:50-26, 54:50-26.1, 54:50-26.2, 54:50-26.3, 54:50-27.

Ch. 58, Laws 2004, which was enacted on June 29, 2004, and took effect immediately, provides a mechanism whereby the Division of Taxation will receive information regarding the identity of entities (including individuals) that are holders of licenses to engage in a particular profession, trade or business in this State, and will then examine their tax records to identify any areas of noncompliance and will give them an opportunity to contest their indebtedness or delinquency or to come in compliance. The Act authorizes the Director to demand the summary suspension of a professional, occupational or business license of an entity that already has an unsatisfied judgment for tax indebtedness, or who fails to remedy any tax indebtedness after receiving the notice provided for under this Act.

¶2019 Liability of Fiduciary Agents for Certain Taxes

Effective October 1, 2007, the law imposes personal liability on certain individuals and entities that, as the State's fiduciary agents, are required to collect and remit

Cape May County tourism sales tax, N.J.S.A. 40:54D-4; Atlantic City luxury tax, N.J.S.A. 40:48-8.15 et seq.; hotel and motel occupancy fee, N.J.S.A. 54:32D-1; 9-1-1 system and emergency response fee, N.J.S.A. 54:17C-18; and cosmetic medical procedures gross receipts tax, N.J.S.A. 54:32E-1. (Ch. 102, Laws 2007).

¶2020　Multiple Taxes: Enhancement of Tax Compliance Measures Enacted

For purposes of all taxes administered by the New Jersey Division of Taxation, legislation was enacted in 2007 that makes several changes to tax collection procedures to increase compliance with state tax laws.

• *Cost of Collection Fees*

Effective June 28, 2007, the legislation authorizes the imposition of a fee for the cost of collection on arbitrary assessments. The fee is the greater of 10% of the tax liability or $200.

• *Reporting of Account Information by Financial Institutions*

Effective June 28, 2007, the Division is authorized to request deposit information from financial institutions about bank accounts when a tax judgment has been secured against a bank customer. Prior to amendment, the law limited access to accounts held solely by the delinquent taxpayer and allowed the financial institution to withhold account information when someone other than the taxpayer had an ownership interest in the account. The law as amended removes the restriction on access to joint accounts, or certain accounts that are held in the name of someone other than the taxpayer, requiring disclosure on such accounts similar to individual accounts.

• *Alcoholic Beverage Retail Licensee Clearance Certificates*

Effective August 1, 2007, a requirement is added to assure that a business pays all state taxes due before the sale, transfer or assignment in bulk of any part or the whole of its business assets. The purchaser must notify the Director of the Division of the sale at least 10 days before taking possession of the assets. The Director must respond within 10 days of receiving the notice and notify the purchaser, transferee or assignee that a possible claim for state taxes exists and include the amount of the state's claim.

If the Director fails to provide timely notice, the purchaser, transferee or assignee may transfer over to the seller, transferrer or assignor any sums of money, property, choses in action, or other consideration to the extent of the amount of the state's claim. The purchaser, transferee or assignee will not be subject to liabilities and remedies and will not be personally liable for the payment to the state of any such taxes theretofore or thereafter determined to be due to New Jersey from the seller, transferrer or assignor. (Ch. 100, Laws 2007).

¶2021　Use of Fraud Prevention Contractors

For purposes of all taxes administered by the New Jersey Division of Taxation, legislation was enacted effective January 25, 2013, that authorizes the use of contractors by the Division to supply fraud prevention services for the purpose of assisting the Division. The Director may enter into agreements with one or more private persons, companies, associations or corporations providing fraud prevention services. (Ch. 20, Laws 2013).

ADMINISTRATION AND PROCEDURE

CHAPTER 21
NEW JERSEY RESOURCES

Division of Taxation—Hotline
50 Barrack St., P.O. Box 269, Trenton NJ 08646 800-323-4400
        Internet: www.state.nj.us/treasury/taxation
—Forms & Refunds
50 Barrack St., P.O. Box 269, Trenton, NJ 08646 609-292-6400
        Internet: www.state.nj.us/treasury/taxation
New Jersey Economic Development Authority
36 West State St., P.O. Box 990, Trenton, NJ 08625 609-292-1800
        Internet: www.njeda.com
—Small Business & Women & Minority Business
20 West State St., P.O. Box 820, Trenton, NJ 08625 609-292-0181
        Internet: www.njeda.com
—Urban Enterprise Zone
20 West State St., P.O. Box 820, Trenton, NJ 08625 609-292-1912
        Internet: www.njeda.com
—Division of International Trade
20 West State St., P.O. Box 820, Trenton, NJ 08625 609-633-3606
        Internet: www.njeda.com

PART X
DOING BUSINESS IN NEW JERSEY
CHAPTER 22
FEES AND TAXES

¶2201	Domestic Corporation and Limited Partnership (LP) Costs
¶2202	Foreign Corporation and Limited Partnership (LP) Costs
¶2203	Domestic Limited Liability Company (LLC) and Limited Liability Partnership (LLP) Costs
¶2204	Foreign Limited Liability Company (LLC) and Limited Liability Partnership (LLP) Costs

¶2201 Domestic Corporation and Limited Partnership (LP) Costs

Law: R.S. 14A:4-5, 14A:15-2, 14A:15-3, 54:10A-2, 54:10A-3, 54:10A-4(d), 54:10A-4(k), 54:10A-5, 54:10A-6, 54:10A-8, 54:10A-9, 54:10A-15, 54:10A-17, 54:10A-19.2, 54:49-5 (CCH NEW JERSEY TAX REPORTS ¶1-120).

The following paragraphs discuss the costs and fees payable by domestic corporations and limited partnerships. For those payable by foreign corporations and foreign limited partnerships, see ¶2202.

CCH Advisory: Annual Reports

Beginning with the 2005 year, all annual report filings have been moved to electronic filing and payment systems. This includes annual reports for corporations, limited liability companies, limited liability partnerships, limited partnerships and non-profit entities. The formation or registration date is the due date for the annual report. To file and pay electronically, visit the Division of Revenue's website at http://www.state.nj.us/njbgs.

• *Initial fees and taxes*

The following filing fees are paid to the Department of Treasury/Division of Revenue:

Certificate of incorporation or limited partnership	$125
Amendment to the certificate	$75
Certificate of abandonment of amendment	$75
Certificate of merger or consolidation	$75
Certificate of abandonment of merger or consolidation	$75
Restated certificate of incorporation	$75
Certificate of dissolution or cancellation	$75
Revocation of dissolution	$75
Change of address of registered office or registered agent, or both	$25
Certificate of change of address of registered agent, where such certificate effects a change in the address of the registered office of one to 499 corporations or of 500 or more corporations in cases where the filing information is not transmitted in a machine readable format agreeable to the Division of Revenue, for each corporation named in the certificate	$25
Certificate of change of address of registered agent, where such certificate effects a change in the address of the registered office of 500 or more corporations in cases where the filing information is transmitted in a machine readable format agreeable to the Division of Revenue (an additional fee may be assessed not to exceed those administrative costs associated with the technical transmission of the filing information)	$5,000
Affidavit of resignation of registered agent	$25
Filing of tax clearance certificate	$20

The following miscellaneous fees are also paid to the Department of Treasury:

Annual report	$50
Reservation of corporate name	$50
Name search[1]	$20
Transfer of a reserved name for corporations	$25
Transfer of a reserved name for limited partnerships	$50
Renewal of reserved corporate or limited partnership name	$25
Certificate of standing	$25
Certificate of standing, including incorporators, officers, directors and authorized shares	$25
Certificate of standing, listing charter documents	$25
Certificate of availability of corporate name	$25
Certificate of registration of alternate name	$50
Renewal of registration of alternate name for corporations	$25
Renewal of registration of alternate name for limited partnerships	$50
Termination of alternate name (corporations only)	$75
Certificate of correction for corporations	$10
Certificate of correction for limited partnerships	$50
Filing and issuing reinstatement of charter for corporations	$295
Filing and issuing reinstatement of charter for limited partnerships	$275
Corporate status reports, per name	$6.25
Service of process	$25

• *Annual fees and taxes*

Corporations subject to tax: Domestic corporations (except utilities, insurance and financial corporations, certain nonprofit corporations, limited dividend housing corporations, and production credit associations) are subject to the corporation business tax, see ¶701.

¶2202 Foreign Corporation and Limited Partnership (LP) Costs

Law: R.S. 14A:3-14, 14A:4-5(3), 14A:15-2, 14A:15-3, 54:10A-2, 54:10A-3, 54:10A-4, 54:10A-4(d), 54:10A-5, 54:10A-6, 54:10A-8, 54:10A-15, 54:10E-1 (CCH New Jersey Tax Reports ¶2-220).

The following paragraphs discuss the costs and fees payable by foreign corporations and foreign limited partnerships. For those payable by domestic corporations and limited partnerships, see ¶2201.

• *Initial fees and taxes*

The following filing fees are paid to the Department of Treasury/Division of Revenue:

Certificate of authority	$125
Application for amended certificate of authority	$75
Application for withdrawal or cancellation from the state	$75
Certificate or decree dissolving corporation or terminating its authority	$75
Change of address of registered office or registered agent, or both	$25
Resignation affidavit of agent	$25
Tax clearance certificate	$20
Reservation of corporate name	$50
Renewal of reserved name	$50
Certificate of registration of alternate name	$50
Renewal of registration of alternate name for corporations	$25
Renewal of registration of alternate name for LP	$50
Certificate of correction for corporations, in addition to any applicable license fee	$10
Certificate of correction for LP, in addition to any applicable license fee	$50
Service of process	$25

See also ¶2201 for fees that may apply to both domestic and foreign corporations.

---

[1] Name searches are available free on-line at http://www.state.nj.us/njbgs.

- *Annual fees and taxes*

Corporations subject to tax: Foreign corporations doing business in New Jersey (except utilities, insurance and financial corporations, certain nonprofit corporations, limited-dividend housing corporations, and production credit associations) are subject to the corporation business tax, see ¶701.

¶2203 Domestic Limited Liability Company (LLC) and Limited Liability Partnership (LLP) Costs

The following costs and filing fees are paid by domestic limited liability companies (LLC's) and limited liability partnerships (LLP's) to the Department of Treasury/Division of Revenue:

Certificate of formation for a limited liability company or a limited liability partnership	$125
Amendment to the certificate of formation	$100
Certificate of merger or consolidation	$100
Certificate of cancellation or withdrawal	$100
Change of address or registered office or registered agent, or both	$25
Annual report	$50
Certificate of change of address of registered agent, where such certificate effects a change in the address of the registered office of one to 499 limited liability companies or limited liability partnerships or of 500 or more limited liability comp anies or limited liability partnerships in cases where the filing information is not transmitted in a machine readable format agreeable to the Division of Revenue, for each corporation named in the certificate	$25
Certificate of change of address of registered agent, where such certificate effects a change in the address of the registered office of 500 or more limited liability companies or limited liability partnerships in cases where the filing information i s not transmitted in a machine readable format agreeable to the Division of Revenue (an additional fee may be assessed not to exceed those administration costs associated with the technical transmission of the filing information)	$25
Resignation of registered agent (with or without appointment of successor)	$25
Affidavit of each effected limited liability company where an agent is resigning	$10
Name search[2]	$20
Reservation of limited liability company or limited liability partnership name	$50
Transfer of a reserved limited liability company or limited liability partnership name	$50
Renewal of a reserved limited liability company or limited liability partnership name	$50
Certificate of standing for a limited liability company or a limited liability partnership (short form)	$50
Certificate of standing for a limited liability company or a limited liability partnership listing charter documents (long form)	$100
Certificate of availability of limited liability company or limited liability partnership name	$50
Certificate of registration of alternate name	$50
Renewal of registration of alternate name	$50
Certificate of correction	$100
Filing and issuing reinstatement of charter	$275
Corporate status reports, per name	$6.25
Service of Process for LLC	$75
Service of Process for LLP	$50

---

[2] Name searches are available free on-line at http://www.state.nj.us/njbgs.

¶2204 Foreign Limited Liability Company (LLC) and Limited Liability Partnership (LLP) Costs

The following costs and filing fees are paid by foreign limited liability companies (LLC's) and limited liability partnerships (LLP's) to the Department of Treasury/ Division of Revenue:

Certificate of Registration for a foreign limited liability company or limited liability partnership	$125
Amendment to the certificate of registration	$100
Certificate of cancellation or withdrawal	$125
Change of address or registered office or registered agent, or both	$25
Certificate of registration of alternate name	$50
Renewal of registration of alternate name	$50
Certificate of correction	$100
Corporate status reports, per name	$6.25
Service of Process for LLC	$75
Service of Process for LLP	$50

PART XI

UNCLAIMED PROPERTY

CHAPTER 23
UNCLAIMED PROPERTY

¶2301 Unclaimed Property

"Escheat" is the vesting of title to unclaimed property in the state. The New Jersey Uniform Unclaimed Property Act, codified as Title 46, Chapter 30B of the Revised Statutes, was essentially adopted from the Uniform Unclaimed Property Act of 1981.

CCH Comment: Escheat

Escheat is an area of potential federal/state conflict. A federal statute may preempt state escheat provisions. For instance, it has been federal policy that the Employee Retirement Income Security Act of 1974 (ERISA) (particularly Sec. 514(a)) generally preempts state laws relating to employee benefit plans. Thus, funds of missing participants in a qualified employee benefit plan stay in the plan pursuant to the federal executive policy that state escheat laws are preempted by ERISA (Advisory Opinion 94-41A, Department of Labor, Pension and Welfare Benefit Administration, Dec. 7, 1994). However, some states have challenged the federal position on this and similar narrowly delineated situations. Thus, practitioners are advised that a specific situation where federal and state policy cross on the issue of escheat may, at this time, be an area of unsettled law.

New Jersey law provides that property held in IRAs, defined benefit plan, or other account or plan that is qualified for tax deferral under federal income tax laws becomes abandoned three years after the earliest of the date of the distribution or attempted distribution of the property, the date of the required distribution as stated in the plan or trust agreement governing the plan, or the date, if determinable by the holder, specified in federal income tax law by which distribution of the property must begin in order to avoid a penalty (Sec. 46:30B-38, R.S.). In addition, in the case of federal tax refunds, IRC Sec. 6408 disallows refunds if the refund would escheat to a state.

Two conditions are necessary for escheat to take place: (1) the property must be abandoned, and (2) there must be some basis for the state taking custody of the property.

- *"Abandoned" property*

Generally, all property that is held, issued, or owing in the ordinary course of a holder's business, whether or not located in New Jersey, that has remained un-claimed by the owner for more than three years after it became payable or distributa-ble is presumed abandoned. (Sec. 46:30B-7, R.S.) Other presumptive periods for abandonment apply to certain types of property, as discussed below.

- *Presumptions of abandonment*

Actual abandonment of property may be proved at any time, but since un-claimed property is usually held under circumstances in which ownership of the property is unknown or uncertain, New Jersey provides the following presumptive periods for abandonment (*New Jersey Unclaimed Property Abandonment Table*, New Jersey Division of Taxation, November 11, 2008):

One-year property

Deposits held by utilities . . . . 1 year after service ends

Class action proceeds . . . . 1 year after initial distribution date

Proceeds to dissolution . . . . 1 year after date of final distribution

Wages . . . . 1 year

Governmental entity—bonds and other intangible items . . . . 1 year

Two-year property

Property held by a superior court or a surrogate for a minor . . . 2 years after the minor reaches majority

Three-year property

Non-governmental bonds . . . . 3 years after maturity

Checks, drafts, certified checks . . . . 3 years

Property held by agents and fiduciaries . . . . 3 years

Credit memos . . . . 3 years after payable

Dividends . . . . 3 years

Money orders . . . . 3 years

Savings, time and demand deposits . . . . 3 years

Traveler's checks . . . . 3 years

Undelivered shares . . . . 3 years

Underlying shares and bonds . . . 3 years and 3 dividend or interest distributions

Unexchanged shares . . . . 3 years

Commission . . . . 3 years

All other intangible property . . . . 3 years

Non-dividend paying securities (NEW) and mutual funds . . . . . 3 years after 2nd mailing is returned by post office or after discontinuation of mailing

Demutualization . . . 3 years after the earlier of the date of distribution or the last contact with policyholder

Retirement account or plan . . . . 3 years

Non-traditional retirement account or plan (Roth) . . . . 3 years

Education IRA . . . . 3 years

Life or endowment policy or annuity contract . . . . 3 years

Health savings account . . . . 3 years

Five-year property

Contents of safe deposit box . . . . 5 years

Stored value cards issued on or after July 1, 2010 . . . . 5 years

Ten-year property

Property held by a superior court and a surrogate . . . . 10 years

Deposits held by utilities: Deposits made to secure payment or advance payment for services remaining unclaimed for more than one year after termination of the service are presumed abandoned. (Sec. 46:30B-29, R.S.)

Refunds held by business associations: Refunds ordered by a court or administrative agency to be refunded by a business association that remains unclaimed for more than one year after it became payable are presumed abandoned. (Sec. 46:30B-30, R.S.)

Property of business associations held in course of dissolution: Property distributable in the course of a dissolution of a business association that remains unclaimed more than one year after the date of final distribution is presumed abandoned. (Sec. 46:30B-36, R.S.)

Unpaid wages: Unpaid wages (including those represented by unpresented payroll checks) owing in the ordinary course of business which remain unclaimed for more than one year after becoming payable are presumed abandoned. (Sec. 46:30B-44, R.S.)

Funds owing under life insurance policies: Funds held or owing under any life or endowment insurance policy or annuity contract that has matured are presumed abandoned if unclaimed for more than three years after the funds became due and payable. (Sec. 46:30B-22, R.S.)

Uncashed checks or drafts: Any sum payable on a check, draft, or similar instrument (but not including traveler's checks and money orders) on which a financial organization is directly liable which has been outstanding for more than three years after it was payable (or after its issuance, if an instrument payable on demand) is presumed abandoned, unless within the three-year period the owner has communicated in writing with the financial organization or otherwise indicated an interest. (Sec. 46:30B-22, R.S.)

Property held by agents and fiduciaries: Property, and any income or increment accruing, held in a fiduciary capacity is presumed abandoned after three years from the time it became payable or distributable, unless within the three-year period the owner increased or decreased the principal, accepted payment of principal or income, communicated concerning the property, or otherwise indicated an interest therein. (Sec. 46:30B-37, R.S.)

Credit memos: A credit balance, customer overpayment, security deposit, refund credit memorandum, unused ticket, or similar instrument that occurs or is issued in the ordinary course of the issuer's business that remains unclaimed by the owner for more than three years after becoming payable or distributable is presumed abandoned. (Sec. 46:30B-42, R.S.)

Gift certificates and gift cards: Paper gift certificates, gift cards, and electronic gift cards are included in the definition of "stored value cards". A stored value card for which there has been no stored value card activity for five years is presumed abandoned. This applies only to any stored value card issued on or after July 1, 2010. Only a stored value card that is exempt pursuant to the provisions of Sec. 46:30B-42.1(e), R.S. and Sec. 46:30B-42.1(f), R.S., will be deemed a gift card or gift certificate. (Sec. 46:30B-6(t), R.S.)

Stored value cards: Effective June 29, 2012, a stored value card for which there has been no stored value card activity for five years is presumed abandoned. This is applicable to any stored value card issued on or after July 1, 2010. (Sec. 46:30B-42.1(a), R.S.)

"Stored value card" means a record that evidences a promise, made for monetary or other consideration, by the issuer or seller of the record that the owner of the record will be provided, solely or a combination of, merchandise, services, or cash in the value shown in the record, which is pre-funded and the value of which is reduced upon each redemption. The term "stored value card" includes, but is not limited to the following items: paper gift certificates, records that contain a microprocessor chip, magnetic stripe or other means for the storage of information, gift cards, electronic gift cards, rebate cards, stored-value cards or certificates, store cards, and similar records or cards. (Sec. 46:30B-6(t), R.S.)

The proceeds of a general purpose reloadable card presumed abandoned will be the value of the card, in money, on the date the general purpose reloadable card is presumed abandoned. The proceeds of any other stored value card presumed abandoned will be 60% of the value of the card, in money, on the date the stored value card is presumed abandoned. (Sec. 46:30B-42.1(b), R.S.) A "general purpose reloadable card" means a stored value card issued by a bank or other similarly regulated financial institution or by a licensed money transmitter that is (1) usable and honored upon presentation at multiple merchants or service providers that are not under common ownership or control for goods or services or at automated teller machines, (2) issued in a requested prepaid amount which amount may be, at the option of the issuer, increased in value or reloaded if requested by the cardholder, and (3) not marketed or labeled as a gift card; the term "reloadable card" includes a temporary non-reloadable card issued solely in connection with a reloadable card. (Sec. 46:30B-42.1(k), R.S.)

The following are exempt from the Uniform Unclaimed Property Act: (1) a stored value card that is distributed by the issuer, directly or indirectly, to a person under a promotional, incentive, rewards, or customer loyalty program or a charitable program for which no direct monetary consideration is paid by the owner; (2) a stored value card that is donated or sold below face value to a nonprofit or charitable organization or an educational organization; (3) a stored value card that is redeemable for admission to events or venues at a particular location or group of affiliated locations, or for goods or services in conjunction with admission to those events or venues, or both, at the event or venue or at specific locations affiliated with and in geographic proximity to the event or venue; and (4) a stored value card issued by an issuer that in the past year sold stored value cards with a face value of $250,000 or less. Sales of stored value cards by businesses that operate either under the same trade name as or under common ownership or control with another business or businesses in New Jersey, or as franchised outlets of a parent business, will be considered sales by a single issuer. (Sec. 46:30B-42.1(e), R.S.)

The State Treasurer is authorized to grant an exemption from the provisions concerning stored value cards for a business or class of businesses that demonstrate good cause. The State Treasurer may consider relevant factors including, but not limited to, the amount of stored value card transactions processed, the technology in place, whether or not stored value cards issued contain a microprocessor chip, magnetic strip, or other means designed to trace and capture information about place and date of purchase, and such other factors as the State Treasurer deems relevant. (Sec. 46:30B-42.1(f), R.S.)

Beginning September 1, 2012, if a stored value card is redeemed and a balance of less than $5 remains on the card after redemption, at the owner's request, the merchant or other entity redeeming the card must refund the balance in cash to the owner. A merchant or other entity required to comply with these provisions will be liable to a penalty of $500 for each violation plus restitution of the amount of the cash value remaining on the stored value card, provided, however, that the amount of the penalty will be trebled for an aggregate of 100 such violations occurring during any 12 month period. Failure to provide the requested cash redemption for each stored value card will be considered a separate violation. The Director of the Division of Consumer Affairs is authorized to hold hearings related to violations, and, upon finding a violation to have been committed, to assess a penalty against the person alleged to have committed the violation. The director must thereafter return to the owner of the card the amount of the cash value remaining on the recovered card. This will be the sole remedy available to the owner for a violation. (Sec. 46:30B-42.1(h), R.S.)

This does not impose on an issuer or merchant or other entity required to comply with these provisions an obligation to advertise the availability of a refund balance redemption. The provisions will not apply to (1) a non-reloadable stored value card with an initial value of $5 or less; (2) a stored value card that is not purchased but is provided in lieu of a refund for returned merchandise; or (3) a stored value card that can be redeemed at multiple merchants that are not under common ownership or control, including, but not limited to, network-branded stored value cards. (Sec. 46:30B-42.1(h), R.S.)

Funds associated with a stored value card sold on or after December 1, 2012, will be valid until redemption and will not expire. (Sec. 46:30B-42.1(i), R.S.)

No fees or charges will be imposed on a stored value card that is sold on or after December 1, 2012, except that the issuer may charge an activation, issuance, purchase or similar fee related to the issuance and purchase of a stored value card and for each occurrence of adding value to an existing stored value card, and a replacement card fee with respect to lost, stolen or damaged stored value cards, provided that these fees are disclosed in writing prior to issuance or referenced on the stored value card or the stored value card packaging. The State Treasurer is authorized to adopt regulations regarding the establishment of activation, issuance, purchase or similar fees, fees for adding value to an existing stored value card and replacement card fees. A general purpose reloadable card is not subject to these provisions* (Sec. 46:30B-42.1(j), R.S.)

See the note on litigation involving stored value cards, below.

Note regarding prepaid phone cards and record maintenance: Effective November 1, 2010, the New Jersey Treasurer is exempting prepaid phone cards from certain requirements of Ch. 25 (A.B. 3002), Laws 2010, concerning the reporting of unredeemed balances to the Office of the Administrator of Unclaimed Property of the New Jersey Department of the Treasury. The law requires that issuers of stored value cards, including but not limited to gift cards, report unredeemed balances from cards where there has been no activity or contact for at least a two-year period. While the language in the amended statute does not exempt prepaid phone cards, the treasurer has determined that further study and review of the use and issuance of prepaid phone cards within the telecommunications industry is required. Therefore, prepaid phone cards redeemable for minutes are exempt from the statutory reporting requirements until further notice. However, stored value cards issued by the telecommunications industry that are used for prepaid services and are redeemable for cash or merchandise are subject to the statutory provisions. (Treasury Announcement 2011-03, State of New Jersey, Office of the State Treasurer, September 23, 2010)

Section 5(c) of the law requires a stored value card issuer to obtain and maintain the name and address of the purchaser or owner of each stored value card issued or sold and, at a minimum, to maintain a record of the zip code. In consideration of the increased burden that recording the names and addresses might impose on businesses, the treasurer has determined that good cause exists to exempt issuers and holders who do not otherwise obtain names and addresses of purchasers in their ordinary course of business from the requirement to obtain the name and address, provided that the issuer obtains and maintains the zip code of the purchaser. (Treasury Announcement 2011-03, State of New Jersey, Office of the State Treasurer, September 23, 2010)

Note regarding litigation on stored value cards: On January 5, 2012, the U.S. Court of Appeals for the Third Circuit upheld preliminary injunctions issued by the U.S. District Court for the District of New Jersey concerning the reporting and remittance of unclaimed stored value cards (SVCs) required under Ch. 25 (A.B. 3002), Laws 2010. The appellate court determined that enforcing Chapter 25 retroactively against issuers of stored value cards with existing stored value card contracts that obligate the issuers to redeem the cards solely for merchandise or services was unconstitutional. Furthermore, it was determined that subsection 5c of Chapter 25 and Treasurer Guidance dated September 23, 2010, which apply a place-of-purchase presumption for all stored value cards, were preempted by federal common law. The data collection provision of subsection 5c of Chapter 25, which provides that an issuer of a stored value card must obtain the name and address of the purchaser or owner of each stored value card issued or sold and must, at a minimum, maintain a record of the ZIP code of the owner or purchaser, is severable from the place-of-purchase presumption. Thus, the data collection provision may stand alone even if the place-of-purchase presumption is preempted under federal common law. (*New Jersey Retail Merchants Assoc. v. Sidamon-Eristoff*, U.S. Court of Appeals, Third Circuit, Dkt. Nos. 10-4551, 10-4552, 10-4553, 10-4714, 10-4715, 10-4716, 11-1141, 11-1164, and 11-1170, January 5, 2012, ¶ 401-616)

On October 29, 2012, the U.S. Supreme Court denied a petition from the state of New Jersey to review the ruling, explained above, by the U.S. Court of Appeals for the Third Circuit that the state was preempted from assuming temporary custody of gift cards and other SVCs sold in the state and not claimed by any other state. Left standing was the ruling by the U.S. Court of Appeals for the Third Circuit that the state's action probably violated the federal Contract Clause. (*Sidamon-Eristoff v. New Jersey Retail Merchants Assn.*, U.S. Supreme Court, Dkt. 12-108, petition for certiorari denied October 29, 2012)

Exemption of prepaid phone cards from certain stored value card requirements: Effective November 1, 2010, the New Jersey State Treasurer is exempting prepaid phone cards from certain requirements of Ch. 25 (A.B. 3002), Laws 2010, concerning the reporting of unredeemed balances to the Office of the Administrator of Unclaimed Property of the New Jersey Department of the Treasury. The law requires that issuers of stored value cards, including but not limited to gift cards, report unredeemed balances from cards where there has been no activity or contact for at least a two-year period. While the language in the amended statute does not exempt prepaid phone cards, the treasurer has determined that further study and review of the use and issuance of prepaid phone cards within the telecommunications industry is required. Therefore, prepaid phone cards redeemable for minutes are exempt from the statutory reporting requirements until further notice. However, stored value cards issued by the telecommunications industry that are used for prepaid services and are redeemable for cash or merchandise are subject to the statutory provisions. (*Treasury Announcement,* State of New Jersey, Office of the State Treasurer, September 23, 2010)

Retirement account or plan: These are presumed abandoned after the earliest of the date of the distribution of the property, or three years from the date of required distribution as stated in the plan or trust agreement of the plan, or three years from the date of required distribution to avoid a federal tax penalty (from the date the owner reaches age 70.5). (Sec. 46:30B-38, R.S.; *New Jersey Unclaimed Property Abandonment Table,* New Jersey Division of Taxation, November 11, 2008)

Non traditional retirement account (Roth): These are presumed abandoned three years after the date of a second returned mailing of a statement or other notification or three years after discontinuation of mailings to the apparent owner. (Sec. 46:30B-38.1, R.S.; *New Jersey Unclaimed Property Abandonment Table,* New Jersey Division of Taxation, November 11, 2008)

Education IRA: These are presumed abandoned three years after the date of required distribution to avoid a federal tax penalty (currently three years from the date the owner reaches age 30 years and one month). (*New Jersey Unclaimed Property Abandonment Table,* New Jersey Division of Taxation, November 11, 2008)

Funds held or owing under any life or endowment policy or annuity contract: These are presumed abandoned three years after the policy has matured or terminated and is due; or three years after the insured has died; or three years after the

¶2301

insured has attained the limiting age under mortality tables, and there are no assignments, readjustments, premium payments, loans or written communication in the last two years. (Sec. 46:30B-22, R.S.; *New Jersey Unclaimed Property Abandonment Table*, New Jersey Division of Taxation, November 11, 2008)

Contents of safe deposit box: All property held in a safe deposit box or other safekeeping repository in the ordinary course of the holder's business that remains unclaimed by the owner for more than five years after the lease on the box has expired is presumed abandoned. (Sec. 46:30B-42, R.S.)

Money orders: Any sum payable on a money order or similar written instrument that has been outstanding for more than three years after its issuance is presumed abandoned, unless within the three-year period the owner has communicated in writing with the issuer or otherwise indicated an interest. (Sec. 46:30B-12, R.S.)

Dividends, stocks and other interests in business associations: Dividends, stocks, or other ownership interest in a business association is presumed abandoned if a dividend, distribution or other sum payable as a result of the interest has remained unclaimed by the owner for the longer of two periods: (a) three years, or (b) such period as would cover at least three such unclaimed distributions by the owner. If within the three-year period the owner has communicated with the association regarding the interest, dividend or other distribution as a result of the interest, the running of the abandonment period is interrupted. (Sec. 46:30B-32, R.S.) The abandonment presumption does not apply in the case of automatic dividend reinvestment plans.

Property held by courts and public agencies: Property held for the owner by a court, state, or other government, governmental agency, public corporation, or public authority that remains unclaimed for more than ten years after becoming payable or distributable is presumed abandoned. (Sec. 46:30B-41, R.S.)

Inactive bank accounts: Any demand, savings, or time deposits presumed abandoned three years after the earlier of the maturity or the date of the last indication by the owner of interest in the property, but a deposit that is automatically renewable is deemed matured upon its initial date of maturity unless the owner has consented to a renewal at or about the time of renewal and the consent is in writing or is evidence by a contemporaneous memorandum or other record on file with the holder. Such abandonment will not be deemed to have occurred if the owner has increased or decreased the balance of his account, established relationship with the bank, communicated in writing with the financial organization or otherwise indicated interest concerning the property. (Sec. 46:30B-18, R.S.)

Traveler's checks: Any sum payable on a traveler's check that has been outstanding for more than three years after its issuance is presumed abandoned, unless within the three-year period the owner has communicated in writing with the issuer or otherwise indicated an interest. (Sec. 46:30B-11, R.S.)

• *Basis for taking custody of the property*

In addition to satisfying a presumptive period of abandonment, the state must have some basis for taking custody of the property. The nexus may consist of any of the following (Sec. 46:30B-10, R.S.):

(1) the records of the holder showing that the apparent owner's last known address is in New Jersey or in another state that does not provide for escheat or whose escheat law does not apply to the property;

(2) if the holder's records do not indicate the owner's identity or last known address, a showing that the last known address of the person entitled to the property is in New Jersey or that the holder is domiciled in New Jersey or is a government entity in New Jersey;

(3) if the apparent owner's last known address as shown on the holder's records is in a foreign nation, a showing that the holder is domiciled in New Jersey, or is a New Jersey government agency; or

(4) if the last known address of the apparent owner or other person entitled to the property is unknown or is in a state that does not allow escheat or whose escheat law does not apply to the property and if the holder is domiciled in a state that does not provide for escheat or whose escheat law does not apply to the property, the fact that the transaction out of which the property arose occurred in New Jersey.

- *Obligations of holder of unclaimed property*

Report filing: A holder of abandoned property must file a verified annual report containing such information concerning the property as is required by the Treasurer of the State of New Jersey (the "administrator"). (Sec. 46:30B-47, R.S.) The due date of the report is as indicated below, but may be extended by the Treasurer on written request.

Companies other than life insurance companies file the report by November 1 as of the preceding June 30th. (Sec. 46:30B-49, R.S.) Life insurance companies file the report by May 1 as of the preceding December 31.

Written notice: Not more than 120 days nor less than 60 days prior to the due date of the annual report, a holder of abandoned property must send written notice to the apparent owner at the last known address informing the owner that the holder is in possession of the property. (Sec. 46:30B-50, R.S.)

Delivery: At the same time as the final date for filing the report, the abandoned property is delivered to the Treasurer, unless the owner in the meantime has established its rights to the property. (Sec. 46:30B-59, R.S.) Delivery or payment of the property relieves the holder of all further liability and entitles him to be defended by the administrator against any third-party claims on the property. (Sec. 46:30B-60, R.S.; Sec. 46:30B-65, R.S.)

Retention of records: A holder of abandoned property must maintain a record of the name and last known address of the apparent owner for five years (three years in the case of traveler's checks and money orders) after the holder files the report. (Sec. 46:30B-95, R.S.; Sec. 46:30B-96, R.S.)

Penalties: Failure to deliver property is subject to a penalty of interest at the rate of 10% above the annual treasury bill discount rate on the value of the property. (Sec. 46:30B-103, R.S.) The penalty for failing to render a report or perform other required duties is $200 per day of violation, in addition to interest. (Sec. 46:30B-104, R.S.) A holder who makes a fraudulent report must pay, in addition to interest, a civil penalty of $1,000 for each day the report is withheld up to a maximum of $250,000, plus 25% of the value of any property that should have been but was not reported. (Sec. 46:30B-105.1, R.S.)

- *Recovery of escheated property*

A person claiming an interest in any property paid or delivered as abandoned property may file a claim with the administrator, who must consider the claim within 120 days and provide notice of its decision to the claimant. (Sec. 46:30B-77, R.S.; Sec. 46:30B-78, R.S.) Under certain circumstances, a state may also file a claim for recovery. (Sec. 46:30B-81, R.S.)

A person aggrieved by a decision of the Treasurer may bring an action to establish the claim in the Appellate Division of the Superior Court of New Jersey. (Sec. 46:30B-84, R.S.)

- *Administrator*

The New Jersey Unclaimed Property Program is administered by the Treasurer of the State of New Jersey. Claim inquiries are sent to the State of New Jersey, Unclaimed Property, CN214, Trenton, NJ 08646-0214, Attention: Claims Section. Taxpayer hotline: 609-588-2200. TaxFax for forms: 609-588-4500.

LAW AND REGULATION LOCATOR

This finding list shows where sections of New Jersey statutory law and administrative regulations referred to in the *Guidebook* are discussed.

LAW

Law Sec.	Discussion at ¶	Law Sec.	Discussion at ¶
5:12-139—5:12.152	1812	40:48F-5	1903
5:47-1.1 *et seq.*	718	40:54D	1909
6:1-97	1604	40:55C-65	1604
9A:10-2.7	222	40A:5-44—40A:5-47	1608
11A:6-8	222	40A:21-1—40A:21-21	1604
13:1D-60	1826	42:1-15	212
13:1E-28	1815	42:2B-69	212, 502
13:1E-28.1	1815	46:15-5—46:15-11	1806
13:1E-28.2	1815	46:16-7	1806
13:1E-49—13:1E.91	1814	48:2-59—48:2-60	1807
13:1E-99.1	1816	48:4-1—48:4-35	1810
13:1E-137—13:1E-176	1815	48:16-23—48:16-28	1810
14A:3-14	2202	48:4-3	1808
14A:4-5	2201	52:17C-18	1825
14A:4-5(3)	2202	52:17C-20	1825
14A:15-2	2201, 2202	52:27D-490 et seq.	718
14A:15-3	2201, 2202	52:27BBB-55	720
17:22-6.59	1802	52:27BBB-57	117
17:22-6.64	1802	52:27H-77	707
17:22-6.75	1802	52:27H-78	707
17:30A-1—17:30A-15	1802	52:27H-79	60, 1315
17:32-15	1802	52:27H-80	1213, 1315
17:33B-58—17:33B-62	1416	52:27H-80.2	1315
17:33B-63	1803	52:27H-86	707, 1315
17:35-8	1802	52:32-44	2017
17:35-19	1802	54:3-21	1609
17B:32A-1—17B:32A-19	1802	54:4-1	1603, 1604, 1902
17B:32B-12	721		
18:24-11.2	1402	54:4-1.5	1604
18:24-25.7(a)(1)	1302	54:4-1.6	1604
18:24-25.7(a)(2)	1302	54:4-1.7	1203, 1302
18:24B-1.4	1402	54:4-1.16	1603
26:2H-18.57	1823	54:4-1.19	1604
26:2J-47	1822	54:4-2.25	1606
27:26A-15	112, 714, 1802, 1807	54:4-2.26	1606
		54:4-2.48	1902
30:6D-40	222	54:4-3.3—54:4-3.33	1604
32:23-58	1818	54:4-3.48	1604
32:23-74	1818	54:4-3.52	1604
34:1B-7.42	713	54:4-3.55	1604
34:1B-207—209	708	54:4-3.56	1604
34:1B-242–249	725B	54:4-3.59	1604
34:18-209.4	725A	54:4-3.60	1604
39:3-1—39:3-42	1803	54:4-3.64	1604
40:48-8.15—40:48-8.44	1904	54:4-3.131	1604
40:48C-1	1906, 1907	54:4-3.138—54:4-3.149	1604
40:48C-1.2	1908	54:4-3.153	1604
40:48C-6—40:48C-8	1906, 1907, 1908	54:4-3.154	1604
		54:4-6.2—54:4-6.12	1605
40:48C-14—40:48C-19	1906, 1907	54:4-8.11	1604
40:48E-1—40:48E-6	1903	54:4-8.15	1604
40:48E-5	1603	54:4-8.41	1604

Law Sec.	Discussion at ¶
54:4-8.57—54:4-8.74	1605
54:4-11.1	1204, 1821
54:4-20	1604
54:4-23	1606, 1607
54:4-23.2	1603
54:4-23.8	1603
54:4-23.12	1603
54:4-34	1608
54:4-66	1608, 1609
54:4-67	1608, 1609
54:4-69	1609
54:4-78	1609
54:8A-69	410
54:8A-119	120
54:8A-122	120, 301
54:10-23.11b	1811
54:10-23.11h	1811
54:10A-2	702, 722, 723, 2201, 2202
54:10A-3	703, 2201, 2202
54:10A-4	702, 724, 730, 801—808, 2201, 2202
54:10A-4.3	713
54:10A-5	702, 704, 705, 724, 728, 801, 901, 2201, 2202
54:10A-5a	704, 901
54:10A-5.1	705
54:10A-5.2	705
54:10A-5.4—54:10A-5.15	711
54:10A-5.16—54:10A-5.21	712
54:10A-5.22	728
54:10A-5.24	713, 715, 802
54:10A-5.29	715
54:10A-5.30	715
54:10A-5.33	723
54:10A-5.38	117A;725
54:10A-5.39	117B; 716; 717
54:10A-5.40	705
54:10A-6	727, 809, 901—905, 2201, 2202
54:10A-6B	904
54:10A-7	905
54:10A-8	808, 902, 906, 2201, 2202
54:10A-9	803, 2201
54:10A-10	808, 906, 1004
54:10A-11	1105
54:10A-13	1001, 1106, 1108
54:10A-15	706, 730, 1001, 1005, 2201, 2202
54:10A-15—54:10A-15.4	1006
54:10A-15.4	1107
54:10A-15.6—54:10A-15.10	729
54:10A-17	732, 901, 1102, 1107, 2201
54:10A-18	1001, 1002
54:10A-19	1001, 1003
54:10A-19.1	1102, 1106, 1107
54:10A-19.2	1103, 1108, 2201
54:10A-21	1107
54:10A-22	1107
54:10A-23	1101
54:10A-31	1106
54:10A-31 et seq.	719
54:10A-34	702, 726
54:10B-2	702
54:10E-1	2202
54:11-3	1603
54:11A-6.1	1902
54:15B-1—54:15B-12	1817
54:16-1—54:18A-11	1802
54:29A-7	1603, 1604, 1606
54:29A-13—54:29A-14	1807
54:29A-16	1603, 1606
54:29A-17	1603
54:29A-44	1807
54:29A-44	1608
54:29A-46	1608, 1807
54:30A-16—54:30A-30	1807
54:30A-49—54:30A-68	1807
54:32B-2	1203, 1204, 1206—1209, 1214, 1215, 1216, 1302, 1303, 1310, 1408
54:32B-2(g)	1302
54:32B-3	1202—1207, 1209, 1213, 1214, 1215, 1216, 1302, 1303, 1313
54:32B-3(b)(2)	1302
54:32B-3.2	1201, 1217
54:32B-3.4	1204
54:32B-4	1204, 1213
54:32B-4.6	1204
54:32B-6	1208, 1211, 1213, 1302, 1304
54:32B-7	1210, 1211, 1215
54:32B-7.1	1203
54:32B-8—54:32B-8.46	1302
54:32B-8	1215
54:32B-8.1	1302
54:32B-8.2	1302
54:32B-8.3	1205
54:32B-8.6	1310
54:32B-8.7	1308
54:32B-8.10	1303
54:32B-8.12	1316
54:32B-8.13	1305, 1306, 1317
54:32B-8.14	1309
54:32B-8.16	1307
54:32B-8.19	1904
54:32B-8.20	1311
54:32B-8.22	1214, 1312
54:32B-8.39	1302
54:32B-8.45	1213

Law Sec.	Discussion at ¶
54:32B-8.56	1302
54:32B-9	1206, 1312, 1313
54:32B-10	1303
54:32B-11	1304
54:32B-12	1209, 1212, 1214, 1215, 1303, 1404, 1405
54:32B-13	1403
54:32B-14	1402, 1403, 1411
54:32B-15	1401
54:32B-16	1406
54:32B-17	1402
54:32B-18	1403
54:32B-19	1409
54:32B-20	1410
54:32B-21	1409
54:32B-22	1407
54:32B-24	1402, 1408
54:32B-26	1402
54:32B-27	1409, 1410
54:32B-40	1215
54:32B-44	1412
54:32D-1	1206
54:32E-1	1820
54:32F-1	1824
54:32G-1	1302
54:33-1	1601
54:34-1	1502—1504, 1601—1604, 1606
54:34-2	1504
54:34-2.1	1504
54:34-3	1504
54:34-4	1605
54:34-5	1606
54:34-9	1606
54:34-12	1902
54:34-13	1903
54:35-1	1803, 1804
54:35-2	1801—1804, 1909
54:35-3	1801, 1905
54:35-4	1906
54:35-5	1904
54:35-5.1	1902, 1910
54:35-8	1803
54:35-10	1907
54:35-11	1907
54:35-15	1909
54:35-16	1909
54:35-19—54:35-23	1910
54:36-2	1606
54:36-5	1803
54:36-6	1906
54:37-3—54:37-8	1909
54:38-1—54:38-12	1505
54:38-3	1510
54:38-6	1904
54:38-10	1903
54:38A-1	1502, 1908
54:38A-2	1502
54:38A-3—54:38A-6	1908
54:39-1—54:39-75	1808
54:39A-1—54:39A-24	1809

Law Sec.	Discussion at ¶
54:40A-1—54:40A-44	1805
54:40B-1—54:40B-14	1805
54:43-1	1804
54:45-1	1804
54:48-1—54:52-19	2001
54:48-2	2010
54:48-4.1	410, 1005, 1403, 1802, 1804, 1805, 1807, 1808, 1809, 1815, 1817
54:49-1	2007
54:49-1—54:50-23	1802
54:49-2	2012
54:49-3	607, 2010
54:49-3.1	1402
54:49-4	2010
54:49-5	1102, 2201
54:49-5—54:49-7	2002
54:49-6	1106, 2010, 2015
54:49-7	1102, 1104, 1409
54:49-8	2003
54:49-9	2003, 2010
54:49-9.1	2010
54:49-11	1102, 2010
54:49-12	2013
54:49-13	2007
54:49-13a	2007
54:49-14—54:49-16	2006
54:49-14	1108
54:49-18	1103, 1409, 2004
54:50-1	1101
54:50-2	2009
54:50-9	2018
54:50-12—54:50-18	2008
54:50-13	722, 723
54:50-14	722, 723, 726
54:50-15	722, 723
54:50-24	2018
54:50-26	2018
54:50-26.1	2018
54:50-26.2	2018
54:50-26.3	2018
54:50-27	2018
54:51A-1	1609
54:51A-13—54:51A-23	2005
54:51A-23	2016
54:52-1 et seq.	1107
54:52-6	607
54:52-8	607, 2011
54:52-10	2011
54:52-14	607
54:52-15	607
54:53-1	609
54:53-1—54:53-15	2014
54:53-4	1109
54:53-7	1109, 609
54A:1-2	102, 106, 501, 502
54A:2-1	102, 103, 111, 201, 501
54A:2-1.1	102, 120, 201, 301, 303, 501

Law Sec.	Discussion at ¶
54A:2-2	102, 502
54A:2-2.1	303
54A:2-3	102
54A:2-4	102, 110, 301
54A:3-1	104, 105, 501
54A:3-1.1	105
54A:3-2	107
54A:3-3	106, 301
54A:3-5	106
54A:3-6	108
54A:3A-15—54A:3A-22	121
54A:4-1	112, 114
54A:4-2	112, 113
54A:4-3	112
54A:4-4	112, 113
54A:4-7	116
54A:5-1	119, 202—217, 219, 728
54A:5-1.c	202
54A:5-1.1	211
54A:5-2	201, 203
54A:5-3	201, 209, 501
54A:5-4	102, 212, 502
54A:5-6	301, 403
54A:5-7	302, 303
54A:5-8	211, 220, 301, 501
54A:5-9	217, 301, 503
54A:5-10	301, 503
54A:5-12	503
54A:5-13	301
54A:5-14	204
54A:5-15	203
54A:6-2	211
54A:6-3	211
54A:6-4—54A:6-7	222
54A:6-8	213
54A:6-9	218
54A:6-10	211
54A:6-11	208, 213
54A:6-13	222
54A:6-14	219
54A:6-14.1	204, 223
54A:6-15	219, 220
54A:6-21	211
54A:6-23	221
54A:6-24	224
54A:6-25	211
54A:6-26	220
54A:6-27	223
54A:6-28	211
54A:7-1	408, 409
54A:7-1.1	408
54A:7-2	410
54A:7-4	410
54A:7-7	410
54A:8-1	401, 405, 407
54A:8-2	110
54A:8-3	117
54A:8-3.1	119, 402, 403
54A:8-4	406
54A:8-5	406, 407
54A:8-6	212, 402, 404, 411, 502
54A:8-7	401
54A:8-8	406
54A:8-10	406

Law Sec.	Discussion at ¶
54A:9-1	601
54A:9-2	602
54A:9-3	602
54A:9-4	606
54A:9-5	607
54A:9-6	406, 607
54A:9-7—54A:9-9	608
54A:9-8.1	1605
54A:9-9	603
54A:9-10	603
54A:9-11	401
54A:9-13	605
54A:9-14	604
54A:9-17	120, 301, 408, 601
55:14A-20	1604
55:19-3	710
55:19-13	710
55:19-23	710
56:6-2	1808
56:6-2.3	1808

Uncodified Laws

	Discussion at ¶
Ch. 320, Laws 1993	301
Ch. 2, Laws 1996	1803
Ch. 162, Laws 1997	703, 1807

REGULATIONS

Reg. Sec.	Discussion at ¶
18:7-1.6	702
18:7-1.7	702
18:7-1.8	702
18:7-1.9	702
18:7-1.14	702
18:7-2.3	730
18:7-2.4	730
18:7-3.6	705
18:7-3.11	706
18:7-3.13	1005, 1006
18:7-3.17	706, 710, 713, 714
18:7-3.19	714
18:7-3.22	711
18:7-3.23	713
18:7-3A.2—3A.5	713
18:7-3B.1—3B.7	117B; 713, 717
18:7-5.2	801, 802, 803, 806
18:7-5.3	803, 806
18:7-5.10	702
18:7-5.11	803
18:7-5.17	805
18:7-7.2	901
18:7-8.1	902
18:7-8.2	902
18:7-8.3	906
18:7-8.4—18:7-8.6	903
18:7-8.7—18:7-8.12	904
18:7-8.13	905
18:7-8.15	905
18:7-11.2	1001
18:7-11.4	1001
18:7-11.6	1001
18:7-11.7	1001
18:7-11.8	1001, 1002
18:7-11.12	1003
18:7-11.15	1004

Reg. Sec.	Discussion at ¶
18:7-12.1—18:7-12.3	731, 732
18:7-12.3	901
18:7-13.1	1106
18:7-13.8	1108
18:7-15.2—18:7-15.5	707
18:7-20.1	731
18:7-20.2	707
18:24-1.4	1209
18:24-2.1—18:24-2.16	1406
18:24-3.2	1206
18:24-4.4	1305
18:24-5.2—18:24-5.12	1214
18:24-6.1—18:24-6.7	1302
18:24-7.4	1209
18:24-7.13	1211
18:24-7.14	1211
18:24-7.15	1203
18:24-8.1—18:24-9.11	1312
18:24-11.2	1402
18:24-11.3	1402
18:24-12.3	1205
18:24-12.5	1205
18:24-12.7	1205
18:24-15.2	1203
18:24-15.5	1203
18:24-17.2	1302
18:24-19.1—18:24-19.6	1307
18:24-23.1—18:24-23.3	1212

Reg. Sec.	Discussion at ¶
18:24-23.2	1410
18:24-25.1	1203, 1204
18:24-25.2	1203, 1204
18:24-27.2	1209
18:25-1.5	1904
18:25-2.4	1904
18:26-9.5	1504
18:26-10.12	1907
18:26-12.8	1802
18:35-1.1	203, 303
18:35-1.2	202
18:35-1.3	202, 212
18:35-1.4	114
18:35-1.23	202
18:35-1.5	503
18:35-2.7	109
18:35-4.4	117B
18:35-5.2	402
18:35-6.1	405
18:35-6.4	402
18:35-7.2	410
18:35-7.3	410
18:35-7.3B.1—3B.7	117B
18:35-7.6	208
18:35-7.8	221, 410
18:35-8.1	411

TOPICAL INDEX

⤳ References are to paragraph (¶) numbers.

A

Accounting periods and methods
. corporation business tax . . . . 731—733
. personal income tax 119

Additions to tax—see Penalties

Administration—see also State Tax Uniform Procedure Law
. corporation business tax 1101
. personal income tax 601
. real property taxes 1609
. sales and use taxes 1408

Admission charges—see Sales and use taxes
. outdoor advertising space
. . fees 1821

Advertising 60; 1302

Agriculture
. real property taxes
. . exemptions 65
. sales and use taxes
. . exemptions 60; 1307

Air pollution control equipment
. real property tax exemption 1604

Air toxics
. surcharge 1826

Aircraft
. real property taxes
. . exemption 1604
. sales tax exemption 1302
. . sales to nonresidents 1303

Alcoholic beverages
. excise taxes 1804
. sales tax
. . Atlantic City 1904
. wholesale sales tax 1216

Alimony or separate maintenance payments
. personal income tax 107; 214

Allocation and apportionment
. adjustment of business allocation factor 906
. corporation business tax . . . . 901—706
. . payroll fraction 905
. . property fraction 903
. . receipts fraction 904
. personal income tax 302

AMA
. tax credit 55, 724

Amnesty
. sales and use 1412

Angel investor tax credit
. personal income tax 117E
. . credit against tax 725C

Annuities
. inheritance tax 1504
. personal income tax 211; 222

Appeals
. corporation business tax 1103
. inheritance tax 1509
. personal income tax 603
. real property taxes 1609
. sales and use taxes 1409
. state tax uniform procedure law 2005
. Tax Court 2005

Apple cider—see Alcoholic beverages

Armed forces—see Military pay; Veterans

Assembling
. sales and use tax exemption 1305

Assessment
. corporation business tax 1102
. HMOs . . . . 602—604
. . interim assessment 1822
. inheritance tax 1509

Assessment—continued
. licensed ambulatory care facilities
. . assessment 1823
. . personal income tax . . . . 602—604
. . limitations of time 606
. . real property tax 1607
. . sales and use taxes 1409
. . state tax uniform procedure law 2002

Assessment date
. real property taxes 1607

Associations—see Personal income tax

Atlantic City luxury tax 1904

Automobiles—see Motor vehicles

Aviation fuel 1808

Awards and prizes
. personal income tax 213

B

Banking corporations—see Corporation business tax

Bankruptcy and receivership
. corporation business tax 1105

Banks—see Corporation business tax

Barges
. sales and use tax exemption 1302; 1316

Basis of property
. personal income tax
. . gain or loss 204

Basis of tax
. corporation business tax 704
. personal income tax 103
. real property taxes 1606
. sales and use taxes . . . . 1209—1212

Beer—see Alcoholic beverages

Beneficiaries—see also Inheritance tax
. personal income tax 209

Beverages—see Food and beverages

Bibles
. sales and use tax exemption 1302

Blind persons
. personal income tax exemption 105

Boats
. sales tax exemption 1302; 1316
. . sales to nonresidents 1303

Bonds, government
. personal income tax 219

Bonuses
. personal income tax 202

Bracket collection schedules
. sales and use taxes 1213

Bulk sales
. sales and use taxes 1407

Buses
. motor fuels use tax 1809
. motor passenger carrier taxes 1810
. sales and use tax exemption 1302

Business allocation factor
. corporation business tax 902
. . adjustment of 906
. . payroll fraction 905
. . property fraction 903
. . receipts fraction 904

Business incentives . . . . 55—70
. corporation business tax
. . credits 55
. . enterprise zones, incentives 55; 65
. . financial incentives 70
. real property taxes 65
. sales and use taxes 60

Business net profits
. personal income tax 203

Business use tax returns 1402

C

Cafeteria plan benefits
. personal income tax
.. exemption 224

Canceled sales 1209

Cape May County tourism tax 1909

Capital gains and losses
. personal income tax 204
.. excluded gains 218; 219

Capital improvement
. certificate of 1204

Carryback and carryover
. personal income tax, not allowed 203

Casino taxes 1812

Casual sales
. sales and use tax exemption 1310

Certificate of authority
. corporation business tax
.. holding, effect on taxable status 702

Certificate of debt 2013

Charitable transfers
. inheritance tax exemption 1504

Chemicals and catalysts
. sales and use tax exemption 1302; 1311

Child care programs
. corporation business tax
.. corporate credit 55

Cigarette and tobacco products tax 1805

Clean Communities and Recycling Act—see Litter control tax

Closing agreements
. corporation business tax 1109
. personal income tax 609
. state tax uniform procedure law 2014

Closure tax
. sanitary landfill facilities 1815

Clothing
. sales and use tax exemption 1302

Cogeneration facilities
. sales and use tax exemption 1306

Coin-operated vending machine sales 1205; 1302

Commercial vehicles
. sales and use tax exemption 1302

Commission income
. personal income tax 202

Commuter transportation benefits
. credits against tax
.. corporation business tax 55; 713
.. personal income tax 115
. exemptions
.. personal income tax 221

Commuters' income taxes
. former provisions 119

Compensation
. personal income tax
.. injuries or sickness, exempt 222
.. wages, etc., taxable 202

Computation of estate tax 1508

Computation of taxable income
. personal income tax . . . . 201—224

Computers
. sales and use tax 1203

Conservation contributions
. personal income tax
.. deductions 108

Consolidated returns
. consolidated returns 1004
. corporation business tax, not permitted 1004

Consolidation
. corporation business tax 722; 727

Containers
. sales and use tax exemption 1302

Contractors
. sales and use taxes
.. in general 1214
.. installation and repair service 1204

Copyright income
. personal income tax 205

Corporate expenses on nonoperational income
. corporation business (excise) tax
.. deduction from federal taxable income 803

Corporate partners
. corporation business tax 730

Corporation business tax
. accounting periods and methods 731
.. differences with federal return 732
.. short period 733
. administration of tax 1101
. allocation of income and net worth . . . . . 901—906
.. business allocation factor 902
. angel investor tax credit 725C
. appeals 1103
. banking corporations
.. imposition of tax 701; 702
.. inclusion of income of merged bank 727; 802
.. privilege period 701
.. rate of tax 705
. bankruptcy and receivership 1105
. banks
.. exempt 703
. basis of tax 704
.. entire net income . . . . 801—809
. business incentives 55
.. credits 55
.. enterprise zones, incentives 55
. certificate of authority, effect on taxable status . . 702
. closing agreements and compromises 1109
. consolidation 722; 727
. corporate partners 730
. corporations subject to tax 702
. credits against tax
.. child care programs 55
.. coordination of credits 706
.. developer's credit 709
.. effluent treatment equipment 719
.. employer-provided commuter transportation . . 55; 714
.. film production 55; 716
.. high technology 55; 715
.. HMO assistance fund 721
.. jobs tax 725B
.. manufacturing equipment and employment
      investment 55; 712
.. municipal rehabilitation and economic recovery . . 720
.. neighborhood revitalization 718
.. new jobs investment 55; 711
.. research activities 55; 713
.. sheltered workshops 55; 725
.. tax improperly paid 706
.. urban development 710
.. urban enterprise zones 707
.. urban transit hub 708
. deficiency assessment 1102
. limitations on 1106
. dissolving corporations 722; 727
. doing business in New Jersey 702
. doing business within and without New Jersey . . 728
. domestic corporations ceasing to possess a franchise . . 722;
      727
. employing or owning capital 702
. employing or owning property 702
. entire net income . . . . 801—809
. allocation of 809; 901
. estimated tax 1005; 1006
. exempt corporations 703
. extension of time 1003
. fair and reasonable tax 808

Corporation business tax—continued
. federal changes, report of 1001
. federal limitations 702
. financial businesses
. . corporate 701; 702
. foreign corporations ceasing to have a taxable status . . 723; 727
. forms 1002
. history and imposition of tax 701
. intercompany pricing 808
. interest and additions to tax
. . estimated tax 1006
. . extensions of time 1003
. . generally 1107
. . interstate commerce 702
. investment companies 726
. jeopardy assessment 1104
. judicial review 1103
. liability for tax 702
. maintaining an office in New Jersey 702
. merger, consolidation or reorganization 727
. minimum tax 705
. partnership association, limited 702
. payment of tax 1005; 1006
. penalties
. . estimated tax 1006
. . extensions of time 1003
. . generally 1107
. period when subject to tax 702
. prepayment of tax 1005; 1006
. rate of tax 705
. real estate investment trusts 726
. refunds 1108
. . estimated tax and prepayments 1006
. regulated investment companies 726
. returns 1001; 1002
. S corporations 702; 729
. . entire net income of 801
. . rate of tax 705
. . returns 1001
. state tax uniform procedure law 1101
. subsidiaries 803
. tax benefit transfer program 713
. taxes paid
. . adjustments to federal income 806
. telecommuting employees 702
. throwout rule 904
. urban enterprise zones
. . credit for business located in 707
. withdrawing corporations 723

Cosmetic medical procedures 1820

Credit card tax payment 1608

Credits against tax
. corporation business tax . . . . 706—716
. . business incentives 55
. . enterprise zones, incentives 55
. . wind energy facility credit 725A
. personal income tax . . . . 112—117B
. real property taxes 65
. . enterprise zones 65
. sales and use taxes 60

Criminal acts, gain from 215

D

Databases
. sales and use tax 1203; 1302

Death benefits
. personal income tax exemption 222

Decedents
. personal income tax
. . estate or trust of 102
. . income in respect of 119; 210
. . return for 402

Declarations of estimated tax
. personal income tax 406

Deductions—see specific taxes

Deficiency assessment—see Assessment

Delivery/installation charges
. sales and use taxes
. . exemption 60; 1302

Dependents
. personal income tax exemption 105

Developer's credit 60

Diesel fuel
. tax rate 1808

Digital media content production expenses 717

Disability benefits—see also Unemployment compensation tax
. disqualification periods 1706
. employee's benefits 1706
. employers subject to tax 1703
. exemptions 1703
. payment 1706
. personal income tax exemption 222
. rates 1704
. returns 1705

Disabled persons, personal income tax
. compensation, exemption 222
. pensions, exemption 712; 222
. personal exemption 105

Disallowance of deductions
. personal income tax 203A

DISCs—see Foreign Sales Corporations

Dissolving taxpayers
. corporation business tax 722; 727

Dividends
. corporation business tax 804
. personal income tax 207; 223

Doing business
. corporation business tax 702
. domestic corporations 2201
. foreign corporations 2202

Domestic corporations
. ceasing to possess franchise 722
. corporation business tax 702
. domestic corporation costs 2201

Domestic International Sales Corporations—see Foreign Sales Corporations

Domestic security fee leases 1819

Drugs
. sales and use tax exemption 1302

E

Earned income credit
. personal income tax 116

Education accounts 211

Effluent treatment equipment credit 719

Electric companies 1807

Electronic funds transfer
. alcoholic beverage tax 1804
. casino control tax 1812
. corporation business (excise) tax 1005
. hazardous substances spill compensation tax 1811
. insurance taxes 1802
. motor fuels tax 1808
. motor fuels use tax 1809
. petroleum products gross receipts tax 1817
. sales and use tax 1403
. sanitary landfill facility taxes 1815
. tobacco products tax 1805
. utility corporations 1807

Elizabeth, City of
. parking tax 1908

Employees
. corporation business tax
. . enterprise zones, incentives 55

Employer payroll tax (Newark) 1906

Employers and employees—see also Withholding of tax
. housing furnished by employer
. . personal income tax 202

Employing or owning capital
. corporation business tax 702

Employing or owning property
. corporation business tax 702

Employment investment tax credit
. corporation business tax 55; 712

Enterprise zones
. corporation business tax
. . credits, incentives 55
. real property taxes
. . credits, incentives 65
. sales and use taxes
. . credits, incentives 60

Entire net income (corporation business tax)
. additions to federal taxable income 802
. adjustments to 808
. allocation of . . . . 809; 901—906
. basis of tax . . . . 801—809
. deduction for net income of international banking
. . facility 807
. deductions from federal taxable income 803
. dividends 804
. federal taxable income as starting point 801
. in general 801
. interest and dividends 804
. interest paid to stockholders 805
. net operating losses 805
. subsidiaries, deduction of dividends of 803
. taxes 806

Environmental fines or penalties 216

Environmental opportunity zones
. real property taxes
. . exemptions 65

Equalization tables 1607

Equipment
. sales and use tax exemptions . . . . . 1302; 1305—1307

Estate tax—see also Inheritance tax
. additional tax for federal credit 25; 1505

Estates
. personal income tax 102; 209; 501

Estimated tax
. corporation business tax 1006
. personal income tax 304; 406; 407

Exemption certificate
. sales and use taxes 2005

Exemptions
. certificates 1318
. corporation business tax 703
. inheritance tax 1502, 1503, 1504
. license fees 1805
. personal income tax
. . employer-provided commuter transportation
. . . benefits 221
. . excluded income . . . . 218—224
. . personal 105
. . persons with low income 110
. . real property taxes 1604
. . reciprocal, nonresidents 301
. . retirement income 211; 220
. sales and use taxes . . . . 1301—1317

Express companies 1807

Extensions of time
. corporation business tax 1003
. personal income tax 405

F

Fabricators
. sales and use taxes 1214

Farm land 1603; 2203

Farming exemption
. sales and use tax 1307

Federal changes, report of
. corporation business tax 1001
. personal income tax 401

Fees and taxes
. domestic corporations 2201
. foreign corporations 2202

Fees received
. personal income tax 202

Fellowships
. personal income tax exemption 213

Fiduciaries
. personal income tax 402

Film production tax credit
. corporation business tax 716

Financial incentives
. corporation business tax 55

Fire suppression systems
. real property taxes
. . exemption 65

Firearm vaults 1302

Fishing boats
. sales and use tax exemption 1302; 1316

Flags 1302

Food and beverages
. sales and use tax 1302

Footwear
. sales and use tax 1302

Foreign corporations
. corporation business tax
. . taxable status 702; 723
. . foreign coporation costs 2202

Foreign Sales Corporations
. corporation business tax 702

Foreign taxes paid on dividends
. corporation business (excise) tax
. . deduction from federal taxable income 803

Forms —see specific taxes

401(k) plans 211

Franchise tax, corporations —see Corporation business tax

FSCs—see Foreign Sales Corporations

Fuel
. sales and use tax exemption 1308

Funeral directors 1302

Fur clothing retail
. miscellaneous taxes 1827

Future interests
. inheritance tax 1509

G

Gains and losses
. personal income tax 204
. . carryover of loss not allowed 203
. . excluded gains 218; 219

Gambling
. casino taxes 1812
. winnings
. . personal income tax 208

Garbage removal
. sale and use taxes 1214

Gas companies 1807

Gasoline tax 1808

Gifts
. personal income tax exemption 222

Gold and silver
. sales and use tax exemption 1302

Government obligations
. personal income tax 219

Government pensions
. personal income tax 211

Gross income tax—see Personal income tax

Gross receipts
. utilities tax 1807

H

Hazardous substances spill compensation tax 1811

Hazardous waste facilities tax 1814

High technology
. corporation business tax credit 55; 715

Highway use—see Motor fuels use tax

Historic property
. real property tax deduction 1604

HMO assistance fund credit 721

Homestead exemption
. real property taxes 1605

Homestead rebate 1605

Host community benefits tax 1815

Hotel room occupancy—see Sales and use taxes; Hotel use or occupancy tax

Hotel use or occupancy tax 1903

Household workers
. personal income tax
. . withholding 410

Housing furnished by employer
. personal income tax 202

Husband and wife—see Personal income tax

I

Import tax surcharge
. sales and use taxes 1209

Imposition of tax
. corporation business tax 701
. inheritance tax 1501
. personal income tax 101
. sales and use taxes . . . . 1201—1208

Incentives—see Business incentives; Financial incentives

Income—see Entire net income (corporation business tax); see also specific taxes

Individual retirement accounts
. personal income tax 211

Industrial banks
. franchise tax
. . corporations—see Corporation business tax

Information at source
. personal income tax 411

Inheritance—see also Inheritance tax
. personal income tax exemption 222

Inheritance tax
. additional tax for federal credit 1504
. appeals 108
. assessment of tax 1509
. . limitation period 1509
. compromise of taxes 1509
. computation of estate tax 1508
. deductions 1507
. exemptions 1502
. forms 1509
. imposition of tax 1501
. in general 1501
. nonresidents
. . computation of tax 1503
. . imposition of tax 1501
. . property subject to tax 1506
. notice 1511
. payment of tax 1510
. property subject to tax 1506
. rate of tax 1502
. release under blanket consent 1511
. returns 1509
. . forms 1509
. small estates
. . waivers 1511

Inheritance tax—continued
. tax on future interests 1509
. tax rates 1502
. taxable transfers 1504
. transfers of assets and waivers consenting to transfer . . 1511

Installment payments
. corporation business tax 1006
. personal income tax 406

Insurance companies 1802

Interest
. administration and procedure
. . rate 2010
. corporation business tax
. . income 802; 804; 805
. . penalty 1003; 1006; 1107
. personal income tax
. . income 206
. . penalty 607

Interest and additions to tax—see Penalties

International banking facility
. business allocation factor 114
. deduction for net income of 807

Internet gaming
. miscellaneous taxes 1813

Interstate commerce
. corporation business tax 702

Investment companies
. allocation of income 1101
. corporation business tax 726

Investment funds 223

IRA's—see Individual retirement accounts

J

Jeopardy assessment
. corporation business tax 1104
. personal income tax 604
. state tax uniform procedure law 2002

Jersey City
. parking tax 1907

Jitney operators 1810

Jobs Tax Credit 725B

Jobs training programs
. financial incentives 70

Judicial review
. corporation business tax 1103
. state tax uniform procedure law 2005

K

Keogh plan contributions
. personal income tax 203

L

Landfill facilities 65; 70; 1815

Laundering
. sales and use tax exemption 1302

Leasehold interests
. realty transfer tax 1806

Leases
. tangible personal property
. . sales and use tax liability 1215

License fees 1805

Licenses
. sales and use tax 1401

Lien of tax
. inheritance tax 1510
. state tax uniform procedure law 2007

Life insurance companies—see Insurance companies

Light, heat and power corporations 1807

LIG

Limitations of time
. assessment
. . corporation business tax 1106
. . inheritance tax 1510
. . personal income tax 606
. . sales and use taxes 1409
. refunds—see Refunds

Limitations on assessment 2015

Limited liability companies 212; 502

Limited liability partnerships 212; 502

Linen
. sales and use taxes
. . rentals 1203

Liquidation
. corporation business tax 727

Liquor, tax on 1804

Litter control tax 1816

Local taxes
. admission surcharges 1912
. alcoholic beverages tax 1904
. Atlantic City luxury tax 1904
. Elizabeth parking tax 1908
. hotel use or occupancy tax 1903
. in general 1901
. Jersey City parking tax 1907
. motor vehicle rental tax 1913
. Newark 1906
. parking tax . . . . 1906—1908
. payroll tax 1906
. real property taxes 1601
. tangible personal property of local exchange
. . telephone, telegraph and messenger systems, tax on . . .
. . . . 1902
. Trenton business license tax 1905

Losses—see Gains and losses

Lottery winnings
. personal income tax 213

Low-income exemption
. personal income tax 110

Luxury vehicle/gas guzzler
. miscellaneous taxes 1828

M

Machinery and equipment
. corporation business tax credit 712
. sales and use tax exemptions . . . 1302; 1305—1307; 1317

Maintaining an office in New Jersey
. corporation business tax 702

Manufactured homes
. real property taxes 1604
. sales and use taxes 1203; 1302

Manufacturing exemption
. corporation business tax 55
. real property taxes 65
. sales and use taxes 60

Meals
. sales and use taxes 1205
. . elderly and disabled persons 1302

Medical aids 1302

Medical expense deduction
. personal income tax 106

Medical savings accounts
. personal income tax 222

Medicines
. sales and use tax exemption 1302

Merger, consolidation or reorganization
. corporation business tax 727

Messenger system companies
. local tax on 1902

Military pay
. personal income tax 222

Minimum tax
. corporation business tax 705

Mobile homes—see Manufactured homes

Motion pictures
. sales and use taxes
. . exemption 60

Motor carriers
. motor passenger road tax 1810

Motor fuels—see also Motor fuels use tax
. gasoline tax 1808
. . liquefied petroleum or natural gas 1808
. sales and use tax exemption 1302

Motor fuels use tax 1809

Motor passenger carrier taxes 1810

Motor vehicles
. registration 1803
. sales and use taxes
. . commercial vehicles, exemption 1302
. . rentals 1203
. . sales to nonresident purchasers 1303
. tires
. . fees 1824

**Municipal rehabilitation and economic recovery
credit** 720

**Municipal surcharge on charges for admission to
major places of amusement** 1911

Mustering-out pay, Armed Services
. personal income tax exemption 222

N

Nazi Holocaust reparations
. personal income tax exemption 222

Neighborhood rehabilitation projects
. real property taxes
. . exemption 65

Neighborhood revitalization tax credit 718D

Net income
. corporation business tax . . . . 801—809

Net operating losses
. deduction 803; 805

Net profits from business
. personal income tax 203

**New Jersey Life and Health Insurance Guaranty
Fund** 1802

**New Jersey School Assessment Valuation Relief Act
(NJSAVER)** 1605

New jobs credit, state
. corporation business (franchise) tax 55; 711

Newark, City of
. employer payroll tax 1906
. parking tax 1906

Newspaper advertising
. sales tax exemption 1302

Newspaper production machinery and equipment
. sales tax exemption 1302

Newspapers, magazines & periodicals
. sales tax exemption 1302

Nonprofit corporations 703

Nonresidents
. inheritance tax 1503; 1504; 1506; 1507
. personal income tax
. . annuities 211
. . composite returns 402
. . definition 102
. . pensions 211
. . taxation of . . . . 301—303
. . withholding 408

Non-residential development fee 1829

O

Occupancy—see Hotel use or occupancy tax; Sales and use taxes

P

Packaging materials
. sales and use tax exemption 60; 1302

Palace, parlor or sleeping car companies 1807

Parking tax
. Elizabeth 1908
. Jersey City 1907
. Newark 1906

Partnerships—see Corporation business tax; Personal income tax

Patents, income from
. personal income tax 205

Payment of tax—see also specific taxes
. corporation business tax 1005; 406
. credit card 1608
. personal income tax 407; 410
. sales and use taxes 1403

Payroll tax
. Newark 1906
. Waterfront Commission of New York harbor 1818

Penalties
. corporation business tax 1003; 1006; 507
. criminal penalties 2011
. environmental 216
. inheritance tax 1510
. personal income tax 406; 607
. state tax uniform procedure law 2010; 2011

Pensions
. personal income tax 211; 222

Personal exemptions
. personal income tax 105

Personal income tax
. accounting periods and methods 119
. administration 601
. alimony or separate maintenance
. . paid, deduction for 107
. . received, taxable income 214
. allocation and apportionment, nonresidents 302
. angel investor tax credit 117E
. annuities and pensions 211; 222
. appeals 603
. Armed Forces payments 222
. assessment . . . . 602—604
. . statute of limitations 606
. awards and prizes 213
. basis of property for gain or loss 204
. basis of tax 103
. beneficiaries, taxation of 209
. blind persons
. . personal exemption 105
. bonds, government
. . exclusion of gains and income from 219
. bonuses, taxable income 202
. business net profits 203
. capital gain and loss 204
. . excluded gains 218; 219
. carryback and carryover
. . not allowed 203
. closing agreements 609
. commissions 202
. commuters' taxes 119
. compensation for injuries or sickness
. . exemption 222
. compromise of tax 609
. computation of taxable income . . . . 201—224
. conservation contributions deductions 108
. copyrights, income from 205
. credits against tax . . . . 112—117B
. criminal acts, gain from 215
. death benefits, exemption 222
. decedents
. . estate or trust of 102; 501
. . income in respect of 119; 210

Personal income tax—continued
. decedents—continued
. . returns for 402
. declarations of estimated tax 406
. deductions . . . . 104—108; 121
. . property tax on principal residence 121
. deficiencies
. . assessment 602
. . penalties 607
. dependents, personal exemption 105
. disabled persons
. . compensation, exemption 222
. . pensions, exemption 211; 222
. . personal exemption 105
. distributions from investment companies 223
. dividends 207
. due dates
. . estimated tax 406
. . extensions 405
. . generally 401; 407
. . withholding of tax 410
. earned income credit 116
. employees' trusts 211
. employers and employees
. . housing furnished by employer 202
. estates and trusts
. . definitions 102
. . taxation 209; 501
. estimated tax 406; 407
. excluded income . . . . 218—224
. exemptions
. . cafeteria plan benefits 224
. . employer-provided commuter transportation
. . . benefits 221
. . medical savings accounts 222
. . personal 105
. . reciprocal, nonresidents 401
. . retirement income 211; 730
. extension of time for filing returns 405
. federal changes, report of 401
. fees, taxable income 202
. fellowships, exemption 213
. fiduciaries, returns by 402
. forms 404; 408; 410; 610
. 401(k) plans 211
. gains and losses 204
. . carryover of loss not allowed 203
. . excluded gains 218; 219
. gambling winnings 208
. . withholding 408
. gifts and inheritances, exemption 222
. government obligations
. . exclusion of gain and income from 219
. government pension benefits 211
. history and imposition 101
. housing furnished by employer 202
. . nonresidents 301
. . returns 403
. information at source 411
. inheritances, exemption 222
. installment payments, estimated tax 406
. interest
. . income 206
. . penalty 607
. jeopardy assessments 604
. Keogh plan contributions 203
. limitations of time, assessments 606
. lottery, New Jersey
. . winnings exempt 213
. . withholding 408
. low-income exemption 110
. medical expense deduction 106
. minors, returns for 402
. mustering-out pay, Armed Services
. . exemption 222
. neighborhood revitalization tax credit 117D
. net profits from business 203
. nonresidents
. . annuities 211
. . commuters' taxes 120
. . composite returns 402
. . definition 102
. . pensions 211
. . taxation of . . . . 301—303

Personal income tax—continued
. nonresidents—continued
. . withholding of tax 408
. partners and partnerships 212; 502
. . information returns 402
. . limited liability companies 212; 502
. . limited liability partnerships 212; 502
. patents, income from 205
. payment of tax 407
. . withheld tax 410
. penalties
. . environmental 216
. . generally 607
. . underpayment of estimated tax 406
. pensions 211; 222
. personal exemptions 105
. persons subject 102
. prizes 213
. profits from business 203
. qualified disaster relief payments 222
. qualified investment fund
. . exclusion of dividends from 223
. Railroad Retirement benefits, exempt 211
. rates 111
. reciprocal exemption, nonresidents 301
. redetermination, petition 603
. refunds 608
. remuneration for services 202
. rents 205
. residence, sale of
. . exclusion of gain 218
. retirement plans
. . contributions 202; 211
. . proceeds from 211; 220; 222
. returns
. . composite 402
. . declarations of estimated tax 406
. . generally . . . . 401—405
. . information 411
. . penalties for failure to file 607
. . specimen 610
. . withholding 410
. rollovers
. . pension or annuity distributions 211
. royalties 205
. S corporations 217
. salary, taxable income 202
. scholarships, exemption 213
. senior citizens
. . personal exemption 105
. . residence, sale of 218
. separate maintenance payments
. . paid, deduction for 107
. . received, taxable income 214
. Social Security benefits, exempt 211
. . personal exemption 105
. social services student loan redemption payments 222
. . personal exemption 105
. taxable income . . . . 201—217
. taxes paid to other jurisdictions
. . credit for 114
. tips 202
. transferee liability 605
. trusts
. . definitions 102
. . taxation 209; 501
. tuition expenses, personal exemption 105
. unemployment compensation, exemption 222
. U.S. obligations
. . exclusion of gain and income from 219
. wages
. . nonresidents 303
. . taxable income 202
. withholding of tax
. . credit for amounts withheld 113
. . forms 408
. . generally 408
. . returns and payment 410
. . tables and methods 409; 412

Personal property—see Real property taxes

Petroleum products
. spill compensation tax 1811

Petroleum products excise tax 1817

Pollution control facilities
. real property taxes
. . exemption 65

Prizes
. personal income tax 213

Procedure—see State Tax Uniform Procedure Law

Processing exemption
. sales and use taxes 1305

Product samples 1211

Production machinery
. sales and use tax exemption 1305
. newspaper production 1302

Profits from business
. personal income tax 203

Property taxes—see Real property taxes

Public utilities
. sales and use tax exemptions 1306; 1308
. taxes on 1807

R

Race horses sold through claiming races
. sales and use taxes 1203

Railroad real property—see Railroads

Railroad Retirement benefits
. personal income tax exemption 211

Railroads
. franchise tax 1807
. property taxation
. . assessment 1606
. . classification of railroad real property 1603
. . exempt property 1604
. . in general 1603
. . payment of tax 1608
. . rate of tax 1608
. . returns 1608
. sales and use taxes 1302

Rate of tax—see also specific taxes
. corporation business tax 10; 705
. corporation income tax 5
. inheritance tax 25; 1502
. personal income tax 1; 111
. sales and use taxes 20; 1213

Real estate investment trusts
. corporation business tax 726

Real property—see also Real property taxes
. inheritance tax 202
. transfer tax 1806

Real property taxes
. administration 1609
. assessment date 1607
. assessment procedure 1607
. attached personal property 1604
. basis of tax 1606
. deduction
. . historic property 1604
. . senior citizens 1604
. . veterans 1604
. equalization 1607
. exemptions 65; 1604
. farm land 1603
. homestead rebate 1605
. imposition of tax 1602
. in general 1601
. incentives 65
. . enterprise zones 65
. payment 1608
. penalties 1609
. personal property attached to realty 1603
. property exempt 1604
. property subject to tax 1603
. railroads 1603; 1606; 1608
. rate of tax 1606
. reduction 1606
. returns 1608
. tenant's rebate 1605
. urban gardens 1604

Realty transfer tax 1806

Receivership—see Bankruptcy and receivership

Recycling
. solid waste disposal
. . sales tax exemption 1302
. . tax on 1814

Recycling equipment
. corporation business tax
. . credit 55
. sales and use taxes
. . exemption 60; 1302

Redetermination of assessment
. personal income tax 603

Refining
. sales and use tax exemption 1305

Refunds—see also specific taxes
. corporation business tax 1006; 1108
. inheritance tax 1510
. personal income tax 608
. sales and use taxes 1410
. state tax uniform procedure law 2006

Regional Efficiency Aid Program (REAP) 1606

Registration
. motor vehicles 1803
. sales and use taxes 1401

Regulated investment companies
. allocation of income 901
. corporation business tax 726
. . rate of tax 705
. dividends
. . personal income tax 207; 223
. interest
. . personal income tax 223

Remedies
. action for damages against the state 2016

Remuneration for services
. personal income tax 202

Rent
. personal income tax 205

Rentals
. sales and use tax liability 1203; 1215

Reorganization—see Merger, consolidation or reorganization

Research activities
. corporation business tax credit 55; 713

Research and development exemption
. sales and use taxes 60; 1309

Residence
. principal, credit for
. . personal income tax 117
. sale of
. . personal income tax 218

Residential heating unit
. services to 1214

Resource recovery investment tax 1815

Retirement income
. personal income 211; 220

Returns—see also Reports
. composite 402
. corporation business tax 1001; 1002
. inheritance tax 1509
. personal income tax 410; 411
. . specimen 610
. real property taxes 1608
. sales and use taxes 1402
. unemployment compensation tax 1705

Rollovers
. pension or annuity distributions
. . personal income tax 211

Roth IRA
. personal income tax 712

Royalties
. personal income tax 205

S

S corporations
. corporation business tax 702; 729; 801
. . net operating carryovers 805; 503
. . rate of tax 705
. personal income tax 503
. . shareholder's pro rata share of income 217
. returns 1001, 402

Safe deposit box
. rental
. . sales and use taxes 1204

Salary
. personal income tax 202

Sales and use taxes—see also Atlantic City luxury tax
. administration 1408
. admission charges 1207
. . exempt 1313
. advertising absorption of tax, illegal 1411
. advertising services 1204
. . out-of-state, exemption 60; 1302
. . yellow pages exemption 1302
. agriculture
. . exemptions 60
. alcoholic beverages 1216
. appeals 1409
. assessment 1409
. basis of tax . . . . 1209—1212
. bracket collection schedules 1213
. building and construction trades 1214
. canceled sales, returned merchandise, bad debts 1209
. Cape May County tourism tax 1909
. casual sales 1310
. catered meals 1205
. chemicals and catalysts used in processing 1311
. cogeneration facilities 1306
. computers 1203; 1302
. contractors 1214
. coupons 1209; 1302
. credit sales 1212
. databases 1203; 1302
. definitions 1201
. delivery/installation charges
. . exemption 60
. digital property 1201
. direct payment permits 1404
. employee leasing services 1204
. enterprise zones 60
. equipment exemptions 1302; 1305; 1306
. exempt admission charges 1313
. exempt meals 1205
. . exempt occupancies 1206
. exempt organizations 1312
. exempt property and services 1302
. exempt transactions 1303
. exemption certificates 1405
. exemptions . . . . 60; 1301—1317; 1320
. farming exemption 1307
. federal excise taxes
. . exclusion and inclusions 1209
. food and drink
. . meals and vending machine sales 1205
. fuel and utilities exemption 1308
. hotel room occupancy 1206
. . exemptions 1206
. import tax surcharge 1209
. imposition of tax . . . . 1201—1208
. incentives 60
. installment sales 1212
. leases 1215
. lessor certifications 1215
. limitations of time
. . assessment 1409
. . refunds 1410
. machinery and equipment exemptions
. . manufacturing and processing 60; 1305
. . newspaper production 1302
. . radio and television broadcast production
     equipment 1317
. . utilities 1306
. manufactured homes 1302
. manufacturer using own product 1211

Sales and use taxes—continued
. meals (restaurant, catered or for off-premises
  consumption) 1205
. motion pictures
. . exemption 60; 1302
. motor vehicles (commercial), exemptions 1302
. occupancy 1206
. . exemptions 1314
. payment of tax 1403
. postconsumer material manufacturing facility 1320
. product samples 1211
. property used out of state and brought into New
  Jersey 1210
. rate of tax 1213
. real estate maintenance and repair 1204
. records 1406
. recycling equipment exemption 60; 1302
. refunds 1410
. registration 1401
. rentals 1203; 1215
. research and development exemption 60; 1309
. retail sales, taxability of 1202
. returns 1402
. sales for resale 1303
. seller liability 1201, 1409
. services, taxability of 1203; 1204
. software 60; 1203; 1302
. solar energy devices
. . exemption 60
. taxable transactions and services . . . . 1202—1208
. telecommunications services 1204; 1302
. telephone debit cards 1204
. tourism tax 1909
. trade-in allowances 1209
. transportation charges 1209
. urban enterprise zones
. . exemption 1302; 1315
. use tax 1208
. use tax exemptions 1304
. utilities exemptions 1308
. . machinery and equipment 1306
. vending machine sales
. . exemption 1302
. . food and drink 1205
. yellow pages exemption 1302

Sales for resale 1303

Salespersons
. wages
. . personal income tax 303

Sanitary landfill facility taxes 1815

Scholarships
. personal income tax exemption 213

Security for payment of tax
. state tax uniform procedure law 2012

Senior citizens
. personal income tax
. . personal exemption 105
. . residence, sale 218
. real property tax deduction 1604

Separate maintenance payments
. personal income tax 107; 214

Services
. commmputer related services 1302
. computer related services 1203
. sales and use tax exemption 1302
. sales and use taxes on 1204

Sewer service
. sales and use taxes 1214

Sewerage companies 1807

Ships
. sales and use tax exemption 1302; 1316

Silver
. sales and use tax exemption 1302

Simplified employee pension plans 211

Small businesses
. basis of tax 705

Social Security benefits
. personal income tax exemption 211

Software
. sales and use tax 60; 1203; 1302

Solar energy devices
. sales and use tax exemption 60; 1302

Solid waste importation tax 1815

Solid waste services tax 1815

Sourcing rules
. sales and use 1217

Spill compensation and control tax 1811

Spouse
. personal income tax
. . personal exemption 105

State Tax Uniform Procedure Law
. appeals 2005
. application 2001
. assessment 2002
. . payment after special assessment 2003
. certificate of debt 2013
. collection of tax 2001; 2013
. examination powers of Director 2009
. in general 2001
. jeopardy assessment 2002
. judicial review 2005
. lien of tax 2007
. payment of tax
. . after special assessment 2003
. . prerequisite for dissolution, withdrawal, merger or
  consolidation 2008
. penalties 2010; 2011
. personal liability of taxpayer 2007
. protest 2004
. refunds 2006
. release of lien 2007
. request for hearing 2004
. security for payment of tax 2012
. use of fraud prevention contractors 2021

Statute of limitations—see Limitations of time

Streamlined Sales and Use Tax Agreement (SSUTA)
. sales and use . . 1203–1205; 1209; 1212; 1215; 1302; 1401;
  1403; 1405; 1410

Streamlined Sales Tax Project 1412

Subchapter S corporations—see S corporations

Subcontractors
. sales and use taxes 1214

Subsidiary
. defined 803
. dividends, deduction from federal taxable income . . . 803

T

Tax Court 2005

Tax rates—see Rate of tax

Taxes—see specific taxes

Taxpayer remedies
. action for damages against the state 2016

Telecommunications
. mobile telecommunications fee 1825
. sales and use taxes 1204; 1302

Telephone and telegraph companies
. franchise tax 1807

Telephone debit cards 1204

Tenants' Property Tax Rebate Act 1605

Textbooks
. sales and use tax exemption 1302

Tips
. personal income tax 202

Tobacco products 1805

Tourism tax 1909

Traction companies 1807

Tractors
. motor fuels use tax 1809

Transferee liability
. personal income tax 605

Transportation charges
. deduction
. . sales and use taxes 1209
. exemption, sales and use tax 1302

Trenton business license tax 1905

Trigger locks 1302

Trucks
. motor fuels use tax 1809
. sales and use tax exemptions 1302

Trusts
. personal income tax 102; 209; 501

Tuition expenses
. personal income tax 105

U

Unclaimed property 2301

Unemployment compensation tax
. disqualification periods 1706
. employee's benefits 1706
. employers subject to tax 1703
. exemptions 1703
. general discussion 1701
. history and imposition 1702
. new hire reporting 1705
. payment 1706
. personal income tax exemption 222
. rate of tax 1704
. returns 1705

Uniform Procedure Law—see State Tax Uniform Procedure Law

United States obligations
. exclusion of gain and income from
. . personal income tax 223

Urban development
. credit against corporate tax 710

Urban Enterprise Zones
. corporation business tax
. . credit 707
. sales and use tax exemption 1315

Urban Transit Hub 708; 117C

Use tax—see Hotel use or occupancy tax; Sales and use taxes

Utilities
. corporation business tax
. . exemptions 703
. personal property taxes 1902
. sales and use tax exemptions 1306; 1308
. taxes on 1807

V

Vehicles—see Commercial vehicles

Vending machine sales 1205; 1302

Vessels
. sales and use tax exemption 1302; 1316
. . sales to nonresidents 1303

Veterans
. real property tax deduction 1604

W

Wages
. personal income tax 202; 303
. withholding from—see Withholding of tax

Waivers consenting to transfer of assets
. inheritance tax 1511

Warrant
. collection of tax 2007

Waste
. hazardous facilities tax 1814
. solid, landfill facilities tax 1815

Water companies 1807

Water pollution control equipment
. real property tax exemption 1604

Waterfront Commission payroll tax (Joint New York—New Jersey Compact) 1818

Widows
. property tax exemptions 1604

Wind Energy Facility Credit
. corporation business tax 725A

Wines—see Alcoholic beverages

Withholding of tax
. personal income tax . . . . 408—412
. . credit for tax withheld 113
. . forms 408
. . household workers 410
. . returns and payment 410
. . tables and methods 409

WIT